Y0-BQG-182

THE DILEMMA
OF AMERICAN
POLITICAL
THOUGHT

THE DILEMMA OF AMERICAN POLITICAL THOUGHT

edited by

Jeffrey L. Prewitt

Appalachian State University

Prentice Hall
Upper Saddle River, New Jersey 07458

Library of Congress Cataloging-in-Publication Data

The dilemma of American political thought / edited by Jeffrey L.
  Prewitt.
    p.   cm.
  Includes bibliographical references.
  ISBN 0-13-371592-2 (pbk.)
    1. Political science—United States—History.   2. United States—
  Politics and government.   I. Prewitt, Jeffrey l., (date).
  JA84.U5D55   1996
  320'.092'273—dc20   95-30163
                                                                              CIP

Editor in Chief: Nancy Roberts
Acquisition Editor: Mike Bickerstaff
Editorial/production supervision,
  interior design, and electronic
  page makeup: Mary Araneo
Editorial assistant: Anita Castro
Buyer: Bob Anderson
Cover designer: Bruce Kenselaar

Excerpts from *Great Political Thinkers: Plato to the Present,*
Fifth Edition by William Ebenstein and Allan O. Ebenstein,
reprinted by permission of Holt, Rinehart and Winston, Inc.

 © 1996 by Prentice-Hall, Inc.
Simon & Schuster/A Viacom Company
Upper Saddle River, New Jersey 07458

Printed in the United States of America

10   9   8   7   6   5   4   3   2   1

ISBN 0-13-371592-2

Prentice-Hall International (UK) Limited, *London*
Prentice-Hall of Australia Pty. Limited, *Sydney*
Prentice-Hall Canada Inc., *Toronto*
Prentice-Hall Hispanoamericana, S.A., *Mexico*
Prentice-Hall of India Private Limited, *New Delhi*
Prentice-Hall of Japan, Inc., *Tokyo*
Simon & Schuster Asia Pte. Ltd., *Singapore*
Editora Prentice-Hall do Brasil, Ltda., *Rio de Janeiro*

This book is dedicated to Edward M. Allen, Jr.

Whatever success I have in the field of political
theory is due to his intellectual ability
and teaching skill.

CONTENTS

ACKNOWLEDGMENTS

The creation of a reader is one of the most complicated projects an individual can undertake. Long hours of reading, pondering, and writing are necessary in order to begin the task of assembling a group of works which represent the embodiment of a subject. Then the selected works must be edited so as to eliminate extraneous information and to fit into the space considerations of a publisher. Once those hurdles have been successfully met, a new reader appears on the market.

Although those hurdles have been met, as demonstrated by the fact that this volume is being read, its success will be determined by a number of factors. Certainly, an editor must possess an understanding of the material in order for the work to have value. But all scholars are products of their teachers. This author owes a debt in that regard to Dr. Edward Allen, Jr., of Appalachian State University and Dr. Daniel Jacobs of Miami University. Dr. Allen, who was the editor's first political theory professor, showed students the wonders of the past and how they had application to the contemporary period. Dr. Jacobs, who was the editor's Soviet politics and Marxist theory professor, continually challenged students to think critically. Hopefully, some of their efforts have bore fruit with the editor.

Appreciation was also due to other scholars whose efforts have produced works which have stimulated the intellectual growth of the editor. Among these are William Ebenstein and Alan O. Ebenstein's classic work, *Great Political Thinkers: Plato to the Present.* The Ebensteins' work has been the classic work on Western political thought in that it presents students with the actual writings of key philosophers and also shows the intellectual and political climate of the time under study. Appreciation was also due to Alpheus Thomas Mason's classic work *Free Government in the Making*. Mason's reader sets a standard by presenting what can only be viewed as the most inclusive set of readings on American political theory. In the preceding decades, scholars have repeatedly attempted to duplicate the nature of that work, but have failed to achieve the degree of scholarship presented by Mason.

The editor would also like to thank various individuals who directly assisted in the creation of this reader. Special thanks are owed to Dr. P. Albert Hughes of Appalachian State University, who was instrumental in proofing the manuscript and making suggestions regarding ideas that were overlooked by the author. The efforts of Ms. Adrienne Hiner and especially Ms. Kate Tillman during the 1994–1995 academic year were crucial in researching questions and references as well as in scanning the existing printed works into an electronic computer language. The editor would also like to thank Ms. Kathy Isaacs of the Hubbard Center for Faculty Development and Staff as well as Ms. Lisa Burwell of the Academic Computing Center, both at Appalachian State University, for their assistance in transferring the reading selections from paper into a computer language. A special thanks is also owed to the American Political Theory classes taught by the editor in 1993, 1994, and 1995, for much of this volume is the product of their inquisitive minds. Additionally, the editor would like to thank the following Prentice Hall reviewers who read the manuscript and offered constructive criticism: Roger Durham of Linfield College, Larry Elowitz of Georgia College, and Michael Johnston of Colgate University.

However, in the final analysis the organization and nature of this work are the responsibility of the editor. As such, mistakes should not be regarded as the responsibility of anyone else.

Jeffrey L. Prewitt

THE DILEMMA
OF AMERICAN
POLITICAL
THOUGHT

Chapter 1

INTRODUCTION

The eternal dilemma of Western political philosophy and certainly American thought is how to devise a political relationship which encourages individual rights and creativity while ensuring societal order. In that society, individual liberty would be maximized so that freedom and equality would be the standard, but not to the degree that one person or a group of people could suppress the well-being or abilities of others. A strong government would exist possessing the authority necessary to resolve societal problems, but not enough so as to dominate the individual or to allow one individual to control the majority. Finally, in the ideal society, an economic system would exist which would encourage human creativity and the development of society without allowing one person to take another's property or to use one's wealth to override the political rights of the majority. This is the dilemma of American political thought which has been evident since the first permanent English settlements were established on the North American continent over three hundred years ago.

Political theory tends to focus on past history in order to develop an outlook about political relationships. Fowler and Orenstein defined political theory as "the search for wisdom and understanding about the ends and means of political life. It is an activity concerned with the search for the best possible political and social lives of today's citizens."[1] Older definitions exist regarding political theory. Jacobson wrote, "political theory develops

---

[1]Robert Booth Fowler and Jeffrey R. Orenstein, *An Introduction to Political Theory* (New York: HarperCollins College Publishers, 1993), p. 1.

out of the needs and practices of its own age; often it arises out of specific issues and controversies."[2] Or as Russell wrote, "Philosophy . . . is something intermediate between theology and science. Like theology, it consists of speculations on matters as to which definite knowledge has, so far, been unascertainable; but like science, it appeals to human reason rather than to authority, whether that of tradition or that of revelation."[3] For the purpose of this reader, political theory is defined as the study of what ought to be national policy regarding the relationship between individual rights, governmental authority, and private property.

Political theory can therefore be described as being the product of a continuing debate over the nature of a political system, for as with all theory it is produced by the needs and practices of a people which are themselves constantly changing. As Tinder wrote, "the history of political thought shows how doubt continually pursues thought and frequently overtakes it."[4] Political theory seeks to examine policy alternatives in terms of values in order to deduce what policies ought to be chosen. Thus even though Americans may be better educated, wealthier, have longer lives, and experience what can only be described as an incredible technological capability, they continue to argue over what ought to be the relationship between individual liberty, government authority, and private property.

This reader examines the interplay between these values which have produced something special called the American political system. However, in an effort to acquaint the student with the analytic framework used in this study, the ideas of individual liberty, government authority, and private property are set forth in the following paragraphs. This framework examines these issues primarily in a European context, for as Mason and Leach noted, "This continent was settled almost entirely by immigrants from England, much of American political thought comes as a direct inheritance from the mother country. It is significant not only that this nation was founded by Englishmen, but also that seventeenth-century English culture served as the filter through which the congenial ideas of the past reached our forefathers."[5] At the same time, the influence of ancient Greece has to be acknowledged, given that it was with the ideas of Socrates, Plato, and Aristotle that Western political thought truly originated.

The key element in the dilemma of American political thought is the concept of individual liberty. Individuals created the state and it is in order to increase their well-being that private property exists. Individual liberty

---

[2]Thornton Anderson, ed., *Jacobson's Development of American Political Thought*, 2nd ed. (New York: Appleton-Century-Crofts, Inc., 1961), p. v.

[3]Bertrand Russell, *A History of Western Philosophy* (New York: Simon and Schuster, 1945), p. xiii. © Bertrand Russell Peace Foundation Ltd.

[4]Glenn Tinder, *Political Thinking*, 5th ed. (New York: HarperCollins Publishers, 1991), p. 16.

[5]Alpheus Thomas Mason and Richard H. Leach, *In Quest of Freedom*, 2nd ed. (Englewood Cliffs, NJ: Prentice-Hall, Inc., 1973), p. 1.

can be defined as the ability to establish one's own future, for humans have generally desired a maximum degree of freedom that would allow them to make their own decisions while remaining independent of the effects of decisions made by others. Implicately, the degree of liberty a person enjoys is related to human nature. If human beings are able to divine the best course of action for themselves without harming others, then a strong governing body is not needed. However, if human beings tend to engage in actions which limit the liberties enjoyed by a portion of the population, then a strong government is needed to establish a degree of equality.

Perhaps the oldest school of thought is that human beings are base creatures. Plato wrote over two thousand years ago of a utopian society in which there was no individual freedom because not all people were capable of perceiving the ideal form of things, and therefore the individual had only the same rights as individuals with similar abilities. Hobbes reached the same conclusion writing nearly nineteen centuries after Plato.

> During the time men live without a common power to keep all in awe, they are in that condition which is called war; and such a war as is of every man against every man. For war consists not in battle only, or the act of fighting, but in a tract of time, wherein the will to contend by battle is sufficiently known; and therefore the notion of time is to be considered in the nature of war, as it is in the nature of the weather.[6]

Apparent in the above quote was a belief that liberty for all was dangerous to the well-being of the community. However, not all writers agreed with this view on the nature of human beings.

Aristotle and John Locke were among those writers who rejected the dark side of human nature. Aristotle was perhaps the earliest writer to believe in the intrinsic goodness of human beings and their rationality in decision making. Where Plato created an oligarchy to control the population with a guardian class, Aristotle saw the people as capable of determining the orientation of the state. Likewise, Locke wrote that "To understand political power aright, and derive it from its original, we must consider, what state all men are naturally in, and that is, a state of perfect freedom to order their actions, and dispose of their possessions and persons, as they think fit, within the bounds of the law of nature, without asking leave, or depending upon the will of any other man."[7] Human beings once existed as rational beings in a state of nature which, according to Locke, they were willing to give up so as to achieve even greater bounties. Leaving the state

---

[6]Thomas Hobbes, *Leviathan*, *Great Political Thinkers: Plato to the Present*, 5th ed., eds. William Ebenstein and Alan O. Ebenstein (Orlando, FL: Holt, Rinehart and Winston, 1991), p. 408.

[7]John Locke, *Two Treatises of Government*, *Great Political Thinkers: Plato to the Present*, 5th ed., eds. William Ebenstein and Alan O. Ebenstein (Orlando, FL: Holt, Rinehart and Winston, 1991), p. 435.

of nature was not designed to deprive human beings of their rights, but to magnify their freedom.

The liberty created in the community takes different forms. Specifically, liberty can take the form of equality of opportunity or equality of outcome. Equality of opportunity invests the individual with the obligation to develop one's own place in society. It assumes that the individual has certain natural rights which government cannot intrude upon. The idea of equality of opportunity is perhaps best exemplified in the American tradition of rugged individualism that held the individual responsible for achieving social, economic, or political status. Conversely, equality of outcome holds government responsible for seeing that individuals share in the benefits of society because human beings tend to obstruct one another's liberty. Individuals thus possess only positive rights, or those privileges determined by government. The degree of liberty is therefore determined not only by the nature of the individual but by the extent of government authority. American political thought, the idea of equality of opportunity, is largely confined to the late nineteenth and twentieth centuries when government sought to limit the inequalities caused by extreme wealth and poverty.

Government is created by the popular demand that certain actions be encouraged or controlled. Government authority is defined as the legitimate use of state powers to direct society. Legitimacy is determined by the nature of a political system. In a democratic system such as the United States, legitimate policies are ones which receive popular support in uniting the population. As Tinder wrote, "politics is the art of reconciliation and that the need for this art always arises from some kind of estrangement."[8] Estrangement has its roots in the violation of people's rights and/or the economic abuse by the few or the many. Government provides people with a sense of direction in that it provides order. Few writers have suggested that government be abolished, for even the most outspoken have realized that government provides order in a society which is needed whether people be good or evil. Specifically, society is composed of individuals who make different and competing demands upon the political authority, and government seeks to arbitrate, mediate, and allocate scarce resources in the polity to benefit the people. Governments produce policies which are used to modify "social environments" in order "to pursue the best political outcomes."[9]

In relation to individual liberty and government authority there exists tension in the form of private property. Private property, the third of the three terms, is defined as the ownership of the means of production which occurs in both artificial (machinery) and natural (land) forms. But is private

[8]Tinder, *Political Thinking*, p. 23.
[9]Fowler and Orenstein, *An Introduction*, p. 177.

property theft or genius? Charles Beard, who was the first theorist to study the impact of economics on the creation of the Constitution, offered a quote by a Professor Seligman in explaining the importance of economics in human society.

> The existence of man depends upon his ability to sustain himself; the economic life is therefore the fundamental condition of all life. Since human life, however, is the life of man in society, individual existence moves within the framework of the social structure and is modified by it. What the conditions of maintenance are to the individual, the similar relations of production and consumption are to the community. To economic causes, therefore, must be traced in the last instance those transformations in the structure of society which themselves condition the relations of social classes and the various manifestations of social life.[10]

This theory suggested the idea of economic determinism; that is, economics determines political and social relationships. More recently, Fowler and Orenstein noted that a relationship existed between politics and economics as a result of the "reality that political decisions and governments cannot operate independently of the economy and resource patterns that they regulate."[11]

A strong government sees property as a source of taxes with which to implement its programs and as a form of inequality. There exists a tension in democratic society when political decisions are determined by majority rule, and those with huge amounts of property are able to appeal the political decision. This paradox is ingrained in the American political system most notably by the fact that the writers of the Constitution were motivated to form a strong central government which would protect their property. However, individuals regarded property as the ability to exercise their higher reasoning ability in providing for their well-being and that of society. The nature of property as a regressive or progressive force has been debated for over two thousand years. In *The Republic*, Plato held that property retarded the development of society's leaders and refused to allow the ruling class to possess it. More recently, a similar view was expressed by Karl Marx when private property was viewed as the means one part of society uses to repress another. Marx and Engels wrote, "the history of all hitherto existing society is the history of class struggles."[12] Only when private property is eliminated or controlled can there be equality of outcome in the

---

[10]Edwin R.A. Seligman, *The Economic Interpretation of History*, p. 3, in Charles Beard, *An Economic Interpretation of the Constitution of the United States* (New York: The Macmillan Company, 1913), p. 15.

[11]Fowler and Orenstein, *An Introduction*, p. 25.

[12]Karl Marx and Friedrich Engels, *The Communist Manifesto*, in *Great Political Thinkers: Plato to the Present*, 5th ed., eds. William Ebenstein and Alan O. Ebenstein (Orlando, FL: Holt, Rinehart and Winston, 1991), p. 737.

form of economic and political capabilities. The implementation of an income tax in the United States was an attempt to control extreme wealth by limiting the political influence of the wealthy and paying the cost of some social programs for the poor.

Supporters of private property rejected the idea that an equality of outcome can be enforced by the state without stunting individual freedom or depriving the community of economic growth. In this regard, Aristotle wrote over two thousand years ago that "property should be in a certain sense common, but, as a general rule, private; for, when every one has a distinct interest, men may not complain of one another, and they will make more progress, because every one will be attending to his own business."[13] Virtue is thus the result of private property. Equality of opportunity enables people to take charge of their lives, and provide for society's well-being. The classic exposition of private property was presented by Locke.

> God, who hath given the world to men in common, hath also given them reason to make use of it to the best advantage of life and convenience . . . Every man has a property in his own person. This nobody has any right to but himself. The labour of his body and the work of his hands . . . are properly his. Whatsoever, then, he removes out of the state that nature hath provided and left it in, he hath mixed his labour with it, and joined to it something that is his own, and thereby makes it his property.[14]

The belief in the individual's natural right to property enhanced the Western idea of individualism. Private property served to encourage individuals to take responsibility for their own well-being, as well as giving them the ability to challenge government decisions that are seen as dictatorial. Thus liberty was created. When Adam Smith registered a basic acceptance of Aristotle and Locke's views about private property in *The Wealth of Nations*, the additional point was made that government has no role in managing the economy. Although neither Aristotle, Locke, nor Smith used the French phrase laissez faire ("let it be") in application with economics, it quickly came to mean in nineteenth century America that the individual knows best how to manage economic relations and government should not interfere.

The Putney Debates stand as possibly the best example of the conflict between individual liberty, government authority, and private property even though they occurred before the birth of Smith and Marx. After the defeat of King Charles I's army, the Parliamentary Army of Oliver Cromwell debated the future direction of England in terms of property, government, and individual rights. Mason and Leach noted in this regard that Cromwell's forces agreed on three basic ideas: government as a social

---

[13]Aristotle, *Politics*, in *Great Political Thinkers: Plato to the Present*, 5th ed., eds. William Ebenstein and Alan O. Ebenstein (Orlando, FL: Holt, Rinehart and Winston, 1991), p. 98.

[14]John Locke, *Two Treatises of Government*, in *Great Political Thinkers*, eds. Ebenstein and Ebenstein, p. 441.

contract, the existence of higher law, and private property.[15] But they disagreed on the relationship between the three.[16] The officers, led by Cromwell and General Henry Ireton, argued that the social contract which established government was the basis for justice in terms of higher law and private property.[17] As General Ireton wrote, "Covenants freely made, freely entered into, must be kept one with another. Take away that I do not know what ground there is of any thing you can call any man's right."[18] To the rank and file soldiers led by Colonel Rainboro, higher law demanded that justice take precedence over the social compact which established government and private property.[19] The officers saw this as opening the way for the propertyless to take the property of the few, for they regarded property as the basis of government. Accordingly, the chief mission of the state was to protect property and thus its owners had the primary interest in a well-run government. General Ireton wrote in that regard,

> What weight there [is in it] lies in this: since there is a falling into a Government, and Government is to preserve property, therefore this cannot be against property. The objection does not lie in that, the making of it [i.e., the franchise more equal] but [in] the introducing of men into an equality of interest in this Government who have no property in this Kingdom, or who have no local permanent interest in it. . . . Why may not those men vote against all property?[20]

Almost in a Burkean sense, what is seen in the above quote is that those who own property are committed to controlling their emotions and thus are more capable in guiding the actions of government. Colonel Rainboro objected to that view and held that participating in elections was a right of all Englishmen in that the poorest man has the right to live as the richest does in terms of the political system.[21]

> Sir, I think it's clear, that every man that is to live under a Government ought first by his own consent to put himself under that Government; and I do think that the poorest man in England is not at all bound in a strict sense to that Government that he has not had a voice to put himself under. . . .[22]

[15]Mason and Leach, *In Quest*, p. 5.

[16]Ibid.

[17]Ibid.

[18]Lt. General Ireton, *Debates on the Putney Project*, in *Free Government in the Making*, 3rd ed., ed. Alpheus Thomas Mason (New York: Oxford University Press, 1965), p. 11.

[19]Ibid.

[20]Ibid, p. 17.

[21]Colonel Rainboro, *Debates on the Putney Project*, in *Free Government in the Making*, 3rd ed., ed. Alpheus Thomas Mason (New York: Oxford University Press, 1965), p. 13.

[22]Ibid.

Political equality requires that all people have the opportunity to be represented in government irrespective of their economic status according to Rainboro. Elections and representative government ensure the presentation of divergent interests and thereby act to suppress violations of the social contract. The Putney Debates stand as a primary example of the dilemma of politics and political theory in uniting individual liberty, government authority, and private property.

While this dilemma was truly given birth through the Putney Debates in 1647, it is alive and well in twentieth-century America. How to create a government with enough authority to act in society while being seen as legitimate? Are the liberties of a people to be based on equality of opportunity or equality of outcome? Is private property to be regarded as the means of encouraging individual and societal achievement while providing that everyone benefits from what is the largest economy on earth? Consider for a moment Fowler and Orenstein's definition of justice. "Justice must honor each of us in some basic . . . fashion; it must honor our moral worth and our very personhood."[23] If Americans are to find justice, then they must first resolve the struggle over the correct balance between individual liberty, government authority, and private property.

The reader is cautioned that there is no conclusion to this story. Creating a more perfect relationship has been the goal of successive generations of American leaders dating from the colonial period. The last three hundred plus years of American history illustrate the continuing struggle between individual liberty, government authority, and private property. In the process, each succeeding generation has contributed individuals possessed of remarkable intellectual talent who have written and debated the dilemma of American politics. As Mason and Leach wrote, "Each generation has made its own peculiar contribution to the stream of American thought . . . resulting in an accumulated storehouse of material continuously drawn upon in today's debate."[24] Knowledge of this "storehouse of material" is requisite to understanding the contemporary debate in American politics. It is in that regard that this reader is offered to the student as a means of developing a grasp of intellectual ideas.

This text organizes this material into eleven chapters each of which deals with a specific time frame with the exceptions of Chapters 7 and 8. (These chapters contain selected works of writers in which they display the truth they have found.) Each chapter begins with an introduction to the period and a set of discussion questions as to the meaning of the material during the time under study as well as the contemporary period. This is followed by a series of readings which exemplify political views of the time. As will be seen, one writer's truth is rarely the truth of their contempo-

[23]Fowler and Orenstein, *An Introduction*, p. 69.
[24]Mason and Leach, *In Quest*, pp. xii.

raries, let alone succeeding generations. However, in their works scholars have offered important clues that may someday allow Americans to create a relationship between individual liberty, governmental authority, and private property that will resolve the dilemma which first began on the American continent in the seventeenth century.

The purpose of the readings presented in the following chapters is twofold. First, the readings seek to inform students about the debates which have occurred in the past. Without political information students can never be expected to be more than ideologues. Secondly, the goal of this reader is to create an analytic framework which students can choose to adopt, or reject, in developing their own philosophy of American politics. The development of a critical thinking ability for adults is paramount in this regard for creating opportunities, particularly in intimate relationships, the workplace, political involvements, and their perceptions of the world.[25] According to Brookfield,

> When we think critically, we come to our judgments, choices, and decisions for ourselves, instead of letting others do this on our behalf. We refuse to relinquish the responsibility for making the choices that determine our indivudual and collective futures to those who presume to know what is in our own best interests. We become actively engaged in creating our personal and social worlds. In short, we take the reality of democracy seriously.[26]

Therefore, critical thinking is the empowerment of the individual in the context of this book, for it means to understand the dilemma of American political thought as well as seek its resolution. Perhaps someone who reads the next eleven chapters will be the person who resolves the dilemma of American political thought.

Chapter 2 begins this study by focusing on the role and attitudes of Puritans and Quakers in settling this continent. Even though Puritans and Quakers shared a common Christian focal point, their religious differences appeared to dictate different views of the state and citizens. For example, whereas the Puritans accepted the need for a strong state and limited rights for colonists, Quakers emphasized the individual as a key to solving societal problems. Individual freedom, or the lack thereof, was used by the early colonists to justify the acquisition of property.

As seen in Chapter 3, the religious hold over colonial affairs was eclipsed by economics after 1700. Seeing their lives less dominated by the goal of establishing the city of God on earth, individuals increasingly focused on acquiring property. A native middle class was created which sought to abolish restrictions on the acquisition of property and to achieve

---

[25]Stephen D. Brookfield, *Developing Critical Thinkers* (San Francisco: Jossey-Bass Publishers, 1987), p. x.
[26]Ibid.

major political roles in colonial affairs. That new-found freedom of action was confronted in the middle eighteenth century with English policies. The result was the intellectual foundations of the Revolutionary War.

Chapter 4 focuses on the formation of a new central government during the 1780s. While the Articles of Confederation provided a central authority for managing the Revolutionary War, they failed to unite the thirteen states after its conclusion. While basically accepting the idea that a new, more centralized government was necessary, two groups, the Federalists and Anti-federalists debated the extent of its powers over the people of this country and over the newly independent states. The Federalists generally saw a strong central government as the only way to hold the states together and to ensure individual liberties and property rights. Anti-federalists regarded a strong central government as much of a threat to individual liberties and private property as a weak one. To some degree that debate was settled with the adoption of the Constitution. Yet, not all Americans achieved political rights under it.

As seen in Chapter 5, the debate resurfaced in preceding years regarding the role of government in securing individual freedom and private property. The presidency of Andrew Jackson saw the reorientation of federal policies from supporting the expansion of commercial property to supporting individuals who created prosperity through their own ingenuity. This philosophy of rugged individualism held that individuals should be allowed to succeed or fail based on their own creativity and that the purpose of government was to eliminate artificial barriers. This emphasis on property led to the creation of the transcendentalist movement and its guiding belief that wealth corrupted the individual thereby destroying the spirit of democracy.

No single issue more polarized the continuing debate between the extent of individual liberty, government authority, and private property than did slavery as seen in Chapter 6. At the most basic level, slavery was a question of the rights Americans enjoyed. Namely, did they come from the Declaration of Independence or were they determined by government? If it was government, then did the federal government have greater competence than the states to make that decision? Finally, slavery was an issue of private property in that it was increasingly competing against the wage labor of Northern industry and the Western family farms.

In Chapter 7, the focus once again is directed on private property, but largely in terms of the impact of artificial property in expanding individual freedom. The rapid industrialization which took place as a result of the Civil War concentrated extreme wealth in the possession of a few. Justification for this fact was presented in terms of laissez-faire economics and the Gospel of Wealth. Subscribers to these doctrines regarded the individual's ability to accumulate wealth as representative of achieving equality. Consequently, the individual should neither seek the aid of government nor allow government to disturb the growth of opportunity which would expand equality.

Chapter 8 examines the expansion of wealth from the perspective that it hindered the opportunities available to the general population and that greater government involvement was necessary to ensure equality. Initially, this took the form of a debate between fundamentalists and revisionists over the extent of government involvement in the economy. However, by the twentieth century, the debate had turned to recognizing the natural rights of women to participate in the American democracy and the issue of whether the U.S. government should seek to promote democracy in other countries.

Federal interaction with the economy to secure individual rights also appears in Chapter 9, which focuses on the period between 1930 and 1940. The rugged individualism and the emphasis of equality of opportunity which characterized American political philosophy for a hundred years was rejected in favor of greater government intervention in the economy to secure equality of outcome. However, this philosophy was challenged by the believers in rugged individualism, but particularly from the extreme right by fascism and from the left by communism. These latter two philosophies sought greater government management if not ownership of the means of production as the only way to eliminate disruptive swings in the American economy.

Chapter 10 focuses on the regulation of individual liberties during the 1950s and 1960s at a time when the U.S. was engaged in a cold war with the Soviet Union. In preparing the nation to oppose Soviet communism a popular mindset emerged which regarded anyone critical of the U.S. government or the American way of life as being a communist sympathizer. Individuals who supported government regulation of the economy and who protested the conformity of ideas were regarded as subversive and thus fired or blacklisted to prevent their employment by other businesses.

The civil rights movements for minorities and women are examined in Chapter 11. Despite the fact that minorities, particularly blacks, and women had achieved de jure equality by 1920, discrimination continued to be practiced which prevented the enjoyment of basic civil and economic liberties. While these movements sought to address historic patterns of discrimination, voices were heard which debated the means by which to achieve equality. Most particularly, two thought patterns emerged, one which stressed individual rights and the ability of individuals to achieve political and economic rewards on their own, while another emphasized the role of government in providing groups with equality in terms of outcome.

Chapter 12 examines trends in political thought during the latter part of the twentieth century at which time the dilemma of American politics remained unresolved. By providing civil liberties for those people who were historically discriminated against, the idea also emerged that American society should give equal weight to the Anglo-American cultures and the cultures of minorities. Likewise, the fact that the American economy had failed to produce the equality necessary for a democracy came under scrutiny. Was this due to the maneuverings of the wealthy to dominate government decision making, or to government's increased regulatory and redistributing roles preventing the rapid expansion of the economy? Finally, James Q. Wilson offers one answer to the dilemma of American political thought with the conclusion that the problems of American society result from the freedom, prosperity, and democracy present in the United States. Americans desire that their elected leaders solve societal problems and at the same time demand freedom from government regulation of their lives and property.

The dilemma of American political thought is still present as witnessed by the contemporary debate over the extent of government's powers in regulating individual rights and private property. This reader is not an attempt to resolve that dilemma once and for all. Rather, this book is an attempt to chronicle the evolution of American political thought in order that students can be aware of reasonings presented in the past and seek the dilemma's resolution in the future.

Chapter 2

THE COLONIAL LEGACY

Freedom has been a key goal of people through the millennia whether it be defined in political or economic terms. The discovery of America provided a unique opportunity for people to flee economic, religious and political oppression in Europe and to experiment with various forms of political relationships in the New World. Individuals such as John Winthrop, Anne Hutchinson, Roger Williams, and William Penn produced in theory and fact new political relationships in regard to individual liberty, governmental authority, and private property.

As detailed in Table 1–1, the late seventeenth and early eighteenth centuries were periods of rapid settlement of the North American continent. Puritans and Quakers arrived in the New World seeking religious freedom as well as the most basic rights which had been denied to them because of their religious beliefs. As Nichols and Nichols noted in that regard,

> The Church of England was the state church and the medieval idea of uniformity was still too strong to brook the notion of more than one organization. Separatists were not only schismatic but unpatriotic and as the Queen (Elizabeth I) sought to subdue those who opposed her rule, she was also determined to destroy those who opposed her church.[1]

Because of their refusal to accept the national religion, nonconformists lost

---

[1]Jeanette P. Nichols and Roy F. Nichols, *The Growth of American Democracy* (New York: D. Appleton-Century Company, 1939), p. 12.

TABLE 1-1   *Total Colonial Population*

	1630	1640	1650	1660	1670	1680	1690
New Hampshire	500	1,055	1,305	1,555	1,805	2,047	4,164
Massachusetts	1,296	10,852	15,603	22,062	35,333	46,152	56,928
Rhode Island		300	785	1,539	2,155	3,017	4,224
Connecticut		1,472	4,139	7,980	12,603	17,246	21,645
New York	350	1,930	4,116	4,936	5,754	9,830	13,909
New Jersey					1,000	3,400	8,000
Pennsylvania						680	11,450
Delaware			185	540	700	1,005	1,482
Maryland		582	4,504	8,426	13,226	17,904	24,024
Virginia	2,500	10,442	18,731	27,020	35,309	43,596	53,046
North Carolina				1,000	3,850	5,430	7,600
South Carolina					200	1,200	3,900

Historical Statistics of the United States, Colonial Times to 1957 (Washington, D.C.: Department of Commerce, 1975), p. 756.

political and economic rights. The New World offered them an opportunity for religious freedom as well as an opportunity to establish a more Godly form of government and to own property. Ill prepared for the challenges in America the colonists generally held their religious views at the spiritual and political center of their communities.

The first movement to arrive in America was Puritanism, which was an offshoot of Calvinism. The Puritans sought to escape the civil domination of the monarchy and the religious authority of the Church of England in order to establish a society based on their understanding of God.[2] According to Miller and Johnson,

> The difference between the Anglican and the Puritan. . . was that the Puritan thought the Bible, the revealed word of God, was the word of God from one end to the other, a complete body of laws, an absolute code in everything it touched upon; the Anglican thought this a rigid, doctrinaire, and utterly unjustifiable extension of the authority of scripture.[3]

Given that the Bible suggested the existence of original sin, it was not surprising that Puritanism regarded human beings as depraved creatures. Since humans were sinful, and yet social beings, a strong coercive government was necessary to encourage civic virtue. This religious relationship was further strengthened by the facts that there was no higher authority to intervene and the settlers were engaged in a constant struggle against the wilderness. Winthrop wrote in this regard,

[2]Thornton Anderson, ed., *Jacobson's Development of American Political Thought*, 2nd ed. (New York: Appleton-Century-Crofts, Inc., 1961), p. 19.

[3]Perry Miller and Thomas H. Johnson, eds., *The Puritans* (New York: American Book Company, 1938), p. 43.

Now the only way to avoid this shipwreck (the destruction of the Puritan colony) and to provide for our posterity is to follow the Council of Micah, to do Justly, to allow mercy, to walk humbly with our God, for this end, we must entertain each other in brotherly affection, we must be willing to abridge our selves of our superfluities, for the supply of others' necessities, we must uphold familiar commerce together in all meekness, gentleness, patience and liberality, we must delight in each other, make our conditions our own, rejoice together, mourn together, labor, and suffer together, always having before our eyes our Commission and Community in the work, our Community as members of the same body, so shall we keep the light of the spirit in the bond of peace . . . that man of shall say of succeeding plantations: the Lord make it like that of New England: for we must consider that we shall be as a City upon a Hill.[4]

In the Puritan state, religious qualifications existed as a prerequisite for participation in politics; the clergy was the most powerful group in civil affairs and religious law took precedence over judicial procedures.[5] A consensual theory of politics was advocated in that all the Puritan settlers were united in a visible body structured by civil obedience to the magistrates and religious obedience to the clergy. Being a member of the Puritan religious community was key to one's ability to participate in politics. Miller and Johnson wrote of Puritanism in this regard,

The natural man was indeed bound in slavery to sin and unable to make exertions toward his own salvation; but the man into whose soul grace had been infused was liberated from that bondage and made free to undertake the responsibilities and obligations of virtue and decency.[6]

Being God's elect, which might be made known through a superior talent like financial success, obligated one to be a leader of the colony. Magistrates were thus responsible for following the Bible in achieving their own salvation as well as for members of the community. Equality was strictly defined in terms of outcome, not opportunity, for what was important was bringing the community closer to God. Miller and Johnson concluded that the Puritan state was:

An active instrument of leadership, discipline, and, whatever necessary, of coercion; it legislated over any or all aspects of human behavior, it not merely regulated misconduct but undertook to inspire and direct all conduct. . . . There was no idea of the equality of men. There was no questioning that men who would not serve the purposes of the society should be whipped into line. The government . . . was a dictatorship; . . . not of a single tyrant, or of an economic class, or of a political faction, but of the holy and regenerate.[7]

[4]John Winthrop, "A Modell of Christian Charity," in *The Puritans*, eds. Perry Miller and Thomas H. Johnson (New York: American Book Company, 1938), pp. 198-99.

[5]Anderson, *Jacobson's Development*, p. 21.

[6]Miller and Johnson, eds., *The Puritans*, p. 188.

[7]Ibid., p. 183.

Thus allowing the individual's conscience to prevail over the assembly was contradictory. Why should the colony's leaders, who were presumed to be the most godly, allow the individual, presumably the most sinful, to oppose their policies when the community alone possessed truth? Why would individuals come to a community whose beliefs they disagreed with unless they sought to destroy it? Submission to the government of the righteous was all-important and those who refused were either punished, exiled, or executed.[8]

Puritans tended to justify their philosophy in terms of Luther's "calling" and the Calvinist idea of "worldly asceticism" in economics and politics. Both ideas suggested that the acquisition of wealth was a potential indicator of one's godliness. Wealth for its own sake was sinful, but righteous when used to promote the glory of God in the community. Not all people would acquire wealth for its acquisition was determined by God. In this regard the Puritan state promoted equality of opportunity in that the purpose of government was not seen as determining who would achieve wealth.

The authoritarian nature of the Puritan government was not accepted by all of its members. The potential for a strong authority with discretion to abuse its powers was seen by individuals like Anne Hutchinson and Roger Williams. Hutchinson, who has been generally regarded as a leader of the Antinomian Crisis during the 1630s, held that the individual was responsible for achieving a "personal sense of communion with God," and therefore did not have to rely on the Puritan church to obtain grace.[9] Each individual was seen as possessing a conscience which was the highest source of authority for that person. Hutchinson wrote in this regard, "The Lord spake this to me with a strong hand, and instructed me that I should not walke in the way of this people."[10] Hutchinson's ideas challenged the Puritan emphasis on works to achieve salvation, and had the practical political effect that all individuals must have the same opportunities to participate in the governance of the colony. Another outspoken critic, Roger Williams, held that the individual's conscience was superior to that of the community, and thus there existed a need to separate the church from the state in order to give the individual the ability to achieve salvation. Williams wrote, "While I plead the Cause of Truth and Innocence against the bloody Doctrine of Persecution for cause of conscience, I judge it not unfit to give alarm to my self, and all men to prepare to be persecuted or hunted for cause of conscience."[11] As the possessors

---

[8]Notable among the punishments were "Quakers whipped, blasphemers punished by the amputation of ears, Antinomians exiled, Anabaptists fined, or witches executed." Ibid., p. 185.

[9]David D. Hall, *The Antinomian Controversy, 1636–1638,* (2nd ed.) Durham, NC: Duke University Press, 1990, p. 18. Reprinted with permission.

[10]Ibid., p. 273.

[11]Roger Williams, "The Bloudy Tenent of Persecution," in *The Puritans*, eds. Perry Miller and Thomas H. Johnson (New York: American Book Company, 1938), p. 216.

of religious truth and state power, the regenerate, or saints, of the Puritan community had the ability to force acceptance of their truth. Individuals like Hutchinson and Williams had no civil protection or religious right to demand their consciences be considered equal with those of the colony's leadership. As a consequence of their activities, both Hutchinson and Williams were exiled from the Puritan community.

The centrality of the individual as seen in the writings of Hutchinson and Williams was confirmed by the Quakers. In the short ten-year period from 1680 to 1690, the Quaker population in America exploded as seen by the increase in Pennsylvania's population from less than seven hundred to more than eleven thousand. The Society of Friends, or Quakers as they were better known, was founded in 1647 as a reaction to the formalism of Anglicanism and the stiffness of Puritanism. Quakers accepted the idea that an inner light existed within all human beings whether they were European or Native American, but whose intensity was determined by the acceptance of Christ's teachings. Whereas Puritans regarded individual failings as the result of original sin, Quakers held that sin was due to individuals' actions and imperfections. Thus Quakers appeared willing to accept the idea of natural equality. Given that individual equality appeared as an assured feature of their religious lives, the Quakers used congregational meetings to resolve problems. Their decisions were based primarily on consensus instead of voting in order to achieve "the corporate inner light."[12]

Generally speaking, Quakers rejected involvement in government until the founding of the Holy Experiment in Pennsylvania by William Penn. Quakers accepted a limited government because of their belief that the inner light did not burn as brightly in all people. As Beitzinger wrote, Quaker political philosophy was to:

> Establish, on the basis of the teachings of the fifth chapter of the Gospel according to St. Matthew and the twelfth chapter of St. Paul's epistle to the Romans, a government in which virtue would rule and the ideals of brotherhood, equality, liberty of conscience, simplicity and purity of life and manners, the sovereignty of the Inner Light, and peace and nonviolence might be realized for all men, regardless of religious persuasion.[13]

Or as Penn concluded, government exists in order to "terrify evildoers" and "to cherish those that do well."[14] Penn's definition thus ensured that those who used their inner light in a progressive manner would be rewarded by government and therefore governmental authority was not restricted to a coercive role. Equality of opportunity appeared as the rule in Pennsylvan-

[12]A.J. Beitzinger, *A History of American Political Thought* (New York: Dodd, Mead & Company, 1972), p. 72.

[13]Ibid., p. 74.

[14]Ibid., p. 75.

ian politics in that Quakers as well as other nonconformists were allowed to participate in politics. As Beitzinger concluded regarding Puritans and Quakers, "the difference between them lay in their answers to the crucial question, who is ultimately to decide what is politically 'good, just and honest'? Winthrop leaned in the direction of magisterial prerogative, whereas Penn . . . emphasized the need for settled, known, just laws based on the consent of freeholders."[15] It was therefore incumbent upon Quakers to be involved in politics so as to ensure their rights.

Both Puritans and Quakers brought their religious attitudes to government in order to create a more perfect society. While private property was important as a right that was denied to them in England, their primary concern was apparently the role of government vis-à-vis the individual. The following writings by John Winthrop, Anne Hutchinson, and Roger Williams are especially pointed in that regard.

A Modell of Christian Charity*

John Winthrop

. . . GOD ALMIGHTIE in his most holy and wise providence hath soe disposed of the Condicion of mankinde, as in all times some must be rich some poore, some highe and eminent in power and dignitie; others meane and in subieccion.

The Reason Hereof.

I. Reas: *First,* to hold conformity with the rest of his workes, being delighted to shewe forthe the glory of his wisdome in the variety and differance of the Creatures and the glory of his power, in ordering all these differences for the preservacion and good of the whole, and the glory of his greatnes that as it is the glory of princes to haue many officers, soe this great King will haue many Stewards counting himselfe more honoured in dispenceing his guifts to man by man, then if hee did it by his owne immediate hand.

2. Reas: *Secondly,* That he might haue the more occasion to manifest the worke of his Spirit: first, vpon the wicked in moderateing and restraineing them: soe that the riche and mighty should not eate vpp the poore, nor the poore, and dispised rise vpp against their superiors, and shake off theire yoake; 2ly in the regenerate in exerciseing his graces in them, as in

---

[15]Ibid., p. 77.

*From John Winthrop, "A Modell of Christian Charity," in *The Puritans,* eds. Perry Miller and Thomas H. Johnson (New York: American Book Company, 1938), pp. 195–99.

the greate ones, theire loue mercy, gentlenes, temperance etc., in the poore
and inferiour sorte, theire faithe patience, obedience etc:

3. Reas: *Thirdly,* That every man might haue need of other, and from
hence they might be all knitt more nearly together in the Bond of brotherly
affeccion: from hence it appeares plainely that noe man is made more hon-
ourable then another or more wealthy etc., out of any perticuler and sin-
guler respect to himselfe but for the glory of his Creator and the Common
good of the Creature, Man; Therefore God still reserues the propperty of
these guifts to himselfe as Ezek: 16. 17. he there calls wealthe his gold and
his silver etc. Prov: 3. 9. he claimes theire seruice as his due honour the Lord
with thy riches etc. All men being thus (by divine providence) rancked into
two sortes, riche and poore; vnder the first, are comprehended all such as
are able to liue comfortably by theire owne meanes duely improued; and all
others are poore according to the former distribution. There are two rules
whereby wee are to walke one towards another: JUSTICE and MERCY.
These are allwayes distinguished in theire Act and in theire obiect, yet may
they both concurre in the same Subiect in eache respect; as sometimes there
may be an occasion of shewing mercy to a rich man, in some sudden danger of distresse, and allsoe doeing of meere Justice to a poor man in regard
of some perticuler contract etc. There is likewise a double Lawe by which
wee are regulated in our conversacion one towardes another: in both the
former respects, the lawe of nature and the lawe of grace, or the morrall
lawe or the lawe of the gospell, to omitt the rule of Justice as not propperly
belonging to this purpose otherwise then it may fall into consideracion in
some perticuler Cases: By the first of these lawes man as he was enabled soe
withall [is] commaunded to loue his neighbour as him selfe vpon this
ground stands all the precepts of the morrall lawe, which concernes our
dealings with men. To apply this to the works of mercy this lawe requires
two things first that every man afford his help to another in every want or
distresse Secondly, That hee performe this out of the same affeccion, which
makes him carefull of his owne good according to that of our Saviour Math:
[7. 12.] Whatsoever ye would that men should doe to you. This was practised by Abraham and Lott in entertaineing the Angells and the old man of
Gibea.

The Lawe of Grace or the Gospell hath some differance from the former as in these respectes first the lawe of nature was giuen to man in the
estate of innocency; this of the gospell in the estate of regeneracy: 2ly, the
former propounds one man to another, as the same fleshe and Image of
god, this as a brother in Christ allsoe, and in the Communion of the same
spirit and soe teacheth vs to put a difference betweene Christians and others. Doe good to all especially to the household of faith; vpon this ground
the Israelites were to putt a difference betweene the brethren of such as
were strangers though not of the Canaanites. 3ly. The Lawe of nature could
giue noe rules for dealeing with enemies for all are to be considered as

freinds in the estate of innocency, but the Gospell commaunds loue to an enemy. proofe[:] If thine Enemie hunger feede him; Loue your Enemies doe good to them that hate you Math: 5. 44.

This Lawe of the Gospell propoundes likewise a difference of seasons and occasions there is a time when a christian must sell all and giue to the poore as they did in the Apostles times. There is a tyme allsoe when a christian (though they giue not all yet) must giue beyond theire abillity, as they of Macedonia. Cor: 2. 6. likewise community of perills calls for extraordinary liberallity and soe doth Community in some speciall seruice for the Churche. *Lastly,* when there is noe other meanes whereby our Christian brother may be releiued in this distresse, wee must help him beyond our ability, rather then tempt God, in putting him vpon help by miraculous or extraordinary meanes. . . .

1. For the persons, wee are a Company professing our selues fellow members of Christ, In which respect onely though wee were absent from eache other many miles, and had our imploymentes as farre distant, yet wee ought to account our selues knitt together, by this bond of loue, and liue in the exercise of it, if wee would haue comforte of our being in Christ, this was notorious in the practise of the Christians in former times, as is testified of the Waldenses. . . from the mouth of one of the adversaries Aeneas Syluius, mutuo [solent amare] pene antequam norint, they vse to loue any of theire owne religion even before they were acquainted with them.

2ly. for the worke wee haue in hand, it is by a mutuall consent through a speciall overruleing providence, and a more then an ordinary approbation of the Churches of Christ to seeke out a place of Cohabitation and Consorteshipp vnder a due forme of Government both ciuill and ecclesiasticall. In such cases as this the care of the publique must oversway all private respects, by which not onely conscience, but meare Ciuill pollicy doth binde vs; for it is a true rule that perticuler estates cannott subsist in the ruine of the publique.

3ly. The end is to improue our liues to doe more seruice to the Lord the comforte and encrease of the body of christe whereof wee are members that our selues and posterity may be the better preserued from the Common corrupcions of this euill world to serue the Lord and worke out our Salvacion vnder the power and purity of his holy Ordinances.

4ly. for the meanes whereby this must bee effected, they are 2fold, a Conformity with the worke and end wee aime at, these wee see are extraordinary, therefore wee must not content our selues with vsuall ordinary meanes whatsoever wee did or ought to haue done when wee liued in England, the same must wee doe and more allsoe where wee goe: That which the most in theire Churches maineteine as a truthe in profession onely, wee must bring into familiar and constant practice, . . . as in this duty of loue wee must loue brotherly without dissimulation, wee must loue one another with a pure hearte feruently wee must beare one anothers burthens, wee must not looke onely on our owne things, but allsoe on the things of our brethren, neither must wee think that the lord will beare with such faileings at our hands as hee dothe from those among whome wee haue liued. . . .

Thus stands the cause betweene God and vs, wee are entered into Covenant with him for this worke, wee haue taken out a Commission, the Lord hath giuen vs leaue to drawe our owne Articles wee haue professed to enterprise these Accions vpon these and these ends, wee haue herevpon besought him of favour and blessing: Now if the Lord shall please to heare vs, and bring vs in peace to the place wee desire, then hath hee ratified this Covenant and sealed our Commission, [and] will expect a strict performance of the Articles contained in it, but if wee shall neglect the observacion of these Articles which are the ends wee haue propounded, and dissembling with our God, shall fall to embrace this present world and prosecute our carnall intencions seekeing great things for our selues and our posterity, the Lord will surely breake out in wrathe against vs be revenged of such a periured people and make vs knowe the price of the breache of such a Covenant. . . .

Now the onely way to avoyde this shipwracke and to provide for our posterity is to followe the Counsell of Micah, to doe Justly, to loue mercy, to walke humbly with our God, for this end, wee must be knitt together in this worke as one man, wee must entertaine each other in brotherly Affeccion, wee must be willing to abridge our selues of our superfluities, for the supply of others necessities, wee must vphold a familiar Commerce together in all meekenes, gentlenes, patience and liberallity, wee must delight in eache other, make others Condicions our owne reioyce together, mourne together, labour, and suffer together, allwayes haueing before our eyes our Commission and Community in the worke, our Community as members of the same body, soe shall wee keepe the vnitie of the spirit in the bond of peace, the Lord will be our God and delight to dwell among vs, as his owne people and will commaund a blessing vpon vs in all our wayes, soe that wee shall see much more of his wisdome power goodnes and truthe then formerly wee haue beene acquainted with, wee shall finde that the God of Israell is among vs, when tenn of vs shall be able to resist a thousand of our enemies, when hee shall make vs a prayse and glory, that men shall say of succeeding plantacions: the lord make it like that of New England: for wee must Consider that wee shall be as a Citty vpon a Hill, the eies of all people are vppon vs; soe that if wee shall deale falsely with our god in this worke wee haue vndertaken and soe cause him to withdrawe his present help from vs, wee shall be made a story and a by-word through the world, wee shall open the mouthes of enemies to speake euill of the wayes of god and all professours for Gods sake; wee shall shame the faces of many of gods worthy seruants, and cause theire prayers to be turned into Cursses vpon vs till wee be consumed out of the good land whether wee are goeing: And to shutt vpp this discourse with that exhortacion of Moses that faithfull seruant of the Lord in his last farewell to Irsaell Deut. 30. Beloued there is now sett before vs life, and good, deathe and euill in that wee are Commaunded this day to loue the Lord our God,and to loue one another to walke in his wayes and to keepe his Commaundements and his Ordinance, and his lawes, and the Articles of our Covenant with him that wee may liue and be multiplyed, and that the Lord our God may blesse vs in the land whether wee goe to possesse it: But if our heartes shall turne away soe that wee will not obey, but shall be seduced and worshipp . . . other Gods our pleasures, and proffitts, and serue them; it is propounded vnto vs this day, wee shall surely perishe out of the good Land whether wee passe over this vast Sea to possesse it . . .

Statement of Mistress Anne Hutchinson*

Anne Hutchinson

When I was in old *England,* I was much troubled at the constitution of the Churches there, so farre, as I was ready to have joyned to the Separation, whereupon I set apart a day for humiliation by my selfe, to seeke direction from God, and then did God discover unto me the unfaithfulnesse of the Churches, and the danger of them, and that none of those Ministers could preach the Lord Jesus aright, for he had brought to my mind, that in the 1 John 4. 3. Every spirit that confesseth not, that Jesus Christ is come in the flesh, is the spirit of Antichrist; I marvelled what this should meane, for I knew that neither Protestants nor Papists did deny that Christ was come in the flesh; and are the Turkes then the onely Antichrists? Now I had none to open the Scripture to me, but the Lord, he must be the Prophet, then he brought to my mind another Scripture, He that denies the Testament, denies the death of the Testator; from whence the Lord did let me see, that every one that did not preach the New Covenant, denies the death of the Testator; then it was revealed to me that the Ministers of *England* were these Antichrists, but I knew not how to beare this, I did in my heart rise up against it, then I begged of the Lord that this Atheisme might not be in my heart: after I had begged this light, a twelve moneth together, at last he let me see how I did oppose Christ Jesus, and he revealed to mee that place in *Esay* 46. 12, 13. and from thence shewed me the Atheisme of my owne heart, and how I did turne in upon a Covenant of works, and did oppose Christ Jesus; from which time the Lord did discover to me all sorts of Ministers, and how they taught, and to know what voyce I heard, which was the voyce of *Moses,* which of *John Baptist,* and which of Christ; the voyce of my

*From Anne Hutchinson, Statement of Mistress Anne Hutchinson, in David D. Hall, ed., *The Antinomian Controversy, 1636–1638,* (2nd ed.), pp 271–73. Durham, NC: Duke University Press, 1990. Reprinted with permission.

beloved, from the voyce of strangers; and thenceforth I was the more care-full whom I heard, for after our teacher Mr. *Cotton,* and my brother *Wheelwright* were put downe, there was none in England that I durst heare. Then it pleased God to reveale himselfe to me in that of *Esay* 30. 20. Though the Lord give thee the bread of adversity, &c. yet thine eyes shall see thy teachers; after this the Lord carrying Mr. *Cotton* to *New England* (at which I was much troubled) it was revealed to me, that I must go thither also, and that there I should be persecuted and suffer much trouble. I will give you another Scripture, *Jer.* 46. Feare not *Jacob* my servant, for I am with thee, I will make a full end of all the Nations, &c. then the Lord did reveale himselfe to me, sitting upon a Throne of Justice, and all the world appearing before him, and though I must come to *New England,* yet I must not feare nor be dismaied. The Lord brought another Scripture to me, *Esay* 8. 9. The Lord spake this to me with a strong hand, and instructed me that I should not walke in the way of this people, &c. I wil give you one place more which the Lord brought to me by immediate revelations, and that doth concerne you all, it is in *Dan.* 6. When the Presidents and Princes could find nothing against him, because he was faithfull, they sought matter against him concerning the Law of his God, to cast him into the Lions denne; so it was revealed to me that they should plot against me, but the Lord bid me not to feare, for he that delivered *Daniel,* and the three children, his hand was not shortened. And see this Scripture fulfilled this day in mine eyes, therefore take heed what yee goe about to doe unto me, for you have no power over my body, neither can you do me any harme, for I am in the hands of the eternall Jehovah my Saviour, I am at his appointment, the bounds of my habitation are cast in Heaven, no further doe I esteeme of any mortall man, then creatures in his hand, I feare none but the great Jehovah, which hath foretold me of these things, and I doe verily beleeve that he will deliver me out of our hands, therefore take heed how you proceed against me; for I know that for this you goe about to doe to me, God will ruine you and your posterity, and this whole State.

The Bloudy Tenent of Persecution*

Roger Williams

WHILE I plead the Cause of *Truth* and *Innocencie* against the bloody Doctrine of Persecution for cause of *conscience,* I judge it not unfit to give alarme to my selfe, and all men to prepare to be persecuted or hunted for cause of *conscience.*

*From Roger Williams, "The Bloudy Tenent of Persecution," in *The Puritans*, eds. Perry Miller and Thomas H. Johnson (New York: American Book Company, 1938), pp. 216–17.

Whether thou standest charged with 10 or but 2 *Talents,* if thou huntest any for cause of *conscience,* how canst thou say thou followest the *Lambe* of *God* who so abhorr'd that practice? . . .

Who can now but expect that after so many scores of yeares *preaching* and professing of more *Truth,* and amongst so many great *contentions* amongst the very best of *Protestants,* a fierie furnace should be heat, and who sees not now the *fires* kindling?

I confesse I have little hopes till those flames are over, that this Discourse against the *doctrine* of *persecution* for cause of *conscience* should passe currant (I say not amongst the *Wolves* and *Lions,* but even amongst the Sheep of Christ themselves) yet . . . I have not hid within my *breast* my *souls* belief: And although sleeping on the bed either of the pleasures or profits of sinne thou thinkest thy conscience bound to smite at him that dares to waken thee? Yet in the middest of all these *civill* and *spirituall Wars* (I hope we shall agree in these particulars.)

First, how ever the proud (upon the advantage of an higher earth or ground) or'elooke the poore and cry out *Schismatickes, Hereticks,* &c. shall *blasphemers* and *seducers* scape unpunished? &c. Yet there is a sorer punishment in the Gospel for despising of Christ then *Moses,* even when the despiser of *Moses* was put to death without mercie, Heb. 10. 28, 29. He that beleeveth not shall bee damned, Marke 16. 16.

Secondly, what ever Worship, Ministry, Ministration, the best and purest are practised without *faith* and true perswasion that they are the true institutions of God, they are sin, sinfull worships, Ministries, &c. And however in Civill things we may be servants unto men, yet in Divine and Spirituall things the poorest *pesant* must disdaine the service of the highest *Prince:* Be ye not the servants of men, I Cor. 14.

Thirdly, without search and triall no man attaines this faith and right perswasion, I Thes. 5. Try all things.

In vaine have *English Parliaments* permitted English Bibles in the poorest *English* houses, and the simplest man or woman to search the Scriptures, if yet against their soules perswasion from the Scripture, they should be forced (as if they lived in *Spaine* or *Rome* it selfe without the sight of a *Bible*) to beleeve as the Church beleeves.

Fourthly, having tried, we must hold fast, I *Thessal.* 5. upon the losse of a Crowne, *Revel.* 13. we must not let goe for all the flea bitings of the present afflictions, &c. having bought Truth deare, we must not sell it cheape, not the least graine of it for the whole World, no not for the saving of Soules, though our owne most precious; least of all for the bitter sweetning of a little vanishing pleasure.

For a little puffe of credit and reputation from the changeable breath of uncertaine sons of men.

For the broken bagges of Riches on Eagles wings: For a dreame of these, any or all of these which on our death-bed vanish and leave tormenting stings behinde them: Oh how much better is it from the love of Truth, from the love of the Father of lights, from whence it comes, from the love of the Sonne of God, who is the way and the Truth, to say as he, *John* 18. 37. For this end was I borne, and for this end came I into the World that I might beare witnesse to the Truth.

DISCUSSION QUESTIONS

1. What role did religion play in the settling of the American colonies?
2. Does the individual or the minority have the right to resist government policy according to the Puritans and Quakers?
3. What is the proper role of government in a society?
4. How was private property a component of individual freedom for the early settlers?

Chapter 3

THE PAMPHLET WAR

During the period from 1750 to 1775, the intellectual foundations were laid for the Revolutionary War. Key among the elements which promoted the conflict were the greater political and economic freedom of the early colonists and the restricted focus of colonial governments.

While the colonial governments offered protection from the hostile environment they were not absolute. Their responsibility was largely limited to providing a few public works, most notable of which was defense from the Native American attacks. Moreover, those who dissented from the actions of local government could migrate to the western territories to find wealth or greater political freedom. As suggested by Fredrick Jackson Turner's frontier thesis, the result of westward migrations was the rise of individualism and liberty culminating in democracy. Miller and Johnson noted regarding the Puritans, "the character of the people underwent a change; they moved further into the frontier, they became more absorbed in business and profits than in religion and salvation, their memories of English social stratification grew dim."[1] The early colonists became less concerned with heaven, and more interested in individualism and the responsiveness of local government.

During the first half of the eighteenth century, the importance of colonial self-government was challenged by the resurgence of divine right theory. As Bailyn noted, by 1750 there were suggestions that the Anglican

---

[1] Perry Miller and Thomas H. Johnson, eds., *The Puritans* (New York: American Book Company, 1938), p. 17.

church in America was reverting to the divine right of kings which promoted the idea of the people's duty of passive submission to their monarch.[2] Its acceptance implied the end of religious toleration as well as self-government, and the reassertion of the English Crown's right to determine political and economic outcomes in the colonies.

Responding to divine right theory, Jonathan Mayhew argued that kingship was not based on God-granted rights, but upon the limited powers surrendered to the king in the form of a social contract. In "A Discourse Concerning Unlimited Submission," Mayhew reiterated the Lockean idea that human beings were invested with natural rights and that certain of these rights were given up freely to the state in exchange for greater protection. The test of a good ruler was whether leadership promoted "the common good."[3] Accordingly, the monarch's powers were limited, since the people were the true sovereigns.

> If we calmly consider the nature of the thing itself, nothing can well be imagined more directly contrary to common sense, than to suppose that millions of people should be subjected to the arbitrary, precarious pleasure of one single man; (who has naturally no superiority over them in point of authority) so that their estates, and every thing that is valuable in life, and even their lives also, shall be absolutely at his disposal, if he happens to be wanton and capricious enough to demand them.[4]

While Mayhew's rejection of divine right theory was not new, it justified the existence of self-government and individualism for early colonial society.

This idea of limited submission to government resurfaced in 1763 when a tract appeared promoting the establishment of a Church of England bishopric in the American colonies.[5] This course of action was inconsistent with the settling of Massachusetts, Connecticut, and Pennsylvania, for they were originally refugees from the Church of England. As for Virginia, where a significant Anglican population existed, the possibility of a bishopric suggested that the British social structure might also be transplanted thereby negating the planters' responsibility for religious and governmental affairs. Mayhew's emphasis on the individual was prominent in defeating the establishment of an Anglican bishopric.

---

[2] Reprinted by permission of the publishers from *Pamphlets of the American Revolution, 1750–1776*, edited by Bernard Bailyn, Cambridge, MA: The Belknap Press of Harvard University Press, Copyright © 1965 by the President and Fellows of Harvard College. I, 206.

[3] A.J. Beitzinger, *A History of American Political Thought* (New York: Dodd, Mead & Company, 1972), p. 109.

[4] Jonathan Mayhew, "A Discourse Concerning Unlimited Submission." Reprinted by permission of the publishers from *Pamphlets of the American Revolution, 1750–1776*, edited by Bernard Bailyn, Cambridge, MA: The Belknap Press of Harvard University Press, Copyright © 1965 by the President and Fellows of Harvard College, I, 235.

[5] Bailyn, *Pamphlets*, p. 5.

While the Episcopate Dispute appeared as the sharpest dispute between Britain and its colonies, trends over the previous seventy years suggested growing British intrusion into colonial affairs. British colonial policy began taking on a new outlook when Charles II granted huge tracts of land to supporters.[6] Implicit in that approach was that individuals settling in the New World accepted the sovereignty of the monarch in exchange for land. Likewise colonial self-government was threatened by King James II's attempt to organize New Hampshire, Massachusetts, Plymouth, Connecticut, Rhode Island, New York, and New Jersey under a royal governor.[7]

The stability of British and American relations were particularly challenged as a result of a series of wars which transpired from 1689 to 1755 and resulted in a colonial debt of 750,000 pounds as well as British war debts which totaled 130,000,000 pounds.[8] In 1763, the British government concluded that the American colonies should help pay the war debts and that efforts were necessary to knit together the far-flung parts of the British Empire.[9] A succession of taxation policies were enacted in 1764 and 1765, including the Revenue, Currency, and Stamp Acts, with the goal of ending the American financial burden on the English Crown. These policies spurred financial difficulties in the colonies as well as protests.

With their economic freedom threatened, the colonial governments sought to reproach Britain for its actions, not declare their independence. Attempts to resist British authority or organize a united opposition resulted in the dissolution of the New York, Massachusetts, and Virginia legislatures.[10] The quarrel over economic rights was quickly transformed into a dispute over the political rights of the colonists which was primarily fought through pamphlets.[11] Pamphlets were central in publicizing the views of James Otis, Martin Howard, Jr., and Thomas Paine, as well as galvanizing public opinion.

Otis argued that the British government was attempting to establish a new colonial relationship in the pamphlet "The Rights of the British Colonies Asserted and Proved." Like other opponents of direct British rule, Paine was not arguing for the end of British authority in the Americas, but that the colonists' natural rights were threatened. Otis acknowledged the power of Parliament to enact legislation but only so long as it did not violate the intrinsic rights of all human beings. Moreover, simply because Par-

[6]Jeanette P. Nichols and Roy F. Nichols, *The Growth of American Democracy* (New York: D. Appleton-Century Company, 1939), p. 18.

[7]Ibid., p. 37.

[8]Ibid., p. 67.

[9]Anderson, *Jacobson's Development*, pp. 95–96.

[10]Nichols and Nichols, *The Growth*, pp. 72, 75.

[11]Pamphlets were composed of a "few printer's sheets" of paper folded to make pages, stitched together but left unbound. Bailyn, *Pamphlets*, p. 3.

liament possessed the ability to pass laws did not make them just. In this regard Otis wrote, "the end of government being the good of mankind points out its great duties: it is above all things to provide for the security, the quiet, and happy enjoyment of life, liberty and property."[12] Governments which existed to increase their power violated the mission of spurring the development of society and were thus in conflict with the popular sovereignty invested in the people. Among Otis's list of grievances against the Crown were: (1) the rights of the colonists as Englishmen were being violated; (2) Parliament lacked the power to tax the colonies without their representation; and (3) the colonies were prohibited from trading with other countries, including British colonies. Otis can be seen as capitalizing on Mayhew's idea that the colonists were not required to submit to an unjust ruler.

Against Otis's contention of natural rights, Martin Howard, Jr., argued a strict positivist view of the colonial-British relationship. In *A Letter from a Gentleman at Halifax*, three arguments were presented supporting English colonial policy. First, Howard argued that there was a difference in terms of political and personal rights. The personal rights of life, liberty, and property were protected by English law, and the political rights of the colonists were amendable in that they were established in colonial charters by acts of the British government. The colonists could not accept the legitimacy of their personal rights and reject their political rights, since both were based on Parliament's authority. Secondly, Howard maintained that Parliament's power was based on common law and therefore the state was competent to determine what was in the best interest of its citizens. The people thus did not have any natural rights. Their rights were restricted to those offered by Parliament. Finally, the American colonies were not unique in that other Englishmen living abroad were also denied representation. Parliament, as the source of political power, could exercise the authority vested in it to make decisions without consulting the people regarding their interests.

In the following years, the views of Otis, Howard, and others would be cited in the debate over British colonial policy. Ultimately, events outpaced attempts to maintain the colonies as part of the British Empire. In 1767, the Townsend Acts placed a colonial import tax on glass, lead, paint, paper, and tea, as well as established special machinery for collecting these taxes and enforcing the laws.[13] The failure to repeal the tea tax with the others, as well as passage of the North Act in 1773 caused further anger. Colonists feared establishment of a tea monopoly would prompt

---

[12]James Otis, "The Rights of the British Colonies Asserted and Proved." Reprinted by permission of the publishers from *Pamphlets of the American Revolution, 1750–1776,* edited by Bernard Bailyn, Cambridge, MA: The Belknap Press of Harvard University Press, copyright © 1965 by the President and Fellows of Harvard College. I, 425.

[13]John W. Caughey and Ernest R. May, *A History of the United States* (Chicago: Rand McNally, 1964), p. 96.

the creation of other monopolies.[14] The refusal to buy tea, and more particularly the tea dumpings, prompted Parliament to assert its powers through: (1) the Boston Port Act, which closed the harbor until the tea was paid for; (2) the Administration of Justice Act, which allowed trials to be moved to England; (3) the Massachusetts Government Act, which made the legislature appointed and restricted town meetings; and (4) the Quartering Act, which allowed the requisitioning of buildings for troop housing.[15] These acts, which were perceived in the colonies as threatening economic freedoms as well as colonial self-government, stimulated the calling of the First Continental Congress. By 1775, the prospect of peaceful resolution of the grievances dissipated as the colonists and British soldiers openly engaged in an armed struggle.

American independence became a prominent theme in early 1776 at the same time Thomas Paine published his pamphlet *Common Sense*. Unlike Otis who accepted Parliament's authority, Paine argued the rights of the colonists were denied by King George III. Moreover, the reliance on political legalism which characterized the works of Otis and Howard was absent from Paine's pamphlet which appeared as a literary spark igniting the political controversy into armed rebellion. The basic tenor of Paine's piece is seen in the following quote.

> As to government matters, 'tis not in the power of Britain to do this continent justice: . . . it will soon be too weighty and intricate to be managed with any tolerable degree of convenience, by a power so distant from us, and so very ignorant of us; for if they cannot conquer us, they cannot govern us. . . . There was a time when it was proper, and there is a proper time for it to cease.[16]

Government must be beneficial in order to curb man's most base instincts. A distant government or one which is base in itself cannot be beneficial to the colonies. Revolution was the only means to address American grievances given the British governments' refusal to consider the needs of the colonists.

Not all people saw the impending revolution as an event likely to establish the idea of freedom in America. One vocal critic was Abigail Adams, who had objected to the fact that women lacked the same political rights as men, and thus were at their mercy. Abigail Adams wrote to John Adams,

> I can not say I think you very generous to the Ladies, for whilst you are proclaiming peace and good will to Men, Emancipating all Nations, you insist

[14]Ibid., p. 97.

[15]Ibid., p. 97.

[16]Thomas Paine, "Thoughts on the Present State of American Affairs," in *The Life and Works of Thomas Paine*, ed. William M. Van der Weyde (New Rochelle, NY: Thomas Paine National Historical Association, 1925), II, 136.

upon retaining an absolute power over Wives. But you must remember that Arbitrary power is like most other things which are very hard, very liable to be broken—and notwithstanding all your wise Laws and Maxims we have it in our power not only to free ourselves but to subdue our Masters, and without violence throw both your natural and legal authority at our feet.[17]

Neither the declaration of Independence nor the Constitution established freedom for all people living in the United States. White males, generally speaking, enjoyed a sense of legal equality, but only those who owned property had the possibility of voting. The states could, and in some cases did, prescribe religious qualifications for voting. For their part, women and people of color had no political rights and did not share in the same legal protections as men.

While the colonial relationship was dissolved within months of the appearance of Paine's work, seven years passed before the dream of American independence became a reality. Men of the caliber of John Adams, Thomas Jefferson, and George Washington provided the leadership which was key to achieving independence. However, it was the writings of individuals like Mayhew, Otis, Howard, and Paine which provided the intellectual stimulus used to justify the positions used by both sides. Furthermore it was writers like Abigail Adams who demonstrated that the Revolutionary War was fought for limited aims, not ones that would establish true equality for all Americans. Examples of the latter individuals' writings appear in the following pages.

Concerning Unlimited Submission and Nonresistance to the Higher Powers*

Jonathan Mayhew

. . . IT is evident that the affair of civil government may properly fall under a *moral* and *religious* consideration, at least so far forth as it relates to the general nature and end of magistracy and to the grounds and extent of that submission which persons of a private character ought to yield to those who are vested with . . . authority. This must be allowed by all who

---

[17]Reprinted by permission of the publishers from *The Book of Abigail and John: Selected Letters of the Adams Family, 1762–1784*, edited by L.H. Butterfield, Cambridge, MA: Harvard University Press, Copyright © 1975 by the Massachusetts Historical Society, p. 127.

*From Jonathan Mayhew, "Concerning Unlimited Submission and Nonresistance to the Higher Powers." Reprinted by permission of the publishers from *Pamphlets of the American Revolution, 1750–1776*, edited by Bernard Bailyn, Cambridge, MA: The Belknap Press of Harvard University Press, Copyright © 1965 by the President and Fellows of Harvard College. I, 215-47.

acknowledge the divine original of Christianity. For although there be a sense, and a very plain and important sense, in which Christ's *kingdom is not of this world,*[1] his inspired apostles have, nevertheless, laid down some general principles concerning the office of civil rulers and the duty of subjects, together with the reason and obligation of that duty. And from hence it follows that it is proper for all who acknowledge the authority of Jesus Christ and the inspiration of his apostles to endeavor to understand what is in fact the doctrine which they have delivered concerning this matter. It is the duty of *Christian* magistrates to inform themselves what it is which their religion teaches concerning the nature and design of their office. And it is equally the duty of all *Christian* people to inform themselves what it is which their religion teaches concerning that subjection which they owe to *the higher powers.* It is for these reasons that I have attempted to examine into the Scripture account of this matter, in order to lay it before you with the same *freedom* which I constantly use with relation to other doctrines and precepts of Christianity; not doubting but you will *judge* upon everything offered to your consideration with the same spirit of *freedom* and *liberty* with which it is *spoken.*

The passage read is the most full and express of any in the New Testament relating to rulers and subjects: and therefore I thought it proper to ground upon it what I had to propose to you with reference to the . . . authority of the civil magistrate and the subjection which is due to him. . . .

The Apostle enters upon his subject thus: *Let every soul be subject unto the higher powers. For there is no power but of God: the powers that be are ordained of God.*[2] Here he urges the duty of obedience from this topic of argument, that civil rulers, as they are supposed to fulfill the pleasure of God, are the ordinance of God. But how is this an argument for obedience to such rulers as do not perform the pleasure of God by doing good but the pleasure of the devil by doing evil, and such as are not, therefore, *God's ministers* but the devil's! *Whosoever, therefore, resisteth the power, resisteth the ordinance of God; and they that resist, shall receive to themselves damnation.*[3] Here the Apostle argues that those who resist a reasonable and just authority which is agreeable to the will of God do really resist the will of God himself, and will, therefore, be punished by Him. But how does this prove that those who resist a lawless, unreasonable power, which is contrary to the will of God, do therein resist the will and ordinance of God? Is resisting those who resist God's will the same thing with resisting God? Or shall those who do so *receive to themselves damnation! For rulers are not a terror to good works, but to the evil. Wilt thou then not be afraid of the power? Do that which is good and*

[1]John xviii, 36.

[2]Romans xiii, verse 1.

[3]Romans xiii, verse 2.

thou shalt have praise of the same. For he is the minister of God to thee for good.[4] Here the Apostle argues more explicitly . . . than he had before done for revering and submitting to magistracy, from this consideration: that such as really performed the duty of magistrates would be enemies only to the evil actions of men and would befriend and encourage the good and so be a common blessing to society. . . .

For, please to observe, that if the end of an civil government be the good of society, if this be the thing that is aimed at in constituting civil rulers, and if the motive and argument for submission to government be taken from the apparent usefulness of civil authority, it follows that when no such good end can be answered by submission there remains no argument or motive to enforce it; and if instead of this good end's being brought about by submission, a *contrary end* is brought about and the ruin and misery of society effected by it, here is a plain and positive reason against submission in all such cases, should they ever happen. And therefore, in such cases a regard to the public welfare ought to make us withhold from our rulers that obedience and subjection which it would, otherwise, be our duty to render to them. If it be our duty, for example, to obey our King merely for this reason, that he rules for the public . . . welfare (which is the only argument the Apostle makes use of), it follows by a parity of reason that when he turns tyrant and makes his subjects his prey to devour and to destroy instead of his charge to defend and cherish, we are bound to throw off our allegiance to him and to resist, and that according to the tenor of the Apostle's argument in this passage. Not to discontinue our allegiance, in this case, would be to join with the sovereign in promoting the slavery and misery of that society the welfare of which we ourselves as well as our sovereign are indispensably obliged to secure and promote as far as in us lies. It is true the Apostle puts no case of such a tyrannical prince; but by his grounding his argument for submission wholly upon the good of civil society it is plain he implicitly authorizes and even requires us to make resistance whenever this shall be necessary to the public safety and happiness. . . .

But it ought to be remembered that if the duty of universal obedience and nonresistance to our king or prince can be argued from this passage, the same unlimited submission under a republican or any other form of government and even to all the subordinate powers in any particular state, can be proved by it as well: which is more than those who allege it for the mentioned purpose would be willing should be inferred from it. So that this passage does not answer their purpose, but really overthrows and confutes it. This matter deserves to be more particularly considered.—The advocates for unlimited submission and passive obedience do, if I mistake not, always speak with reference to kingly or monarchical government as distinguished

[4]Romans xiii, verse 3d and part of the 4th.

from all other forms and with reference to submitting to the will of the king in distinction from all subordinate officers acting beyond their commission and the authority which they have received from the crown. It is not pretended that any persons besides kings have a divine right to do what they please so that no one may resist them without incurring the guilt of factitousness and rebellion. If any other supreme powers oppress the . . . people it is generally allowed that the people may get redress, by resistance if other methods prove ineffectual. And if any officers in a kingly government go beyond the limits of that power which they have derived from the crown (the supposed original source of all power and authority in the state), and attempt, illegally, to take away the properties and lives of their fellow subjects, they may be *forcibly* resisted, at least till application can be made to the crown. But as to the sovereign himself, he may not be resisted in any case, nor any of his officers while they confine themselves within the bounds which he has prescribed to them. This is, I think, a true sketch of the principles of those who defend the doctrine of passive obedience and nonresistance. Now there is nothing in Scripture which supports this scheme of political principles. As to the passage under consideration, the Apostle here speaks of civil rulers in *general*, of all persons in *common* vested with authority for the good of society, without any particular reference to one form of government more than to another or to the supreme power in any particular state more than to subordinate powers. The Apostle does not concern himself with the different forms of government.[5] This he supposes left entirely to human . . . prudence and discretion. Now the consequence of this is that unlimited and passive obedience is no more enjoined in this passage under monarchical government, or to the supreme power in any state, than under all other species of government which answer the end of government, or to all the subordinate degrees of civil authority, from the highest to the lowest. Those, therefore, who would from this passage infer the guilt of resisting kings in all cases whatever, though acting ever so contrary to the design of their office, must, if they will be consistent, go much farther, and infer from it the guilt of resistance under all other forms of government and of resisting *any petty officer* in the state, though acting beyond his commission, in the most arbitrary, illegal manner possible. The argument holds equally strong in both cases. All civil rulers, as such, are the *ordinance* and *ministers of God*; and they are all, by the nature of their office

---

[5]The essence of government (I mean *good* government, and this is the only government which the Apostle treats of in this passage) consists in the *making* and *executing of good laws*—laws attempered to the common felicity of the *governed*. And if this be, *in fact*, done, it is evidently in itself a thing of no consequence at all what the *particular* form of government is—whether the legislative and executive power be lodged in *one and the same* person or in *different* persons; whether in *one* person, whom we call an *absolute monarch;* whether in a *few*, so as to constitute an *aristocracy;* whether in *many*, so as to constitute a *republic;* or whether in *three co-ordinate branches*, in such manner as to make the government *partake* something of *each* of these forms, and to be at the same time *essentially different* from them *all*. . . .

and in their respective spheres and stations, bound to consult the public welfare. With the same reason, therefore, that any deny unlimited and passive obedience . . . to be here enjoined under a republic or aristocracy or any other established form of civil government or to subordinate powers acting in an illegal and oppressive manner, with the same reason others may deny that such obedience is enjoined to a king or monarch or any civil power whatever. For the Apostle says nothing that is *peculiar to kings;* what he says extends equally to *all* other persons whatever, vested with any civil office. They are all, in exactly the same sense, the *ordinance of God* and the *ministers of God;* and obedience is equally enjoined to be paid to them all. For, as the Apostle expresses it, *there is* NO POWER *but of God:* and we are required to *render to* ALL *their* DUES, and not MORE than their DUES. And what these *dues* are, and to *whom* they are to be *rendered*, the Apostle *saith not* but leaves to the reason and consciences of men to determine.

Thus it appears that the common argument, grounded upon this passage, in favor of universal and passive obedience really overthrows itself by proving too much, if it proves anything at all; namely, that no civil officer is, in any case whatever, to be resisted, though acting in express contradiction to the design of his office; which no man in his senses ever did or can assert.

If we calmly consider the nature of the thing itself, nothing can well be imagined more directly contrary to common sense than to suppose that *millions* of people should be subjected to the arbitrary, precarious pleasure of *one single man* (who has *naturally* no superiority over them in point of authority) so that their estates, and everything that is valuable in life, and even their lives also shall be absolutely at his disposal, if he happens to be wanton and capricious enough to demand them. What unprejudiced man can think that God made ALL to be thus subservient to the lawless pleasure and frenzy of ONE so that it shall always be a sin to resist him! Nothing but the most plain and express revelation from Heaven could make a sober impartial man believe such a monstrous, unaccountable doctrine; and, indeed, the thing itself appears so shocking—so out of all *proportion,* that it may be questioned whether all the *miracles* that ever were wrought could make it credible that this doctrine *really* came from God. At present, there is not the least syllable in Scripture which gives any countenance to it. The hereditary, indefeasible, divine right of kings, and the doctrine of nonresistance, which is built upon the supposition of such a right, are altogether as fabulous and chimerical as transubstantiation or any of the most absurd reveries of ancient or modern visionaries. These notions are fetched neither from divine revelation nor human reason; and if they are derived from neither of those sources, it is not much matter from *whence they come, or whither they go.* Only it is a pity that such doctrines should be propagated in society, to raise factions and rebellions, as we see they have in fact been, both in the *last* and in the *present* REIGN. . . .

. . . A PEOPLE really oppressed to a great degree by their sovereign cannot well be insensible when they are so oppressed. And such a people (if I may allude to an ancient *fable* have, like the Hesperian fruit, a DRAGON . . . for their *protector* and *guardian;* nor would they have any reason to mourn if some HERCULES should appear . . . to dispatch him. For a nation thus abused to arise unanimously and to resist their prince, even to the dethroning him, is not criminal, but a reasonable way of vindicating their liberties and just rights; it is making use of the means, and the only means, which God has put into their power for mutual and self-defense. And it would be highly criminal in them not to make use of this means. It would be stupid tameness and unaccountable folly for whole nations to suffer one unreasonable, ambitious, and cruel man to wanton and riot in their misery. And in such a case it would, of the two, be more rational to suppose that they did NOT *resist* than that they who did would *receive to themselves damnation.* . . .

To conclude: Let us all learn to be *free* and to be *loyal.* Let us not profess ourselves vassals to the lawless pleasure of any man on earth. But let us remember, at the same time, government is *sacred* and not to be *trifled* with. It is our happiness to live under the government of a PRINCE who is satisfied with ruling according to law, as every other good prince will. We enjoy under his administration all the liberty that is proper and expedient . . . for us. It becomes us, therefore, to be contented and dutiful subjects. Let us prize our freedom but not *use our liberty for a cloak of maliciousness.*[6] There are men who strike at *liberty* under the term *licentiousness.* There are others who aim at *popularity* under the disguise of *patriotism.* Be aware of both. *Extremes* are dangerous. There is at present amongst *us,* perhaps, more danger of the *latter* than of the *former.* For which reason I would exhort you to pay all due regard to the government over us, to the KING and all in authority, and to lead a *quiet and peaceable life.*[7] And while I am speaking of loyalty to our *earthly prince,* suffer me just to put you in mind to be loyal also to the supreme RULER of the universe, *by whom kings reign and princes decree justice.*[8] To which King eternal, immortal, invisible, even to the ONLY WISE GOD[9] be all honor and praise, DOMINION and thanksgiving, through JESUS CHRIST our LORD. AMEN.

[6]I Peter ii, 16.
[7]I Timothy ii, 2.
[8]Proverbs viii, 15.
[9]I Timothy i, 17.

Of the Political and Civil Rights of the British Colonists*

James Otis

Here indeed opens to view a large field; but I must study brevity.–Few people have extended their inquiries after the foundation of any of their rights beyond a charter from the crown. There are others who think when they have got back to old *Magna Carta* that they are at the beginning of all things. They imagine themselves on the borders of chaos (and so indeed in some respects they are), and see creation rising out of the unformed mass or from nothing. Hence, say they, spring all the rights of men and of citizens. But liberty was better understood and more fully enjoyed by our ancestors before the coming in of the first Norman tyrants than ever after, till it was found necessary for the salvation of the kingdom to combat the arbitrary and wicked proceedings of the Stuarts. . . .

I also lay it down as one of the first principles from whence I intend to deduce the civil rights of the British colonies, that all of them are subject to and dependent on Great Britain, and that therefore as over subordinate governments the Parliament of Great Britain has an undoubted power and lawful authority to make acts for the general good that, by naming them, shall and ought to be equally binding as upon the subjects of Great Britain within the realm. This principle, I presume, will be readily granted on the other side the Atlantic. It has been practised upon for twenty years to my knowledge, in the province of the *Massachusetts Bay;* and I have ever received it that it has been so from the beginning in this and the sister provinces through the continent. . . .

I am aware some will think; it is time for me to retreat, after having expressed the power of the British Parliament in quite so strong terms. But 'tis from and under this very power and its acts, and from the common law, that the political and civil rights of the colonists are derived: and upon those grand pillars of liberty shall my defense be rested. At present, therefore, the reader may suppose that there is not one provincial charter on the continent; he may, if he pleases, imagine all taken away, without fault or forfeiture, without trial or notice. All this really happened to some of them in the last century. I would have the reader carry his imagination still further, and suppose a time may come when instead of a process at common law the Parliament shall give a decisive blow to every charter in America, and declare them all void. Nay it shall also be granted that 'tis barely possible the time may come when the real interest of the whole may require an act of Parliament to annihilate all those charters. What could follow from all this that would shake one of the essential, natural, civil, or religious rights of the colonists? Nothing. They would be men, citizens and British subjects after all. No act of Parliament can deprive them of the liberties of such, unless any will contend that an act of Parliament can make slaves not only of one but of two millions of the commonwealth. And if so, why not of the whole? I freely own that I can find nothing in the laws of my country that would justify the . . . Parliament in making one slave, nor did they ever professedly undertake to make one. . . .

Every British subject born on the continent of America or in any other of the British dominions is by the law of God and nature, by the common law, and by act of Parliament (exclusive of all charters from the crown) entitled to all the natural, essential, inherent, and inseparable rights of our fellow subjects in Great Britain. Among those rights are the following, which it is humbly conceived no man or body of men, not excepting the Parliament, justly, equitably, and consistently with their own rights and the constitution can take away.

First. *That the supreme and subordinate powers of legislation should be free and sacred in the hands where the community have once rightfully placed them.*

Secondly. *The supreme national legislative cannot be altered justly till the commonwealth is dissolved, nor a subordinate legislative taken away without forfeiture or other good cause. . . .*

Thirdly. *No legislative, supreme or subordinate, has a right to make itself arbitrary. . . .*

Fourthly. *The supreme legislative cannot justly assume a power of ruling by extempore arbitrary decrees, but is bound to dispense justice by known settled rules and by duly authorized independent judges. . . .*

Fifthly. *The supreme power cannot take from any man any part of his property, without his consent in person or by representation.*

Sixthly. *The legislature cannot transfer the power of making laws to any other hands.*

These are their bounds, which by God and nature are fixed; hitherto have they a right to come, and no further.

1. *To govern by stated laws.*
2. *Those laws should have no other end ultimately but the good of the people.*
3. *Taxes are not to be laid on the people but by their consent in person or by deputation.*
4. *Their whole power is not transferable. . . .*

These are the first principles of law and justice, and the great barriers of a free state and of the British constitution in particular. I ask, I want, no more. Now let it be shown how 'tis reconcilable with these principles, or to many other fundamental maxims of the British constitution, as well as the natural and civil rights which by the laws of their country all British subjects are entitled to as their best inheritance and birthright, that all the northern colonies, who are without one representative in the House of Commons, should be taxed by the British Parliament.

That the colonists, black and white, born here are freeborn British subjects, and entitled to all the essential civil rights of such is a truth not only manifest from the provincial charters, from the principles of the common law, and acts of Parliament, but from the British constitution, which was re-established at the Revolution with a professed design to secure the liberties of all the subjects to all generations. . . .

I can see no reason to doubt but that the imposition of taxes, whether on trade, or on land, or houses, or ships, on real or personal, fixed or floating property, in the colonies is absolutely irreconcilable with the rights of the colonists as British subjects and as men. I say men, for in a state of nature no man can take my property from me without my consent: if he does, he deprives me of my liberty and makes me a slave. If such a proceeding is a breach of the law of nature, no law of society can make it just. The very act of taxing exercised over those who are not represented appears to me to be depriving them of one of their most essential rights as freemen, and if continued seems to be in effect an entire disfranchisement of every civil right. For what one civil right is worth a rush after a man's property is subject to be taken from him at pleasure without his consent? If a man is not his *own assessor* in person or by deputy, his liberty is gone or lays entirely at the mercy of others. . . .

We all think ourselves happy under Great Britain. We love, esteem, and reverence our mother country, and adore our King. And could the choice of independency be offered the colonies or subjection to Great Britain upon any terms above absolute slavery, I am convinced they would accept the latter. The ministry in all future generations may rely on it that British America will never prove undutiful till driven to it as the last fatal resort against ministerial oppression, which will make the wisest mad, and the weakest strong.

These colonies are and always have been "entirely subject to the crown," in the legal sense of the terms. But if any politician of "tampering activity, of wrong-headed inexperience, misled to be meddling," . . . means by "curbing the colonies in time" and by "being made entirely subject to the crown" that this subjection should be absolute and confined to the crown, he had better have suppressed his wishes. This never will nor can be done without making the colonists vassals of the crown. Subjects they are; their lands they hold of the crown by common socage, the freest feudal tenure by which any hold their lands in England or anywhere else. Would these gentlemen carry us back to the state of the Goths and Vandals, and revive all the military tenures and bondage which our forefathers could not bear? It may be worth noting here that few if any instances can be given where colonies have been disposed to forsake or disobey a tender mother; but history is full of examples that armies stationed as guards over provinces have seized the prey for their general and given him a crown at the expense of his master. Are all ambitious generals dead? Will no . . . more rise up hereafter? The danger of a standing army in remote provinces is much greater to the metropolis than at home. Rome found the truth of this assertion in her Sullas, her Pompeys, and Caesars; but she found it too late. Eighteen hundred years have rolled away since her ruin. A continuation of the same liberties that have been enjoyed by the colonists since the Revolution, and the same moderation of government exercised towards them will bind them in perpetual lawful and willing subjection, obedience, and love to Great Britain: she and her colonies will both prosper and flourish. The monarchy will remain in sound health and full vigor at that blessed period when the proud arbitrary tyrants of the continent shall either unite in the deliverance of the human race or resign their crowns. Rescued human nature must and will be from the general slavery that has so long triumphed over the species. Great Britain has done much towards it: what a glory will it be for her to complete the work throughout the world! . . .

The sum of my argument is: that civil government is of God; that the administrators of it were originally the whole people; that they might have devolved it on whom they pleased; that this devolution is fiduciary, for the good of the whole; that by the British constitution this devolution is on the King, Lords and Commons, the supreme, sacred and uncontrollable legislative power not only in the realm but through the dominions; that by the abdication, the original compact was broken to pieces; that by the Revolution it was renewed and more firmly established, and the rights and liberties of the subject in all parts of the dominions more fully explained and confirmed; that in consequence of this establishment and the acts of succession and union, His Majesty GEORGE III is rightful King and sovereign, and, with his Parliament, the supreme legislative of Great Britain, France, and Ireland, and the dominions thereto belonging; that this constitution is the most free one and by far the best now existing on earth; that by this constitution every man in the dominions is a free man; that no parts of His Majesty's dominions can be taxed without their consent; that every part has a right to be represented in the supreme or some subordinate legislature; that the refusal of this would seem to be a contradiction in practice to the theory of the constitution; that the colonies are subordinate dominions and are now in such a state as to make it best for the good of the whole that they should not only be continued in the enjoyment of subordinate legislation but be also represented in some proportion to their number and estates in the grand legislature of the nation; that this would firmly unite all parts of the British empire in the greatest peace and prosperity, and render it invulnerable and perpetual.

A *Letter from a Gentlemen at Halifax**

Martin Howard, Jr.

MY DEAR SIR,

I thank you very kindly for the pamphlets and newspapers you was so obliging as to send me. I will, according to your request, give you a few miscellaneous strictures on that pamphlet, wrote by Mr. *H-p-s,* your governor, entitled *The Rights of Colonies Examined.* . . .

However disguised, polished, or softened the expression of this pamphlet may seem yet everyone must see that its professed design is sufficiently prominent throughout, namely, to prove *that the colonies have rights independent of, and not controllable by the authority of Parliament.* It is upon this dangerous and indiscreet position I shall communicate to you my real sentiments. . . .

The sum of His Honor's argument is this: the people of Great Britain have not any sort of power over the Americans; the House of Commons have no greater authority than the people of Great Britain who are their constituents; *ergo,* the House of Commons *have not any sort of power over the Americans.* This is indeed a curious invented syllogism, the sole merit of which is due to the first magistrate of an English colony.

I have endeavored to investigate the true natural relation, if I may so speak, between colonies and their mother state, abstracted from compact or positive institution, but here I can find nothing satisfactory. Till this relation is clearly defined upon a rational and natural principle, our reasoning upon the measure of the colonies' obedience will be desultory and inconclusive. . . . The ancients have transmitted to us nothing that is applicable to the state of modern colonies because the relation between these is formed by political compact, and the condition of each, variant in their original and from each other. The honorable author has not freed this subject from any of its embarrassments: vague and diffuse talk of rights and privileges, and ringing the changes upon the words liberty and slavery only serve to convince us that words may affect without raising images or affording any repose to a mind philosophically inquisitive. For my own part, I will shun the walk of metaphysics in my inquiry, and be content to consider the colonies' rights upon the footing of their charters, which are the only plain avenues that lead to the truth of this matter. . . .

*From Martin Howard, Jr., "A Letter from a Gentleman at Halifax." Reprinted by permission of the publishers from *Pamphlets of the American Revolution, 1750-1776,* edited by Bernard Bailyn, Cambridge, MA: The Belknap Press of Harvard University Press, Copyright © 1965 by the President and Fellows of Harvard College. I, 532–44.

The several New England charters ascertain, define, and limit the respective rights and privileges of each colony, and I cannot conceive how it has come to pass that the colonies now claim any other or greater rights than are therein expressly granted to them. I fancy when we speak or think of the rights of freeborn Englishmen, we confound those rights which are personal with those which are political: there is a distinction between these which ought always to be kept in view. . . .

Our personal rights, comprehending those of life, liberty, and estate, are secured to us by the common law, which is every subject's birthright, whether born in Great Britain, on the ocean, or in the colonies; and it is in this sense we are said to enjoy all the rights and privileges of Englishmen. The political rights of the colonies or the powers of government communicated . . . to them are more limited, and their nature, quality, and extent depend altogether upon the patent or charter which first created and instituted them. As individuals, the colonists participate of every blessing the English constitution can give them: as corporations created by the crown, they are confined within the primitive views of their institution. Whether, therefore, their indulgence is scanty or liberal can be no cause of complaint; for when they accepted of their charters they tacitly submitted to the terms and conditions of them.

The colonies have no rights independent of their charters; they can claim no greater than those give them; by those the Parliamentary jurisdiction over them is not taken away, neither could any grant of the King abridge that jurisdiction, because it is founded upon common law, as I shall presently show, and was prior to any charter or grant to the colonies: every Englishman, therefore, is subject to this jurisdiction, and it follows him wherever he goes. It is of the essence of government that there should be a supreme head, and it would be a solecism in politics to talk of members independent of it.

With regard to the jurisdiction of Parliament, I shall endeavor to show that it is attached to every English subject wherever he be, and I am led to do this from a clause in page nine of His Honor's pamphlet, where he says "That the colonies do not hold their rights as a privilege granted them, nor enjoy them as a grace and favor bestowed, but possess them as an inherent, indefeasible right." This postulatum cannot be true with regard to political rights, for I have already shown that these are derived from your charters, and are held by force of . . . the King's grant; therefore these inherent, indefeasible rights, as His Honor calls them, must be personal ones, according to the distinction already made. Permit me to say that inherent and indefeasible as these rights may be, the jurisdiction of Parliament over every English subject is equally as inherent and indefeasible: that both have grown out of the same stock, and that if we avail ourselves of the one we must submit to and acknowledge the other.

It might here be properly enough asked, Are these personal rights self-existent? Have they no original source? I answer, They are derived from the constitution of England, which is the common law; and from the same fountain is also derived the jurisdiction of Parliament over us.

But to bring this argument down to the most vulgar apprehension: The common law has established it as a rule or maxim that the plantations are bound by British acts of Parliament if particularly named; and surely no Englishman in his senses will deny the force of a common law maxim. One cannot but smile at the inconsistency of these inherent, indefeasible men: if one of them has a suit at law, in any part of New England, upon a question of land, property, or merchandise, he appeals to the common law to support his claim or defeat his adversary, and yet is so profoundly stupid as to say that an act of Parliament does not bind him when perhaps the same page in a law book which points him out a remedy for a libel or a slap in the face would inform him that it does. In a word, the force of an act of Parliament over the colonies is predicated upon the common law, the origin and basis of all those inherent rights and privileges which constitute the boast and felicity of a Briton. . . .

It is the opinion of the House of Commons, and may be considered as a law of Parliament, that they are the representatives of every British subject, wheresoever he be. In this view of the matter, then, the aforegoing maxim is fully vindicated in practice, and the whole benefit of it, in substance and effect, extended and applied to the *colonies.* Indeed the maxim . . . must be considered in this latitude, for in a literal sense or construction it ever was, and ever will be, impracticable. Let me ask, Is the Isle of Man, Jersey, or Guernsey represented? What is the value or amount of each man's representation in the kingdom of Scotland, which contains near two millions of people, and yet not more than three thousand have votes in the election of members of Parliament? But to show still further that in fact and reality this right of representation is not of that consequence it is generally thought to be, let us take into the argument the moneyed interest of Britain, which, though immensely great, has no share in this representation. A worthless freeholder of forty shillings per annum can vote for a member of Parliament, whereas a merchant, though worth one hundred thousand pounds sterling, if it consist only in personal effects, has no vote at all. But yet let no one suppose that the interest of the latter is not equally the object of Parliamentary attention with the former. Let me add one example more. Copyholders in England of one thousand pounds sterling per annum, whose estates in land are nominally but not intrinsically inferior to a freehold cannot, by law, vote for members of Parliament; yet we never hear that these people *"murmur with submissive fear, and mingled rage."* They don't set up their private humor against the constitution of their country, but submit with cheerfulness to those forms of government which providence, in its goodness, has placed them under. . . .

The jurisdiction of Parliament being established, it will follow that this jurisdiction cannot be apportioned; it is transcendent and entire, and may levy internal taxes as well as regulate trade. There is no essential difference in the rights: a stamp duty is confessedly the most reasonable and equitable that can be devised, yet very far am I from desiring to see it established among us; but I fear the shaft is sped and it is now too late to prevent the blow. . . .

You'll easily perceive that what I have said is upon the general design of His Honor's pamphlet; if he had divided his argument with any precision, I would have followed him with somewhat more of method. The dispute between Great Britain and the colonies consists of two parts: first, the jurisdiction of Parliament, and, secondly, the exercise of that jurisdiction. His Honor hath blended these togther, and nowhere marked the division between them. The first I have principally remarked upon. As to the second, it can only turn upon the expediency or utility of those schemes which may, from time to time, be adopted by Parliament relative to the colonies. Under this head, I readily grant, they are at full liberty to remonstrate, petition, write pamphlets and newspapers without number, to prevent any improper or unreasonable imposition. Nay, I would have them do all this with that spirit of freedom which Englishmen always have, and I hope ever will, exert; but let us not use our liberty for a cloak of maliciousness. Indeed I am very sure the loyalty of the colonies has ever been irreproachable; but from the pride of some and the ignorance of others the cry against mother country has spread from colony to colony; . . . and it is to be feared that prejudices and resentments are kindled among them which it will be difficult ever thoroughly to soothe or extinguish. It may become necessary for the supreme legislature of the nation to frame some code, and therein adjust the rights of the colonies with precision and certainty, otherwise Great Britain will always be teased with new claims about liberty and privileges. . . .

I have no ambition in appearing in print, yet if you think what is here thrown together is fit for the public eye you are at liberty to publish it. . . . I the more cheerfully acquiesce in this because it is with real concern I have observed that, notwithstanding the frequent abuse poured forth in pamphlets and newspapers against the mother country, not one filial pen in America hath as yet been drawn, to my knowledge, in her vindication. . . .

Thoughts on the Present State of American Affairs*

Thomas Paine

IN the following pages I offer nothing more than . . . simple facts, plain arguments, and common sense: and have no other preliminaries to settle with the reader, than that he will divest himself of prejudice and preposses-

*Thomas Paine, "Thoughts on the Present State of American Affairs," in *The Life and Works of Thomas Paine*, ed. William M. Van der Weyde (New Rochelle, NY: Thomas Paine National Historical Association, 1925), II, 122–50.

sion, and suffer his reason and his feelings to determine for themselves: that he will put on, or rather that he will not put off, the true character of a man, and generously enlarge his views beyond the present day. . . .

The sun never shone on a cause of greater worth. 'Tis not the affair of a city, a county, a province, or a kingdom; but of a continent—of at least one eighth part of the habitable globe. 'Tis not the concern of a day, a year, or an age; posterity are virtually involved in the contest, and will be more or less affected even to the end of time, by the proceedings now. Now is the seed-time of continental union, faith and honor. The least fracture now will be like a name engraved with the point of a pin on the tender rind of a young oak; the wound would enlarge with the tree, and posterity read it in full grown characters. . . .

I have heard it asserted by some, that as America has flourished under her former connection with Great Britain, the same connection is necessary towards her future happiness, and will always have the same effect. Nothing can be more fallacious than this kind of argument. We may as well assert that because a child has thrived upon milk, that it is never to have meat, or that the first twenty years of our lives is to become a precedent for the next twenty. But even this is admitting more than is true; for I answer roundly, that America would have flourished as much, and probably much more, had no European power taken any notice of her. The commerce by which she hath enriched herself are the necessaries of life, and will always have a market while eating is the custom of Europe. . . .

Alas! we have been long led away by ancient prejudices and made large sacrifices to superstition. We have boasted the protection of Great Britain, without considering, that her motive was *interest not attachment;* and that she did not protect us from *our enemies* on *our account;* but from *her enemies* on *her own account,* from those who had no quarrel with us on any *other account,* and who will always be our enemies on the *same account.* Let Britain waive her pretensions to the continent, or the continent throw off the dependance, and we should be at peace with France and Spain, were they at war with Britain. The miseries of Hanover's last war ought to warn us against connections. . . .

The authority of Great Britain over this continent, is a form of government, which sooner or later must have an end. And a serious mind can draw no true pleasure by looking forward, under the painful and positive conviction that what he calls "the present constitution" is merely temporary. . . .

As to government matters, 'tis not in the power of Britain to do this continent justice: the business of it will soon be too weighty and intricate to be managed with any tolerable degree of convenience, by a power so distant from us, and so very ignorant of us; for if they cannot conquer us, they cannot govern us. To be always running three or four thousand miles with a tale or a petition, waiting four or five months for an answer, which, when obtained, requires five or six more to explain it in, will in a few years be looked upon as folly and childishness. There was a time when it was proper, and there is a proper time for it to cease.

Small islands not capable of protecting themselves are the proper objects for government . . . to take under their care; but there is something absurd, in supposing a Continent to be perpetually governed by an island. In no instance hath nature made the satellite larger than its primary planet; and as England and America, with respect to each other, reverse the common order of nature, it is evident that they belong to different systems. England to Europe: America to itself.

I am not induced by motives of pride, party or resentment to espouse the doctrine of separation and independence; I am clearly, positively, and conscientiously persuaded that it is the true interest of this continent to be so; that everything short of that is mere patchwork, that it can afford no lasting felicity,—that it is leaving the sword to our children, and shrinking back at a time when a little more, a little further, would have rendered this continent the glory of the earth. . . .

But admitting that matters were now made up, what would be the event? I answer, the ruin of the continent. And that for several reasons.

First. The powers of governing still remaining in the hands of the king, he will have a negative over the whole legislation of this continent. And as he hath shown himself such an inveterate enemy to liberty, and discovered such a thirst for arbitrary power, is he, or is he not, a proper person to say to these colonies, *You shall make no laws but what I please!?* And is there any inhabitant of America so ignorant as not to know, that according to what is called the *present Constitution,* this continent can make no laws but what the king gives leave to; and is there any man so unwise as not to see, that (considering what has happened) he will suffer no law to be made here but such as suits *his* purpose? We may be as effectually enslaved by the want of laws in America, as by submitting to laws made for us in England. After matters are made up (as it is called) can there be any doubt, but the whole power of the crown will be exerted to keep this continent as low and humble as possible? . . .

America is only a secondary object in the system of British politics. England consults the good of this country no further than it answers her own purpose. Wherefore, her own interest leads her to suppress the growth of ours in every case which doth not promote her advantage, or in the least interferes with it. A pretty state we should soon be in under such a second hand government, considering what has happened! . . .

Secondly. That as even the best terms which we can expect to obtain can amount to no more than a temporary expedient, or a kind of government by guardianship, which can last no longer than till the colonies come of age, so the general face and state of things in the interim will be unsettled and unpromising. Emigrants of property will not choose to come to a country whose form of government hangs but by a thread, and who is every day tottering on the brink of commotion and disturbance; and numbers of the present inhabitants would lay hold of the interval to dispose of their effects, and quit the continent.

But the most powerful of all arguments is, that nothing but independance, *i.e.* a continental form of government, can keep the peace of the continent and preserve it inviolate from civil wars. I dread the event of a reconciliation with Britain now, as it is more than probable that it will be followed by a revolt some where or other, the consequences of which may be far more fatal than all the malice of Britain. . . .

Ye that tell us of harmony and reconciliation, can ye restore to us the time that is past? Can ye give to prostitution its former innocence? Neither can ye reconcile Britain and America. The last cord now is broken, the people of England are presenting addresses against us. There are injuries which nature cannot forgive; she would cease to be nature if she did. As well can the lover forgive the ravisher of his mistress, as the continent forgive the murders of Britain. The Almighty hath implanted in us these unextinguishable feelings for good and wise purposes. They are the guardians of his image in our hearts. They distinguish us from the herd of common animals. The social compact would dissolve, and justice be extirpated from the earth, or have only a casual existence were we callous to the touches of affection. The robber and the murderer would often escape unpunished, did not the injuries which our tempers sustain, provoke us into justice.

O! ye that love mankind! Ye that dare oppose not only the tyranny but the tyrant, stand forth! Every spot of the old world is overrun with oppression. Freedom hath been hunted round the globe. Asia and Africa have long expelled her. Europe regards her like a stranger, and England hath given her warning to depart. O! receive the fugitive, and prepare in time an asylum for mankind.

Abigail Adams's Letter to John Adams, March 31, 1776*

Abigail Adams

. . . I have sometimes been ready to think that the passion for Liberty cannot be Eaquelly Strong in the Breasts of those who have been accustomed to deprive their fellow Creatures of theirs. Of this I am certain that it is not founded upon that generous and christian principal of doing to others as we would that others should do unto us. . . .

*From Abigail Adams, "Abigail Adams's Letter to John Adams, March 31, 1776." Reprinted by permission of the publisher, from *The Book of Abigail and John: Selected Letters of the Adams Family, 1762–1784*, edited by L.H. Butterfield, Cambridge, MA: Harvard University Press, Copyright © 1975 by the Massachusetts Historical Society. Pp. 120–21.

I feel very differently at the approach of spring to what I did a month ago. We knew not then whether we could plant or sow with safety, whether when we had toild we could reap the fruits of our own industery, whether we could rest in our own Cottages, or whether we should not be driven from the sea coasts to seek shelter in the wilderness, but now we feel as if we might sit under our own vine and eat the good of the land. . . .

Tho we felicitate ourselves, we sympathize with those who are trembling least the Lot of Boston should be theirs. But they cannot be in similar circumstances unless pusilanimity and cowardise should take possession of them. They have time and warning given them to see the Evil and shun it.—I long to hear that you have declared an independancy—and by the way in the new Code of Laws which I suppose it will be necessary for you to make I desire you would Remember the Ladies, and be more generous and favourable to them than your ancestors. Do not put such unlimited power into the hands of the Husbands. Remember all Men would be tyrants if they could. If perticuliar care and attention is not paid to the Laidies we are determined to foment a Rebelion, and will not hold ourselves bound by any Laws in which we have no voice, or Representation.

That your Sex are Naturally Tyrannical is a Truth so thoroughly established as to admit of no dispute, but such of you as wish to be happy willingly give up the harsh title of Master for the more tender and endearing one of Friend. Why then, not put it out of the power of the vicious and the Lawless to use us with cruelty and indignity with impunity. Men of Sense in all Ages abhor those customs which treat us only as the vassals of your Sex. Regard us then as Beings placed by providence under your protection and in immitation of the Supreem Being make use of that power only for our happiness.

DISCUSSION QUESTIONS

1. How did the issue of property lead to the political confrontation between the colonies and Great Britain?
2. What were the sources of the colonists' rights according to early colonial writers? How did they disagree? What are the sources of Americans' contemporary rights?
3. How can it be said that Mayhew, Otis, and Paine laid the intellectual foundations of the Revolutionary War?

Chapter 4

FORMATION OF THE NATION

The American colonies operated as thirteen independent governments prior to the Revolution. Only when faced with British subjugation did the colonies accept a unified authority in the form of the Articles of Confederation.

> This plan provided for a "perpetual union" of the states in a confederation, to be governed by a congress similar to the Continental Congress, consisting of one house composed of delegates from each state. In legislating each state had one vote and the agreement of nine states was necessary to pass a bill. The states jealously guarded their control of commerce and the taxing power and the Congress of the Confederation could only ask the states for what it needed.[1]

While the states were united in this "perpetual union," Congress's authority was limited largely to foreign policy. Political power continued to reside at the state level where government was equated with democracy in that the people possessed the ability to direct and limit its actions. Indeed, the American Revolution had been fought to preserve freedom and democracy from the British government which, because of the vast distance, was seen as uncaring about local needs and often dictatorial in manner. When the Revolutionary War officially ended in 1783, the purpose which enabled the Articles of Confederation to function ceased to exist. This was especially made evident given that: (1) the loyalty of the delegates was to the states

---

[1]Jeanette P. Nichols and Roy F. Nichols, *The Growth of American Democracy* (New York: D. Appleton-Century Company, 1939), p. 83.

which paid their salaries; (2) meetings of Congress were infrequent due to the inability to achieve a quorum; and (3) Congress was poorly financed in that it could not collect taxes or issue a strong currency. The Continental Congresses served to coordinate policy in the form of recommendations to the states or implementing their consensus, the most notable example being issuance of the Declaration of Independence.

A strong central government was generally opposed, for it was regarded as a threat to state authority and the natural rights of the individual. Colonists had only to look at the actions of Great Britain to conclude that a strong central government was a dangerous creature, for it infringed on the political and economic rights of the American people. The colonial experience with local self-government suggested that that type of relationship was best in terms of responsiveness to popular needs. However, that relationship failed to unite the American people and in fact encouraged the dissolution of the confederation as noted by Nichols and Nichols. "The people were restless, the states were quarrelling, westerners talked secession, foreign nations slighted the government, business was bad, and state governments had `gone radical.' Congress was helpless, without power, without funds, without adequate armed force, worst of all, without prestige."[2] Shays' Rebellion was illustrative of these troubles in that poor economic conditions of the time led to a division between creditors and debtors. This event and the near failure of the Massachusetts government in suppressing this rebellion can be seen to have served as a catalyst for the Continental Congress to call for the revision of the Articles of Confederation in order to create a stronger central government.

For all intents and purposes, the delegates to the Constitutional Convention scrapped the Articles of Confederation and started work on a new constitution. The delegates who attended the convention were motivated to produce a more effective government if for no other reason than to protect their property from similar events as Shays' Rebellion. Dye and Zeigler concluded that the writers of the Constitution were the economic elite of the period. In their analysis, Dye and Zeigler concluded that "at least forty of the fifty-five delegates (at the Constitutional Convention) were known to be holders of public securities; fourteen were land speculators; twenty-four were moneylenders and investors; eleven were engaged in commerce or manufacturing; and fifteen owned large plantations."[3] Beard wrote in that regard, "the Constitution-is a secondary or derivative feature arising from the nature of the economic groups seeking positive action and negative restraint."[4] Because of their wealth, the founding fathers appeared to establish protections on property while allowing for the acquisition of property.

[2]Ibid., pp. 91–*92.

[3]Thomas R. Dye and L. Harmon Zeigler, *The Irony of Democracy* 4th ed. (North Scituate, MA: Duxbury Press, 1978), p. 33.

[4]Charles Beard, *An Economic Interpretation of the Constitution of the United States* (New York: The Macmillan Company, 1913), p. 13.

When submitted to the states, Federalist and Anti-federalist groups quickly appeared and debated the desirability of the Constitution. Key among their members were Alexander Hamilton, John Jay, James Madison, Governor Edmund Randolph, and Robert Yates. Madison and Yates used their records of the Constitutional Convention to champion the causes of the Federalists and Anti-federalists, respectively. Generally, Federalists shared the views presented in the Constitution, whereas Anti-federalists opposed it on the grounds that too much power was allocated to the central government. As Beitzinger has noted, the differences between Federalists and Anti-federalists were most apparent in the areas of free government, human nature, consent of the governed, and constitutional limitations. Anti-federalists generally held that a free government would degenerate into despotism, for a vast country composed of diverse population would not maintain a democratic, central government. Federalists countered that the thirteen states would become one nation with the people having direct control over the House of Representatives, and a more limited role in the Senate and choosing a president. Anti-federalists also criticized the Constitution for failing to recognize the baseness of human nature and to incorporate appropriate safeguards against self-aggrandizement. Federalists, while also recognizing the base aspects of humankind, saw it as being controlled by the checks and balances featured in the Constitution. The Federalist view that government was based on the consent of the people was also rejected by the Anti-federalists. They held that since the states declared their independence in 1776, and were granted it formally in 1783, the authority of the central government rested on the states, not the people. Federalists for their part referred to a literal meaning of the Preamble to the Constitution which begins, "We the People," to assert it was a compact among a people, not of states. Finally, in terms of constitutional limitations, the most important Anti-federalist criticism was the lack of a national Bill of Rights to protect individual freedoms, as the states' bills of rights would not be applicable to the federal government.[5] While each of the thirteen colonies eventually approved the Constitution, ratification was a point of contention especially in Virginia and New York.

To advance the Federalist cause in those states Alexander Hamilton, James Madison, and John Jay produced a series of essays known as *The Federalist Papers* which stated the need for a strong representative government. John Jay in "The Federalist No. 2," held that the union of the American people was a logical act, given how closely they identified with one another. Jay wrote,

> With equal pleasure I have as often taken notice, that Providence has been pleased to give this one connected country, to one united people; a people

---

[5]A.J. Beitzinger, *A History of American Political Thought* (New York: The Macmillan Company, 1929), pp. 214–16.

descended from the same ancestors, speaking the same language, professing the same religion, attached to the same principles of government, very similar in their manners and customs and who, by their joint counsels, arms and efforts, fighting side by side throughout a long and bloody war, have nobly established their general Liberty and Independence.[6]

The human need for government coupled with the fact that the American people possessed common bonds, predisposed them towards one, single authority according to Jay. One finds in "The Federalist No. 10," Madison's belief that society is composed of factions and that a republican form of government is necessary to unite these groups.[7] Another example of these essays was "The Federalist No. 21" by Alexander Hamilton in which the weaknesses of the Confederation system were addressed in terms of the need of a central government capable of self-defense as well as protecting the state governments.[8] In "The Federalist No. 51," Madison offered reassurance that the federal government would not lead to the rise of a tyrant due to the constitutional feature of separation of powers which would prevent the interests of one group from dominating others.[9] In "The Federalist No. 84," Hamilton addressed charges that the rights of the citizenry were being endangered and concluded that the Constitution was in itself a Bill of Rights to protect the people from too powerful a government.[10]

These views were contested by the Anti-federalists. One of the most prominent was Edmund Randolph. Unlike most Anti-federalists, Randolph did not reject the new Constitution on the grounds it created too powerful a government. Indeed, the fact that it created a strong central government capable of defending the states and people was applauded. Rather, Randolph criticized the failure to provide term limitations and the need to enhance the rights and powers of the people as well as the states. More importantly, the states were not given the opportunity to offer amendments to be considered by a second Constitutional Convention.[11] A more mainstream example of Anti-federalist views was presented by Robert Yates, a justice on the New York Supreme Court, in the form of a series of letters

[6]John Jay, "The Federalist No. 2," in *The Federalist Papers*, 2E, ed. Roy P. Fairfield (Baltimore, MD: The Johns Hopkins University Press, 1981), p. 6.

[7]James Madison, "The Federalist No. 10," in *The Federalist Papers*, 2E, ed. Roy P. Fairfield (Baltimore, MD: The Johns Hopkins University Press, 1981), pp. 16–23.

[8]Alexander Hamilton, "The Federalist No. 21," in *The Federalist Papers*, 2E, ed. Roy P. Fairfield (Baltimore, MD: The Johns Hopkins University Press, 1981), pp. 45–49.

[9]James Madison, "The Federalist No. 51," in *The Federalist Papers*, 2E, ed. Roy P. Fairfield (Baltimore, MD: The Johns Hopkins University Press, 1981), pp. 158–63.

[10]Alexander Hamilton, "The Federalist No. 84," in *The Federalist Papers*, 2E, ed. Roy P. Fairfield (Baltimore, MD: The Johns Hopkins University Press, 1981), pp. 259–69.

[11]Edmund Randolph, "Letter from Edmund Randolph Giving His Reasons for Refusing His Signature To The Proposed Federal Constitution," in *The Complete Anti-Federalist*, ed. Herbert J. Storing (Chicago: University of Chicago Press, 1981), II, 86–98.

under the pseudonym Brutus. In the first and second of these works, the chief concerns were that the proposed federal government would become too strong to be controlled by the states, and eventually one person or group would dominate the government. Likewise, the fact that no Bill of Rights was incorporated into the Constitution to ensure citizen's natural rights was also regarded as highly dangerous.[12] Indeed the fact that there was no Bill of Rights was perhaps the most contentious issue, for Federalists such as Hamilton saw the Constitution as establishing a limited government, already constrained by the protections guaranteed in the state constitutions, while to Anti-Federalists such as Yates it was regarded as establishing a government of almost unlimited powers.

In the following sections, writings by John Jay, Alexander Hamilton, James Madison, Edmund Randolph, and Robert Yates appear.

The Federalist No. 2*

John Jay

To the People of the State of New York:
When the people of America reflect that they are now called upon to decide a question, which, in its consequences, must prove one of the most important, that ever engaged their attention, the propriety of their taking a very comprehensive, as well as a very serious, view of it, will be evident.

Nothing is more certain than the indispensable necessity of Government, and it is equally undeniable, that whenever and however it is instituted the people must cede to it some of their natural rights, in order to vest it with requisite powers. It is well worthy of consideration, therefore, whether it would conduce more to the interest of the people of America, that they should, to all general purposes, be one nation, under one Federal Government, or that they should divide themselves into separate confederacies, and give to the head of each, the same kind of powers which they are advised to place in one national Government.

It has until lately been a received and uncontradicted opinion, that the prosperity of the people of America depended on their continuing firmly united, and the wishes, prayers, and efforts of our best and wisest Citizens have been constantly directed to that object. But Politicians now appear, who insist that this opinion is erroneous, and that instead of looking for

---

[12]Robert Yates, "Essays of Brutus," in *The Complete Anti-Federalist*, ed. Herbert J. Storing, (Chicago: University of Chicago Press, 1981), II, 363–78.

*From John Jay, "The Federalist No. 2," in *The Federalist Papers*, 2E, ed. Roy P. Fairfield (Baltimore, MD: The Johns Hopkins University Press, 1981), pp. 5–9.

safety and happiness in union, we ought to seek it in a division of the States into distinct confederacies or sovereignties. However extraordinary this new doctrine may appear, it nevertheless has its advocates; and certain characters who were much opposed to it formerly, are at present of the number. Whatever may be the arguments or inducements which have wrought this change in the sentiments and declarations of these Gentlemen, it certainly would not be wise in the people at large to adopt these new political tenets without being fully convinced that they are founded in truth and sound Policy.

It has often given me pleasure to observe that Independent America was not composed of detached and distant territories, but that one connected, fertile, wide-spreading country was the portion of our western sons of liberty. Providence has in a particular manner blessed it with a variety of soils and productions, and watered it with innumerable streams, for the delight and accommodation of its inhabitants. A succession of navigable waters forms a kind of chain round its borders, as if to bind it together; while the most noble rivers in the world, running at convenient distances, present them with highways for the easy communication of friendly aids, and the mutual transportation and exchange of their various commodities.

With equal pleasure I have as often taken notice, that Providence has been pleased to give this one connected country, to one united people; a people descended from the same ancestors, speaking the same language, professing the same religion, attached to the same principles of government, very similar in their manners and customs and who, by their joint counsels, aims and efforts, fighting side by side throughout a long and bloody war, have nobly established their general Liberty and Independence. . . .

Similar sentiments have hitherto prevailed among all orders and denominations of men among us. To all general purposes we have uniformly been one people; each individual citizen everywhere enjoying the same national rights, privileges and protection. As a nation we have made peace and war: as a nation we have vanquished our common enemies: as a nation we have formed alliances and made treaties, and entered into various compacts and conventions with foreign States. . . .

A strong sense of the value and blessings of Union induced the people, at a very early period, to institute a Federal Government to preserve and perpetuate it. They formed it almost as soon as they had a political existence; nay, at a time, when their habitations were in flames, when many of their Citizens were bleeding, and when the progress of hostility and desolation—left little room for those calm and mature inquiries and reflections, which must ever precede the formation of a wise and well-balanced government for a free people. It is not to be wondered at, that a Government instituted in times so inauspicious, should on experiment be found greatly deficient and inadequate to the purpose it was intended to answer. . . .

This Convention, composed of men who possessed the confidence of the people, and many of whom had become highly distinguished by their patriotism, virtue, and wisdom, in times which tried the minds and hearts of men, undertook the arduous task. In the mild season of peace, with minds unoccupied by other subjects, they passed many months in cool, uninterrupted, and daily consultation; and finally, without having been awed by power, or influenced by any passions except love for their Country, they presented and recommended to the people the plan produced by their joint and very unanimous councils. . . .

They considered that the Congress was composed of many wise and experienced men. That being convened from different parts of the country, they brought with them and communicated to each other a variety of useful information. That in the course of the time they passed together in inquiring into and discussing the true interests of their country, they must have acquired very accurate knowledge on that head. That they were individually interested in the public liberty and prosperity, and therefore that it was not less their inclination than their duty, to recommend only such measures as after the most mature deliberation they really thought prudent and advisable.

These and similar considerations then induced the people to rely greatly on the judgment and integrity of the Congress; and they took their advice, notwithstanding the various arts and endeavors used to deter and dissuade them from it. But if the people at large had reason to confide in the men of that Congress, few of whom had then been fully tried or generally known, still greater reason have they now to respect the judgment and advice of the Convention, for it is well known that some of the most distinguished members of that Congress, who have been since tried and justly approved for patriotism and abilities, and who have grown old in acquiring political information, were also members of this Convention, and carried into it their accumulated knowledge and experience.

It is worthy of remark, that not only the first, but every succeeding Congress, as well as the late Convention, have invariably joined with the people in thinking that the prosperity of America depended on its Union. To preserve and perpetuate it, was the great object of the people in forming that Convention, and it is also the great object of the plan which the Convention has advised them to adopt. With what propriety, therefore, or for what good purposes, are attempts at this particular period, made by some men, to depreciate the importance of the Union? Or why is it suggested that three or four confederacies, would be better than one? I am persuaded in my own mind, that the people have always thought right on this subject, and that their universal and uniform attachment to the cause of the Union rests on great and weighty reasons, which I shall endeavor to develop and explain in some ensuing papers. They who promote the idea of substituting a number of distinct confederacies in the room of the plan of the Convention, seem clearly to foresee that the rejection of it would put the continuance of the Union in the utmost jeopardy: that certainly would be the case, and I sincerely wish that it may be as clearly foreseen by every good Citizen, that whenever the dissolution of the Union arrives, America will have reason to exclaim in the words of the Poet, "FAREWELL! A LONG FAREWELL TO ALL MY GREATNESS." PUBLIUS

The Federalist No. 10*

James Madison

To the People of the State of New York:

Among the numerous advantages promised by a well-constructed Union, none deserves to be more accurately developed than its tendency to break and control the violence of faction. The friend of popular governments never finds himself so much alarmed for their character and fate, as when he contemplates their propensity to this dangerous vice. He will not fail, therefore, to set a due value on any plan which, without violating the principles to which he is attached, provides a proper cure for it. The instability, injustice, and confusion introduced into the public councils, have, in truth, been the mortal diseases under which popular governments have everywhere perished; as they continue to be the favorite and fruitful topics from which the adversaries to liberty derive their most specious declamations. . . .

By a faction, I understand a number of citizens, whether amounting to a majority or minority of the whole, who are united and actuated by some common impulse of passion, or of interest, adverse to the rights of other citizens, or to the permanent and aggregate interests of the community. . . .

There are two methods of curing the mischiefs of faction: the one, by removing its causes; the other, by controlling its effects.

There are again two methods of removing the causes of faction: the one, by destroying the liberty which is essential to its existence; the other, by giving to every citizen the same opinions, the same passions, and the same interests.

It could never be more truly said than of the first remedy, that it is worse than the disease. Liberty is to faction what air is to fire, an aliment without which it instantly expires. But it could not be less folly to abolish liberty, which is essential to political life, because it nourishes faction, than

*From James Madison, "The Federalist No. 10," in *The Federalist Papers*, 2E, ed. Roy P. Fairfield (Baltimore, MD: The Johns Hopkins University Press, 1981), pp. 16–23.

it would be to wish the annihilation of air, which is essential to animal life, because it imparts to fire its destructive agency.

The second expedient is as impracticable as the first would be unwise. As long as the reason of man continues fallible, and he is at liberty to exercise it, different opinions will be formed. As long as the connection subsists between his reason and his self-love, his opinions and his passions will have a reciprocal influence on each other; and the former will be objects to which the latter will attach themselves. The diversity in the faculties of men, from which the rights of property originate, is not less an insuperable obstacle to a uniformity of interests. The protection of these faculties is the first object of government. From the protection of different and unequal faculties of acquiring property, the possession of different degrees and kinds of property immediately results; and from the influence of these on the sentiments and views of the respective proprietors, ensues a division of the society into different interests and parties.

The latent causes of faction are thus sown in the nature of man; and we see them everywhere brought into different degrees of activity, according to the different circumstances of civil society. A zeal for different opinions concerning religion, concerning government, and many other points, as well of speculation as of practice; an attachment to different leaders ambitiously contending for pre-eminence and power; or to persons of other descriptions whose fortunes have been interesting to the human passions, have, in turn, divided mankind into parties, inflamed them with mutual animosity, and rendered them much more disposed to vex and oppress each other than to co-operate for their common good. . . . So strong is this propensity of mankind to fall into mutual animosities, that where no substantial occasion presents itself, the most frivolous and fanciful distinctions have been sufficient to kindle their unfriendly passions and excite their most violent conflicts. But the most common and durable source of factions has been the various and unequal distribution of property. . . . Those who hold and those who are without property have ever formed distinct interests in society. Those who are creditors, and those who are debtors, fall under a like discrimination. A landed interest, a manufacturing interest, a mercantile interest, a moneyed interest, with many lesser interests, grow up of necessity in civilized nations, and divide them into different classes, actuated by different sentiments and views. . . . The regulation of these various and interfering interests forms the principal task of modern legislation, and involves the spirit of party and faction in the necessary and ordinary operations of the government. . . .

It is in vain to say that enlightened statesmen will be able to adjust these clashing interests and render them all subservient to the public good. Enlightened statesmen will not always be at the helm. . . .

The inference to which we are brought is, that the causes of faction cannot be removed, and that relief is only to be sought in the means of controlling its *effects.*

If a faction consists of less than a majority, relief is supplied by the republican principle, which enables the majority to defeat its sinister views by regular vote. It may clog the administration, it may convulse the society; but it will be unable to execute and mask its violence under the forms of the Constitution. When a majority is included in a faction, the form of popular government, on the other hand, enables it to sacrifice to its ruling passion or interest both the public good and the rights of other citizens. To secure the public good and private rights against the danger of such a faction, and at the same time to preserve the spirit and the form of popular government, is then the great object to which our inquiries are directed. . . .

By what means is this object attainable? Evidently by one of two only. Either the existence of the same passion or interest in a majority at the same time must be prevented, or the majority, having such coexistent passion or interest, must be rendered by their number and local situation unable to concert and carry into effect schemes of oppression. If the impulse and the opportunity be suffered to coincide, we well know that neither moral nor religious motives can be relied on as an adequate control. They are not found to be such on the injustice and violence of individuals, and lose their efficacy in proportion to the number combined together, that is, in proportion as their efficacy becomes needful.

From this view of the subject it may be concluded that a pure democracy, by which I mean a society consisting of a small number of citizens, who assemble and administer the government in person, can admit of no cure for the mischiefs of faction. . . . A common passion or interest will, in almost every case, be felt by a majority of the whole; a communication and concert result from the form of government itself; and there is nothing to check the inducements to sacrifice the weaker party or an obnoxious individual. Hence it is that such democracies have ever been spectacles of turbulence and contention; have ever been found incompatible with personal security or the rights of property; and have in general been as short in their lives as they have been violent in their deaths. Theoretic politicians, who have patronized this species of government, have erroneously supposed that by reducing mankind to a perfect equality in their political rights, they would, at the same time, be perfectly equalized and assimilated in their possessions, their opinions, and their passions.

A republic, by which I mean a government in which the scheme of representation takes place, opens a different prospect, and promises the cure for which we are seeking. Let us examine the points in which it varies from pure democracy, and we shall comprehend both the nature of the cure and the efficacy which it must derive from the Union.

The two great points of difference between a democracy and a republic are: first, the delegation of the government in the latter to a small number of citizens elected by the rest; secondly, the greater number of citizens and greater sphere of country over which the latter may be extended.

The effect of the first difference is, on the one hand, to refine and enlarge the public views, by passing them through the medium of a chosen body of citizens, . . . whose wisdom may best discern the true interest of their country, and whose patriotism and love of justice will be least likely to sacrifice it to temporary or partial considerations. Under such a regulation, it may well happen that the public voice, pronounced by the representatives of the people, will be more consonant to the public good than if pronounced by the people themselves, convened for the purpose. On the other hand, the effect may be inverted. Men of factious tempers, of local prejudices, or of sinister designs, may by intrigue, by corruption, or by other means, first obtain the suffrages, and then betray the interests of the people. The question resulting is, whether small or extensive republics are more favorable to the election of proper guardians of the public weal; and it is clearly decided in favor of the latter by two obvious considerations.

In the first place, it is to be remarked that, however small the republic may be, the representatives must be raised to a certain number in order to guard against the cabals of a few; and that, however large it may be, they must be limited to a certain number in order to guard against the confusion of a multitude. Hence, the number of representatives in the two cases not being in proportion to that of the two constituents, and being proportionally greater in the small republic, it follows that, if the proportion of fit characters be not less in the large than in the small republic, the former will present a greater option and consequently a greater probability of a fit choice.

In the next place, as each representative will be chosen by a greater number of citizens in the large than in the small republic, it will be more difficult for unworthy candidates to practise with success the vicious arts by which elections are too often carried; and the suffrages of the people being more free, will be more likely to centre in men who possess the most attractive merit and the most diffusive and established characters.

It must be confessed that in this, as in most other cases, there is a mean, on both sides of which inconveniences will be found to lie. By enlarging too much the number of electors, you render the representative too little acquainted with all their local circumstances and lesser interests: as by reducing it too much, you render him unduly attached to these, and too little fit to comprehend and pursue great and national objects. The federal Constitution forms a happy combination in this respect; the great and aggregate interests being referred to the national, the local and particular to the State legislatures.

The other point of difference is, the greater number of citizens and extent of territory which may be brought within the compass of republican than of democratic government; and it is this circumstance principally which renders factious combinations less to be dreaded in the former than in the latter. The smaller the society, the fewer probably will be the distinct parties and interests composing it; the fewer the distinct parties and interests, the more frequently will a majority be found of the same party; and the smaller the number of individuals composing a majority, and the smaller the compass within which they are placed, the more easily will they concert and execute their plans of oppression. Extend the sphere, and you take in a greater variety of parties and interests; you make it less probable that a majority of the whole will have a common motive to invade the rights of other citizens; or if such a common motive exists, it will be more difficult for all who feel it to discover their own strength and to act in unison with each other. Besides other impediments, it may be remarked that, where there is a consciousness of unjust or dishonorable purposes, communication is always checked by distrust in proportion to the number whose concurrence is necessary. . . .

Hence, it clearly appears that the same advantage which a republic has over a democracy in controlling the effects of faction is enjoyed by a large over a small republic,—is enjoyed by the Union over the States composing it. . . . Does the advantage consist in the substitution of representatives whose enlightened views and virtuous sentiments render them superior to local prejudices and to schemes of injustice? It will not be denied that the representation of the Union will be most likely to possess these requisite endowments. Does it consist in the greater security afforded by a greater variety of parties, against the event of any one party being able to outnumber and oppress the rest? In an equal degree does the increased variety of parties comprised within the Union, increase this security. Does it, in fine, consist in the greater obstacles opposed to the concert and accomplishment of the secret wishes of an unjust and interested majority? Here, again, the extent of the Union gives it the most palpable advantage. . . .

The influence of factious leaders may kindle a flame within their particular States, but will be unable to spread a general conflagration through the other States. A religious sect may degenerate into a political faction in a part of the Confederacy; but the variety of sects dispersed over the entire face of it must secure the national councils against any danger from that source. A rage for paper money, for an abolition of debts, for an equal division of property, or for any other improper or wicked project, will be less apt to pervade the whole body of the Union than a particular member of it; in the same proportion as such a malady is more likely to taint a particular county or district, than an entire State.

In the extent and proper structure of the Union, therefore, we behold a republican remedy for the diseases most incident to republican government. And according to the degree of pleasure and pride we feel in being republicans, ought to be our zeal in cherishing the spirit and supporting the character of Federalists. PUBLIUS

The Federalist No. 21*

Alexander Hamilton

To the People of the State of New York:

. . . The next most palpable defect of the subsisting Confederation, is the total want of a SANCTION to its laws. The United States, as now composed, have no powers to exact obedience or punish disobedience to their resolutions, either by pecuniary mulcts, by a suspension or divestiture of privileges, or by any other constitutional mode. There is no express delegation of authority to them to use force against delinquent members; and if such a right should be ascribed to the federal head, as resulting from the nature of the social compact between the States, it must be by inference and construction in the face of that part of the second article by which it is declared, "that each State shall retain every power, jurisdiction, and right, not *expressly* delegated to the United States in Congress assembled" [sic]. . . . There is, doubtless, a striking absurdity in supposing that a right of this kind does not exist, but we are reduced to the dilemma either of embracing that supposition, preposterous as it may seem, or of contravening or explaining away a provision, which has been of late a repeated theme of the eulogies of those who oppose the new Constitution; and the want of which, in that plan, has been the subject of much plausible animadversion, and severe criticism. If we are unwilling to impair the force of this applauded provision, we shall be obliged to conclude, that the United States afford the extraordinary spectacle of a government destitute even of the shadow of constitutional power to enforce the execution of its own laws. It will appear from the specimens which have been cited that the American Confederacy, in this particular, stands discriminated from every other institution of a similar kind, and exhibits a new and unexampled phenomenon in the political world.

The want of a mutual guaranty of the State governments is another capital imperfection in the federal plan. There is nothing of this kind declared in the articles that compose it; and to imply a tacit guaranty from considerations of utility would be a still more flagrant departure from the clause which has been mentioned, than to imply a tacit power of coercion from the like considerations. The want of a guaranty, though it might in its consequences endanger the Union, does not so immediately attack its existence as the want of a constitutional sanction to its laws.

Without a guaranty the assistance to be derived from the Union in

*From Alexander Hamilton, "The Federalist No. 21," in *The Federalist Papers*, 2E, ed. Roy P. Fairfield (Baltimore, MD: The Johns Hopkins University Press, 1981), pp. 45–49.

repelling those domestic dangers which may sometimes threaten the existence of the State constitutions must be renounced. Usurpation may rear its crest in each State, and trample upon the liberties of the people, while the national government could legally do nothing more than behold its encroachments with indignation and regret. A successful faction may erect a tyranny on the ruins of order and law, while no succor could constitutionally be afforded by the Union to the friends and supporters of the government. The tempestuous situation from which Massachusetts has scarcely emerged evinces that dangers of this kind are not merely speculative. Who can determine what might have been the issue of her late convulsions if the malcontents had been headed by a Caesar or by a Cromwell? Who can predict what effect a despotism, established in Massachusetts, would have upon the liberties of New Hampshire or Rhode Island, of Connecticut or New York? . . .

The inordinate pride of State importance has suggested to some minds an objection to the principle of a guaranty in the federal government, as involving an officious interference in the domestic concerns of the members. A scruple of this kind would deprive us of one of the principal advantages to be expected from union, and can only flow from a misapprehension of the nature of the provision itself. It could be no impediment to reforms of the State constitutions by a majority of the people in a legal and peaceable mode. This right would remain undiminished. The guaranty could only operate against changes to be effected by violence. Towards the preventions of calamities of this kind, too many checks cannot be provided. The peace of society and the stability of government depend absolutely on the efficacy of the precautions adopted on this head. Where the whole power of the government is in the hands of the people, there is the less pretence for the use of violent remedies in partial or occasional distempers of the State. The natural cure for an ill-administration, in a popular or representative constitution, is a change of men. A guaranty by the national authority would be as much levelled against the usurpations of rulers as against the ferments and outrages of faction and sedition in the community. . . .

The Federalist No. 51*

James Madison

To the People of the State of New York:
    To what expedient, then, shall we finally resort for maintaining in practice the necessary partition of power among the several departments as

*From James Madison, "The Federalist No. 51," in *The Federalist Papers*, 2E, ed. Roy P. Fairfield (Baltimore, MD: The Johns Hopkins University Press, 1981), pp. 158–63.

laid down in the Constitution? The only answer that can be given is, that as all these exterior provisions are found to be inadequate, the defect must be supplied by so contriving the interior structure of the government as that its several constituent parts may, by their mutual relations, be the means of keeping each other in their proper places. . . .

In order to lay a due foundation for that separate and distinct exercise of the different powers of government, which to a certain extent is admitted on all hands to be essential to the preservation of liberty, it is evident that each department should have a will of its own; and consequently should be so constituted that the members of each should have as little agency as possible in the appointment of the members of the others. Were this principle rigorously adhered to, it would require that all the appointments for the supreme executive, legislative, and judiciary magistracies should be drawn from the same fountain of authority, the people, through channels having no communication whatever with one another. Perhaps such a plan of constructing the several departments would be less difficult in practice than it may in contemplation appear. Some difficulties, however, and some additional expense would attend the execution of it. Some deviations, therefore, from the principle must be admitted. In the constitution of the judiciary department in particular, it might be inexpedient to insist rigorously on the principle: first, because peculiar qualifications being essential in the members, the primary consideration ought to be to select that mode of choice which best secures these qualifications; secondly, because the permanent tenure by which the appointments are held in that department must soon destroy all sense of dependence on the authority conferring them.

It is equally evident, that the members of each department should be as little dependent as possible on those of the others for the emoluments annexed to their offices. Were the executive magistrate or the judges not independent of the legislature in this particular, their independence in every other would be merely nominal.

But the great security against a gradual concentration of the several powers in the same department, consists in giving to those who administer each department the necessary constitutional means and personal motives to resist encroachments of the others. The provision for defence must in this as in all other cases, be made commensurate to the danger of attack. Ambition must be made to counteract ambition. The interest of the man must be connected with the constitutional rights of the place. It may be a reflection on human nature, that such devices should be necessary to control the abuses of government. But what is government itself, but the greatest of all reflections on human nature? If men were angels, no government would be necessary. . . . If angels were to govern men, neither external nor internal controls on government would be necessary. . . . In framing a government which is to be administered by men over men, the great difficulty lies in this: you must first enable the government to control the governed; and in the next place oblige it to control itself. A dependence on the people is, no doubt, the primary control on the government; but experience has taught mankind the necessity of auxiliary precautions.

This policy of supplying, by opposite and rival interests, the defect of better motives might be traced through the whole system of human affairs, private as well as public. We see it particularly displayed in all the subordinate distributions of power, where the constant aim is to divide and arrange the several offices in such a manner as that each may be a check on the other—that the private interest of every individual may be a sentinel over the public rights. These inventions of prudence cannot be less requisite in the distribution of the supreme powers of the State.

But it is not possible to give to each department an equal power of self-defence. In republican government the legislative authority necessarily predominates. The remedy for this inconveniency is to divide the legislature into different branches; and to render them, by different modes of election and different principles of action, as little connected with each other as the nature of their common functions and their common dependence on the society will admit. It may even be necessary to guard against dangerous encroachments by still further precautions. As the weight of the legislative authority requires that it should be thus divided, the weakness of the executive may require, on the other hand, that it should be fortified. An absolute negative on the legislature appears, at first view, to be the natural defence with which the executive magistrate should be armed. But perhaps it would be neither altogether safe nor alone sufficient. On ordinary occasions it might not be exerted with the requisite firmness, and on extraordinary occasions it might be perfidiously abused. May not this defect of an absolute negative be supplied by some qualified connection between this weaker department and the weaker branch of the stronger department, by which the latter may be led to support the constitutional rights of the former, without being too much detached from the rights of its own department?

If the principles on which these observations are founded be just . . . and they be applied as a criterion to the several State constitutions and to the federal Constitution, it will be found that if the latter does not perfectly correspond with them, the former are infinitely less able to bear such a test.

There are, moreover, two considerations particularly applicable to the federal system of America, which place that system in a very interesting point of view.

First. In a single republic, all the power surrendered by the people is submitted to the administration of a single government; and the usurpations are guarded against by a division of the government into distinct and separate departments. In the compound republic of America, the power surrendered by the people is first divided between two distinct governments, and then the portion allotted to each subdivided among distinct and separate departments. Hence a double security arises to the rights of the people. The different governments will control each other, at the same time that each will be controlled by itself.

Second. It is of great importance in a republic not only to guard the society against the oppression of its rulers, but to guard one part of the society against the injustice of the other part. Different interests necessarily exist in different classes of citizens. If a majority be united by a common interest, the rights of the minority will be insecure. There are but two methods of providing against this evil: the one by creating a will in the community independent of the majority—that is, of the society itself; the other by comprehending in the society so many separate descriptions of citizens as will render an unjust combination of a majority of the whole very improbable, if not impracticable. . . . The first method prevails in all governments possessing an hereditary or self-appointed authority. This, at best, is but a precarious security; because a power independent of the society may as well espouse the unjust views of the major, as the rightful interests of the minor party, and may possibly be turned against both parties. The second method will be exemplified in the federal republic of the United States. Whilst all authority in it will be derived from and dependent on the society, the society itself will be broken into so many parts, interests and classes of citizens, that the rights of individuals or of the minority will be in little danger from interested combinations of the majority. . . . Justice is the end of government. It is the end of civil society. . . . It ever has been and ever will be pursued until it be obtained, or until liberty be lost in the pursuit. . . . In the extended republic of the United States and among the great variety of interests, parties, and sects which it embraces, a coalition of a majority of the whole society could seldom take place on any other principles than those of justice and the general good; whilst there being thus less danger to a minor from the will of a major party, there must be less pretext, also, to provide for the security of the former, by introducing into the government a will not dependent on the latter, or, in other words, a will independent of the society itself. It is no less certain than it is important, notwithstanding the contrary opinions which have been entertained, that the larger the society, provided it lie within a practical sphere, the more duly capable it will be of self-government. And happily for the *republican cause,* the practicable sphere may be carded to a very great extent by a judicious modification and mixture of the *federal principle.* PUBLIUS

The Federalist No. 84*

Alexander Hamilton

To the People of the State of New York:
   In the course of the foregoing review of the Constitution, I have taken notice of, and endeavored to answer most of the objections which have appeared against it. There, however, remain a few which either did not fall naturally under any particular head or were forgotten in their proper places. . . .
   The most considerable of the remaining objections is that the plan of the convention contains no bill of rights. Among other answers given to this, it has been upon different occasions remarked that the constitutions of several of the States are in a similar predicament. I add that New York is of the number. And yet the opposers of the new system, in this State, who profess an unlimited admiration for its constitution, are among the most intemperate partisans of a bill of rights. To justify their zeal in this matter, they allege two things: one is that, though the constitution of New York has no bill of rights prefixed to it, yet it contains, in the body of it, various provisions in favor of particular privileges and rights, which, in substance, amount to the same thing; the other is, that the Constitution adopts, in their full extent, the common and statute law of Great Britain, by which many other rights, not expressed in it, are equally secured.
   To the first I answer, that the Constitution proposed by the convention contains, as well as the constitution of this State, a number of such provisions.
   Independent of those which relate to the structure of the government, we find the following: Article 1, section 3, clause 7—"Judgment in cases of impeachment shall not extend further than to removal from office, and disqualification to hold and enjoy any office of honor, trust, or profit under the United States; but the party convicted shall, nevertheless, be liable and subject to indictment, trial, judgment, and punishment according to law." Section 9, of the same article, clause 2—'The privilege of the writ of *habeas corpus* shall not be suspended, unless when in cases of rebellion or invasion the public safety may require it." Clause 3—"No bill of attainder or *ex-post-facto* law shall be passed. Clause 7—"No title of nobility shall be granted by the United States; and no person holding any office of profit or trust under them, shall, without the consent of the Congress, accept of any present,

*From Alexander Hamilton, "The Federalist No. 84," in *The Federalist Papers*, 2E, ed. Roy P. Fairfield (Baltimore, MD: The Johns Hopkins University Press, 1981), pp. 259–69.

emolument, office, or title of any kind whatever, from any king, prince, or foreign state." Article 3, section 2, clause 3—"The trial of all crimes, except in cases of impeachment, shall be by jury; and such trial shall be held in the State where the said crimes shall have been committed; but when not committed within any State, the trial shall be at such place or places as the Congress may by law have directed." Section 3, of the same article—"Treason against the United States shall consist only in levying war against them, or in adhering to their enemies, giving them aid and comfort. No person shall be convicted of treason, unless on the testimony of two witnesses to the same overt act, or on confession in open court." And clause 3 [sic], of the same section—"The Congress shall have power to declare the punishment of treason; but no attainder of treason shall work corruption of blood, or forfeiture, except during the life of the person attainted." . . .

But a minute detail of particular rights is certainly far less applicable to a Constitution like that under consideration, which is merely intended to regulate the general political interests of the nation, than to a constitution which has the regulation of every species of personal and private concerns. If, therefore, the loud clamors against the plan of the convention, on this score, are well founded, no epithets of reprobation will be too strong for the constitution of this State. But the truth is, that both of them contain all which, in relation to their objects, is reasonably to be desired.

I go further, and affirm that bills of rights, in the sense and to the extent in which they are contended for, are not only unnecessary in the proposed Constitution, but would even be dangerous. They would contain various exceptions to powers not granted; and, on this very account, would afford a colorable pretext to claim more than were granted. For why declare that things shall not be done which there is no power to do? Why, for instance, should it be said that the liberty of the press shall not be restrained, when no power is given by which restrictions may be imposed? I will not contend that such a provision would confer a regulating power; but it is evident that it would furnish, to men disposed to usurp, a plausible pretence for claiming that power. . . . This may serve as a specimen of the numerous handles which would be given to the doctrine of constructive powers by the indulgence of an injudicious zeal for bills of rights.

On the subject of the liberty of the press—as much as has been said, I cannot forbear adding a remark or two: in the first place, I observe that there is not a syllable concerning it in the constitution of this State; in the next, I contend that whatever has been said about it in that of any other State, amounts to nothing. What signifies a declaration, that "the liberty of the press shall be inviolably preserved." What is the liberty of the press? Who can give it any definition which would not leave the utmost latitude for evasion? I hold it to be impracticable; and from this I infer that its security, whatever fine declarations may be inserted in any constitution respecting it, must altogether depend on public opinion, and on the general spirit of the people and of the government. And here, after all, as is intimated upon another occasion, must we seek for the only solid basis of all our rights.

There remains but one other view of this matter to conclude the point. The truth is, after all the declamations we have heard, that the Constitution is itself, in every rational sense and to every useful purpose, A BILL OF RIGHTS. The several bill of rights in Great Britain form its Constitution, and conversely the constitution of each State is its bill of rights. And the proposed Constitution, if adopted, will be the bill of rights of the Union. Is it one object of a bill of rights to declare and specify the political privileges of the citizens in the structure and administration of the government? This is done in the most ample and precise manner in the plan of the convention; comprehending various precautions for the public security, which are not to be found in any of the State constitutions. Is another object of a bill of rights to define certain immunities and modes of proceeding, which are relative to personal and private concerns? This we have seen has also been attended to, in a variety of cases, in the same plan. Adverting therefore to the substantial meaning of a bill of rights, it is absurd to allege that it is not to be found in the work of the convention. It may be said that it does not go far enough, though it will not be easy to make this appear; but it can with no propriety be contended that there is no such thing. It certainly must be immaterial what mode is observed as to the order of declaring the rights of the citizens, if they are to be found in any part of the instrument which establishes the government. And hence it must be apparent that much of what has been said on this subject rests merely on verbal and nominal distinctions, entirely foreign from the substance of the thing. . . .

A Letter of His Excellency Edmund Randolph, Esquire, on the Federal Constitution*

Edmund Randolph

Sir,

The Constitution, which I inclosed to the General Assembly in a late official letter, appears without my signature. This circumstance, although trivial in its own nature, has been rendered rather important to myself at

---

*From Edmund Randolph, "A Letter of His Excellency Edmund Randolph, Esquire, on the Federal Constitution," in *The Complete Anti-Federalist*, ed. Herbert J. Storing (Chicago: University of Chicago Press, 1981), II, pp. 86–89.

least, by being misunderstood by some, and misrepresented by others—As I disdain to conceal the reasons for with-holding my subscription, I have always been, still am, and ever shall be, ready to proclaim them to the world. To the legislature therefore, by whom I was deputed to the Federal Convention. I beg leave now to address them; affecting no indifference to public opinion, but resolved not to court it by an unmanly sacrifice of my own judgment. . . .

Before my departure for the Convention, I believed, that the confederation was not so eminently defective, as it had been supposed. But after I had entered into a free communication with those, who were best informed of the condition and interest of each state; after I had compared the intelligence derived from them, with the properties, which ought to characterize the government of our union, I became persuaded, that the confederation was destitute of every energy, which a constitution of the United States ought to possess. . . .

For the objects proposed by its institution were, that it should be a shield against foreign hostility, and a firm resort against domestic commotion: that it should cherish trade, and promote the prosperity of the states under its care.

But these are not among the attributes of our present union. Severe experience under the pressure of war—a ruinous weakness, manifested since the return of peace—and the contemplation of these dangers, which darken the future prospect, have condemned the hope of grandeur and of safety under the auspices of the confederation. . . .

I saw however that the confederation was tottering from its own weakness, and that the sitting of the convention was a signal of its total insufficiency. I was therefore ready to assent to a scheme of government, which was proposed, and which went beyond the limits of the confederation, believing, that without being too extensive it would have preserved our tranquility, until that temper and that genius should be collected.

But when the plan which is now before the General Assembly, was on its passage through the convention, I moved, that the state-conventions should be at liberty to amend, and that a second general Convention should be holden to discuss the amendments, which should be suggested by them. This motion was in some measure justified by the manner, in which the confederation was forwarded originally, by Congress to the state-legislatures, in many of which amendments were proposed, and those amendments were afterwards examined in Congress. Such a motion was doubly expedient here, as the delegation of so much more power was sought for. But it was negatived. I then expressed my unwillingness to sign. My reasons were the following. . . .

1. It is said in the resolutions, which accompany the constitution, that it is to be submitted to a convention of Delegates, chosen in each state by

the people thereof, for their assent and ratification. The meaning of these terms is allowed universally to be, that the Convention must either adopt the constitution in the whole, or reject it in the whole, and is positively forbidden to amend. . . . With this consequence before my eyes and with a determination to attempt an amendment, I was taught by a regard for consistency not to sign.

2. My opinion always was, and still is, that every citizen of America, let the crisis be what it may, ought to have a full opportunity to propose through his representatives any amendment, which in his apprehension tends to the public welfare—By signing I should have contradicted this sentiment.

3. A constitution ought to have the hearts of the people on its side. But if at a future day it should be burthensome, after having been adopted in the whole, and they should insinuate, that it was in some measure forced upon them, by being confined to the single alternative of taking or rejecting it altogether, under my impressions and with my opinions I should not be able to justify myself had I signed.

4. I was always satisfied, as I have now experienced, that this great subject, would be placed in new lights and attitudes by the criticism of the world, and that no man can assure himself, how a constitution will work for a course of years, until at least he shall have heard the observations of the people at large. I also fear more from inaccuracies in a constitution, than from gross errors in any other composition; because our dearest interests are to be regulated by it, and power, if loosely given, especially where it will be interpreted with great latitude, may bring sorrow in its execution. Had I signed with these ideas, I should have virtually shut my ears against the information, which I ardently desired.

5. I was afraid, that if the Constitution was to be submitted to the people, to be wholly adopted or wholly rejected by them, they would not only reject it, but bid a lasting farewell to the union. This formidable event I wished to avert, by keeping myself free to propose amendments, and thus, if possible, to remove the obstacles to an effectual government. . . .

Again may I be asked, why the mode pointed out in the Constitution for its amendment, may not be a sufficient security against its imperfections, without now arresting it in its progress?—My answers are, 1. that it is better to amend, while we have the Constitution in our power, while the passions of designing men are not yet enlisted and while a bare majority of the states may amend, than to wait for the uncertain assent of three fourths of the states. 2. That a bad feature in government becomes more and more fixed every day. 3. That frequent changes of a Constitution even if practicable ought not to be wished, but avoided as much as possible: and 4. That in the present case it may be questionable, whether, after the particular advantages of its operation shall be discerned, three fourths of the states can be induced to amend . . .

I should now conclude this letter, which is already too long, were it not incumbent on me from having contended for amendments, to set forth the particulars, which I conceive to require correction. . . .

The two first points are the equality of suffrage in the Senate, and the submission of commerce to a mere majority in the legislature, with no other check than the revision of the President. I conjecture that neither of these things can be corrected; and particularly the former; without which we must have risen perhaps in disorder.

But I am sanguine in hoping, that in every other, justly obnoxious clause, Virginia, will be seconded by a majority of the states. I hope, that she will be seconded 1. in causing all ambiguities of expression to be precisely explained: 2. in rendering the President ineligible after a given number of years: 3. in taking from him either the power of nominating to the judiciary offices, or of filling up vacancies which therein may happen during the recess of the senate, by granting commissions which shall expire at the end of their next session: 4. in taking from him the power of pardoning for treason, at least before conviction: 5. in drawing a line between the powers of Congress and individual states; and in defining the former; so as to leave no clashing of jurisdictions nor dangerous disputes: and to prevent the one from being swallowed up by the other, under the cover of general words, and implication: 6. in abridging the power of the Senate to make treaties the supreme laws of the land: 7. in providing a tribunal instead of the Senate for the impeachment of Senators: 8. in incapacitating the Congress to determine their own salaries: and often limiting and defining the judicial power.

The proper remedy must be consigned to the wisdom of the convention: and the final step, which Virginia shall pursue, if her overtures shall be discarded, must also rest with them.

But as I affect neither mystery nor subtilty, in politics, I hesitate not to say, that the most fervent prayer of my soul is the establishment of a firm, energetic government; that the most inveterate curse, which can befal us, is a dissolution of the union; and that the present moment, if suffered to pass away unemployed, can never be recalled. These were my opinions, while I acted as a Delegate; they sway me, while I speak as a private citizen. I shall therefore cling to the union, as the rock of our salvation, and urge Virginia to finish the salutary work, which she has begun. And if after our best efforts for amendments they cannot be obtained, I scruple not to declare, (notwithstanding the advantage, which such a declaration may give to the enemies of my proposal,) that I will, as an individual citizen, accept the constitution; because I would regulate myself by the spirit of America. . . .

Essays of Brutus, I*

Robert Yates

To the Citizens of the State of New-York.

When the public is called to investigate and decide upon a question in which not only the present members of the community are deeply interested, but upon which the happiness and misery of generations yet unborn is in great measure suspended, the benevolent mind cannot help feeling itself peculiarly interested in the result. . . .

Perhaps this country never saw so critical a period in their political concerns. We have felt the feebleness of the ties by which these United States are held together, and the want of sufficient energy in our present confederation, to manage, in some instances, our general concerns. Various expedients have been proposed to remedy these evils, but none have succeeded. At length a Convention of the states has been assembled, they have formed a constitution which will now, probably, be submitted to the people to ratify or reject, who are the fountain of all power, to whom alone it of right belongs to make or unmake constitutions, or forms of government, at their pleasure. The most important question that was ever proposed to your decision, or to the decision of any people under heaven, is before you, and you are to decide upon it by men of your own election, chosen specially for this purpose. If the constitution, offered to your acceptance, be a wise one, calculated to preserve the invaluable blessings of liberty, to secure the inestimable rights of mankind, and promote human happiness, then, if you accept it, you will lay a lasting foundation of happiness for millions yet unborn; generations to come will rise up and call you blessed. . . . But if, on the other hand, this form of government contains principles that will lead to the subversion of liberty—if it tends to establish a despotism, or, what is worse, a tyrannic aristocracy; then, if you adopt it, this only remaining assylum for liberty will be shut up, and posterity will execrate your memory. . . .

With these few introductory remarks, I shall proceed to a consideration of this constitution:

The first question that presents itself on the subject is, whether a confederated government be the best for the United States or not? . . . Or in other words, whether the thirteen United States should be reduced to one great republic, governed by one legislature, and under the direction of one executive and judicial; or whether they should continue thirteen confederat-

---

*From Robert Yates, "Essays of Brutus, I," in *The Complete Anti-Federalist,* ed. Herbert J. Storing (Chicago: University of Chicago Press, 1981), II, 363-72.

ed republics, under the direction and controul of a supreme federal head for certain defined national purposes only?

This enquiry is important, because, although the government reported by the convention does not go to a perfect and entire consolidation, yet it approaches so near to it, that it must, if executed, certainly and infallibly terminate in it.

This government is to possess absolute and uncontroulable power, legislative, executive and judicial, with respect to every object to which it extends, for by the last clause of section 8th, article 1st, it is declared "that the Congress shall have power to make all laws which shall be necessary and proper for carrying into execution the foregoing powers, and all other powers vested by this constitution, in the government of the United States; or in any department or office thereof." And by the 6th article, it is declared "that this constitution, and the laws of the United States, which shall be made in pursuance thereof, and the treaties made, or which shall be made, under the authority of the United States, shall be the supreme law of the land; and the judges in every state shall be bound thereby, any thing in the constitution, or law of any state to the contrary notwithstanding." It appears from these articles that there is no need of any intervention of the state governments, between the Congress and the people, to execute any one power vested in the general government, and that the constitution and laws of every state are nullified and declared void, so far as they are or shall be inconsistent with this constitution, or the laws made in pursuance of it, or with treaties made under the authority of the United States.—The government then, so far as it extends, is a complete one, and not a confederation. . . . The powers of the general legislature extend to every case that is of the least importance—there is nothing valuable to human nature, nothing dear to freemen, but what is within its power. It has authority to make laws which will affect the lives, the liberty, and property of every man in the United States; nor can the constitution or laws of any state, in any way prevent or impede the full and complete execution of every power given. The legislative power is competent to lay taxes, duties, imposts, and excises; . . . —there is no limitation to this power, unless it be said that the clause which directs the use to which those taxes, and duties shall be applied, may be said to be a limitation: but this is no restriction of the power at all, for by this clause they are to be applied to pay the debts and provide for the common defence and general welfare of the United States; but the legislature have authority to contract debts at their discretion; they are the sole judges of what is necessary to provide for the common defence, and they only are to determine what is for the general welfare; this power therefore is neither more nor less, than a power to lay and collect taxes, imposts, and excises, at their pleasure; not only [is] the power to lay taxes unlimited, as to the amount they may require, but it is perfect and absolute to raise them in any mode they please. No state legislature, or any power in the state governments, have any more to do in carrying this into effect, than the authority of one state has to do with that of another. In the business therefore of laying and collecting taxes, the idea of confederation is totally lost, and that of one entire republic is embraced. It is proper here to remark, that the authority to lay and collect taxes is the most important of any power that can be granted; it connects with it almost all other powers, or at least will in process of time draw all other after it; it is the great mean of protection, security, and defence, in a good government, and the great engine of oppression and tyranny in a bad one. . . . Every one who has thought on the subject, must be convinced that but small sums of money can be collected in any country, by direct taxe[s], when the federal government begins to exercise the right of taxation in all its parts, the legislatures of the several states will find it impossible to raise monies to support their governments. Without money they cannot be supported, and they must dwindle away, and, as before observed, their powers absorbed in that of the general government. . . .

The judicial power of the United States is to be vested in a supreme court, and in such inferior courts as Congress may from time to time ordain and establish. . . . The powers of these courts are very extensive; their jurisdiction comprehends all civil causes, except such as arise between citizens of the same state; and it extends to all cases in law and equity arising under the constitution. One inferior court must be established, I presume, in each state, at least, with the necessary executive officers appendant thereto. It is easy to see, that in the common course of things, these courts will eclipse the dignity, and take away from the respectability, of the state courts. These courts will be, in themselves, totally independent of the states, deriving their authority from the United States, and receiving from them fixed salaries; and in the course of human events it is to be expected, that they will swallow up all the powers of the courts in the respective states.

How far the clause in the 8th section of the 1st article may operate to do away all idea of confederated states, and to effect an entire consolidation of the whole into one general government, it is impossible to say. The powers given by this article are very general and comprehensive, and it may receive a construction to justify the passing almost any law. A power to make all laws, which shall be *necessary* and *proper*, for carrying into execution, all powers vested by the constitution in the government of the United States, or any department or officer thereof, is a power very comprehensive and definite [indefinite?], and may, for ought I know, be exercised in a such manner as entirely to abolish the state legislatures. . . .

Let us now proceed to enquire, as I at first proposed, whether it be best the thirteen United States should be reduced to one great republic, or not? It is here taken for granted, that all agree in this, that whatever government we adopt, it ought to be a free one; that it should be so framed as to secure the liberty of the citizens of America, and such an one as to admit of a full, fair, and equal representation of the people. The question then will be, whether a government thus constituted, and founded on such principles, is practicable, and can be exercised over the whole United States, reduced into one state?

History furnishes no example of a free republic, any thing like the extent of the United States. The Grecian republics were of small extent; so also was that of the Romans. Both of these, it is true, in process of time, extended their conquests over large territories of country; and the consequence was, that their governments were changed from that of free governments to those of the most tyrannical that ever existed in the world.

Not only the opinion of the greatest men, and the experience of mankind are against the idea of an extensive republic, but a variety of reasons may be drawn from the reason and nature of things, against it. In every government, the will of the sovereign is the law. In despotic governments, the supreme authority being lodged in one, his will is law, and can be as easily expressed to a large extensive territory as to a small one. In a pure democracy the people are the sovereign, and their will is declared by themselves; for this purpose they must all come together to deliberate, and decide. This kind of government cannot be exercised, therefore, over a country of any considerable extent; it must be confined to a single city, or at least limited to such bounds as that the people can conveniently assemble, be able to debate, understand the subject submitted to them, and declare their opinion concerning it.

In a free republic, although all laws are derived from the consent of the people, yet the people do not declare their consent by themselves in person, but by representatives, chosen by them, who are supposed to know the minds of their constituents, and to be possessed of integrity to declare this mind. . . .

In every free government, the people must give their assent to the laws by which they are governed. This is the true criterion between a free government and an arbitrary one. The former are ruled by the will of the whole, expressed in any manner they may agree upon; the latter by the will of one, or a few. If the people are to give their assent to the laws, by persons chosen and appointed by them, the manner of the choice and the number chosen, must be such, as to possess, be disposed, and consequently qualified to declare the sentiments of the people; for if they do not know, or are not disposed to speak the sentiments of the people, the people do not govern, but the sovereignty is in a few. Now, in a large extended country, it is impossible to have a representation, possessing the sentiments, and of integrity, to declare the minds of the people, without having it so numerous and unwieldly, as to be subject in great measure to the inconveniency of a democratic government.

The territory of the United States is of vast extent; it now contains near three millions of souls, and is capable of containing much more than ten times that number. Is it practicable for a country, so large and so numerous as they will soon become, to elect a representation, that will speak their sentiments, without their becoming so numerous as to be incapable of transacting public business? It certainly is not. . . .

In a republic, the manners, sentiments, and interests of the people should be similar. If this be not the case, there will be a constant clashing of opinions; and the representatives of one part will be continually striving against those of the other. . . . This will retard the operations of government, and prevent such conclusions as will promote the public good. If we apply this remark to the condition of the United States, we shall be convinced that it forbids that we should be one government. The United States includes a variety of climates. The productions of the different parts of the union are very variant, and their interests, of consequence, diverse. Their manners and habits differ as much as their climates and productions; and their sentiments are by no means coincident. The laws and customs of the several states are, in many respects, very diverse, and in some opposite; each would be in favor of its own interests and customs, and, of consequence, a legislature, formed of representatives from the respective parts, would not only be too numerous to act with any care or decision, but would be composed of such heterogeneous and discordant principles, as would constantly be contending with each other.

In a republic of such vast extent as the United States, the legislature cannot attend to the various concerns and wants of its different parts. It cannot be sufficiently numerous to be acquainted with the local condition and wants of the different districts, and if it could, it is impossible it should have sufficient time to attend to and provide for all the variety of cases of this nature, that would be continually arising.

In so extensive a republic, the great officers of government would soon become above the controul of the people, and abuse their power to the purpose of aggrandizing themselves, and oppressing them. The trust committed to the executive offices, in a country of the extent of the United States, must be various and of magnitude. The command of all the troops and navy of the republic, the appointment of officers, the power of pardoning offences, the collecting of all the public revenues, and the power of expending them, with a number of other powers, must be lodged and exercised in every state, in the hands of a few. When these are attended with great honor and emolument, as they always will be in large states, so as greatly to interest men to pursue them, and to be proper objects for ambitious and designing men, such men will be ever restless in their pursuit after them. They will use the power, when they have acquired it, to the purposes of gratifying their own interest and ambition, and it is scarcely possible, in a very large republic, to call them to account for their misconduct, or to prevent their abuse of power. . . .

These are some of the reasons by which it appears, that a free republic cannot long subsist over a country of the great extent of these states. If then this new constitution is calculated to consolidate the thirteen states into one, as it evidently is, it ought not to be adopted. . . .

Essays of Brutus, II*

Robert Yates

To the Citizens of the State of New-York.

I flatter myself that my last address established this position, that to reduce the Thirteen States into one government, would prove the destruction of your liberties.

But lest this truth should be doubted by some, I will now proceed to consider its merits.

Though it should be admitted, that the argument[s] against reducing all the states into one consolidated government, are not sufficient fully to establish this point; yet they will, at least, justify this conclusion, that in forming a constitution for such a country, great care should be taken to limit and definite its powers, adjust its parts, and guard against an abuse of authority. How far attention has been paid to these objects, shall be the subject of future enquiry. When a building is to be erected which is intended to stand for ages, the foundation should be firmly laid. The constitution proposed to your acceptance, is designed not for yourselves alone, but for generations yet unborn. The principles, therefore, upon which the social compact is founded, ought to have been clearly and precisely stated, and the most express and full declaration of rights to have been made—But on this subject there is almost an entire silence.

If we may collect the sentiments of the people of America, from their own most solemn declarations, they hold this truth as self evident, that all men are by nature free. No one man, therefore, or any class of men, have a right, by the law of nature, or of God, to assume or exercise authority over their fellows. The origin of society then is to be sought, not in any natural right which one man has to exercise authority over another, but in the united consent of those who associate. The mutual wants of men, at first dictated the propriety of forming societies; and when they were established, protection and defence pointed out the necessity of instituting government. . . . The common good, therefore, is the end of civil government, and common consent, the foundation on which it is established. To effect this end, it was necessary that a certain portion of natural liberty should be surrendered, in

---

*From Robert Yates, "Essays of Brutus, II," in *The Complete Anti-Federalist*, ed. Herbert J. Storing (Chicago: University of Chicago Press, 1981), II, 372–76.

order, that what remained should be preserved: how great a proportion of natural freedom is necessary to be yielded by individuals, when they submit to government, I shall not now enquire. So much, however, must be given up, as will be sufficient to enable those, to whom the administration of the government is committed, to establish laws for the promoting the happiness of the community, and to carry those laws into effect. But it is not necessary, for this purpose, that individuals should relinquish all their natural rights. Some are of such a nature that they cannot be surrendered. Of this kind are the rights of conscience, the right of enjoying and defending life, etc. Others are not necessary to be resigned, in order to attain the end for which government is instituted, these therefore ought not to be given up. To surrender them, would counteract the very end of government, to wit, the common good. . . . From these observations it appears, that in forming a government on its true principles, the foundation should be laid in the manner I before stated, by expressly reserving to the people such of their essential natural rights, as are not necessary to be parted with. . . . But rulers have the same propensities as other men; they are as likely to use the power with which they are vested for private purposes, and to the injury and oppression of those over whom they are placed, as individuals in a state of nature are to injure and oppress one another. It is therefore as proper that bounds should be set to their authority, as that government should have at first been instituted to restrain private injuries. . . .

This principle, which seems so evidently founded in the reason and nature of things, is confirmed by universal experience. Those who have governed, have been found in all ages ever active to enlarge their powers and abridge the public liberty. This has induced the people in all countries, where any sense of freedom remained, to fix barriers against the encroachments of their rulers. . . . I presume, to an American, then, that this principle is a fundamental one, in all the constitutions of our own states; there is not one of them but what is either founded on a declaration or bill of rights, or has certain express reservation of rights interwoven in the body of them. From this it appears, that at a time when the pulse of liberty beat high and when an appeal was made to the people to form constitutions for the government of themselves, it was their universal sense, that such declarations should make a part of their frames of government. It is therefore the more astonishing, that this grand security, to the rights of the people, is not to be found in this constitution.

It has been said, in answer to this objection, that such declaration[s] of rights, however requisite they might be in the constitutions of the states, are not necessary in the general constitution, because, "in the former case, every thing which is not reserved is given, but in the latter the reverse of the proposition prevails, and every thing which is not given is reserved." . . . It requires but little attention to discover, that this mode of reasoning is rather specious than solid. The powers, rights, and authority, granted to the general government by this constitution, are as complete, with respect to every object to which they extend, as that of any state government—It reaches to every thing which concerns human happiness—Life, liberty, and property, are under its controul. There is the same reason, therefore, that the exercise of power, in this case, should be restrained within proper limits, as in that of the state governments. To set this matter in a clear light, permit me to instance some of the articles of the bills of rights of the individual states, and apply them to the case in question.

For the security of life, in criminal prosecutions, the bills of rights of most of the states have declared, that no man shall be held to answer for a crime until he is made fully acquainted with the charge brought against him; he shall not be compelled to accuse, or furnish evidence against himself—The witnesses against him shall be brought face to face, and he shall be fully heard by himself or counsel. That it is essential to the security of life and liberty, that trial of facts be in the vicinity where they happen. Are not provisions of this kind as necessary in the general government, as in that of a particular state? The powers vested in the new Congress extend in many cases to life; they are authorised to provide for the punishment of a variety of capital crimes, and no restraint is laid upon them in its exercise, save only, that "the trial of all crimes, except in cases of impeachment, shall be by jury: and such trial shall be in the state where the said crimes shall have been committed." . . .

For the security of liberty it has been declared, "that excessive bail should not be required, nor excessive fines imposed, nor cruel or unusual punishments inflicted—That all warrants, without oath or affirmation, to search suspected places, or seize any person, his papers or property, are grievous and oppressive." . . .

These provisions are as necessary under the general government as under that of the individual states; for the power of the former is as complete to the purpose of requiring bail, imposing fines, inflicting punishments, granting search warrants, and seizing persons, papers, or property, in certain cases, as the other.

For the purpose of securing the property of the citizens, it is declared by all the states, "that in all controversies at law, respecting property, the ancient mode of trial by jury is one of the best securities of the rights of the people, and ought to remain sacred and inviolable." . . .

Does not the same necessity exist of reserving this right, under this national compact, as in that of these states? Yet nothing is said respecting it. In the bills of rights of the states it is declared, that a well regulated militia is the proper and natural defence of a free government—That as standing armies in time of peace are dangerous, they are not to be kept up, and that the military should be kept under strict subordination to, and controuled by the civil power. . . .

The same security is as necessary in this constitution, and much more so; for the general government will have the sole power to raise and to pay armies, and are under no controul in the exercise of it; yet nothing of this is to be found in this new system.

I might proceed to instance a number of other rights, which were as necessary to be reserved, such as, that elections should be free, that the liberty of the press should be held sacred; but the instances adduced, are sufficient to prove, that this argument is without foundation.—Besides, it is evident, that the reason here assigned was not the true one, why the framers of this constitution omitted a bill of rights; if it had been, they would not have made certain reservations, while they totally omitted others of more importance. We find they have, in the 9th section of the 1st article, declared, that the writ of habeas corpus shall not be suspended, unless in cases of rebellion—that no bill of attainder, or expost facto law, shall be passed—that no title of nobility shall be granted by the United States, &c. If every thing which is not given is reserved, what propriety is there in these exceptions? . . . Does this constitution any where grant the power of suspending the habeas corpus, to make expost facto laws, pass bills of attainder, or grant titles of nobility? It certainly does not in express terms. The only answer that can be given is, that these are implied in the general powers granted. With equal truth it may be said, that all the powers, which the bills of right, guard against the abuse of, are contained or implied in the general ones granted by this constitution.

So far it is from being true, that a bill of rights is less necessary in the general constitution than in those of the states, the contrary is evidently the fact.—This system, if it is possible for the people of America to accede to it, will be an original compact; and being the last, will, in the nature of things, vacate every former agreement inconsistent with it. For it being a plan of government received and ratified by the whole people, all other forms, which are in existence at the time of its adoption, must yield to it. This is expressed in positive and unequivocal terms, in the 6th article, "That this constitution and the laws of the United States, which shall be made in pursuance thereof, and all treaties made, or which shall be made, under the authority of the United States, shall be the supreme law of the land; and the judges in every state shall be bound thereby, any thing in the *constitution* or laws of any state, *to the contrary* notwithstanding.

"The senators and representatives before-mentioned, and the members of the several state legislatures, and all executive and judicial of officers, both of the United States, and of the several states, shall be bound, by oath or affirmation, to support this constitution."

It is therefore not only necessarily implied thereby, but positively expressed, that the different state constitutions are repealed and entirely done away, so far as they are inconsistent with this, with the laws which shall be made in pursuance thereof, or with treaties made, or which shall be made under the authority of the United States; of what avail will the constitutions of the respective states be to preserve the rights of its citizens? Should they be plead, the answer would be, the constitution of the United States, and the laws made in pursuance thereof, is the supreme law, and all legislatures and judicial officers, whether of the general or state governments, are bound by oath to support it. No priviledge, reserved by the bills of rights, or secured by the state government, can limit the power granted by this, or restrain any laws made in pursuance of it. It stands therefore on its own bottom, and must receive a construction by itself without any reference to any other . . . —And hence it was of the highest importance, that the most precise and express declarations and reservations of rights should have been made. . . .

So clear a point is this, that I cannot help suspecting, that persons who attempt to persuade people, that such reservations were less necessary under this constitution than under those of the states, are wilfully endeavouring to deceive, and to lead you into an absolute state of vassalage. . . .

DISCUSSION QUESTIONS

1. What role did property play in the creation of the Constitution?
2. How did the Federalists and Anti-Federalists use geographic and cultural views of America to support their positions on the Constitution?
3. Why was government necessary according to the Federalists? Why were the Anti-Federalists concerned with this view?
4. How were the rights of individuals and states seen as a means of limiting the powers of a central government according to the Anti-Federalists?

Chapter 5

JACKSONIAN
AND
INTELLECTUAL DEMOCRACY

The first twelve years of the American nation was characterized by a debate over the role of the federal government in expanding the economy and individual freedom. During the Washington and Adams administrations the focus was on enhancing the economic well-being of the commercial classes in the belief that that would strengthen the national and international position of the U.S. Along this line Washington's Secretary of the Treasury, Alexander Hamilton, promoted the establishment of a strong central government by its assumption of the states' war debts and the creation of the Bank of the United States in order to expand credit and commerce. Hamilton's political philosophy justified this course of action through the belief that the federal government must apply the broadest interpretation of the "general welfare" clause of the Constitution. Promoting commerce was regarded as the best means of encouraging the prosperity of the majority and gaining the allegiance of those with the most to lose in the event it failed. In fact, the Federalist attitude toward the economy tended to work in favor of those of established wealth and against those trying to prosper. Given that most states provided political rights only to the propertied class, the mass of Americans were denied the most rudimentary ability to participate in politics, to vote.

Increasing popular discontentment resulted in Congress passing the Alien and Sedition Acts during the Adams administration, which made it a crime to criticize the government. Statutory law thereby limited the protections for speech and press offered in the Bill of Rights in violation of the Constitution. The Alien and Sedition Acts provoked Jefferson and Madison to respectively offer in the Kentucky and Virginia Resolutions the view that the states could declare null and void acts of the federal government when they exceeded the authority of the central government.

> Whensoever the general government assumes undelegated powers, its acts are unauthoritative, void, and of no force: that to this compact each State acceded as a State, and is an integral party, its co-States forming, as to itself, the other party: that the government created by this compact was not made the exclusive or final judge of the extent of the powers delegated to itself; since that would have made its discretion, and not the Constitution, the measure of its powers; but that, as in all other cases of compact among powers having no common judge, each party has an equal right to judge for itself, as well of infractions as of the mode and measure of redress.[1]

Federalist activities to control popular political activity enabled the Democratic-Republicans to gain control of the presidency and Congress in the election of 1800. Subsequently, the Alien and Sedition Acts were allowed to expire, aborting the need for an inquiry into the relationship of federal and state governments.

However, the issue of federal involvement in the economy continued. Whereas the Federalists sought to promote capital, paper money, and securities (artificial property), the Democratic-Republicans sought equal treatment for those whose wealth was based on land (natural property).[2] Jefferson's democratic agrarianism held that government should support both the agrarian and commercial interests. As Hofstadter wrote, Jefferson "accepted competitive laissez-faire economics with its assumption that, so long as men were equal in law, and government played no favorites, wealth would be distributed in accordance with `industry and skill.'"[3] Thus the role of government was to promote and expand political equality in order for individuals to seek economic opportunity. Accordingly, the size of government was reduced in order to pay off the national debt and to reduce the interference of the central government in people's lives. Federal monies were used to stimulate the well-being of Federalists and Democratic-Republicans alike.

Between 1790 and 1820 the United States underwent a series of transformations of which the most important was the Louisiana Purchase. The purchase of territory contradicted Jefferson's belief in a smaller, limited federal government for it set the precedent of the central government capable

---

[1]"The Kentucky Resolutions," in *The Complete Jefferson*, assembled and arranged by Saul K. Padover (Freeport, NY: Books for Libraries Press, 1969), p. 129.

[2]A.J. Beitzinger, *A History of American Political Thought* (New York: Dodd, Mead & Company, 1972), p. 337.

[3]From *The American Political Tradition*, by Richard Hofstadter. Copyright © 1948 by Alfred A. Knopf Inc. and renewed 1976 by Beatrice Hofstadter. Reprinted by permission of the publisher, p. 50.

TABLE 5-1   *Territory and Population in the United States, 1790—1830*

	Territory (in square miles)	Population Urban	Rural	Total	Population Per Sq. Mile
1790	888,811	201,655	3,727,559	3,929,214	4.5
1800	888,811	322,371	4,986,112	5,308,483	6.1
1810	1,716,003	525,459	6,714,422	7,239,881	4.3
1820	1,788,006	693,255	8,945,198	9,638,453	5.6
1830	1,788,006	1,127,247	11,738,773	12,866,020	7.4

Historical Statistics of the United States, Colonial Times to 1957 (Washington, DC: Department of Commerce), pp. 8, 14.

of expanding the union territorially and eventually creating new states. Federal authority was expanded in that with the power to create states came the potential to control the most important check on national power, the states. But the Louisiana Purchase supported Jefferson's idea of democratic agrarianism, given the prospect of greater expansion of the farming population which in turn would control a greater number of states and thereby the federal government. As shown in Table 5–1, expansions of U.S. territory were paralleled by increases in the population. Yet, the density of the population did not surpass the 1800 mark of 6.1 until 1830 when the population mark rose to 7.4. These population changes are suggestive of a westward movement in which Americans searched for fame and fortune. The westward movement also tended to empower people. Individuals were able to own land and take responsibility for their economic futures. Also, frontier society tended to be more democratic than in the eastern part of the country in that fewer restrictions were placed on political participation. In summarizing the political and economic impact of the westward migration, Hofstadter wrote,

> As poor farmers and workers gained the ballot, there developed a type of politician that had existed only in embryo in the Jefferson period—the technician of mass leadership, the caterer to a mass sentiment; it was a coterie of such men in all parts of the country that converged upon the prominent figure of Jackson between 1815 and 1824. Generally subordinated in the political corporation and remote from the choicest spoils, these leaders encouraged the common feeling that popular will should control the choice of public officers and the formation of public policy.[4]

Andrew Jackson was a product of the democratic agrarianism produced by the westward movement. As Hofstadter noted,

> The Jacksonian movement grew out of expanding opportunities and a common desire to enlarge these opportunities still further by removing restric-

[4]Ibid., p. 65.

tions and privileges that had their origin in acts of government; thus, with some qualifications, it was essentially a movement of laissez-faire, an attempt to divorce government and business."[5]

The election of 1828 saw the formation of a political coalition consisting of Martin Van Buren, representing the factory workers of the North, John C. Calhoun, the slaveholders of the South, and Andrew Jackson, the family farmers of the West, which gained control of the federal government.

The political ideology of the Jackson administration espoused the existence of a natural aristocracy composed of self-made men who achieved power and wealth. This type of rugged individualism was considered a more positive force on government, since these people created equality through their genius rather than inherited wealth. Accordingly, those people from the frontier or northern workshops who had achieved this new status were regarded as more responsible for government than the northern financial and business establishment. In this regard, the principle of Democratic-Republicanism operated to make government an uninterested arbitrator whose purpose was to actively restrain segments of the population from doing harm to one another while allowing them to succeed or fail on their own merits. Mason and Leach wrote, "whereas the Jeffersonians urged weak government as a first principle, Jackson seemed to favor a strong government, active in behalf of the people, instead of the landed and moneyed aristocracy that flourished in the absence of such a harmonizing agent."[6] Jacksonian democracy, unlike that of Jefferson, held that a strong, activist government was necessary to strike down the barriers which harmed the majority of the population. This point was illustrated by Jackson's message on vetoing the renewal of the Bank of the United States' charter.

> It is to be regretted that the rich and powerful too often bend the acts of government to their selfish purposes. Distinctions in society will always exist under every just government. Equality and talents, of education, or of wealth cannot be produced by human institutions. In the full employment of the gifts of Heaven and the fruits of superior industry, economy, and virtue, every man is equally entitled to protection by law; but when the laws undertake to add to these natural and just advantages artificial distinctions, . . . to make the rich richer and the potent more powerful, the humble members of society— the farmers, mechanics, and labors—who have neither the time nor means of securing like favors to themselves, have a right to complain of the injustice of Government. . . . If we cannot at once, in justice to interests vested under improvident legislation, make our Government what it ought to be, we can at least take a stand against all new grants of monopolies and exclusive privileges, against any prostitution of our Government to the advancement of the

---

[5]Ibid., p. 72.

[6]Alpheus Thomas Mason and Richard H. Leach, *In Quest of Freedom*, 2nd ed. (Englewood Cliffs, N.J.: Prentice-Hall, Inc., 1973), p. 192.

few at the expense of the many, and in favor of compromise and gradual reform in our code of laws and system of political economy.[7]

The purpose of government was not to encourage wealth by the few but to allow individuals the freedom to acquire property so as to expand their political and economic well-being. The crux of Jacksonian ideology was perhaps best summed up by John L. O'Sullivan in the 1838 edition of *The United States Magazine and Democratic Review*.

> As far as superior knowledge and talent confer on their possessor a natural charter of privilege to control his associates, and exert an influence on the direction of the general affairs of the community, the free and natural action of that privilege is best secured by a perfectly free democratic system, which will abolish all artificial distinctions, and, preventing the accumulation of any social obstacles to advancement, will permit the free development of every germ of talent, wherever it may chance to exist, whether on the proud mountain summit, in the humble valley, or by the wayside of common life.[8]

Jackson's veto of the rechartering of the Bank of the United States was thus supported by the popular view that the bank was responsible for the deflationary and inflationary economic trends which harmed the majority of Americans.[9] Federal deposits in the Bank of the United States expanded the credit available to established northern wealth. However, this same credit was denied to westerners. Under Jackson, federal funds were withdrawn and placed in state chartered banks where credit would be made available to members of this natural aristocracy.

Central to the tenets of Jacksonian democracy was equality of opportunity. In the 1830s, Alexis de Tocqueville toured America and produced the book *Democracy in America* in which the source of democracy was analyzed. Central to de Tocqueville's explanation was popular sovereignty. De Tocqueville wrote, "In America, the principle of the sovereignty of the people is not either barren or concealed, as it is with some other nations; it is recognized by the customs and proclaimed by the laws; it spreads freely, and arrives without impediment at its most remote consequences."[10] Political power was based in the people and they in turn determined the direction of the nation. In this regard, Beitzinger wrote, "De Tocqueville believed that American democracy emphasized equality above liberty but aimed at

---

[7]Andrew Jackson, "Veto Message of the Renewal of the Bank of the United States' Charter," quoted in Alpheus Thomas Mason, *Free Government in the Making*, 3rd ed. (New York: Oxford University Press, 1965), p. 443.

[8]John L. O'Sullivan, "Introduction," *The United States Magazine and Democratic Review* 1, no. 1, (1838), p. 5.

[9]Hofstadter, *The American*, pp. 74–75.

[10]Alexis de Tocqueville, *Democracy in America*, ed. Richard D. Heffner (New York: Mentor Books, 1956), p. 54.

an equality in freedom."[11] Class distinctions had not arisen in the United States as they existed in Europe for American society was based on the talents of the individual which allowed people's position in society and government to change. In this context, equality of opportunity served to guarantee the political rights contained in the Constitution.

Opposition to Jacksonian democracy came from a variety of sources of which the most important were intellectuals known as transcendentalists. Among its prominent members were Ralph Waldo Emerson, Henry David Thoreau, and Walt Whitman. Transcendentalists opposed the emphasis placed on expanding property and wealth as well as the new entrepreneurs in government. Caughey and May wrote in describing this movement that:

> Transcendentalism drew on certain Quaker and Puritan insights and on some of the principles enunciated in the political theorizing of the Revolutionary period. The Declaration of Independence and the Bill of Rights, along with being equalitarian, saw a worth and a nobility inherent in every individual. . . . Another central tenet was that there is more to know than man can discover by mind alone, that things sensed and felt or mystically apprehended go beyond and transcend what the mind can achieve. This stress on intuition was a carry-over from the older doctrine of the "inner light," which held that individuals without the necessity of priestly intermediaries can discover divine truth.[12]

Therefore a talent in commerce did not necessarily equip the individual with the ability to govern. Rather the transcendentalists generally believed that those who directed the American nation needed to understand the importance of the individual in a democratic society rather than emphasizing the artifical distinctions produced by one's wealth.

Generally, transcendentalists exalted individuals in terms of their ability to emotionally sustain democracy, whereas the Jacksonian movement emphasized the individual's ability to achieve property and thus the equality offered in a democratic society. Only after becoming a moral force did the individual have the ability to act as a lawgiver for society. In this regard, Emerson argued the concept of "the sufficiency of the private man." Only after using their reasoning ability to become a well-rounded individual were individuals equipped for a policy-making role. As Emerson stated,

> Hence the less government we have the better,—the fewer laws, and the less confided power. The antidote to this abuse of formal Government is the influence of private character, the growth of the Individual; the appearance of the principle to supersede the proxy; the appearance of the wise man; of whom the existing government is, it must be owned, but a shabby imitation.[13]

[11]Beitzinger, *A History*, p. 314.

[12]John W. Caughey and Ernest R. May, *A History of the United States* (Chicago: Rand McNally, 1964), p. 197.

[13]Ralph Waldo Emerson, "Politics," *Essays* (New York: United States Book Company, 1890), p. 178.

Democracy based on rule by the numerical majority had the potential for undermining the democratic traditions of the country and devolving into mob rule. Individual notions of right and wrong would be restrained by majority rule under the idea of democracy thereby reducing the individual to a mere cog in a system dominated by government.

Likewise, to Thoreau, government was a necessary evil, but one which had to be restrained by a sense of individualism. Thoreau regarded the achievement of individual freedom as bringing the person closer in understanding the law of nature and thereby possessing the ability to perfect government. Thus, the ideal government exalted the individual because of the respect placed on the citizen's conscience. This view was evident when Thoreau wrote,

> I think that we should be men first, and subjects afterward. It is not desirable to cultivate a respect for the law, so much as for the right. The only obligation which I have a right to assume is to do at any time what I think right. It is truly enough said, that a corporation has no conscience; but a corporation of conscientious men is a corporation with a conscience.[14]

Government policies which supported a war with Mexico and slavery in the American South led Thoreau to refuse its demand for taxes. In this regard Thoreau developed the idea that the individual should follow a policy of civil disobedience. Accordingly, the individual should refuse to follow the acts of government which violated his or her conscience, but accept the state's punishment. By doing so the individual demonstrates the importance of one's conscience to oneself as well as society at large. In this way the decisions of government can be questioned without suggesting anarchy.

Unlike Emerson and Thoreau who honored the individual, Whitman held that the unity of the American people was key to the success of the country.

> The meaning of America is Democracy. The meaning of Democracy is to put in practice the idea of the sovereignty, license, sacredness of the individual. This idea gives identity and isolation to every man and woman—but the idea of Love fuses and combines all with irresistible power. . . . A third idea, also, is or shall be put there,—namely Religion,—the idea which swallows up and purifies all other ideas and things—and gives endless meaning and destiny to a man and condenses him in all things.[15]

Americans were simultaneously isolated as individuals and united in the community according to Whitman. The individual gives expression to ideas, and by presenting them within the community, fraternal bonds are

[14]Henry D. Thoreau, "Civil Disobedience," *The Works of Thoreau,* ed. Henry Seidel Canby (Boston, MA: Houghton Mifflin Company, 1937), pp. 790–91..

[15]Walt Whitman, Introduction to *Leaves of Grass,* p. 171, in A.J. Beitzinger, *A History of American Political Thought* (New York: Dodd, Mead & Company, 1972), p. 333.

created which porduce freedom. Freedom serves to check individual aspirations while ensuring the presentation of divergent views.

In summation, during the first half of the eighteenth century, the idea
of rugged individualism took root in the United States. The Jefferson and
Jacksonian administrations served to enhance the economic responsibility
of individuals and to establish their role in political affairs. The purpose of
the government was to promote the economic creativity of the people by
striking down artificial barriers. However, transcendentalists like Emerson,
Thoreau, and Whitman believed individualism should be promoted in
democratic terms as opposed to economic ones. Selections appear in the following chapter from the writings of John L. O'Sullivan, Alexis de Tocqueville, Ralph Waldo Emerson, and Henry David Thoreau.

Introduction*

John L. O'Sullivan

THE character and design of the work of which the first number is here
offered to the public, are intended to be shadowed forth in its name, the
"United States Magazine and *Democratic Review.*" It has had its origin in a
deep conviction of the necessity of such work, at the present critical stage of
our national progress, for the advocacy of that high and holy DEMOCRAT-
IC PRINCIPLE which was designed to be the fundamental element of the
new social and political system created by the 'American experiment;' for
the vindication of that principle from the charges daily brought against it,
of responsibility for every evil result growing out, in truth, of adventitious
circumstances, and the adverse elements unhappily combined with it in our
institutions; for its purification from those corruptions and those hostile
influences, by which we see its beneficent and glorious tendencies, to no
slight extent, perverted and paralysed; for the illustration of truth, which
we see perpetually darkened and confused by the arts of wily error; for the
protection of those great interests, not alone of our country, but of humanity, looking forward through countless ages of the future, which we believe
to be vitally committed with the cause of American Democracy. This is in,
broad terms, the main motive in which this undertaking has had its origin:
this is the objective towards which, in all its departments, more or less
directly, its efforts will tend.

We believe, then, in the principle of *democratic republicanism,* in its
strongest and purest sense. We have an abiding confidence in the virtue,

*From John L. O'Sullivan, "Introduction," *The United States Magazine and Democratic Review,* 1,
no. 1 (1838), 1–15.

intelligence, and full capacity for self-government, of the great mass of our people—our industrious, honest, manly, intelligent millions of freemen.

We are opposed to all self-styled "wholesome restraints" on the free action of the popular opinion and will, other than those which have for their sole object the prevention of precipitate legislation. This latter object is to be attained by the expedient of the division of power, and by causing all legislation to pass through the ordeal of successive forms; to be sifted through the discussions of co-ordinate legislative branches, with mutual suspensive veto powers. Yet all should be dependant with equal directness and promptness on the influence of public opinion; the popular will should be equally the animating and moving spirit of them all, and ought never to find in any of its own creatures a self-imposed power, capable (when misused either by corrupt ambition or honest error) of resisting itself, and defeating its own determined object. We cannot, therefore, look with an eye of favor on any such forms of representation as, by length of tenure of delegated power, tend to weaken that universal and unrelaxing responsibility to the vigilance of public opinion, which is the true conservative principle of our institutions. . . .

The great question here occurs, which is of vast importance to this country, (was it not once near dissolving the Union, and plunging it into the abyss of civil war?)—of the relative rights of majorities and minorities. Though we go for the republican principle of the supremacy of the will of the majority, we acknowledge, in general, a strong sympathy with minorities, and consider that their rights have a high moral claim on the respect and justice of majorities; a claim not always fairly recognised in practice by the latter, in the full sway of power, when flushed with triumph, and impelled by strong interests. This has ever been the point of the democratic cause most open to assault, and the most difficult to defend. This difficulty does not arise from any intrinsic weakness. The democratic theory is perfect and harmonious in all its parts; and if this point is not so self-evidently clear as the rest is generally, in all candid discussion, conceded to be, it is because of certain false principles of government which have, in all practical experiments of the theory, been interwoven with the democratic portions of the system, being borrowed from the example of anti-democratic systems of government. We shall always be willing to meet this question frankly and fairly. . . .

It is not our purpose, in this place, to carry out the discussion of this question. The general scope and tendency of the present work are designed to be directed towards the refutation of this sophistical reasoning and inference. It will be sufficient here to allude to the leading ideas by which they are met by the advocate of the pure democratic cause.

In the first place, the greatest number are *more likely*, at least, as a general rule, to understand and follow their own greatest good, than is the minority.

In the second, a minority is much more likely to abuse power for the promotion of its own selfish interests, at the expense of the majority of numbers—the substantial and producing mass of the nation—than the latter is to oppress unjustly the former. The social evil is also, in that case, proportionately greater. This is abundantly proved by the history of all aristocratic interests that have existed, in various degrees and modifications, in the world. A majority cannot subsist upon a minority; while the natural, and in fact uniform, tendency of a minority entrusted with governmental authority is, to surround itself with wealth, splendor, and power, at the expense of the producing mass, creating and perpetuating those artificial social distinctions which violate the natural equality of rights of the human race, and at the same time offend and degrade the true dignity of human nature.

In the third place, there does not naturally exist any such original superiority of a minority class above the great mass of a community, in intelligence and competence for the duties of government—even putting out of view its constant tendency to abuse from selfish motives, and the safer honesty of the mass. The general diffusion of education; the facility of access to every species of knowledge important to the great interests of the community; the freedom of the press whose very licentiousness cannot materially impair its permanent value, in this country at least, make the pretensions of those self-styled "better classes" to the sole possession of the requisite intelligence for the management of public affairs, too absurd to be entitled to any other treatment than an honest, manly contempt. As far as superior knowledge and talent confer on their possessor a natural charter of privilege to control his associates, and exert an influence on the direction of the general affairs of the community, the free and natural action of that privilege is best secured by a perfectly free democratic system, which will abolish all artificial distinctions, and, preventing the accumulation of any social obstacles to advancement, will permit the free developement of every germ of talent, wherever it may chance to exist, whether on the proud mountain summit, in the humble valley, or by the wayside of common life. . . .

It is under the word *government,* that the subtle danger lurks. Understood as a central consolidated power, managing and directing the various general interests of the society, all government is evil, and the parent of evil. A strong and active democratic *government,* in the common sense of the word, is an evil, differing only in degree and mode of operation, and not in nature, from a strong despotism. This difference is certainly vast, yet, inasmuch as these strong governmental powers must be wielded by human agents, even as the powers of despotism, it is, after all, only a difference in degree; and the tendency to demoralization and tyranny is the same, though the developement of the evil results is much more gradual and slow in the one case than in the other. . . .

The best government is that which governs least. No human depositories can, with safety, be trusted with the power of legislation upon the general interests of society so as to operate directly or indirectly on the industry and property of the community. Such power must be perpetually liable to the most pernicious abuse, from the natural imperfection, both in wisdom of judgment and purity of purpose, of all human legislation, exposed constantly to the pressure of partial interests; interests which, at the same time that they are essentially selfish and tyrannical, are ever vigilant, persevering, and subtle in all the arts of deception and corruption. In fact, the whole history of human society and government may be safely appealed to, in evidence that the abuse of such power a thousand fold more than overbalances its beneficial use. Legislation has been the fruitful parent of nine-tenths of all the evil, moral and physical, by which mankind has been afflicted since the creation of the world, and by which human nature has been self-degraded, fettered, and oppressed. Government should have as little as possible to with the general business and interests of the people. If it once undertakes these functions as its rightful province of action, it is impossible to say to it 'thus far shalt thou go, and no farther.' It will be impossible to confine it to the public interests of the *commonwealth*. It will be perpetually tampering with private interests, and sending forth seeds of corruption which will result in the demoralization of the society. Its domestic action should be confined to the administration of justice, for the protection of the natural equal rights of the citizen, and the preservation of social order. In all other respects, the VOLUNTARY PRINCIPLE, the principle of FREEDOM, suggested to us by the analogy of the divine government of the Creator, and already recognised by us with perfect success in the great social interest of Religion, affords the true 'golden rule' which is alone abundantly competent to work out the best possible general result of order and happiness from that chaos of characters, ideas, motives, and interests—human society. Afford but the single nucleus of a system of administration of justice between man and man, and, under the sure operation of this principle, the floating atoms will distribute and combine themselves, as we see in the beautiful natural process of crystallization, into a far more perfect and harmonious result than if government, with its 'fostering hand,' undertake to disturb, under the plea of directing, the process. The natural laws which will establish themselves and find their own level are the best laws. The same hand was the Author of the moral, as of the physical world; and we feel clear and strong in the assurance that we cannot err in trusting, in the former, to the same fundamental principles of spontaneous action and self-regulation which produce the beautiful order of the latter. . . .

Such is, then, our democracy. It of course places us in the school of strictest construction of the constitution; and in that appears to be involved a full committal of opinion on all the great political questions which now agitate the public mind, and to which we deem it unnecessary here to advert in detail. One necessary inference from the views expressed above is, that we consider the preservation of the present ascendency of the democratic party as of great, if not vital, importance to the future destintes of this holy cause. Most of its leading members we know to possess all the qualifications that should entitle men to the confidence and attachment of their country; and the arduous functions of the executive department of the government are administered with an efficiency, and a strictness and purity of principle, which, considering their nature, extent, and complexity, are indeed remarkable. And even without a particular knowledge of the men, the principle alone would still of necessity attach us to that party. The acquisition of the vast influence of the executive department by the Opposition principles, we could not look upon but as a staggering blow to the cause of democracy, and all the high interests committed with it; from which it would take a long and indefinite period of years to recover—even if the loss of time in national progress would not, in that event, have to be reckoned by generations! We shall therefore, while devoting ourselves to preserve and improve the purity of our democratic institutions, labor to sustain the present democratic administration, by fair appeal to argument, with all the earnestness due to the gravity of the principles and interests involved. . . .

The Sovereignty of the People in America*

Alexis de Tocqueville

Whenever the political laws of the United States are to be discussed, it is with the doctrine of the sovereignty of the people that we must begin. . . .

In America, the principle of the sovereignty of the people is not either barren or concealed, as it is with some other nations; it is recognized by the customs and proclaimed by the laws; it spreads freely, and arrives without impediment at its most remote consequences. If there be a country in the world where the doctrine of the sovereignty of the people can be fairly appreciated, where it can be studied in its application to the affairs of society, and where its dangers and its advantages may be judged, that country is assuredly America.

I have already observed that, from their origin, the sovereignty of the people was the fundamental principle of most of the British colonies in America. It was far, however, from then exercising as much influence on

---

*From Alexis de Tocqueville, "The Sovereignty of the People in America," *Democracy in America*, edited by Richard D. Heffner (New York: Mentor Books, 1956), pp. 53–58.

the government of society as it now does. Two obstacles—the one external, the other internal—checked its invasive progress.

It could not ostensibly disclose itself in the laws of colonies which were still constrained to obey the mother country; it was therefore obliged to rule secretly in the provincial assemblies, and especially in the townships.

American society at that time was not yet prepared to adopt it with all its consequences. Intelligence in New England, and wealth in the country to the south of the Hudson, (as I have shown in the preceding chapter,) long exercised a sort of aristocratic influence, which tended to keep the exercise of social power in the hands of a few. Not all the public functionaries were chosen by popular vote, nor were all the citizens voters. The electoral franchise was everywhere somewhat restricted, and made dependent on a certain qualification, which was very low in the North, and more considerable in the South.

The American Revolution broke out, and the doctrine of the sovereignty of the people came out of the townships, and took possession of the State. Every class was enlisted in its cause; battles were fought and victories obtained for it; it became the law of laws.

A change almost as rapid was effected in the interior of society, where the law of inheritance completed the abolition of local influences.

As soon as this effect of the laws and of the Revolution became apparent to every eye, victory was irrevocably pronounced in favor of the democratic cause. All power was, in fact, in its hands, and resistance was no longer possible. The higher orders submitted without a murmur and without a struggle to an evil which was thenceforth inevitable. The ordinary fate of falling powers awaited them: each of their members followed his own interest; and as it was impossible to wring the power from the hands of a people whom they did not detest sufficiently to brave, their only aim was to secure its good-will at any price. The most democratic laws were consequently voted by the very men whose interests they impaired: and thus, although the higher classes did not excite the passions of the people against their order, they themselves accelerated the triumph of the new state of things; so that, by a singular change, the democratic impulse was to be most irresistible in the very States where the aristocracy had the firmest hold. The State of Maryland, which had been founded by men of rank, was the first to proclaim universal suffrage, and to introduce the most democratic forms into the whole of its government.

When a nation begins to modify the elective qualification, it may easily be foreseen that, sooner or later, that qualification will be entirely abolished. There is no more invariable rule in the history of society: the further electoral rights are extended, the greater is the need of extending them; for after each concession the strength of the democracy increases, and its demands increase with its strength. The ambition of those who are below the appointed rate is irritated in exact proportion to the great number of those who are above it. The exception at last becomes the rule, concession follows concession, and no stop can be made short of universal suffrage.

At the present day the principle of the sovereignty of the people has acquired, in the United States, all the practical development which the imagination can conceive. It is unencumbered by those fictions which are thrown over it in other countries, and it appears in every possible form, according to the exigency of the occasion. Sometimes the laws are made by the people in a body, as at Athens; and sometimes its representatives, chosen by universal suffrage, transact business in its name, and under its immediate supervision.

In some countries, a power exists which, though it is in a degree foreign to the social body, directs it, and forces it to pursue a certain track. In others, the ruling force is divided, being partly within and partly without the ranks of the people. But nothing of the kind is to be seen in the United States; there society governs itself for itself. All power centres in its bosom; and scarcely an individual is to be met with who would venture to conceive, or, still less, to express, the idea of seeking it elsewhere. The nation participates in the making of its laws by the choice of its legislators, and in the execution of them by the choice of the agents of the executive government; it may almost be said to govern itself, so feeble and so restricted is the share left to the administration, so little do the authorities forget their popular origin and the power from which they emanate. The people reign in the American political world as the Deity does in the universe. They are the cause and the aim of all things; everything comes from them, and everything is absorbed in them.

Politics*

Ralph Waldo Emerson

IN dealing with the State we ought to remember that its institutions are not aboriginal, though they existed before we were born; that they are not superior to the citizen; that every one of them was once the act of a single man; every law and usage was a man's expedient to meet a particular case; that they all are imitable, all alterable; we may make as good, we may make better. . . .

The theory of politics which has possessed the mind of men, and which they have expressed the best they could in their laws and in their

*From Ralph Waldo Emerson, "Politics," *Essays*, (New York: United States Book Company, 1890), pp. 163–83.

revolutions, considers persons and property as the two objects for whose protection government exists. Of persons, all have equal rights, in virtue of being identical in nature. This interest of course with its whole power demands a democracy. Whilst the rights of all as persons are equal, in virtue of their access to reason, their rights in property are very unequal. One man owns his clothes, and another owns a county. This accident, depending primarily on the skill and virtue of the parties, of which there is every degree, and secondarily on patrimony, falls unequally, and its rights of course are unequal. Personal rights, universally the same, demand a government framed on the ratio of the census; property demands a government framed on the ratio of owners and of owning. . . .

That principle no longer looks so self-evident as it appeared in former times, partly because doubts have arisen whether too much weight had not been allowed in the laws to property, and such a structure given to our usages as allowed the rich to encroach on the poor, and to keep them poor; but mainly because there is an instinctive sense, however obscure and yet inarticulate, that the whole constitution of property, on its present tenures, is injurious, and its influence on persons deteriorating and degrading; that truly the only interest for the consideration of the State is persons; that property will always follow persons; that the highest end of government is the culture of men; and that if men can be educated, the institutions will share their improvement and the moral sentiment will write the law of the land. . . .

The boundaries of personal influence it is impossible to fix, as persons are organs of moral or supernatural force. Under the dominion of an idea which possesses the minds of multitudes, as civil freedom, or the religious sentiment, the powers of persons are no longer subjects of calculation. A nation of men unanimously bent on freedom or conquest can easily confound the arithmetic of statists, and achieve extravagant actions, out of all proportion to their means; as the Greeks, the Saracens, the Swiss, the Americans, and the French have done. . . .

We must trust infinitely to the beneficent necessity which shines through all laws. Human nature expresses itself in them as characteristically as in statues, or songs, or railroads; and an abstract of the codes of nations would be a transcript of the common conscience. Governments have their origin in the moral identity of men. Reason for one is seen to be reason for another, and for every other. There is a middle measure which satisfies all parties, be they never so many or so resolute for their own. Every man finds a sanction for his simplest claims and deeds, in decisions of his own mind, which he calls Truth and Holiness. In these decisions all the citizens find a perfect agreement, and only in these; not in what is good to eat, good to wear, good use of time, or what amount of land or of public aid each is entitled to claim. This truth and justice men presently endeavor to make application of to the measuring of land, the apportionment of service, the protection of life and property. Their first endeavors, no doubt, are very awkward. Yet absolute right is the first governor; or, every government is an impure theocracy. The idea after which each community is aiming to make and mend its law, is the will of the wise man. The wise man it cannot find in nature, and it makes awkward but earnest efforts to secure his government by contrivance; as by causing the entire people to give their voices on every measure; or by a double choice to get the representation of the whole; or by a selection of the best citizens; or to secure the advantages of efficiency and internal peace by confiding the government to one, who may himself select his agents. All forms of government symbolize an immortal government, common to all dynasties and independent of numbers, perfect where two men exist, perfect where there is only one man. . . .

The tendencies of the times favor the idea of self-government, and leave the individual, for all code, to the rewards and penalties of his own constitution; which work with more energy than we believe whilst we depend on artificial restraints. The movement in this direction has been very marked in modern history. Much has been blind and discreditable, but the nature of the revolution is not affected by the vices of the revolters; for this is a purely moral force. It was never adopted by any party in history, neither can be. It separates the individual from all party, and unites him at the same time to the race. It promises a recognition of higher rights than those of personal freedom, or the security of property. A man has a right to be employed, to be trusted, to be loved, to be revered. The power of love, as the basis of a State has never been tried. We must not imagine that all things are lapsing into confusion if every tender protestant be not compelled to bear his part in certain social conventions; nor doubt that roads can be built, letters carried, and the fruit of labor secured, when the government of force is at an end. Are our methods now so excellent that all competition is hopeless? Could not a nation of friends even devise better ways? On the other hand, let not the most conservative and timid fear anything from a premature surrender of the bayonet and the system of force. For, according to the order of nature, which is quite superior to our will, it stands thus; there will always be a government of force where men are selfish; and when they are pure enough to abjure the code of force they will be wise enough to see how these public ends of the post-office, of the highway, of commerce and the exchange of property, of museums and libraries, of institutions of art and science can be answered.

We live in a very low state of the world, and pay unwilling tribute to governments founded on force. There is not, among the most religious and instructed men of the most religious and civil nations, a reliance on the moral sentiment and a sufficient belief in the unity of things, to persuade them that society can be maintained without artificial restraints, as well as the solar system, or that the private citizen might be reasonable and a good neighbor, without the hint of a jail or a confiscation. What is strange too, there never was in any man sufficient faith in the power of rectitude to inspire him with the broad design of renovating the State on the principle of right and love. All those who have pretended this design have been partial reformers, and have admitted in some manner the supremacy of the bad State. I do not call to mind a single human being who has steadily denied the authority of the laws, on the simple ground of his own moral nature. Such designs, full of genius and full of faith as they are, are not entertained except avowedly as air-pictures. If the individual who exhibits them dare to think them practicable, he disgusts scholars and churchmen; and men of talent and women of superior sentiments cannot hide their contempt. Not the less does nature continue to fill the heart of youth with suggestions of this enthusiasm, and there are now men,—if indeed I can speak in the plural number,—more exactly, I will say, I have just been conversing with one man, to whom no weight of adverse experience will make it for a moment appear impossible that thousands of human beings might exercise towards each other the grandest and simplest sentiment, as well as a knot of friends, or a pair of lovers.

Civil Disobedience*

Henry D. Thoreau

I HEARTILY accept the motto,—'That government is best which governs least;' and I should like to see it acted up to more rapidly and systematically. Carried out, it finally amounts to this, which also I believe,—'That government is best which governs not at all;' and when men are prepared for it, that will be the kind of government which they will have. Government is at best but an expedient; but most governments are usually, and all governments are sometimes, inexpedient. The objections which have been brought against a standing army, and they are many and weighty, and deserve to prevail, may also at last be brought against a standing government. The standing army is only an arm of the standing government. The government itself, which is only the mode which the people have chosen to execute their will, is equally liable to be abused and perverted before the people can act through it. Witness the present Mexican war, the work of comparatively a few individuals using the standing government as their tool; for, in the outset, the people would not have consented to this measure.

This American government,—what is it but a tradition, though a recent one, endeavoring to transmit itself unimpaired to posterity, but each

---

*From Henry D. Thoreau, "Civil Disobedience," in *The Works of Thoreau*, ed. Henry Seidel Canby (Boston, MA: Houghton Mifflin Company, 1937), pp. 789-808.

instant losing some of its integrity? It has not the vitality and force of a single living man; for a single man can bend it to his will. It is a sort of wooden gun to the people themselves. But it is not the less necessary for this; for the people must have some complicated machinery or other, and hear its din, to satisfy that idea of government which they have. Governments show thus how successfully men can be imposed on, even impose on themselves, for their own advantage. It is excellent, we must allow. Yet this government never of itself furthered any enterprise, but by the alacrity with which it got out of its way. *It* does not keep the country free. *It* does not settle the West. *It* does not educate. The character inherent in the American people has done all that has been accomplished; and it would have done somewhat more, if the government had not sometimes got in its way. . . .

But, to speak practically and as a citizen, unlike those who call themselves no-government men, I ask for, not at once no government, but *at once* a better government. Let every man make known what kind of government would command this respect, and that will be one step toward obtaining it.

After all, the practical reason why, when the power is once in the hands of the people, a majority are permitted, and for a long period continue, to rule is not because they are most likely to be in the right, nor because this seems fairest to the minority, but because they are physically the strongest. But a government in which the majority rule in all cases cannot be based on justice, even as far as men understand it. Can there not be a government in which majorities do not virtually decide right and wrong, but conscience?—in which majorities decide only those questions to which to rule of expediency is applicable? Must the citizen ever for a moment, or in the least degree, resign his conscience to the legislator? Why has every man a conscience, then? I think that we should be men first, and subjects afterward. It is not desirable to cultivate a respect for the law, so much as for the right. The only obligation which I have a right to assume is to do at any time what I think right. It is truly enough said that a corporation has no conscience; but a corporation of conscientious men is a corporation *with* a conscience. Law never made men a whit mor just; and, by means of their respect for it, even the well-disposed are daily made the agents of injustice. A common and natural result of an undue respect for law is, that you may see a file of soldiers, colonel, captain, corporal, privates, powder-monkeys, and all, marching in admirable order over hill and dale to the wars, against their wills, ay, against their common sense and consciences, which makes it very steep marching indeed, and produces a palpitation of the heart. They have no doubt that it is a damnable business in which they are concerned; they are all peaceably inclined. Now, what are they? Men at all? or small movable forts and magazines, at the service of some unscrupulous man in power? Visit the Navy-Yard, and behold a marine, such a man as an American government can make, or such as it can make a man with its black arts—a mere shadow and reminiscence of humanity, a man laid out alive and standing, and already, as one may say, buried under arms with funeral accompaniments, . . .

The mass of men serve the state thus, not as men mainly, but as machines, with their bodies. They are the standing army, and the militia, jailors, constables, *posse comitatus*, etc. In most cases there is no free exercise whatever of the judgment or of the moral sense; but they put themselves on a level with wood and earth and stones; and wooden men can perhaps be manufactured that will serve the purpose as well. . . . Yet such as these even are commonly esteemed good citizens. Others—as most legislators, politicians, lawyers, ministers, and office-holders—serve the state chiefly with their heads; and, as they rarely make any moral distinctions, they are as likely to serve the Devil, without *intending* it, as God. A very few—as heroes, patriots, martyrs, reformers in the great sense, and *men*—serve the state with their consciences also, and so necessarily resist it for the most part; and they are commonly treated as enemies by it. . . .

All voting is a sort of gaming, like checkers or backgammon, with a slight moral tinge to it, a playing with right and wrong, with moral questions; and betting naturally accompanies it. The character of the voters is not staked. I cast my vote, perchance, as I think right; but I am not vitally concerned that that right should prevail. I am willing to leave it to the majority. Its obligation, therefore, never exceeds that of expediency. Even voting *for the right* is *doing* nothing for it. It is only expressing to men feebly your desire that it should prevail. A wise man will not leave the right to the mercy of chance, nor wish it to prevail through the power of the majority. There is but little virtue in the action of masses of men. . . .

Unjust laws exist: shall we be content to obey them, or shall we endeavor to amend them, and obey them until we have succeeded, or shall we transgress them at once? Men generally, under such a government as this, think that they ought to wait until they have persuaded the majority to alter them. They think that, if they should resist, the remedy would be worse than the evil. But it is the fault of the government itself that the remedy is worse than the evil. *It* makes it worse. . . .

If the injustice is part of the necessary friction of the machine of government, let it go, let it go: perchance it will wear smooth,—certainly the machine will wear out. If the injustice has a spring, or a pulley, or a rope, or a crank, exclusively for itself, then perhaps you may consider whether the remedy will not be worse than the evil; but if it is of such a nature that it requires you to be the agent of injustice to another, then, I say, break the law. Let your life be a counter-friction to stop the machine. What I have to do is see, at any rate, that I do not lend myself to the wrong which I condemn. . . .

Under a government which imprisons any unjustly, the true place for a just man is also a prison. The proper place today, the only place which Massachusetts has provided for her freer and less desponding spirits, is in her prisons, to be put out and locked out of the Senate by her own act, as they have already put themselves out by their principles. It is there that the fugitive slave, and the Mexican prisoner on parole, and the Indian come to plead the wrongs of his race should find them; on that separate, but more free and honorable ground, where the State places those who are not *with* her, but *against* her,—the only house in a slave State in which a free man can abide with honor. If any think that their influence would be lost there, and their voices no longer afflict the ear of the State, that they would not be as an enemy within its walls, they do not know by how much truth is stronger than error, nor how much more eloquently and effectively he can combat injustice who has experienced a little in his own person. Cast your whole vote, not a strip of paper merely, but your whole influence. A minority is powerless while it conforms to the majority; it is not even a minority then; but it is irresistible when it clogs by its whole weight. If the alternative is to keep all just men in prison, or give up war and slavery, the State will not hesitate which to choose. If a thousand men were not to pay their tax-bills this year, that would not be a violent and bloody measure, as it would be to pay them, and enable the State to commit violence and shed innocent blood. This is, in fact, the definition of a peaceable revolution, if any such is possible. . . .

Thus the State never intentionally confronts a man's sense, intellectual or moral, but only his body, his senses. It is not armed with superior wit or honesty, but with superior physical strength. I was not born to be forced. I will breathe after my own fashion. Let us see who is the strongest. What force has a multitude? They only can force me who obey a higher law than I. They force me to become like themselves. I do not hear of *men* being *forced* to live this way or that by masses of men. What sort of life were that to live? When I meet a government which says to me, "Your money or your life," why should I be in haste to give it my money? It may be in a great strait, and not know what to do: I cannot help that. It must help itself; do as I do. It is not worth the while to snivel about it. I am not responsible for the successful working of the machinery of society. I am not the son of the engineer. I perceive that, when an acorn and a chestnut fall side by side, the one does not remain inert to make way for the other, but both obey their own laws, and spring and grow and flourish as best they can, till one, perchance, overshadows and destroys the other. If a plant cannot live according to its nature, it dies; and so a man. . . .

No man with a genius for legislation has appeared in America. They are rare in the history of the world. There are orators, politicians, and eloquent men, by the thousand; but the speaker has not yet opened his mouth to speak who is capable of settling the much-vexed questions of the day. We love eloquence for its own sake, and not for any truth which it may utter, or any heroism it may inspire. Our legislators have not yet learned the comparative value of free-trade and of freedom, of union, and of rectitude, to a nation. They have no genius or talent for comparatively humble questions of taxation and finance, commerce and manufactures and agriculture. If we were left solely to the wordy wit of legislators in Congress for our guidance, uncorrected by the seasonable experience and the effectual complaints of the people, America would not long retain her rank among the nations. . . .

The authority of government, even such as I am willing to submit to,—for I will cheerfully obey those who know and can do better than I, and in many things even those who neither know nor can do so well,—is still an impure one: to be strictly just, it must have the sanction and consent of the governed. It can have no pure right over my person and property but what I concede to it. The progress from an absolute to a limited monarchy, from a limited monarchy to a democracy, is a progress toward a true respect for the individual. . . . There will never be a really free and enlightened State until the State comes to recognize the individual as a higher and independent power, from which all its own power and authority are derived, and treats him accordingly. I please myself with imagining a State at last which can afford to be just to all men, and to treat the individual with respect as a neighbor; which even would not think it inconsistent with its own repose if a few were to live aloof from it, not meddling with it, nor embraced by it, who fulfilled all the duties of neighbors and fellow-men. A State which bore this kind of fruit, and suffered it to drop off as fast as it ripened, would prepare the way for a still more perfect and glorious State, which also I have imagined, but not yet anywhere seen.

DISCUSSION QUESTIONS

1. How was the Jacksonian ideology produced by demographic changes in the U.S.? What role did property play in these political changes?
2. Was de Tocqueville writing of equality of opportunity or equality of outcome? Explain.
3. How did the Jacksonians and transcendentalists differ over what qualified some people to govern?
4. How can the transcendentalist movement be seen as preparing the way for future changes such as the civil rights movement and the anti-war movement?

Chapter 6

DEFINING THE UNION

Two issues remained unresolved in American politics by the mid-nineteenth century. The first and perhaps most important was slavery. Since the first Africans were brought in bondage to the North American continent in 1619, blacks were viewed by some as a form of property, while others regarded them as human beings with the ability to participate in society. Slavery was a prominent issue of the nineteenth century. A slave was a person who was held as property for the production of labor-intensive agriculture products such as cotton and tobacco. As noted in Table 6–1, between 1790 and 1860 slavery tended to die out in commercial areas such as the Northeast, and to expand in agricultural areas like the South. The second issue was the nature of the union. The founding fathers failed to adequately address in the Constitution the relationship of the federal government to the states. In this regard the Kentucky and Virginia Resolutions suggested that the federal government was created by the states and therefore the states were the final authority on its powers. Together these issues stimulated a revision in the way individual liberties, government authority, and private property were understood in the U.S.

At its most basic level, slavery was an issue of individual rights. Abolitionists, the opponents of slavery, generally relied upon arguments that stressed the natural rights of all people, but they were not united regarding the role of blacks in American society and politics. The most notable were the Perfectionists who stressed the need to end slavery and establish blacks and whites as political and social equals. This trend was best exemplified in

TABLE 6–1   *Black Free and Slave Populations by Region*

	Northeast		North Central		South		West	
	Free	Slave	Free	Slave	Free	Slave	Free	Slave
1790	27,070	40,354			32,457	657,327		
1800	46,696	36,370	500	135	61,239	857,097		
1810	75,156	27,081	3,630	3,304	107,660	1,160,977		
1820	92,723	18,001	6,931	11,329	133,980	1,508,692		
1830	122,434	2,780	15,664	25,879	181,501	1,980,384		
1840	141,559	765	30,743	58,604	213,991	2,427,986		
1850	149,526	236	48,185	87,422	235,569	3,116,629	1,215	26
1860	155,983	18	69,291	114,948	258,346	4,097,111	4,450	29

Historical Statistics of the United States, Colonial Times to 1957 (Washington, DC: Department of Commerce, 1975), pp. 11–12. The Northeast region consisted of Maine, New Hampshire, Vermont, Massachusetts, Rhode Island, Connecticut, New York, New Jersey, and Pennsylvania. The North Central Region consisted of Ohio, Indiana, Illinois, Michigan, Wisconsin, Minnesota, Iowa, Missouri, North Dakota, South Dakota, Nebraska, and Kansas. The South Region consisted of Delaware, Maryland, the District of Columbia, Virginia, West Virginia, North Carolina, South Carolina, Georgia, Florida, Kentucky, Tennessee, Alabama, Mississippi, Arkansas, Louisiana, Oklahoma, and Texas. The West Region consisted of Montana, Idaho, Wyoming, Colorado, New Mexico, Arizona, Utah, Nevada, Washington, Oregon, and California.

the writings of William Lloyd Garrison, who organized the American Anti-Slavery Society, and in the writings of Frederick Douglass. Perfectionists like Garrison stressed the equality and liberty of all people, no matter what the color of their skin, in opposing slavery. Slavery was a violation of God's law by government according to Garrison as seen in the statement of purpose for *The Liberator.*

> Another motto we have chosen is, UNIVERSAL EMANCIPATION. . . .
> Henceforth we shall use it in its widest latitude: the emancipation of our whole race from the domination of man, from the thraldom of self, from the government of brute force, from the bondage of sin—and bringing them under the dominion of god, the control of an inward spirit, the government of the law of love, and into the obedience and liberty of Christ. . . .[1]

As seen in the above quote, slavery was allowed to exist in order to promote the interests of self. These selfish interests undermined and corrupted government resulting in the denial of individual's natural rights. A similar position was presented by Frederick Douglass.

> But truth is "from everlasting to everlasting" and can never pass away. Such is the truth of man's right to liberty. It existed in the very idea of man's creation. It was his even before he comprehended it. He was created in it, endowed with it, and it can never be taken from him. No laws, no statutes, no

[1]William Lloyd Garrison, "Prospectus of the Liberator, Volume VIII, " in *Documents of Upheaval,* ed. Truman Nelson (New York: Hill and Wang, 1966), p. 140.

compacts, no compromises, no constitutions, can abrogate or destroy it. . . . Slavery is a sin, in that it comprehends a monstrous violation of the great principle of human liberty. . . . In this respect, it is a direct war upon the government of God.[2]

Not all abolitionists accepted the political and social equality of blacks and whites. The American Colonization Society rejected the institution of slavery as well as black participation in American politics. Their solution was to return blacks to Africa in order to end slavery in the U.S. and establish democracy on the African continent. Most notable of their efforts was the founding of Liberia by former slaves. Still other groups like the Free Soil Movement rejected slavery as a political and economic institution, but refused the return of blacks to Africa. Mason and Leach noted in that regard, "with each extension of slavery into the west, the free farmers . . . saw their homesteads menaced by the prospect of slave labor. Cotton became a monster, consuming the land, degrading the labor market, and driving free white farmers out of existence."[3] The 1854 remarks of Abraham Lincoln were indicative of this view.

> Let it not be said I am contending the establishment of political and social equality between the whites and blacks. I have already said the contrary. I am not now combating the argument of necessity, arising from the fact that the blacks are already amongst us; but I am combating what is set up as moral argument for allowing them to be taken where they have never yet been—arguing against the extension of a bad thing, which where it already exists, we must of necessity, manage as we best can.[4]

When considered from the perspective that blacks were virtually banned from free states, Lincoln's remark appeared to suggest that blacks were to be confined to the South where they would be free but lack political or social equality.[5] While abolitionists could sympathize with the plight of slaves as portrayed in Harriet Beecher Stowe's *Uncle Tom's Cabin; or Life, Among the Lowly,* they lacked agreement on the political role of blacks.

Not all writers of the period accepted the idea of natural rights for blacks and the accompanying view that slavery was a violation of individ-

---

[2]Frederick Douglass, "Lecture of Slavery, No. 2," in *The Life and Writings of Frederick Douglass,* ed. Philip S. Foner (New York: International Publishers, 1950), II, 140.

[3]Alpheus Thomas Mason and Richard H. Leach, *In Quest of Freedom,* 2nd ed. (Englewood Cliffs: Prentice-Hall, Inc., 1973), p. 243.

[4]Abraham Lincoln, "Speech at Peoria, Illinois," in *The Collected Works of Abraham Lincoln,* ed. Roy P. Basler (New Brunswick, NJ: Rutgers University Press, 1953), II, 266.

[5]Slavery was prohibited in Illinois but free blacks were forbidden migration to it. Blacks who sought to live there were threatened with fines and those unable to pay were threatened with slavery. From *The American Political Tradition,* by Richard Hofstadter, p. 144. Copyright 1948 by Alfred A. Knopf Inc. and renewed 1976 by Beatrice Hofstadter. Reprinted by permission of the publisher.

ual rights. Southern writers such as William Harper rejected the natural rights of man and instead stressed the idea that individual rights were established by the state. These individuals regarded slavery as a progressive force in transforming a backward people due to the natural inequality of human beings. Indeed, supporters of slavery generally pointed to the fact that the institution of slavery was condoned in ancient Hebrew, Greek, and Roman societies because of the natural inequality of human beings.

Slavery was not only a question of individual freedom, but of the federal government's authority to decide the issue. Nowhere in the Constitution was the federal government given the explicit authority to deal with slavery, and the Tenth Amendment did conclude all powers not delegated to the federal government, nor prohibited, were "reserved to the states." The states increasingly became embroiled in the slavery question while the national government sought to influence the debate in the territories seeking entry into the Union. The addition of new territory, and the subsequent creation of new states offered the prospect that either view would be victorious at the federal level. When one side controlled three-fourths of the states and population, legislation to amend the Constitution could be enacted that would either destroy or permanently establish slavery in the U.S. But did the federal government have the power to decide the issue of slavery? As already seen, the states appeared to have sole authority to deal with the slavery question under the Constitution. But what if the abolitionist cause gained enough strength to modify the legal status of slavery through legislation or Constitutional amendment?

Slavery was an intricate part of Southern life. In an effort to save their economic system, as well as their liberty, southern writers enunciated a theory of states' rights based on three interrelated elements: (1) state sovereignty; (2) state nullification of federal laws; and (3) the right of the states to succeed from the union if the law was upheld by the other states.[6] John C. Calhoun, one of the most noted advocates of states' rights, held that true sovereignty was invested in the states, since they became independent when the Revolutionary War ended. The states were the creators of the Union as a compact in which sovereignty was not surrendered. Moreover, the states acted as a check on the federal government. Acts of the federal government had to be in accordance with the interest of the states as previously noted in the Kentucky and Virginia Resolutions, and as Calhoun noted during the Fort Hill Address (1831).

> Where the interests are the same, that is, where the laws that may benefit one will benefit all, or the reverse, it is just and proper to place them under the control of the majority; but where they are dissimilar, so that the law that may benefit one portion may be ruinous to another, it would be, on the contrary,

---

[6]Thornton Anderson, ed., *Jacobson's Development of American Political Thought*, 2nd ed. (New York: Appleton-Century-Crofts, Inc., 1961), p. 398.

unjust and absurd to subject them to its will; and such I conceive to be the theory on which our Constitution rests.[7]

The states possessed the power to override acts of the federal government when those laws were not in the interest of the states according to Calhoun, much as Jefferson and Madison had argued. Should the majority of states accept a federal law, then the dissenting state had either to accept it or secede from the union.

Calhoun's views appeared at a point in time when the North clearly dominated the House of Representatives and was gaining control of the Senate. The danger posed by these shifts in control over the federal government was that it would allow an anti-southern majority to pass laws, and possibly even Constitutional amendments, that would invalidate the nature of southern society, economics, and politics. Like Montesquieu's checks and balances, Calhoun's concurrent majority provided the southern states with the ability to veto any unfavorable policies. For southerners this would end the fear that a northern numerical majority in both houses of Congress would subvert southern white control.[8] For the northern states, the failure to acquire control of Congress despite their electoral superiority appeared to deny them their equal role in the political process guaranteed by the Constitution. However, the southern view of the states' right to succeed from the Union was not accepted by all.

The indissoluble nature of the Union had been a constant theme, albeit a challenged one, in theory and practice prior to the Civil War. The basis for this was first laid under the Articles of Confederation, which was the legal predecessor of the Constitution. The former called for a "perpetual union" of the states thereby suggesting that the states surrendered their sovereignty, and the ability to succeed, upon adopting the Articles of Confederation. Also present was the Constitution's provision for the supremacy of federal law in both national and state courts. Yates noted the supremacy of federal law and federal judges as a primary reason for rejecting the Constitution in that it would eliminate the ability of the states to check an expansion of federal authority. In practice, the indissoluble nature of the Union was accepted. Jefferson, the author of the Kentucky Resolution, did not press the issue of state's rights upon becoming president. Likewise, Jackson, who is often regarded as an advocate of state powers, rejected South Carolina's Nullification Act of 1832 and prepared to crush any attempt by that state to secede from the Union. Nevertheless, the ability of the federal government to decide issues like slavery, which were of concern to the states, was contested.

---

[7]John C. Calhoun, *The Fort Hill Address of John C. Calhoun, July 26, 1831* (Richmond, VA: The Virginia Commission on Constitutional Government, 1960), p. 5.

[8]Southerners feared that the end of slavery would mean black citizenship thereby allowing the North to achieve political domination of the South. Hofstadter, *The American*, p. 103.

Ultimately, the question of slavery was removed from federal jurisdiction and placed under the authority of the states. The Compromise of 1850 established the idea of popular sovereignty whereby the people of a territory could decide for themselves whether or not they would be a slave or free state. Likewise in the Dred Scott decision, the Supreme Court ruled that slavery was a form of property and therefore could only be dealt with by the states.[9] The Compromise of 1850 and the Dred Scott case thereby reversed the trend towards greater federal regulation and established the principle that only the states possessed the authority for regulating slavery. Thus slavery became bound up in the issue of states' rights. This emphasis on popular sovereignty was in keeping with the tradition that the Constitution was a compact among the states and the federal government was their creation. As applied to slavery, emphasis on states' rights or popular sovereignty placed the states on a collision course with one another and promoted the sponsorship of pro- and anti-slavery elements into the West. The result was that conflicting claims arose which escalated into armed conflicts earning areas such as the Kansas territory the title "Bleeding Kansas."

Slavery was also an issue of economics in that slaves were regarded by some as a natural form of property and was the form of capitalism dominating the southern United States. In fact, the slave system was one of three economic systems which flourished in the United States between 1800 and 1860. In the North, a commercial system existed based on a system of wages. The Western economy was based on a system of family farms in which the owners performed the manual labor. In the South, an agricultural system existed which was dependent on slavery to produce the labor intensive crops.

Slavery as a means of economic production tended to be viewed in critical terms, especially in the northern states. As shown in Table 6–1, slavery declined in the northeastern states during the period 1790 to 1860. Slavery was not a viable means of production in the manufacturing North where factory owners considered it cheaper to hire people to come and work for a daily or hourly wage and not have to take care of them twenty-four hours a day. Indeed, if examined from the perspective of the northern economy, slavery was an out-dated form of capitalism in light of the advances produced by industrialism.

To southerners slavery was first and foremost an institution of capitalist society. As Mason and Leach wrote,

Slaves were themselves a form of capital, the value of which rose as the plan-

---

[9]In *Scott v. Sanford*, commonly known as the Dred Scott case, the Supreme Court ruled that slaves were property and therefore under the Fifth Amendment the federal government lacked the authority to deprive an individual of his property without due process. The possibility of effective legislation to restrict or abolish slavery, as well as to compensate slave owners, was thereby ruled out, short of amending the Constitution.

tation system became more profitable. As Negroes learned mechanical trades, they could easily be exchanged for all kinds of goods or be sold for cash. Finally, slaves made possible the creation of an aristocracy, freed from the necessity of labor.[10]

Slavery was also regarded in the South as more humane than wage labor, for the slave owner provided for their well-being. In the book, *Cannibals All,* Fitzhugh wrote,

> When the day's labor is ended, he (the white wage-earner) is free, but is overburdened with the cares of family and household, which make his freedom an empty and delusive mockery. But his employer is really free, and may enjoy the profits made by others' labor, without a care or a trouble, as to their well-being. The negro slave is free, too, when the labors of the day are over, and free in mind as well as body; for the master provides food, raiment, house, fuel, and everything else necessary to the physical well-being of himself and family.[11]

Slavery was a means of acquiring wealth in the capitalist system and to abolish or limit slavery was indicative of a movement towards abolishing private property. Certainly slavery was dominate in the southern states as shown in Table 6–1. Even Abraham Lincoln as a Free Soiler acknowledged slavery's necessity for the southern economy in 1854.

> When southern people tell us they are no more responsible for the origin of slavery, than we; I acknowledge the fact. When it is said that the institution exists; and that it is very difficult to get rid of it, in any satisfactory way, I can understand and appreciate the saying. I surely will not blame them for not doing what I should not know how to do myself.[12]

Lincoln's statement suggested that slavery was a concern in the north-central states because it was an economic means of production that threatened the family farm. As seen in Table 6–1, the black population in the north-central states was divided nearly in half between blacks who were free and blacks who were slaves. Increases in the slave population suggested the deeper penetration of plantation-type farming enterprises into the north-central and western regions. Slavery appeared in the western states not until between 1840 and 1850. The expansion of slavery was necessary to produce cotton and tobacco which tended to drain the land of the minerals

---

[10]Alpheus Thomas Mason and Richard H. Leach, *In Quest of Freedon,* 2nd ed. (Englewood Cliffs, NJ: Prentice-Hall, Inc., 1973), pp. 231-32.

[11]Reprinted by permission of the publishers from *Cannibals All? or Slaves without Masters,* by George Fitzhugh, edited by C. Van Woodward, Cambridge, MA: The Belknap Press of Harvard University Press, Copyright © 1960, 1988 by the President and Fellows of Harvard College. Pp. 15–16.

[12]Lincoln, "Speech at Peoria, Illinois," p. 255.

necessary for profitable crops. One can speculate that had slavery not been allowed to spread outside of the South, it would have died out. However as additional territory was acquired and slavery was allowed to expand into it through political compromises between 1820 and 1854, slavery was revitalized as an economic institution.

The question of slavery as a form of private property created an intersection between that area and those of individual liberty and government authority. In this regard, the Dred Scott decision suggested that: (1) slaves were a form of property and therefore had no rights under the Constitution; (2) the federal government had no right to interfere under the guise of the Bill of Rights; and (3) power to regulate slavery was centered in the states thereby enhancing the theory of states' rights. Consequently, the question of slavery was not a simple one of human rights, as all too often suggested, but one that defined issues of individual rights, private property, and governmental authority. Seen in this regard, bleeding Kansas, the Dred Scott decision, John Brown's raid on the federal arsenal at Harper's Ferry, and the election of Abraham Lincoln were sparks which ignited these divergent views into the military conflict generally known as the Civil War. In the following section, the intellectual and emotional basis of that conflict can be seen in the writings of William Lloyd Garrison, Frederick Douglass, Abraham Lincoln, John C. Calhoun, and George Fitzhugh.

Prospectus of the Liberator, Volume VIII*

William Lloyd Garrison

. . . In commencing this publication, we had but a single object in view—the total abolition of American slavery, and as a just consequence, the complete enfranchisement of our colored countrymen. . . .

In entering upon our eighth volume, the abolition of slavery will still be the grand object of our labors, though not, perhaps, so exclusively as heretofore. There are other topics, which, in our opinion, are intimately connected with the great doctrine of inalienable human rights; and which, while they conflict with no religious sect, or political party, as such, are pregnant with momentous consequences to the freedom, equality and happiness of mankind. These we shall discuss as time and opportunity may permit.

The motto upon our banner has been from the commencement of our moral warfare, 'OUR COUNTRY IS THE WORLD—OUR COUNTRYMEN ARE ALL

*From William Lloyd Garrison, "Prospectus of the Liberator, Volume VIII," in *Documents of Upheaval*, ed. Truman Nelson (New York: Hill and Wang, 1966), pp. 140–44.

MANKIND." We trust that it will be our only epitaph. Another motto we have chosen is, 'UNIVERSAL EMANCIPATION.' Up to this time, we have limited its application to those who are held in this country, by southern taskmasters, as marketable commodities, goods and chattels, and implements of husbandry. Henceforth, we shall use it in its widest latitude: the emancipation of our whole race from the dominion of man, from the thraldom of self, from the government of brute force, from the bondage of sin—and bringing them under the dominion of God, the control of an inward spirit, the government of the law of love, and into the obedience and liberty of Christ, who is '*the same,* yesterday, TO-DAY, and forever.' . . .

Next to the overthrow of slavery, the cause of PEACE will command our attention. The doctrine of non-resistance, as commonly received and practised by Friends, and certain members of other religious denominations, we conceive to be utterly indefensible in its application to national wars;—not that it 'goes too far,' but that it does not go far enough. If a nation may not redress its wrongs by physical force—if it may not repel or punish a foreign enemy who comes to plunder, enslave or murder its inhabitants—then it may not resort to arms to quell an insurrection, or send to prison or suspend upon a gibbet any transgressors upon its soil. *If the slaves of the South have not an undoubted right to resist their masters in the last resort, then no man, or body of men, may appeal to the law of violence in self-defence—for none have suffered, or can suffer, more than they.* [Italics mine—T.N.] If, when men are robbed of their earnings, their liberties, their personal ownership, their wives and children, they may not resist, in no case can physical resistance be allowable, either in an individual or collective capacity. Now, the doctrine we shall endeavor to inculcate is, that the kingdoms of this world are to become the kingdoms of our Lord and of his Christ; consequently, that they are all to be supplanted, whether they are called despotic, monarchical or republican, and he only who is King of kings, and Lord of lords, is to rule in righteousness. The kingdom of God is to be established IN ALL THE EARTH, and it shall never be destroyed, but it shall 'BREAK IN PIECES AND CONSUME ALL OTHERS:' its elements are righteousness and peace, and joy in the Holy Ghost: without are dogs, and sorcerers, and whoremongers and murderers, and idolators, and whatsoever loveth and maketh a lie. Its government is one of love, not of military coercion or physical restraint: its laws are not written upon parchment, but upon the hearts of its subjects—they are not conceived in the wisdom of man, but framed by the Spirit of God: its weapons are not carnal, but spiritual: its soldiers are clad in the whole armor of God . . .Hence, when smitten on the one cheek, they turn the other also; being defamed, they entreat; being reviled, they bless; being persecuted, they suffer it; they take joyfully the spoiling of their goods; they rejoice, inasmuch as they are partakers of Christ's sufferings; they are sheep in the midst of wolves; in no extremity whatever, even if their enemies are determined to nail them to the cross

with Jesus, and if they like him could summon legions of angels to their res-
cue, will they resort to the law of violence.

As to the governments of this world, whatever their titles or forms, we
shall endeavor to prove, that, in their essential elements, and as at present
administered, they are all Anti-Christ; that they can never, by human wisdom, be brought into conformity to the will of God; that they cannot be
maintained, except by naval and military power; that all their penal enact-
ments being a dead letter without an army to carry them into effect, are virtually written in human blood; and that the followers of Jesus should
instinctively shun their stations of honor, power and emolument—at the
same time 'submitting to every ordinance of man for the Lord's sake,' and
offering no *physical* resistance to any of their mandates, however unjust or
tyrannical. . . .

Human governments are to be viewed as judicial punishments. If a
people turn the grace of God into lasciviousness, or make their liberty an
occasion for anarchy,—or if they refuse to belong to the 'one fold and one
Shepherd,'—they shall be scourged by the governments of their own choosing, and burdened with taxation, and subjected to physical control, and
torn by factions, and made to eat the fruit of their evil doings, until they are
prepared to receive the liberty and the rest which remain, on earth as well
as in heaven, for THE PEOPLE OF GOD. . . .

So long as men condemn the perfect government of the Most High,
and will not fill up the measure of Christ's sufferings in their own persons,
just so long will they desire to usurp authority over each other—just so long
will they pertinaciously cling to human governments, *fashioned in the like-
ness and administered in the spirit of their own disobedience.* Now, if the prayer
of our Lord be not a mockery; if the kingdom of God is to come universally,
and his will be done ON EARTH AS IT IS IN HEAVEN; and if, in that kingdom, no carnal weapon can be wielded, and swords are beaten into
ploughshares, and spears into pruning hooks, and there is none to molest
or make afraid, and no statute-book but the bible, and no judge but Christ;
then why are not Christians obligated to come out NOW, and be separate
from 'the kingdoms of this world,' which are all based upon THE PRINCIPLE
OF VIOLENCE, and which require their officers and servants to govern and be
governed by that principle? How, then, is the wickedness of men to be
overcome? Not by lacerating their bodies, or incarcerating them in dun-
geons, or putting them upon tread-mills, or exiling them from their native
country, or suspending them upon gibbets—O no!—but simply by returning good for evil, and blessing for cursing; by using those spiritual weapons
which are 'mighty, through God, to the pulling down of strongholds'; by
the power of that faith which overcomes the world; by ceasing to look to
man for a redress of injuries, however grievous, but committing the soul in
well-doing, as unto a faithful Creator, and leaving it with God to bestow
recompense—'for it is written, Vengence is mine; I will repay, saith the
Lord.'

These are among the views we shall offer in connection with the heaven-originated cause of PEACE,—views which any person is at liberty to controvert in our columns, and for which no man or body of men is responsible but ourselves. If any man shall affirm that the anti-slavery cause, as such, or any anti-slavery society, is answerable for our sentiments on this subject, to him may be justly applied the apostolic declaration, 'the truth is not in him.' We regret, indeed, that the principles of abolitionists seem to be quite unsettled upon a question of such vast importance, and so vitally connected with the bloodless overthrow of slavery. It is time for all our friends to know where they stand. If those, whose yokes they are endeavoring to break by the fire and hammer of God's word, would not, in their opinion, be justified in appealing to physical force, how can they justify others of a different complexion in doing the same thing? And if they conscientiously believe that the slaves would be guiltless in shedding the blood of their merciless oppressors, let them say so unequivocally—for there is no neutral ground in this matter, and the time is near at hand when they will be compelled to take sides. . . .

Lecture on Slavery, No. 1*

Frederick Douglass

I come before you this evening to deliver the first lecture of a course which I purpose to give in this city, during the present winter, on the subject of American Slavery. . . .

The fact is, we are in the midst of a great struggle. The public mind is widely and deeply agitated; and bubbling up from its perturbed waters, are many and great impurities, whose poisonous miasma demands a constant antidote. . . .

A very slight acquaintance with the history of American slavery is sufficient to show that it is an evil of which it will be difficult to rid this country. It is not the creature of a moment, which to-day is, and to-morrow is not; it is not a pigmy, which a slight blow may demolish; it is no youthful upstart, whose impertinent pratings may be silenced by a dignified contempt. No: it is an evil of gigantic proportions, and of long standing.

Its origin in this country dates back to the landing of the pilgrims on Plymouth rock.—It was here more than two centuries ago. The first spot poisoned by its leprous presence, was a small plantation in Virginia. The slaves, at that time, numbered only twenty. They have now increased to the frightful number of three millions; and from that narrow plantation, they

*From Frederick Douglass, "Lecture on Slavery, No. 1," in *The Life and Writings of Frederick Douglass*, ed. Philip S. Foner (New York: International Publishers, 1950) II, 132-39.

are now spread over by far the largest half of the American Union. Indeed, slavery forms an important part of the entire history of the American people. Its presence may be seen in all American affairs. It has become interwoven with all American institutions, and has anchored itself in the very soil of the American Constitution. It has thrown its paralysing arm over freedom of speech, and the liberty of the press; and has created for itself morals and manners favorable to its own continuance. It has seduced the church, corrupted the pulpit, and brought the powers of both into degrading bondage; and now, in the pride of its power, it even threatens to bring down that grand political edifice, the American Union, unless every member of this republic shall so far disregard his conscience and his God as to yield to its infernal behests.

That must be a powerful influence which can truly be said to govern a nation; and that slavery governs the American people, is indisputably true. . . . Having said thus much upon the power and prevalence of slavery, allow me to speak of the nature of slavery itself; and here I can speak, in part, from experience—I can speak with the authority of positive knowledge. . . .

First of all, I will state, as well as I can, the legal and social relation of master and slave. A master is one (to speak in the vocabulary of the Southern States) who claims and exercises a right of property in the person of a fellow man. This he does with the force of the law and the sanction of Southern religion. The law gives the master absolute power over the slave. He may work him, flog him, hire him out, sell him, and, in certain contingencies, *kill* him, with perfect impunity. The slave is a human being, divested of all rights—reduced to the level of a brute—a mere "chattel" in the eye of the law—placed beyond the circle of human brotherhood—cut off from his kind—his name, which the "recording angel" may have enrolled in heaven, among the blest, is impiously inserted in a *master's ledger*, with horses, sheep and swine. In law, the slave has no wife, no children, no country, and no home. He can own nothing, possess nothing, acquire nothing, but what must belong to another. To eat the fruit of his own toil, to clothe his person with the work of his own hands, is considered stealing. He toils that another may reap the fruit; he is industrious that another may live in idleness; he eats unbolted meal, that another may eat the bread of fine flour; he labors in chains at home, under a burning sun and a biting lash, that another may ride in ease and splendor abroad; he lives in ignorance, that another may be educated; he is abused, that another may be exalted; he rests his toil-worn limbs on the cold, damp ground, that another may repose on the softest pillow; he is clad in coarse and tattered raiment, that another may be arrayed in purple and fine linen; he is sheltered only by the wretched hovel, that a master may dwell in a magnificent mansion; and to this condition he is bound down as by an arm of iron.

From this monstrous relation, there springs an unceasing stream of most revolting cruelties. The very accompaniments of the slave system, stamp it as the offspring of hell itself. To ensure good behavior, the slave-holder relies on *the whip;* to induce proper humility, he relies on *the whip;* to rebuke what he is pleased to term insolence, he relies on *the whip;* to supply the place of wages, as an incentive to toil, he relies on *the whip;* to bind down the spirit of the slave, to imbrute and to destroy his manhood, he relies on *the whip,* the chain, the gag, the thumb-screw, the pillory, the bowie-knife, the pistol, and the blood-hound. These are the necessary and unvarying accompaniments of the system. . . .

Nor is slavery more adverse to the conscience than it is to the mind.

This is shown by the fact that in every State of the American Union, where slavery exists, except the State of Kentucky, there are laws, *absolutely* prohibitory of education among the slaves. The crime of teaching a slave to read is punishable with severe fines and imprisonment, and, in some instances, with *death itself.* . . .

It is perfectly well understood at the South that to educate a slave is to make him discontented with slavery, and to invest him with a power which shall open to him the treasures of freedom; and since the object of the slave-holder is to maintain complete authority over his slave, his constant vigilance is exercised to prevent everything which militates against, or endangers the stability of his authority. Education being among the menacing influences, and, perhaps, the most dangerous, is, therefore, the most cautiously guarded against. . . .

As a general rule, then, darkness reigns over the abodes of the enslaved, and "how great is that darkness!"

We are sometimes told of the contentment of the slaves, and are entertained with vivid pictures of their happiness. We are told that they often dance and sing; that their masters frequently give them wherewith to make merry; in fine, that that they have little of which to complain. I admit that the slave *does* sometimes sing, dance, and appear to be merry. But what does this prove? It only proves to my mind, that though slavery is armed with a thousand stings, it is not able entirely to kill the elastic spirit of the bondman. That spirit will rise and walk abroad, despite of whips and chains, and extract from the cup of nature, occasional drops of joy and gladness. No thanks to the slaveholder, nor to slavery, that the vivacious captive may sometimes dance in his chains, his very mirth in such circumstances, stands before God, as an accusing angel against his enslaver. . . .

Why is it that all the reports of contentment and happiness among the slaves at the South come to us upon the authority of slaveholders, or (what is equally significant,) of slaveholder's friends? *Why* is it that we do not hear from the slaves direct? The answer to this question furnishes the darkest features in the American slave system. . . .

While this nation is guilty of the enslavement of three millions of innocent men and women, it is as idle to think of having a sound and lasting peace, as it is to think there is no God, to take cognizance of the affairs of men. There can be no peace to the wicked while slavery continues in the land, it will be condemned, and while it is condemned there will be agitation; Nature must cease to be nature; Men must become monsters; Humanity must be transformed; Christianity must be exterminated; all ideas of justice, and the laws of eternal goodness must be utterly blotted out from the human soul, ere a system so foul and infernal can escape condemnation, or this guilty Republic can have a sound and enduring Peace. . . .

Lecture on Slavery, No. 2.*

Frederick Douglass

In my lecture of Sunday evening last, I strove to impress those who kindly gave me their attention, with a slight idea of the all-controlling power of American slavery in the affairs of the nation. . . .

This evening I shall aim to expose further the wickedness of the slave system—to show that its evils are not confined to the Southern States; but that they overshadow the whole country; and that every American citizen is responsible for its existence, and is solemnly required, by the highest convictions of duty and safety, to labor for its utter extirpation from the land.

By some who will hear me, these propositions will be, perhaps, regarded as far too tame for the basis of a lecture on slavery at this exciting period. But I would beg such persons to remember that they are the few, not the many; and that being the exception, they afford no criterion for the course I ought to pursue on the present occasion. By them, the anti-slavery alphabet was learned perhaps twenty years ago; but the great mass of the American people, I am sorry to say, have that simple lesson yet to learn. I design, therefore, to speak to opponents, rather than to friends, and although I may not be able to entertain the latter by the utterance of new truths, I may afford them the satisfaction of hearing those truths enforced which they have so long cherished.

Indeed, I ought to state, what must be obvious to all, that, properly speaking, there is no such thing as *new* truth; for truth, like the God whose attribute it is, is eternal. In this sense, there is, indeed, nothing new under the sun. Error may be properly designated as *old* or *new*, since it is but a misconception, or an incorrect view of the truth. Misapprehensions of what truth is, have their beginnings and their endings. They pass away as the

*From Frederick Douglass, "Lecture on Slavery, No. 2," in *The Life and Writings of Frederick Douglass*, ed. Philip S. Foner (New York: International Publishers, 1950), II, 139–49.

race moves onward. But truth is "from everlasting to everlasting" and can never pass away.

Such is the truth of man's right to liberty. It existed in the very idea of man's creation. It was *his* even before he comprehended it. He was created in it, endowed with it, and it can never be taken from him. No laws, no statutes, no compacts, no compromises, no constitutions, can abrogate or destroy it. It is beyond the reach of the strongest earthly arm, and smiles at the ravings of tyrants from its hiding place in the bosom of God. Men may hinder its exercise, they may act in disregard of it, they are even permitted to war against it; but they fight against heaven and their career must be short, for Eternal Providence will speedily vindicate the right. . . .

Slavery is a sin, in that it comprehends a monstrous violation of the great principle of human liberty, to which I have endeavored thus to draw your attention. In this respect, it is a direct war upon the government of God. In subjecting one man to the arbitrary control of another, it contravenes the first command of the decalogue; and as upon that command rests the whole superstructure of justice, purity and brotherly kindness, slavery may be justly regarded as a warfare against all the principles of infinite goodness. . . .

In contemplating the sin of slavery, and the guilt of slaveholders, I have marvelled at the coolness and self-complacency with which persons at the North often speak of having friends and relatives who are slaveholders at the South. They speak of the fact without a blush of shame, and even as though honor were conferred upon them by their slaveholding friends and relatives. What a commentary is this on the state of morals among us! Why, if the moral sentiment of the North were what it ought to be, a lady would as soon tell of an abandoned sister or a pirate brother, as boast of having slaveholding relatives, for there is nothing in piracy, nothing in lewdness, that is not to be found in the slave system—indeed, slavery is a system of lewdness and piracy. Every slaveholder is the legalized keeper of a house of ill-fame; no matter how high he may stand in Church or in State. . . .

Absolute and arbitrary power can never be maintained by one man over the body and soul of another man, without brutal chastisement and enormous cruelty.

To talk of *kindness* entering into a relation in which one party is robbed of wife, of children, of his hard earnings, of home, of friends, of society, of knowledge, and of all that makes this life desirable, is most absurd, wicked, and preposterous.

I have shown that slavery is wicked—wicked, in that it violates the great law of liberty, written on every human heart—wicked, in that it violates the first command of the decalogue—wicked, in that it fosters the most disgusting licentiousness—wicked, in that it mars and defaces the image of God by cruel and barbarous inflictions—wicked, in that it contravenes the

laws of eternal justice, and tramples in the dust all the humane and heaven-
ly precepts of the New Testament. . . .

The northern people have been long connected with slavery; they
have been linked to a decaying corpse, which has destroyed the moral
health. The union of the government; the union of the north and south, in
the political parties; the union in the religious organizations of the land,
have all served to deaden the moral sense of the northern people, and to
impregnate them with sentiments and ideas forever in conflict with what as
a nation we call *genius of American institutions.* Rightly viewed, this is an
alarming fact, and ought to rally all that is pure, just, and holy in one determined effort to crush the monster of corruption, and to scatter "its guilty
profits" to the winds. In a high moral sense, as well as in a national sense,
the whole American people are responsible for slavery, and must share, in
its guilt and shame, with the most obdurate men-stealers of the south. . . .

I would invoke the spirit of patriotism, in the name of the law of the
living God, natural and revealed, and in the full belief that "righteousness
exalteth a nation, while sin is a reproach to any people." "He that walketh
righteously, and speaketh uprightly; he that despiseth the gain of oppressions, that shaketh his hands from the holding of bribes, he shall dwell on
high, his place of defense shall be the munitions of rocks, bread shall be
given him, his water shall be sure."

We have not only heard much lately of patriotism, and of its aid being
invoked on the side of slavery and injustice, but the very prosperity of this
people has been called in to deafen them to the voice of duty, and to lead
them onward in the pathway of sin. Thus has the blessing of God been converted into a curse. In the spirit of genuine patriotism, I warn the American
people, by all that is just and honorable, to beware!

I warn them that, strong, proud, and prosperous though we be, there
is a power above us that can "bring down high looks; at the breath of
whose mouth our wealth may take wings; and before whom every knee
shall bow;" and who can tell how soon the avenging angel may pass over
our land, and the sable bondmen now in chains, may become the instruments of our nation's chastisement! Without appealing to any higher feeling, I would warn the American people, and the American government, to
be wise in their day and generation. I exhort them to remember the history
of other nations; and I remind them that America cannot always sit "as a
queen," in peace and repose; that prouder and stronger governments than
this have been shattered by the bolts of a just God; that the time *may* come
when those they now despise and hate, may be needed; when those whom
they now compel by oppression to be enemies, may be wanted as friends.
What has been, may be again. There is a point beyond which human
endurance cannot go. The crushed worm may yet turn under the heel of the
oppressor. I warn them, then, with all solemnity, and in the name of ret-
ributive justice, *to look to their ways;* for in an evil hour, those sable arms that

have, for the last two centuries, been engaged in cultivating and adorning the fair fields of our country, may yet become the instruments of terror, desolation, and death, throughout our borders.

It was the sage of the Old Dominion that said—while speaking of the possibility of a conflict between the slaves and the slaveholders—"God has no attribute that could take sides with the oppressor in such a contest. I tremble for my country when I reflect that God *is just,* and that his justice cannot sleep forever." Such is the warning voice of Thomas Jefferson; and every day's experience since its utterance until now, confirms its wisdom, and commends its truth.

Speech at Peoria, Illinois*

Abraham Lincoln

. . . The repeal of the Missouri Compromise, and the propriety of its restoration, constitute the subject of what I am about to say. . . .

In order to [get?] a clear understanding of what the Missouri Compromise is, a short history of the preceding kindred subjects will perhaps be proper. When we established our independence, we did not own, or claim, the country to which this compromise applies. Indeed, strictly speaking, the confederacy then owned no country at all; the States respectively owned the country within their limits; and some of them owned territory beyond their strict State limits. . . . These territories, together with the States themselves, constituted all the country over which the confederacy then claimed any sort of jurisdiction. We were then living under the Articles of Confederation, which were superceded by the Constitution several years afterwards. The question of ceding these territories to the general government was set on foot. Mr. Jefferson . . . prevailed on the Virginia Legislature to adopt his views, and to cede the territory, making the prohibition of slavery therein, a condition of the deed. . . . Congress accepted the cession, with the condition; and in the first Ordinance (which the acts of Congress were then called) for the government of the territory, provided that slavery should never be permitted therein. . . . It is now what Jefferson foresaw and intended—the happy home of teeming millions of free, white, prosperous people, and no slave amongst them. . . .

But to return to history. In 1803 we purchased what was then called Louisiana, of France. It included the now states of Louisiana, Arkansas, Missouri, and Iowa; also the territory of Minnesota, and the present bone of

*From Abraham Lincoln, "Speech at Peoria, Illinois," in *The Collected Works of Abraham Lincoln,* ed. Roy P. Basler (New Brunswick, NJ: Rutgers University Press, 1953), II, 247–83.

contention, Kansas and Nebraska. Slavery already existed among the French at New Orleans; and, to some extent, at St. Louis. In 1812 Louisiana came into the Union as a slave state, without controversy. In 1818 or '19, Missouri showed signs of a wish to come in with slavery. This was resisted by northern members of Congress; and thus began the first great slavery agitation in the nation. This controversy lasted several months, and became very angry and exciting; the House of Representatives voting steadily for the prohibition of slavery in Missouri, and the Senate voting as steadily against it. Threats of breaking up the Union were freely made; and the ablest public men of the day became seriously alarmed. At length a compromise was made, in which, like all compromises, both sides yielded something. It was a law passed on the 6th day of March, 1820, providing that Missouri might come into the Union *with* slavery, but that in all the remaining part of the territory purchased of France, which lies north of 36 degrees and 30 minutes north latitude, slavery should never be permitted. This provision of law, *is the Missouri Compromise.* In excluding slavery North of the line, the same language is employed as in the Ordinance of '87. It directly applied to Iowa, Minnesota, and to the present bone of contention, Kansas and Nebraska. Whether there should or should not, be slavery south of that line, nothing was said in the law; but Arkansas constituted the principal remaining part, south of the line; and it has since been admitted as a slave state without serious controversy. More recently, Iowa, north of the line, came in as a free state without controversy. Still later, Minnesota, north of the line, had a territorial organization without controversy. Texas principally south of the line, and West of Arkansas; though originally within the purchase from France, had, in 1819, been traded off to Spain, in our treaty for the acquisition of Florida. It had thus become a part of Mexico. Mexico revolutionized and became independent of Spain. American citizens began settling rapidly, with their slaves in the southern part of Texas. Soon they revolutionized against Mexico, and established an independent government of their own, adopting a constitution, with slavery, strongly resembling the constitutions of our slave states. By still another rapid move, Texas, claiming a boundary much further West, than when we parted with her in 1819, was brought back to the United States, and admitted into the Union as a slave state. There then was little or no settlement in the northern part of Texas, a considerable portion of which lay north of the Missouri line; and in the resolutions admitting her into the Union, the Missouri restriction was expressly extended westward across her territory. This was in 1845, only nine years ago.

Thus originated the Missouri Compromise, and thus has it been respected down to 1845. . . .

These points all needed adjustment; and they were all held up, perhaps wisely to make them help to adjust one another. The Union, now, as in 1820, was thought to be in danger; and devotion to the Union rightfully inclined men to yield somewhat, in points where nothing else could have so inclined them. A compromise was finally effected. The south got their new fugitive-slave law; and the North got California, (the far best part of our acquisition from Mexico,) as a free State. The south got a provision that New Mexico and Utah, *when admitted as States*, may come in *with* or *without* slavery as they may then choose; and the north got the slave-trade abolished in the District of Columbia. The north got the western boundary of Texas, thence further back eastward than the south desired; but, in turn, they gave Texas ten millions of dollars, with which to pay her old debts. This is the Compromise of 1850. . . .

During this long period of time Nebraska had remained, substantially an uninhabited country, but now emigration to, and settlement within it began to take place. It is about one third as large as the present United States, and its importance so long overlooked, begins to come into view. The restriction of slavery by the Missouri Compromise directly applies to it; in fact, was first made, and has since been maintained, expressly for it. In 1853, a bill to give it a territorial government passed the House of Representatives, and, in the hands of Judge Douglas, failed of passing the Senate only for want of time. This bill contained no repeal of the Missouri Compromise. Indeed, when it was assailed because it did not contain such repeal, Judge Douglas defended it in its existing form. On January 4th, 1854, Judge Douglas introduces a new bill to give Nebraska territorial government. He accompanies this bill with a report, in which last, he expressly recommends that the Missouri Compromise shall neither be affirmed nor repealed.

Before long the bill is so modified as to make two territories instead of one; calling the Southern one Kansas.

Also, about a month after the introduction of the bill, on the judge's own motion, it is so amended as to declare the Missouri Compromise inoperative and void; and, substantially, that the People who go and settle there may establish slavery, or exclude it, as they may see fit. In this shape the bill passed both branches of congress, and became a law.

This is the *repeal* of the Missouri Compromise. The foregoing history may not be precisely accurate in every particular; but I am sure it is sufficiently so, for all the uses I shall attempt to make of it, and in it, we have before us, the chief material enabling us to correctly judge whether the repeal of the Missouri Compromise is right or wrong.

I think, and shall try to show, that it is wrong; wrong in its direct effect, letting slavery into Kansas and Nebraska—and wrong in its prospective principle, allowing it to spread to every other part of the wide world, where men can be found inclined to take it.

This *declared* indifference, but as I must think, covert real *zeal* for the spread of slavery, I can not but hate. I hate it because of the monstrous injustice of slavery itself. I hate it because it deprives our republican example of its just influence in the world—enables the enemies of free institutions, with plausibility, to taunt us as hypocrites—causes the real friends of freedom to doubt our sincerity, and especially because it forces so many really good men amongst ourselves into an open war with the very fundamental principles of civil liberty—criticising the Declaration of Independence, and insisting that there is no right principle of action but *self-interest.*

Before proceeding, let me say I think I have no prejudice against the Southern people. They are just what we would be in their situation. If slavery did not now exist amongst them, they would not introduce it. If it did now exist amongst us, we should not instantly give it up. This I believe of the masses north and south. Doubtless there are individuals, on both sides, who would not hold slaves under any circumstances; and others who would gladly introduce slavery anew, if it were out of existence. We know that some southern men do free their slaves, go north, and become tip-top abolitionists; while some northern ones go south, and become most cruel slave-masters.

When southern people tell us they are no more responsible for the origin of slavery, than we; I acknowledge the fact. When it is said that the institution exists; and that it is very difficult to get rid of it, in any satisfactory way, I can understand and appreciate the saying. I surely will not blame them for not doing what I should not know how to do myself. If all earthly power were given me, I should not know what to do, as to the existing institution. My first impulse would be to free all the slaves, and send them to Liberia,—to their own native land. But a moment's reflection would convince me, that whatever of high hope, (as I think there is) there may be in this, in the long run, its sudden execution is impossible. If they were all landed there in a day, they would all perish in the next ten days; and there are not surplus shipping and surplus money enough in the world to carry them there in many times ten days. What then? Free them all, and keep them among us as underlings? Is it quite certain that this betters their condition? I think I would not hold one in slavery, at any rate; yet the point is not clear enough for me to denounce people upon. What next? Free them, and make them politically and socially, our equals? My own feelings will not admit of this; and if mine would, we well know that those of the great mass of white people will not. Whether this feeling accords with justice and sound judgment, is not the sole question, if indeed, it is any part of it. A universal feeling, whether well or ill-founded, can not be safely disregarded. We can not, then, make them equals. It does seem to me that systems of gradual emancipation might be adopted; but for their tardiness in this, I will not undertake to judge our brethren of the south.

When they remind us of their constitutional rights, I acknowledge them, not grudgingly, but fully, and fairly; and I would give them any legislation for the reclaiming of their fugitives, which should not, in its stringency, be more likely to carry a free man into slavery, than our ordinary criminal laws are to hang an innocent one.

But all this; to my judgment, furnishes no more excuse for permitting slavery to go into our own free territory, than it would for reviving the African slave trade by law. The law which forbids the bringing of slaves *from* Africa; and that which has so long forbid the taking them *to* Nebraska, can hardly be distinguished on any moral principle; and the repeal of the former could find quite as plausible excuses as that of the latter. . . .

The Missouri Compromise ought to be restored. For the sake of the Union, it ought to be restored. We ought to elect a House of Representatives which will vote its restoration. If by any means, we omit to do this, what follows? Slavery may or may not be established in Nebraska. But whether it be or not, we shall have repudiated—discarded from the councils of the Nation—the SPIRIT of COMPROMISE; for who after this will ever trust in a national compromise? The spirit of mutual concession—that spirit which first gave us the constitution, and which has thrice saved the Union—we shall have strangled and cast from us forever. And what shall we have in lieu of it? The South flushed with triumph and tempted to excesses; the North, betrayed, as they believe, brooding on wrong and burning for revenge. One side will provoke; the other resent. The one will taunt, the other defy; one agrees [aggresses?], the other retaliates. Already a few in the North, defy all constitutional restraints, resist the execution of the fugitive slave law, and even menace the institution of slavery in the states where it exists.

Already a few in the South, claim the constitutional right to take to and hold slaves in the free states—demand the revival of the slave trade; and demand a treaty with Great Britain by which fugitive slaves may be reclaimed from Canada. As yet they are but few on either side. It is a grave question for the lovers of the Union, whether the final destruction of the Missouri Compromise, and with it the spirit of all compromise will or will not embolden and embitter each of these, and fatally increase the numbers of both. . . .

But even if we fail to technically restore the compromise, it is still a great point to carry a popular vote in favor of the restoration. The moral weight of such a vote can not be estimated too highly. The authors of Nebraska are not at all satisfied with the destruction of the compromise—an endorsement of this PRINCIPLE, they proclaim to be the great object. With them, Nebraska alone is a small matter—to establish a principle, for FUTURE USE, is what they particularly desire.

That future use is to be the planting of slavery wherever in the wide world, local and unorganized opposition can not prevent it. Now if you wish to give them this endorsement—if you wish to establish this principle—do so. I shall regret it; but it is your right. On the contrary if you are opposed to the principle—intend to give it no such endorsement—let no wheedling, no sophistry, divert you from throwing a direct vote against it. . . .

Fellow countrymen—Americans south, as well as north, shall we make no effort to arrest this? Already the liberal party throughout the world, express the apprehension "that the one retrograde institution in America, is undermining the principles of progress, and fatally violating the noblest political system the world ever saw." This is not the taunt of enemies, but the warning of friends. Is it quite safe to disregard it—to despise it? Is there no danger to liberty itself, in discarding the earliest practice, and first precept of our ancient faith? In our greedy chase to make profit of the negro, let us beware, lest we "cancel and tear to pieces" even the white man's charter of freedom.

Our republican robe is soiled, and trailed in the dust. Let us repurify it. Let us turn and wash it white, in the spirit, if not the blood, of the Revolution. Let us turn slavery from its claims of "moral right," back upon its existing legal rights, and its arguments of "necessity." Let us return it to the position our fathers gave it; and there let it rest in peace. Let us re-adopt the Declaration of Independence, and with it, the practices, and policy, which harmonize with it. Let north and south—let all Americans—let all lovers of liberty everywhere—join in the great and good work. If we do this, we shall not only have saved the Union; but we shall have so saved it, as to make, and to keep it, forever worthy of the saving. We shall have so saved it, that the succeeding millions of free happy people, the world over, shall rise up, and call us blessed, to the latest generations. . . .

A Disquisition on Government*

John C. Calhoun

IN order to have a clear and just conception of the nature and object of government, it is indispensable to understand correctly what that constitution or law of our nature is, in which government originates; or, to express it more fully and accurately,—that law, without which government would not, and with which, it must necessarily exist. . . . The first question, accordingly, to be considered is,—What is that constitution or law of our nature, without which government would not exist, and with which its existence is necessary?

In considering this, I assume, as an incontestable fact, that man is so constituted as to be a social being. His inclinations and wants, physical and

*From John C. Calhoun, "A Disquisition on Government," in *The Works of John C. Calhoun*, ed. Richard K. Cralle (New York: D. Appleton & Company, 1854), I, 1–107.

moral, irresistibly impel him to associate with his kind; and he has, accordingly never been found, in any age or country, in any state other than the social. In no other, indeed, could he exist; and in no other,—were it possible for him to exist,—could he attain to a full development of his moral and intellectual faculties, or raise himself, in the scale of being, much above the level of the brute creation.

I next assume, also, as a fact not less incontestable, that, while man is so constituted as to make the social state necessary to his existence and the full development of his faculties, this state itself cannot exist without government. The assumption rests on universal experience. In no age or country has any society or community ever been found, whether enlightened or savage, without government of some description.

Having assumed these, as unquestionable phenomena of our nature, I shall, without further remark, proceed to the investigation of the primary and important question,—What is that constitution of our nature, which, while it impels man to associate with his kind, renders it impossible for society to exist without government?

The answer will be found in the fact, (not less incontestable than either of the others,) that, while man is created for the social state, and is accordingly so formed as to feel what affects others, as well as what affects himself, he is, at the same time, so constituted as to feel more intensely what affects him directly, than what affects him indirectly through others; or, to express it differently, he is so constituted, that his direct or individual affections are stronger than his sympathetic or social feelings. I intentionally avoid the expression, *selfish* feelings, as applicable to the former; because, as commonly used, it implies an unusual excess of the individual over the social feelings, in the person to whom it is applied; and, consequently, something depraved and vicious. My object is, to exclude such inference, and to restrict the inquiry exclusively to facts in their bearings on the subject under consideration, viewed as mere phenomena appertaining to our nature,—constituted as it is; and which are as unquestionable as is that of gravitation, or any other phenomenon of the material world. . . .

But that constitution of our nature which makes us feel more intensely what affects us directly than what affects us indirectly through others, necessarily leads to conflict between individuals. Each, in consequence, has a greater regard for his own safety or happiness, than for the safety or happiness of others; and, where these come in opposition, is ready to sacrifice the interests of others to his own. And hence, the tendency to a universal state of conflict, between individual and individual; accompanied by the connected passions of suspicion, jealousy, anger and revenge,—followed by insolence, fraud and cruelty;—and, if not prevented by some controlling power, ending in a state of universal discord and confusion, destructive of the social state and the ends for which it is ordained. This controlling power, wherever vested, or by whomsoever exercised, is GOVERNMENT.

It follows, then, that man is so constituted, that government is neces-sary to the existence of society, and society to his existence, and the perfec-tion of his faculties. It follows, also, that government has its origin in this twofold constitution of his nature; the sympathetic or social feelings consti-tuting the remote,—and the individual or direct, the proximate cause. . . .

But government, although intended to protect and preserve society, has itself a strong tendency to disorder and abuse of its powers, as all expe-rience and almost every page of history testify. The cause is to be found in the same constitution of our nature which makes government indispens-able. The powers which it is necessary for government to possess, in order to repress violence and preserve order, cannot execute themselves. They must be administered by men in whom, like others, the individual are stronger than the social feelings. And hence, the powers vested in them to prevent injustice and oppression on the part of others, will if left unguard-ed, be by them converted into instruments to oppress the rest of the com-munity. That, by which this is prevented, by whatever name called, is what is meant, by CONSTITUTION, in its most comprehensive sense, when applied to GOVERNMENT. . . .

How government, then, must be constructed, in order to counteract, through its organism, this tendency on the part of those who make and exe-cute the laws to oppress those subject to their operation, is the next question which claims attention.

There is but one way in which this can possibly be done; and that is, by such an organism as will furnish the ruled with the means of resisting successfully this tendency on the part of the rulers to oppression and abuse. Power can only be resisted by power,—and tendency by tendency. Those who exercise power and those subject to its exercise,—the rulers and the ruled,—stand in antagonistic relations to each other. . . .

Nothing is more difficult than to equalize the action of the govern-ment, in reference to the various and diversified interests of the community; and nothing more easy than to pervert its powers into instruments to aggrandize and enrich one or more interests by oppressing and impoverish-ing the others; and this too, under the operation of laws, couched in general terms;—and which, on their face, appear fair and equal. Nor is this the case in some particular communities only. It is so in all; the small and the great,—the poor and the rich,—irrespective of pursuits, productions, or degrees of civilization;—with, however, this difference, that the more exten-sive and populous the country, the more diversified the condition and pur-suits of its population, and the richer, more luxurious, and dissimilar the people, the more difficult is it to equalize the action of the government,—and the more easy for one portion of the community to pervert its powers to oppress, and plunder the other. . . .

As, then, the right of suffrage, without some other provision, cannot counteract this tendency of government, the next question for consideration is—What is that other provision?. . . . It is, indeed, emphatically, that principle which *makes* the constitution, in its strict and limited sense.

From what has been said, it is manifest, that this provision must be of a character calculated to prevent any one interest, or combination of interests, from using the powers of government to aggrandize itself at the expense of the others. . . . There is but one certain mode in which this result can be secured; and that is, by the adoption of some restriction or limitation, which shall so effectually prevent any one interest, or combination of interests, from obtaining the exclusive control of the government, as to render hopeless all attempts directed to that end. There is, again, but one mode in which this can be effected; and that is, by taking the sense of each interest or portion of the community, which may be unequally and injuriously affected by the action of the government, separately, through its own majority, or in some other way by which its voice may be fairly expressed; and to require the consent of each interest, either to put or to keep the government in action. This, too, can be accomplished only in one way,—and that is, by such an organism of the government,—and, if necessary for the purpose, of the community also,—as will, by dividing and distributing the powers of government, give to each division or interest, through its appropriate organ, either a concurrent voice in making and executing the laws, or a veto on their execution. It is only by such an organism, that the assent of each can be made necessary to put the government in motion; or the power made effectual to arrest its action, when put in motion,—and it is only by the one or the other that the different interests, orders, classes, or portions, into which the community may be divided, can be protected, and all conflict and struggle between them prevented,—by rendering it impossible to put or to keep it in action, without the concurrent consent of all.

Such an organism as this, combined with the right of suffrage, constitutes, in fact, the elements of constitutional government. The one, by rendering those who make and execute the laws responsible to those on whom they operate, prevents the rulers from oppressing the ruled; and the other, by making it impossible for any one interest or combination of interests or class, or order, or portion of the community, to obtain exclusive control, prevents any one of them from oppressing the other. It is clear, that oppression and abuse of power must come, if at all, from the one or the other quarter. From no other can they come. It follows, that the two, suffrage and proper organism combined, are sufficient to counteract the tendency of government to oppression and abuse of power; and to restrict it to the fulfilment of the great ends for which it is ordained. . . .

The necessary consequence of taking the sense of the community by the concurrent majority is, as has been explained, to give to each interest or portion of the community a negative on the others. It is this mutual negative among its various conflicting interests, which invests each with the power of protecting itself;—and places the rights and safety of each, where only they can be securely placed, under its own guardianship. Without this there can be no systematic, peaceful, or effective resistance to the natural tendency of each to come into conflict with the others: and without this there can be no constitution. It is this negative power,—the power of preventing or arresting the action of the government,—be it called by what term it may,—veto, interposition, nullification, check, or balance of power,—which, in fact, forms the constitution. They are all but different names for the negative power. In all its forms, and under all its names, it results from the concurrent majority. Without this there can be no negative; and, without a negative, no constitution. The assertion is true in reference to all constitutional governments, be their forms what they may. It is, indeed, the negative power which makes the constitution,—and the positive which makes the government. The one is the power of acting;—and the other the power of preventing or arresting action. The two, combined, make constitutional governments.

But, as there can be no constitution without the negative power, and no negative power without the concurrent majority;—it follows, necessarily, that where the numerical majority has the sole control of the government, there can be no constitution; as constitution implies limitation or restriction,—and, of course, is inconsistent with the idea of sole or exclusive power. And hence, the numerical, unmixed with the concurrent majority, necessarily forms, in all cases, absolute government.

It is, indeed, the single, or *one power*, which excludes the negative, and constitutes absolute government; and not the *number* in whom the power is vested. The numerical majority is as truly a *single power*, and excludes the negative as completely as the absolute government of one, or of the few. The former is as much the absolute government of the democratic, or popular form, as the latter of the monarchical or aristocratical. It has, accordingly, in common with them, the same tendency to oppression and abuse of power. . . .

Among the other advantages which governments of the concurrent have over those of the numerical majority,—and which strongly illustrates their more popular character, is,—that they admit, with safety, a much greater extension of the right of suffrage. It may be safely extended in such governments to universal suffrage: that is,—to every male citizen of mature age, with few ordinary exceptions; but it cannot be so far extended in those of the numerical majority, without placing them ultimately under the control of the more ignorant and dependent portions of the community. For, as the community becomes populous, wealthy, refined, and highly civilized, the difference between the rich and the poor will become more strongly marked; and the number of the ignorant and dependent greater in proportion to the rest of the community. With the increase of this difference, the tendency to conflict between them will become stronger; and, as the poor and dependent become more numerous in proportion, there will be, in governments of the numerical majority, no want of leaders among the wealthy and ambitious, to excite and direct them in their efforts to obtain the control.

The case is different in governments of the concurrent majority. There, mere numbers have not the absolute control; and the wealthy and intelligent being identified in interest with the poor and ignorant of their respective portions or interests of the community, become their leaders and protectors. And hence, as the latter would have neither hope nor inducement to rally the former in order to obtain the control, the right of suffrage, under such a government, may be safely enlarged to the extent stated, without incurring the hazard to which such enlargement would expose governments of the numerical majority.

In another particular, governments of the concurrent majority have greatly the advantage. I allude to the difference in their respective tendency, in reference to dividing or uniting the community. That of the concurrent, as has been shown, is to unite the community, let its interests be ever so diversified or opposed; while that of the numerical is to divide it into two conflicting portions, let its interests be, naturally, ever so united and identified. . . .

It follows, from all that has been said, that the more perfectly a government combines power and liberty,—that is, the greater its power and the more enlarged and secure the liberty of individuals, the more perfectly it fulfils the ends for which government is ordained. To show, then, that the government of the concurrent majority is better calculated to fulfil them than that of the numerical, it is only necessary to explain why the former is better suited to combine a higher degree of power and a wider scope of liberty than the latter. I shall begin with the former.

The concurrent majority, then, is better suited to enlarge and secure the bounds of liberty, because it is better suited to prevent government from passing beyond its proper limits, and to restrict it to its primary end,—the protection of the community. But in doing this, it leaves, necessarily, all beyond it open and free to individual exertions; and thus enlarges and secures the sphere of liberty to the greatest extent which the condition of the community will admit, as has been explained. The tendency of government to pass beyond its proper limits is what exposes liberty to danger, and renders it insecure; and it is the strong counteraction of governments of the concurrent majority to this tendency which makes them so favorable to liberty. . . .

The Universal Trade*

George Fitzhugh

We are all, North and South, engaged in the White Slave Trade, and he who succeeds best is esteemed most respectable. It is far more cruel than the Black Slave Trade, because it exacts more of its slaves, and neither protects nor governs them. We boast that it exacts more when we say, "that the *profits* made from employing free labor are greater than those from slave labor." The profits, made from free labor, are the amount of the products of such labor, which the employer, by means of the command which capital or skill gives him, takes away, exacts, or "exploitates" from the free laborer. The profits of slave labor are that portion of the products of such labor which the power of the master enables him to appropriate. These profits are less, because the master allows the slave to retain a larger share of the results of his own labor than do the employers of free labor. But we not only boast that the White Slave Trade is more exacting and fraudulent (in fact, though not in intention) than Black Slavery; but we also boast that it is more cruel, in leaving the laborer to take care of himself and family out of the pittance which skill or capital have allowed him to retain. When the day's labor is ended, he is free, but is overburdened with the cares of family and household, which make his freedom an empty and delusive mockery. But his employer is really free, and may enjoy the profits made by others' labor, without a care, or a trouble, as to their well-being. The negro slave is free, too, when the labors of the day are over, and free in mind as well as body; for the master provides food, raiment, house, fuel, and everything else necessary to the physical well-being of himself and family. The master's labors commence just when the slave's end. No wonder men should prefer white slavery to capital, to negro slavery, since it is more profitable, and is free from all the cares and labors of black slave-holding.

Now, reader, if you wish to know yourself—to "descant on your own deformity"—read on. But if you would cherish self-conceit, self-esteem, or self-appreciation, throw down our book; for we will dispel illusions which have promoted your happiness, and show you that what you have considered and practiced as virtue is little better than moral Cannibalism. But you will find yourself in numerous and respectable company; for all good and respectable people are "Cannibals all" who do not labor, or who are suc-

---

*Reprinted by permission of the publishers from "The Universal Trade," *Cannibals All! Or Slaves without Masters*, by George Fitzhugh, ed. C. Vann Woodward, Cambridge, MA: The Belknap Press of Harvard University Press, Copyright © 1960, 1988 by the President and Fellows of Harvard College. Pp. 15—20.

cessfully trying to live without labor, on the unrequited labor of other people:—Whilst low, bad, and disreputable people, are those who labor to support themselves, and to support said respectable people besides. Throwing the negro slaves out of the account, and society is divided in Christendom into four classes: the rich, or independent respectable people, who live well and labor not at all, the professional and skillful respectable people, who do a little light work, for enormous wages; the poor hard-working people, who support everybody, and starve themselves; and the poor thieves, swindlers, and sturdy beggars, who live like gentlemen, without labor, on the labor of other people. The gentlemen exploitate, which being done on a large scale and requiring a great many victims, is highly respectable—whilst the rogues and beggars take so little from others that they fare little better than those who labor.

But, reader, we do not wish to fire into the flock. "Thou art the man!" You are a Cannibal! and if a successful one, pride yourself on the number of your victims quite as much as any Fiji chieftain, who breakfasts, dines, and sups on human flesh—and your conscience smites you, if you have failed to succeed, quite as much as his, when he returns from an unsuccessful foray.

Probably, you are a lawyer, or a merchant, or a doctor, who has made by your business fifty thousand dollars, and retired to live on your capital. But, mark! not to spend your capital. That would be vulgar, disreputable, criminal. That would be, to live by your own labor; for your capital is your amassed labor. That would be to do as common working men do; for they take the pittance which their employers leave them to live on. They live by labor; for they exchange the results of their own labor for the products of other people's labor. It is, no doubt, an honest, vulgar way of living, but not at all a respectable way. The respectable way of living is to make other people work for you, and to pay them nothing for so doing—and to have no concern about them after their work is done. Hence, white slave-holding is much more respectable than negro slavery—for the master works nearly as hard for the negro as he for the master. But you, my virtuous, respectable reader, exact three thousand dollars per annum from white labor (for your income is the product of white labor) and make not one cent of return in any form. You retain your capital, and never labor, and yet live in luxury on the labor of others. Capital commands labor, as the master does the slave. Neither pays for labor; but the master permits the slave to retain a larger allowance from the proceeds of his own labor, and hence "free labor is cheaper than slave labor." You, with the command over labor which your capital gives you, are a slave owner—a master, without the obligations of a master. They who work for you, who create your income, are slaves, without the rights of slaves. Slaves without a master! Whilst you were engaged in amassing your capital, in seeking to become independent, you were in the White Slave Trade. To become independent is to be able to make other people support you, without being obliged to labor for *them*. Now, what man in society is not seeking to attain this situation? He who attains it is a slave owner, in the worst sense. He who is in pursuit of it is engaged in the slave trade. You, reader, belong to the one or other class. The men without property, in free society, are theoretically in a worse condition than slaves. Practically, their condition corresponds with this theory, as history and statistics everywhere demonstrate. The capitalists, in free society, live in ten times the luxury and show that Southern masters do, because the slaves to capital work harder and cost less than negro slaves.

The negro slaves of the South are the happiest, and, in some sense, the freest people in the world. The children and the aged and infirm work not at all, and yet have all the comforts and necessaries of life provided for them. They enjoy liberty, because they are oppressed neither by care nor labor. The women do little hard work, and are protected from the despotism of their husbands by their masters. The negro men and stout boys work, on the average, in good weather, not more than nine hours a day. The balance of their time is spent in perfect abandon. Besides, they have their Sabbaths and holidays. White men, with so much of license and liberty, would die of ennui; but negroes luxuriate in corporeal and mental repose. With their faces upturned to the sun, they can sleep at any hour; and quiet sleep is the greatest of human enjoyments. "Blessed be the man who invented sleep." 'Tis happiness in itself—and results from contentment with the present, and confident assurance of the future. We do not know whether free laborers ever sleep. They are fools to do so; for, whilst they sleep, the wily and watchful capitalist is devising means to ensnare and exploitate them. The free laborer must work or starve. He is more of a slave than the negro, because he works longer and harder for less allowance than the slave, and has no holiday, because the cares of life with him begin when its labors end. He has no liberty, and not a single right. We know, 'tis often said, air and water are common property, which all have equal right to participate and enjoy; but this is utterly false. The appropriation of the lands carries with it the appropriation of all on or above the lands, *usque ad coelum, aut ad inferos*.[1] A man cannot breathe the air without a place to breathe it from, and all places are appropriated. All water is private property "to the middle of the stream," except the ocean, and that is not fit to drink.

Free laborers have not a thousandth part of the rights and liberties of negro slaves. Indeed, they have not a single liberty, unless it be the right or liberty to die. But the reader may think that he and other capitalists and employers are freer than negro slaves. Your capital would soon vanish, if you dared indulge in the liberty and abandon of negroes. You hold your wealth and position by the tenure of constant watchfulness, care, and circumspection. You never labor; but you are never free.

---

[1] "Even to heaven or to hell."

Where a few own the soil, they have unlimited power over the balance of society, until domestic slavery comes in to compel them to permit this balance of society to draw a sufficient and comfortable living from *terra mater*. Free society asserts the right of a few to the earth—slavery maintains that it belongs, in different degrees, to all.

But, reader, well may you follow the slave trade. It is the only trade worth following, and slaves the only property worth owning. All other is worthless, a mere *caput mortuum*,[2] except in so far as it vests the owner with the power to command the labors of others—to enslave them. Give you a palace, ten thousand acres of land, sumptuous clothes, equipage, and every other luxury; and with your artificial wants you are poorer than Robinson Crusoe, or the lowest working man, if you have no slaves to capital, or domestic slaves. Your capital will not bring you an income of a cent, nor supply one of your wants, without labor. Labor is indispensable to give value to property, and if you owned every thing else, and did not own labor, you would be poor. But fifty thousand dollars means, and is, fifty thousand dollars worth of slaves. You can command, without touching on that capital, three thousand dollars' worth of labor per annum. You could do no more were you to buy slaves with it, and then you would be cumbered with the cares of governing and providing for them. You are a slaveholder now, to the amount of fifty thousand dollars, with all the advantages, and none of the cares and responsibilities of a master.

"Property in man" is what all are struggling to obtain. Why should they not be obliged to take care of man, their property, as they do of their horses and their hounds, their cattle and their sheep. Now, under the delusive name of liberty, you work him "from morn to dewy even"—from infancy to old age—then turn him out to starve. You treat your horses and hounds better. Capital is a cruel master. The free slave trade, the commonest, yet the cruellest of trades.

DISCUSSION QUESTIONS

1. What is (are) the legitimate form or forms of property?
2. How did abolitionists, free-soilers, and southerners agree, or disagree, over the nature of individual rights?
3. How did slavery come to be associated with the idea of states' rights?
4. What should be the relationship between the states and federal government in the contemporary period?

[2]"Worthless residue."

Chapter 7

TRIUMPHANT DEMOCRACY

Prior to the Civil War, the U.S. was economically divided into an agrarian South and a simple manufacturing North. In order to successfully conclude the Civil War enormous expenditures of men and supplies were required of the federal government as seen in Table 7–1. Increases in the federal budget and the national debt were suggestive of the massive amounts of money pumped into the American economy which appeared to start a major economic expansion in the succeeding years.

Charles Francis Adams, Jr., wrote in 1871 regarding this transformation,

> History scarcely affords a parallel to the rapid development of character which took place in America during the five years of the late civil war. . . . The

TABLE 7–1 *Federal Spending, 1860–1865*

Year	Federal Expenditures	Federal Debt
1860	$ 63,131,000	$ 64,844,000
1861	66,547,000	90,582,000
1862	474,762,000	524,178,000
1863	714,741,000	1,119,774,000
1864	865,323,000	1,815,831,000
1865	1,297,555,000	2,677,929,000

Historical Statistics of the United States (Washington, DC: Department of Commerce, 1975), pp. 718, 720.

TABLE 7–2   *Indicators of Economic Growth*

	1860	1870	1880	1890	1900
Bituminous Coal (1,000 tons)	9,057	20,471	50,757	111,302	212,316
Crude Oil + (Per 1,000 barrels)	500	5,261	26,286	45,824	63,621
Steel (Long tons)	NA	68,750	1,247,335	4,277,071	10,188,329
Railroads (Mileage operated)	30,626	52,922	93,262	166,703	NA

Historical Statistics of the United States (Washington, DC: Department of Commerce, 1975), pp. 4–27, 356–57, 359–61, 416–17.

NA: not available

most noticeable of these is perhaps to be found in a greatly enlarged grasp of enterprise and increased facility of combination. The great operations of war, the handling of large masses of men, the influence of discipline, the lavish expenditure of unprecedented sums of money, the immense financial operations, the possibilities of effective co-operation were lessons not likely to be lost on men quick to receive and to apply all new ideas.[1]

Best exemplifying those changes in productivity, as detailed in Table 7–2, were increases in coal, crude oil, and steel production as well as the railroad mileage.

Highlighting those changes was the railroad, which by 1869 connected the Atlantic and Pacific coasts thereby connecting the regional markets to form one national economy. Railroads proved to be the economic lifeline whose health determined the financial well-being of the nation.[2]

Generally seen as lasting from 1870 to 1900, this period of rapid economic growth was christened by Andrew Carnegie "triumphant democracy." Triumphant democracy consisted of two distinct parts: a belief in laissez-faire economics as well as in the gospel of wealth.

Laissez faire, a French phrase meaning "let it be," was applied to economics and politics to mean government should not interfere in the nation's business. The philosophical roots of laissez-faire economics appeared in John Locke's formulation of private property.

God, who hath given the world to men in common, hath also given them reason to make use of it to the best advantage of life and convenience. . . . Every man has a property in his own person. This nobody has any right to but himself. The labour of his body and the work of his hands . . . are properly his.

---

[1]Charles Francis Adams, Jr., "An Erie Raid," *The North American Review*, 112, no. 231 (April 1871), 241. Used by permission of the University of Northern Iowa.

[2]Sean Dennis Cashman, *America in the Gilded Age*, 2nd ed. (New York: New York University Press, 1988), pp. 32–36.

> Whatsoever, then, he removes out of the state that nature hath provided and
> left it in, he hath mixed his labour with it, and joined to it something that is his
> own, and thereby makes it his property.[3]

An individual uses their liberty to acquire property and in the process
expands their freedom. The belief in the individual's natural right to property established individualism as a major component of laissez-faire economics.[4]

Laissez-faire economics was largely elaborated in the nineteenth century by Herbert Spencer in England and William Sumner in the U.S.
Spencer transposed the biological studies of Darwin into economics as well
as politics, and argued that government regulation disrupted the natural
evolution of human associations. Government regulation disturbed the
equality of opportunity and created creatures reared on the equality of outcome that could not survive. To Spencer, the well-being of society was
dependent upon individuals, who because of their natural abilities and the
lack of government regulation, pursued more efficient industrial relationships. As if to emphasize Spencer's ideas in the U.S., Sumner wrote,

> The millionaires are a product of natural selection, acting on the whole body
> of men, to pick out those who can meet the requirement of certain work to be
> done. In this respect they are just like the great statesmen, or scientific men, or
> military men. It is because they are thus selected that wealth aggregates under
> their hands—both their own and that intrusted to them. . . . They may fairly
> be regarded as the naturally selected agents of society for certain work. They
> get high wages and live in luxury, but the bargain is a good one for soci-
> ety. . . . This will bring discipline and correction of arrogance and masterful-
> ness.[5]

The purpose of government was not to create economic equality, but to
remove those "artificial impediments to the natural law of the 'survival of
the fittest'."[6] Individualism to Sumner meant that the abilities of people
were unequal and harnessing the most productive members to the ineptitude of the majority would lead to disaster. If the natural evolutionary
process was to be played out: (1) government could not support one group
over another; (2) one group had no obligation to help another; and (3) individuals must pursue their own interests. Government theoretically

---

[3]John Locke, *Two Treatises of Government*, in *Great Political Thinkers:Plato to the Present*, 5th ed.,
eds. William Ebenstein and Alan O. Ebenstein (Orlando, FL: Holt, Rinehart and Winston,
1991), p. 441.

[4]William Ebenstein and Alan O. Ebenstein, eds., *Great Political Thinkers: Plato to the Present*, 5th
ed. (Orlando, FL: Holt, Rinehart and Winston, 1991), p. 843.

[5]William G. Sumner, "Consolidation of Wealth: Economic Aspects," *The Independent*, 54, no.
2787 (May 1, 1902), 1040.

[6]A.J. Beitzinger, *A History of American Political Thought* (New York: Dodd, Mead & Company,
1972), p. 399.

assumed the role of mediating agent in society to ensure political rights albeit without economic responsibilities. Governmental regulation of industry was as dangerous to economic prosperity as was government following the dictates of industrialists regarding political freedom.

Despite their desire for wealth, industrialists were generally of two types. As Cashman noted, the first generation were composed of people such as Daniel Drew and Jay Gould, who as "rogue financiers" sought to create personal wealth no matter the cost to "economic or political stability."[7] In the second generation, individuals such as John Pierpoint Morgan, Andrew Carnegie, and John Rockefeller sought to secure wealth by creating a sound commercial structure through the organization of trusts.[8] A trust was an organization of businesses generally producing the same products and therefore able to regulate their supply and price. The purpose of trusts was well illustrated by Cashman in regard to Standard Oil.

> What Rockefeller wanted to do was to bring all units within one industry into a group under one leader; to get rid of less economical plants; to pool resources to achieve economy and improvement; to limit production and keep the surplus oil off the market until demand exceeded supply; and to stabilize prices.[9]

While trusts served to regulate and preserve industries, they were seen to victimize the population by setting prices and bribing politicians in order to achieve selected goals. The power of trusts provoked outcries for their regulation. Initially, the legal ability of government to regulate corporations was decided by the Supreme Court in the "Slaughterhouse cases" (1873) and *Santa Clara County* v. *Southern Pacific Railroad* (1886). Supporters of laissez-faire economics used the Fourteenth Amendment to advocate constitutional protection for property owners. By providing that "Nor shall any State deprive any person of life, liberty, or property without due process of law," the Supreme Court considered a corporation as having the same legal rights as an individual.

In the same period that laissez-faire economics was promoted, the "gospel of wealth" was advocated by Russell Conwell, William Lawrence, and Andrew Carnegie.

The societal accomplishments of industrialists were used to explain why so few had a right to control so much. One of the most noted advocates was Conwell who toured the country delivering the "Acres of Diamonds" speech. Conwell, who was a Baptist minister, stated that God had given the ability to be wealthy to all people, but one had to seize the oppor-

---

[7]Cashman, *America*, pp. 36–37.
[8]Ibid., pp. 38–44.
[9]Ibid., p. 63.

tunity. Equality of opportunity existed for all people, but only certain individuals actively pursued it. Like the Puritans who tended to regard the achievement of wealth as a sign of superior spirituality, Conwell argued that it was one's Christian duty to utilize the opportunities God provided. Likewise Lawrence, an Episcopalian bishop, viewed wealth as a sign of God's blessings and societal advancement.

> In other words, to seek for and earn wealth is a sign of a natural, vigorous, and strong character. . . . The search for material wealth is therefore as natural and necessary to the man as is the pushing out of its roots for more moisture and food to the oak. This is man's play, his exercise, the expression of his powers, his personality. . . . For one man who seeks money for its own sake there are ten who seek it for satisfaction of the seeking, the power there is in it, and the use they can make of it.[10]

Both Conwell and Lawrence regarded the achievement of wealth as a natural right of all people and beneficial to the Christian community.

Taking a positivist approach, Andrew Carnegie argued that wealth was achieved only through the hard work of the individual. Carnegie, who was a self-made man, argued that success or failure rests upon the initiative of the individual and that the accumulation of wealth was necessary so the industrious few could materially benefit society.

> This, then, is the duty of the man of wealth: To set an example of modest, unostentatious living, shunning display or extravagance; to provide moderately for the legitimate wants of those dependent upon him; and after doing so, to consider all surplus revenues . . . as trust funds, which he is called upon to administer, and strictly bound as a matter of duty to administer in the manner which, in his judgment, is best calculated to provide the most beneficial results for the community—the man of wealth thus becoming the mere trustee and agent for his poorer brethren, bringing to their service his superior wisdom, experience, and ability to administer, doing for them better than they would or could do for themselves.[11]

This attitude toward wealth can be seen in Carnegie's numerous donations of libraries and his endowment of the Carnegie Corporation of New York to promote learning and understanding. Others such as Cornelius Vanderbilt and James Duke built or endowed universities which continue to bear their family names.

In the following sections of this chapter the philosophies of laissez-faire economics and the gospel of wealth are presented in the form of writings by Sumner, Lawrence, and Carnegie.

---

[10]William Lawrence, "The Relation of Wealth to Morals," *World's Work*, 1, no. 3 (January 1901), 288.

[11]Andrew Carnegie, "Wealth," *The North American Review*, 148, no. 391 (June 1889), 661–62. Used by permission of the University of Northern Iowa.

Consolidation of Wealth: Economic Aspects*

William G. Sumner

The concentration of wealth I understand to include the aggregation of wealth into large masses, and its concentration under the control of a few.

In this sense the concentration of wealth is indispensable to the successful execution of the tasks which devolve upon society in our time. Every task of society requires the application of capital, and involves an economic problem, in the form of the most expedient application of material means to ends. Two features most prominently distinguish the present age from all which have preceded it; those are, first, the great scale on which all societal undertakings must be carried out; second, the transcendent importance of competent management—that is, of the personal element in direction and control. I speak of "societal undertakings" because it is important to notice that the prevalent modes and forms are not confined to industrial undertakings, but are universal to all the institutions and devices which have for their purpose to satisfy any wants of society. . . . To a correct understanding of our subject it is essential to recognize the concentration of wealth and control as a universal societal phenomenon, not merely as a matter of industrial power, or social sentiment, or political policy.

Stated in the concisest terms the phenomenon is that of a more perfect integration of all societal functions. The concentration of power (wealth), more dominant control, intenser discipline, and stricter methods are but modes of securing more perfect integration. When we perceive this we see that the concentration of wealth is but one feature of a grand step in societal evolution.

Some may admit that the concentration of wealth is indispensable, but may desire to distinguish between joint stock aggregations on the one side, and individual fortunes on the other. This distinction is a product of the current social prejudice and is not valid. The predominance of the individual and personal element in control is seen in the tendency of all joint stock enterprises to come under the control of very few persons. Every age is befooled by the notions which are in fashion in it. Our age is befooled by "democracy." We hear arguments about the industrial organization which are deductions from democratic dogmas, or which appeal to prejudice by using analogies drawn from democracy to affect sentiment about industrial relations. Industry may be republican; it can never be democratic, so long as men differ in productive power and in industrial virtue. In our time joint

*From William G. Sumner, "Consolidation of Wealth: Economic Aspects," *The Independent*, 54, no. 2787 (May 1, 1902), 1036–40.

stock companies, which are in form, republican, are drifting over into oligarchies or monarchies, because one or a few get greater efficiency of control and greater vigor of administration. They direct the enterprise in a way which produces more, or more economically. This is the purpose for which the organization exists, and success in it outweighs everything else. We see the competent men refuse to join in the enterprise, unless they can control it, and we see the stockholders willingly put their property in the hands of those who are, as they think, competent to manage it successfully. The strongest and most effective organizations for industrial purposes which are formed nowadays are those of a few great capitalists, who have great personal confidence in each other, and who can bring together adequate means for whatever they desire to do. Some such nucleus of individuals controls all the great joint stock companies. . . .

There seems to be a great readiness in the public mind to take alarm at these phenomena of growth. There might seem to be rather reason for public congratulation. We want to be provided with things abundantly and cheaply. That means that we want increased economic power. All these enterprises are efforts to satisfy that want. They promise to do it. Especially the public seems to turn to the politician to preserve them from the captain of industry. When has anybody ever seen a politician who was a match for a captain of industry? One of the latest phenomena is a competition of the legislatures of several States for the profit of granting acts of incorporation. Of course, this competition consists in granting greater and greater powers and exacting less and less responsibility.

It is not my duty in this symposium to make a judicial statement of the good and ill of the facts that I mention. I leave to others to suggest the limitations and safeguards which are required. It is enough to say here that of course all power is liable to abuse. If anybody is dreaming about a millennial state of society in which all energy will be free, yet fully controlled by paradisaic virtue, argument with him is vain. . . . It is in this light that we should view the evils (if there are any) from the concentration of wealth. I do not say that "he who desires the end desires the means," because I do not believe that that dictum is true, but he who will not forego the end must be patient with the incidental ills which attend the means. It is ridiculous to attempt to reach the end while making war on the means. In matters of societal policy the problem always is to use the means and reach the end as well as possible under the conditions. It is proper to propose checks and safeguards, but an onslaught on the concentration of wealth is absurd, and a recapitulation of its "dangers" is idle.

In fact, there is a true correlation between (a) the great productiveness of modern industry and the consequent rapid accumulation of capital from one period of production to another, and (b) the larger and larger aggregations of capital which are required by modern industry from one period of production to another. We see that the movement is constantly accelerated, that its scope is all the time widening, and that the masses of material with which it deals are greater and greater. The great cause of all this is the application of steam and electricity to transportation, and the communication of intelligence; things which we boast about as great triumphs of the nineteenth century. They have made it possible to extend efficient control, from a given central point, over operations which may be carried on at a great number of widely separated points, and to keep up a close, direct and intimate action and reaction between the central control and the distributed agents. That means that it has become possible for the organization to be extended in its scope and complexity, and at the same time intensified in its activity. . . . In it the economic advantage is greatest. There is therefore a gravitation toward this degree of organization. To make an artificial opposition to this tendency from political or alleged moral, or religious, or other motives would be irrational. The society would no longer have any real rule of action. It would have submitted itself to the control of warring motives without any real standards or tests.

It is a consequence of the principle just stated that at every point in the history of civilization it has always been necessary to concentrate capital in large amounts relatively to existing facts. . . . If we could get rid of some of our notions about liberty and equality, and could lay aside this eighteenth century philosophy, according to which human society is to be brought into a state of blessedness, we might get some insight into the might of the societal organization; what it does for us, and what it makes us do. Every day that passes brings us new phenomena of struggle and effort between parts of the societal organization. What do they all mean? They mean that all the individuals and groups are forced against each other in a ceaseless war of interests, by their selfish and mutual efforts to fulfill their career on earth, within the conditions set for them by the state of the arts, the facts of the societal organization, and the current dogmas of world philosophy. As each must win his living, or his fortune, or keep his fortune, under these conditions it is difficult to see what can be meant in the sphere of industrial or economic effort, by a "free man." It is no wonder that we so often hear angry outcries about being "a slave" from persons who have had a little experience of the contrast between the current notions and the actual facts. . . .

I am quite well aware that, in what I have said, I have not met the thoughts and feelings of people who are most troubled about the "concentration of wealth." I have tried to set forth the economic necessity for the concentration of wealth. I maintain that this is the controlling consideration. Those who care most about the concentration are indifferent to this consideration. What strikes them most is the fact that there are some rich men. I will, therefore, try to show that this fact also is only another economic justification of the concentration of wealth.

I often see statements published, in which the objectors lay stress upon the great inequalities of fortune, and, having set forth the contrast between rich and poor, they rest their case. What law of nature, religion, ethics, or the State is not violated by *inequalities* of fortune? The inequalities prove nothing. Others argue that great fortunes are won by privileges created by law and not by legitimate enterprise and ability. This statement is true, but it is entirely irrelevant. We have to discuss the concentration of wealth within the facts of the institutions, laws, usages and customs which our ancestors have bequeathed to us and which we allow to stand. If it is proposed to change any of these parts of the societal order, that is a proper subject of discussion, but it is aside from the concentration of wealth. So long as tariffs, patents, etc., are a part of the system in which we live, how can it be expected that people will not take advantage of them? What else are they for? As for franchises, a franchise is only an X until it has been developed. It never develops itself. It requires capital and skill to develop it. When the enterprise is in the full bloom of prosperity the objectors complain of it, as if the franchise, which never was anything but an empty place where something might be created, had been the completed enterprise. . . . Hence the modern methods offer very great opportunities, and the rewards of those men who can "size up" a situation, and develop its controlling elements with sagacity and good judgment, are very great. It is well that they are so, because these rewards stimulate to the utmost all the ambitions and able men, and they will make it certain that great and useful inventions will not long remain unexploited as they did formerly. Here comes, then, a new reaction on the economic system. New energy is infused into it, with hope and confidence. We could not spare this stimulus and keep up our work of production. I may add that we could not spare it and keep up the air of contentment and enthusiastic cheerfulness which characterizes our society. No man can acquire a million without helping a million men to increase their little fortunes all the way down through all the social grades. In some points of view it is an error that we fix our attention so much upon the very rich and overlook the prosperous mass, but the compensating advantage is that the great successes stimulate emulation the most powerfully.

What matters it then that some millionaires are idle, or silly, or vulgar, that their ideas are sometimes futile, and their plans grotesque, when they turn aside from money-making? How do they differ in this from any other class? The millionaires are a product of natural selection, acting on the whole body of men, to pick out those who can meet the requirement of certain work to be done. In this respect they are just like the great statesmen, or scientific men, or military men. It is because they are thus selected that wealth aggregates under their hands—both their own and that intrusted to them. Let one of them make a mistake and see how quickly the concentration gives way to dispersion. They may fairly be regarded as the naturally selected agents of society for certain work. They get high wages and live in luxury, but the bargain is a good one for society. There is the intensest competition for their place and occupation. This assures us that all who are competent for this function will be employed in it, so that the cost of it will be reduced to the lowest terms, and furthermore that the competitors will study the proper conduct to be observed in their occupation. This will bring discipline and the correction of arrogance and masterfulness.

The Relation of Wealth to Morals*

The Right Reverend William Lawrence

There is a certain distrust on the part of our people as to the effect of material prosperity on their morality. We shrink with some foreboding at the great increase of riches, and question whether in the long run material prosperity does not tend toward the disintegration of character. . . .

MAN "BORN TO BE RICH"

Now we are in a position to affirm that neither history, experience, nor the Bible necessarily sustains the common distrust of the effect of material wealth on morality. Our path of study is made more clear. Two positive principles lead us out on our path.

The first is that man, when he is strong, will conquer Nature, open up her resources, and harness them to his service. This is his play, his exercise, his divine mission. . . .

The other principle is that, in the long run, it is only to the man of morality that wealth comes. We believe in the harmony of God's Universe. We know that it is only by working along His laws natural and spiritual that we can work with efficiency. Only by working along the lines of right thinking and right living can the secrets and wealth of Nature be revealed. We, like the Psalmist, occasionally see the wicked prosper, but only occasionally. . . .

Now we return with an easier mind and clearer conscience to the problem of our twenty-five billion dollars in a decade.

My question is: Is the material prosperity of this Nation favorable or unfavorable to the morality of the people?

The first thought is, Who has prospered? Who has got the money?

I take it that the loudest answer would be, "The millionaires, the capitalists, and the incompetent but luxurious rich"; and, as we think of that twenty-five billion, our thoughts run over the yachts, the palaces, and the luxuries that flaunt themselves before the public.

---

*From William Lawrence, "The Relation of Wealth to Morals," *World's Work*, I, (January 1901), 286–92.

WHO THE RICH ARE

As I was beginning to write this paper an Irishman with his horse and wagon drew up at my back door. Note that I say his horse and wagon. Twenty years ago that Irishman, then hardly twenty years old, landed in Boston, illiterate, uncouth, scarcely able to make himself understood in English. There was no symptom of brains, alertness, or ambition. He got a job to tend a few cows. Soon the American atmosphere began to take hold. He discovered that here every man has his chance. With his first earnings he bought a suit of clothes; he gained self-respect. Then he sent money home; then he got a job to drive a horse; he opened an account at the savings bank; then evening school; more money in the bank. He changed to a better job, married a thrifty wife, and to-day he owns his house, stable, horse, wagon, and bicycle; has a good sum at the bank, supports five children, and has half a dozen men working under him. He is a capitalist, and his yearly earnings represent the income on $30,000. He has no "pull"; he has made his own way by grit, physical strength, and increasing intelligence. He has had material prosperity. His older brother, who paid his passage over, has had material prosperity, and his younger brother, whose passage my friend paid, has had material prosperity.

Now we are beginning to get an idea as to where the savings are. They are in the hands of hundreds of thousands of just such men, and of scores of thousands of men whose incomes ten years ago were two and five thousand, and are now five and ten thousand; and of thousands of others whose incomes have risen from ten to thirty thousand. So that, when you get to the multi-millionaires, you have only a fraction to distribute among them. And of them the fact is that only a small fraction of their income can be spent upon their own pleasure and luxury; the bulk of what they get has to be reinvested, and becomes the means by whereby thousands earn their wages. They are simply trustees of a fraction of the national property.

When, then, the question is asked, "Is the material prosperity of this nation favorable or unfavorable to the morality of the people?" I say with all emphasis, "In the long run, and by all means, favorable!" . . .

In the first place, and as I have already suggested, the effort to make his living and add to his comforts and power gives free play to a man's activities and leads to a development of his faculties. In an age and country where the greater openings are in commercial lines, there the stronger men and the mass of them will move. It is not a question of worldliness or love of money, but of the natural use and legitimate play of men's faculties. An effort to suppress this action is not a religious duty, but a disastrous error, sure to fail.

SELF-RESPECT AND SELF-MASTERY

Besides this natural play of the faculties comes the development of self-respect and ambition. In the uprise from a lower to higher civilization, these are the basal elements. Watch the cart-loads of Polish or Italian immigrants as they are hauled away from the dock. Study their lifeless expression, their hang-dog look, and their almost cowering posture. Follow them and study them five years later: note the gradual straightening of the body, and the kindling of the eye, and the alertness of the whole person as the men, women, and children begin to realize their opportunities, bring in their wages, and move to better quarters. Petty temptations and deep degradations that might have overwhelmed them on their arrival cannot now touch them.

To be sure, a certain fraction wilt under the strain, take to drink, to lust, to laziness. There is always the thin line of stragglers behind every army, but the great body of the American people are marching upwards in prosperity through the mastery of their lower tastes and passions to the development of the higher. From rags to clothes, from filth to cleanliness, from disease to health; from bare walls to pictures; from ignorance to education; from narrow and petty talk to books and music and art; from superstition to a more rational religion; from crudity to refinement; from self-centralization to the conception of a social unity.

Here in this last phrase we strike the next step in development. In this increase of wealth, this rapid communication which goes with it, this shrinking of the earth's surface and unifying of peoples through commerce, men and women are realizing their relations.

That there are those who in the deepest poverty sustain the spirit of unselfishness and exhibit a self-sacrifice for others which puts their richer neighbors to the blush we know by experience. At the same time, the fact is that for the mass and in the long run grinding poverty does grind down the character: in the struggle for bare existence and for the very life of one's children there is developed an intense self-centralization and a hardness which is destructive of the social instinct and of the finer graces. When, however, through the increase of wealth man has extended his interests, his vision, and his opportunities, "he is thoroughly related." . . .

THE PRIVILEGE OF GRATEFUL SERVICE

In other days we have heard much of "the sweet uses of adversity": the note still lingers in sermons and will linger as long as Christianity stands. There is, however, the other note that sounds strong in these days—the privilege of grateful service.

I have in mind now a man of wealth (you can conjure up many like him) who lives handsomely and entertains; he has everything that purveys to his health and comfort. All these things are tributary to what? To the man's efficiency in his complete devotion to the social, educational, and charitable interests to which he gives his life. He is Christ's as much as was St. Paul, he is consecrated as was St. Francis of Assisi; and in recognition of the bounty with which God has blessed him he does not sell all that he has, but he uses all that he has, and, as he believes, in the wisest way, for the relief of the poor, the upbuilding of social standards, and the upholding of righteousness among the people. . . . And if ever Christ's words have been obeyed to the letter, they are obeyed to-day by those who are living out His precepts of the stewardship of wealth.

Again I feel a silent protest. Is not the writer going rather far? We did not believe that our twenty-five billions would lead to orgies; but is he not getting rather close to the millennium? Are there no shadows and dark spaces in the radiance which he seems to think that wealth is shedding around us?

Yes, my friendly critic, there are, and to a mention of a few of them I give the pages that are left.

THE SPIRIT OF COMMERCIALISM

First and most pervasive, I name the spirit of commercialism. It crops up in many forms and places, hydra-headed.

Is it any wonder? When one realizes that in the last ten years seventy millions of people have earned their living, paid their bills, and have at the same time increased the property of the Nation by twenty-five billions of dollars, we reach a slight conception of the intensity, the industry, the enterprise, and the ability with which those people have thought, worked, and reaped. One wonders that religion, charity, or culture have survived the strain at all. When the eye and ambition of a strong man are set upon a purpose, he sometimes neglects other considerations; he is not over nice about the rights of others; he occasionally overrides the weak, crushes out the helpless, and forgets to stop and pick up those that have fallen by the way. . . .

As conditions change, much remains to do. The better adjustment of rights, wages, and taxes will call for the highest intelligence and strongest character. Again, the small tradesman has driven away the little counter where a widow earned her living, the larger tradesman has wiped out the small tradesman, and the department store is now finishing off some of the large tradesmen. It is hard, but it is a part of the great economic movement. It endangers some of the fundamentals of morality, and destroys for the time some of the finer graces.

Beyond these rudimentary forms of commercialism, there is another, even more dangerous, because it threatens the liberties and rights of the people. The eye of the public is on it now. I refer to the relation of concentrated masses of wealth to the public service.

I have no time to more than suggest a few of the conditions that have led up to this. Industrial enterprise has drawn many of the strongest and ablest men from political to commercial interests; society and legislation now do for the people what in other days the landlord did; they are concerned more and more with industrial, commercial, and financial questions, from the national tariff to the size of a house-drain. Just at this time, and because of our great industrial development and prosperity, a horde of ignorant voters waiting to be moulded by any strong leader have come to this shore. The wide distribution of wealth has driven merchants and mechanics, widows and trustees of orphans, doctors and ministers, to invest their savings in great enterprises, corporations, and trusts, which, to succeed, must be directed by a few men. We have therefore this situation: a few men responsible for the safekeeping and development of enormous properties, depending upon legislation, and a great mass of voters, many of them ignorant, represented by their own kind in city or state government, strongly organized by a leader who is in it for what he can get out of it, and who is ever alert with all his legislative cohorts to "strike" the great corporations. The people believe that the officers of great corporations so manage that they can get what they want, call it by assessment, bribery, ransom, or what you will, and they brand those otherwise respectable men as cowards and traitors to public liberty. . . .

THE DANGER FROM LUXURY

One other dark shadow, and I am done. The persistent companion of riches,—luxury and an ability to have what you want. That vice and license are rampant in certain quarters is clear; that vulgar wealth flaunts itself in the face of the people is beyond question; and that the people are rather amused at the spectacle must be confessed. . . .

With all this said, the great mass of the people are self-restrained and simple. Material prosperity has come apace, and on the whole it uplifts. Responsibility sobers men and nations. We have learned how to win wealth: we are learning how to use and spend it. Every year marks a long step in advance in material prosperity, and character must march in step. Without wealth, character is liable to narrow and harden. Without character, wealth will destroy. Wealth is upon us, increasing wealth. The call of to-day is, then, for the uplift of character,—the support of industry, education, art, and every means of culture; the encouragement of the higher life; and, above all, the deepening of the religious faith of the people; the rekindling of the spirit, that clothed with her material forces, the great personality of this Nation may fulfil her divine destiny. . . .

In the investment of wealth in honest enterprise and business, lies our path of character. In the investment of wealth in all that goes towards the uplift of the people in education, art, and religion is another path of character. Above all, and first of all, stands the personal life. The immoral rich man is a traitor to himself, to his material as well as spiritual interests. Material prosperity is upon us; it is marching with us. Character must keep step, ay, character must lead. We want great riches; we want also great men.

Wealth*

Andrew Carnegie

The problem of our age is the proper administration of wealth, so that the ties of brotherhood may still bind together the rich and poor in harmonious relationship. The conditions of human life have not only been changed, but revolutionized, within the past few hundred year. . . . The contrast between the palace of the millionaire and the cottage of the laborer with us to-day measures the change which has come with civilization.

This change, however, is not to be deplored, but welcomed as highly beneficial. It is well, nay, essential for the progress of the race, that the houses of some should be homes for all that is highest and best in literature and the arts, and for all the refinements of civilization, rather than that none should be so. Much better this great irregularity than universal squalor. Without wealth there can be no Maecenas. The "good old times" were not good old times. Neither master nor servant was as well situated then as to-day. A relapse to old conditions would be disastrous to both—not the least so to him who serves—and would sweep away civilization with it. But whether the change be for good or ill, it is upon us; beyond our power to alter, and therefore to be accepted and made the best of. It is a waste of time to criticise the inevitable. . . .

The price which society pays for the law of competition, like the price it pays for cheap comforts and luxuries, is also great; but the advantages of this law are also greater still, for it is to this law that we owe our wonderful material development, which brings improved conditions in its train. But, whether the law be benign or not, we must say of the change in the conditions of men to which we have referred: It is here; we cannot evade it; no substitutes for it have been found; and while the law may be sometimes hard for the individual, it is best for the race, because it insures the survival of the fittest in every department. We accept and welcome, therefore, as

*From Andrew Carnegie, "Wealth," *The North American Review*, 148, no. 391, (June 1889), 653–64. Used by permission of the University of Northern Iowa.

conditions to which we must accommodate ourselves, great inequality of environment, the concentration of business, industrial and commercial, in the hands of a few, and the law of competition between these, as being not only beneficial, but essential for the future progress of the race. . . . It is a law, as certain as any of the others named, that men possessed of this peculiar talent for affairs, under the free play of economic forces, must, of necessity, soon be in receipt of more revenue than can be judiciously expended upon themselves; and this law is as beneficial for the race as the others.

We start, then, with a condition of affairs under which the best interests of the race are promoted, but which inevitably gives wealth to the few. Thus far, accepting conditions as they exist, the situation can be surveyed and pronounced good. The question then arises,—and, if the foregoing be correct, it is the only question with which we have to deal,—What is the proper mode of administering wealth after the laws upon which civilization is founded have thrown it into the hands of the few? And it is of this question that I believe I offer the true solution. It will be understood that *fortunes* are here spoken of, not moderate sums saved by many years of effort, the returns from which are required for the comfortable maintenance and education of families. This is not *wealth,* but only *competence,* which it should be the aim of all to acquire.

There are but three modes in which surplus wealth can be disposed of. It can be left to the families of the decedents; or it can be bequeathed for public purposes; or, finally, it can be administered during their lives by its possessors. Under the first and second modes most of the wealth of the world that has reached the few has hitherto been applied. Let us in turn consider each of these modes. The first is the most injudicious. . . . Why should men leave great fortunes to their children? If this is done from affection, is it not misguided affection? Observation teaches that, generally speaking, it is not well for the children that they should be so burdened. Neither is it well for the state. Beyond providing for the wife and daughters moderate sources of income, and very modest allowances indeed, if any, for the sons, men may well hesitate, for it is no longer questionable that great sums bequeathed oftener work more for the injury than for the good of the recipients. Wise men will soon conclude that, for the best interests of the members of their families and of the state, such bequests are an improper use of their means. . . .

As to the second mode, that of leaving wealth at death for public uses, it may be said that this is only a means for the disposal of wealth, provided a man is content to wait until he is dead before it becomes of much good in the world. Knowledge of the results of legacies bequeathed is not calculated to inspire the brightest hopes of much posthumous good being accomplished. The cases are not a few in which the real object sought by the testator is not attained, nor are they few in which his real wishes are thwarted. In many cases the bequests are so used as to become only monuments of his folly. It is well to remember that it requires the exercise of not less ability than that which acquired the wealth to use it so as to be really beneficial to the community. . . .

There remains, then, only one mode of using great fortunes; but in this we have the true antidote for the temporary unequal distribution of wealth, the reconciliation of the rich and the poor—a reign of harmony—another ideal, differing, indeed, from that of the Communist in requiring only the further evolution of existing conditions, not the total overthrow of our civilization. It is founded upon the present most intense individualism, and the race is prepared to put it in practice by degrees whenever it pleases. Under its sway we shall have an ideal state, in which the surplus wealth of the few will become, in the best sense, the property of the many, because administered for the common good, and this wealth, passing through the hands of the few, can be made a much more potent force for the elevation of our race than if it had been distributed in small sums to the people themselves. Even the poorest can be made to see this, and to agree that great sums gathered by some of their fellow-citizens and spent for the public purposes, from which the masses reap the principal benefit, are more valuable to them than if scattered among them through the course of many years in trifling amounts. . . .

Poor and restricted are our opportunities in this life; narrow our horizon; our best work most imperfect; but rich men should be thankful for one inestimable boon. They have it in their power during their lives to busy themselves in organizing benefactions from which the masses of their fellows will derive lasting advantage, and thus dignify their own lives. The highest life is probably reached, not by such imitation of the life of Christ as Count Tolstoi gives us, but, while animated by Christ's spirit, by recognizing the changed conditions of this age, and adopting modes of expressing this spirit suitable to the changed conditions under which we live; still laboring for the good of our fellows, which was the essence of his life and teaching, but laboring in a different manner.

This, then, is held to be the duty of the man of Wealth: First, to set an example of modest, unostentatious living, shunning display or extravagance; to provide moderately for the legitimate wants of those dependent upon him; and after doing so to consider all surplus revenues which come to him simply as trust funds, which he is called upon to administer, and strictly bound as a matter of duty to administer in the manner which, in his judgment, is best calculated to produce the most beneficial results for the community—the man of wealth thus becoming the mere agent and trustee for his poorer brethren, bringing to their service his superior wisdom, experience, and ability to administer, doing for them better than they would or could do for themselves. . . .

Thus is the problem of Rich and Poor to be solved. The laws of accumulation will be left free: the laws of distribution free. Individualism will continue, but the millionaire will be but a trustee for the poor; intrusted for a season with a great part of the increased wealth of the community, but administering it for the community far better than it could or would have done for itself. The best minds will thus have reached a stage in the development of the race in which it is clearly seen that there is no mode of disposing of surplus wealth creditable to thoughtful and earnest men whose hands it flows save by using it year by year for the general good. This day already dawns. But a little while, and although, without incurring the pity of their fellows, men may die sharers in great business enterprises from which their capital cannot be or has not been withdrawn, and is left chiefly at death for public uses, yet the man who dies leaving behind him millions of available wealth, which was his to administer during life, will pass away "unwept, unhonored, and unsung," no matter to what uses he leaves the dross which he cannot take with him. Of such as these the public verdict will then be: "The man who dies thus rich dies disgraced."

Such, in my opinion, is the true Gospel concerning Wealth, obedience to which is destined some day to solve the problem of the Rich and the Poor, and the bring "Peace on earth, among men Good-Will."

DISCUSSION QUESTIONS

1. What was the relationship between nineteenth-century laissez-faire capitalism and social Darwinism?
2. What was the nature of individual rights according to Sumner?
3. What dangers does laissez faire pose for government?
4. Who is entitled to wealth and for what purposes?
5. Would the abuses inherent in laissez-faire economics outweigh the benefits of economic growth in the contemporary period?

Chapter 8

THE AGE OF CHANGE

The post–Civil War period was denoted not only by advances in production capabilities, but a renewed belief in the supremacy of the individual in the face of uncontrolled power exerted by the money monopoly. Writing of their power in 1869 regarding the Albany & Susquehanna Railroad, Charles Francis Adams, Jr., concluded, "these modern potentates have declared war, negotiated peace, reduced courts, legislatures, and sovereign States to an unqualified obedience to their will, disturbed trade, agitated the currency, imposed taxes, and, boldly setting both law and public opinion at defiance, have freely exercised many other attributes of sovereignty."[1] The reform movements of the period rejected claims that individual liberty and good government were created by the wealthy. Instead, individuals were seen to possess certain natural rights which could not be voided by the potentates simply because of the ownership of property. Anderson noted in this regard that the reform movement was composed of fundamentalists and revisionists.[2]

Fundamentalists like Edward Bellamy and Eugene Debs rejected the idea of capitalism and sought to reorganize the economic sector so equality would exist in terms of outcome. Equality of opportunity, as denoted by the

[1]Charles Francis Adams, Jr., "An Erie Raid," *The North American Review*, 112, no. 231 (April 1871), 242. Used by permission of the University of Northern Iowa.

[2]Thornton Anderson, ed., *Jacobson's Development of American Political Thought*, 2nd ed. (New York: Appleton-Century-Crofts, Inc., 1961), p. 477.

waste produced by capitalism, was the reason for the inequality in a land of plenty according to Bellamy in *Looking Backward*.

> The wastes which resulted from leaving the conduct of industry to irresponsible individuals, wholly without mutual understanding or concert, were mainly four: first, the waste by mistaken undertakings; second, the waste from the competition and mutual hostility of those engaged in industry; third, the waste by periodic gluts and crises, with the consequent interruptions of industry; fourth, the waste from idle capital and labor, at all times. Any one of these four great leaks, were all the others stopped, would suffice to make the difference between wealth and poverty on the part of a nation.[3]

In place of capitalism Bellamy proposed the idea of national socialism as the means of utilizing the available resources for the benefit of the entire population. National socialism meant government ownership of industry and the regulation of production in order to eliminate waste. The result would be material abundance for all Americans. Bellamy's rejection of capitalism was paralleled by Eugene Debs, president of the American Railroad Union, who was especially critical of the moneyed monopoly.

> As long as a relatively few men own the railroads, the telegraph, the telephone, own the oil fields and the gas fields and the steel mills and the sugar refineries and the leather tanneries—own, in short, the sources and means of life—they will corrupt our politics, they will enslave the working class, they will impoverish and debase society, they will do all things that are needful to perpetuate their power as the economic masters and the political rulers of the people. Not until these great agencies are owned and operated by the people can the people hope for any material improvement in their social condition.[4]

To Debs, private property was a form of theft in that the owners of industry were able to live securely and dominate the population through their commanding economic position as well as their manipulation of political leaders. Debs desired to reform the system through the popular election of socialist candidates who would end the inequalities caused by artificial property through the nationalization of major industries. Fundamentalists such as Bellamy and Debs regarded capitalism as depriving society of the prosperity which was all around it and saw public ownership as the only means of restoring what rightfully belonged to the people.

In contrast, revisionists embraced capitalism but concluded changes were required to control its negative aspects. The revisionist attitude was generally dominated by the Populist Party and the Progressive movement.

---

[3]Edward Bellamy, *Looking Backward: 2000–1887*, in Thornton Anderson *Jacobson's Development of Political Thought*, (New York: Appleton-Century-Crofts, Inc., 1961), p. 528.

[4]Eugene V. Debs, *Writings and Speeches of Eugene V. Debs*, ed. Joseph M. Bernstein (New York: Hermitage Press, Inc., 1948), pp. 298–99.

These organizations arose in succession between 1870 and 1920 as counterweights to the triumph of democracy and fundamentalist reformers.

The Populist Party appeared largely as a western and southern agrarian backlash to northern industrialism. In the aftermath of the Civil War, farmers were reduced to virtual slavery by the crop-lien system in which crops were signed over to local merchants in exchange for merchandise. At harvest time, the farmer would seek to settle the debt, often to learn the crop was insufficient. The merchant would offer to carry the debt for another year in exchange for the next crop, but ultimately farmers had to sign over their land to settle accounts. The crop-lien system was the means of operating because of low agricultural prices and the fees charged by bankers, railroads, and grain elevators.[5] The Populist Party arose as an attempt to counter the influence of the wealthy few.

Key among the theoreticians of Populism was Henry Demarest Lloyd. Lloyd concluded that laissez faire had forced Americans to follow the self-interest of the few resulting in the destruction of the rights and abilities of the many. Whereas individuals such as Sumner and Carnegie championed the individual's freedom to achieve for self and community, Lloyd defined capitalism as letting "the individual do what the individual can do best, and also to let the community do what the community can do best."[6] In explaining why government was able to take on this responsibility, Lloyd concluded, "men have become so intelligent, so responsive and responsible, so cooperative, that they can be intrusted in great masses with the care of vast properties owned entirely by others and with the operation of complicated processes."[7] The potentates of the period were not necessarily endowed to promote the well-being of society, for their motivation was basically to provide for their own comfort. Lloyd was thus a critic of unrestrained laissez-faire capitalism as well as government ownership of property. Government's purpose was to act as a moderator for the well-being of the general population and to protect private property.

Populist candidates sought elected office in order to make the economic system favorable for the farmers. In their 1892 convention, the premise of the Populist platform was that "wealth belongs to him who creates it," an idea consistent with Jackson's rugged individualism.[8]

> The Omaha platform specifically called for the free and unlimited coinage of silver at the ratio of 16 to 1, a currency of at least $50 per person in circulation, a graduated income tax, postal savings banks, federal ownership of telegraphs and railroads, . . . reclamation of lands held by railroads and other corpora-

[5]Sean Dennis Cashman, *America in the Gilded Age*, 2nd ed. (New York: New York University Press, 1988), pp. 291–92.

[6]Anderson, *Jacobson's Development*, p. 480.

[7]Ibid., p. 481.

[8]Cashman, *America*, p. 306.

tions for speculation (as well as) . . . immigration restriction, an eight-hour day on government works, an end to the use of injunctions against labor, and the outlawing of the Pinkerton mercenaries. . . .[9]

Some of these ideas were presented by Lyman Trumbull, who in 1894 was seen as a likely Populist candidate for the U.S. Senate from Illinois. However, election of Populist candidates was often to no avail when other branches were controlled by Republicans or Democrats, or when one of the major parties demanded concessions for its support.[10]

The free silver debate polarized American politics during the elections of 1896 and 1900. Populists saw the limited supply of gold as favoring industrialists at the expense of farmers and thus demanded an expansion of the money supply through silver coinage. Indicative of the Populist view was Luman Frank Baum's novel *The Wonderful Wizard of Oz* in 1900. According to the story, Dorothy (representing the common man) joins forces with the Scarecrow (midwestern farmers), the Tin Woodsman (urban workers), and the Cowardly Lion (William Jennings Bryan). They journey on the yellow brick road (the gold standard) to the Emerald City (Washington), but are deceived by the Wizard (the president) and attacked by the Wicked Witch of the East (eastern bankers). Working together, the Wicked Witch was defeated and Dorothy used the silver slippers (the silver standard) to gain freedom.[11] The political implication was that the unity of farmers and workers was necessary to achieve elected office and make their goals national policy.

Free silver became a central component of the 1896 Democratic Party platform under the leadership of William Jennings Bryan. Bryan argued that the limited money supply was discriminatory against workers and farmers because it prevented natural property owners from prospering. During the platform debate Bryan stated,

> Having behind us the producing masses of this nation and the world, supported by the commercial interests, the laboring interests, and the toilers everywhere, we will answer their demand for a gold standard by saying to them: You shall not press down upon the brow of labor this crown of thorns, you shall not crucify mankind upon a cross of gold.[12]

Ultimately, the Populist Party was split by the silver issue. Some joined the Democratic Party, seeing it as the only means to make the Pop-

---

[9]Ibid., p. 306.

[10]Ibid., p. 309.

[11]Peter Dreier, *Today Journal*, 14 February 1986, p. 11, in Kenneth Janda, Jeffrey M. Berry, and Jerry Goldman, *The Challenge of Democracy*, 3rd ed. (Boston: Houghton Mifflin Company, 1992), p. 277.

[12]William Jennings Bryan, "Speech Concluding Debate on the Chicago Platform," *The First Battle* (Chicago: W.B. Conkey Company, 1896), p. 206.

ulist Party's goals a reality. In the election of 1896, William Jennings Bryan served as the candidate of both the Democratic and the Populist Parties. After the election of 1896, the Populist Party declined in influence, and virtually disappeared from the political landscape around 1900.

In the following decades, the Progressives dominated the reform movement. Whereas the Populists formed a political party, Progressives belonged to the Republican and Democratic Parties.[13] Progressives were members of the urban middle class, as opposed to farmers of the Populist Party. Both Populists and Progressives saw economic potential being circumscribed by extreme wealth. The Progressive reform agenda was largely conditioned by the belief that changes were necessary to secure the equality of political and economic opportunity. Central to this goal was limiting the power of the money monopoly. As Cashman concluded, "Progressives wanted to limit the power of big business, to make the political system more representative, democratic, and impartial, and to extend the role of government in order to protect the public interest and to ameliorate poverty and social distress."[14] To enhance democracy, Progressives supported changes in the political system. Robert M. LaFollette, a one-time Progressive nominee for president, sought to bring government under the control of the electorate by devices like "direct election of senators, the direct primary, the initiative, the referendum, and the recall."[15]

During the first decades of the twentieth century, Progressives specifically relied on the power of the presidency. Theodore Roosevelt's square deal expanded the regulatory power of the government, particularly in the areas of transportation, food inspection, and conservation, while ensuring that American business continued to have a primary role for societal advancement.[16] But the most important development was the ascendancy of Woodrow Wilson to the presidency in 1912. Wilson supported the idea of laissez-faire capitalism, but saw the trusts as stifling individual creativity and American society. Laws were thus required to control the economic and political power of the trusts in order to eliminate the barriers to competition. In seeking this goal, Wilson asked and answered the following question.

> What is it that is wrong with the business of this country? In the first place, certain monopolies, or virtual monopolies, have been established in ways which have been unrighteous and have been maintained in ways that were unrighteous; and have been used and intended for monopolistic purposes. In

[13]A Progressive Party was formed in 1912 with Theodore Roosevelt as its nominee. John W. Caughey and Ernest R. May, *A History of the United States* (Chicago: Rand McNally, 1964), p. 421.

[14]Cashman, *America*, p. 350.

[15]Anderson, *Jacobson's Development*, p. 484.

[16]Caughey and May, *A History*, p. 401.

the second place, the business of the country has come near to being regulated, at one crisis and another, by what is no business at all, but the mere manipulation of those securities which represent business. The chief things that have gone wrong with the business of the country have not been based upon monopolistic undertakings at all, but have been based upon such things as over-capitalization and the foisting upon the public, that does not know the process by which this thing has been done, of securities that were not worth the purchase price that was paid for them. . . .[17]

According to Anderson, Wilson's view of government and business was largely conditioned by the belief that "a trust does not bring efficiency to the aid of business; it buys efficiency out of business."[18] Thus the breakup of the trusts was seen as producing competition and progress as well as preventing political equality from being subverted by economic inequality.

An equally important change was the expansion of the electorate by women's suffrage. Various organizations had worked to secure women the right to vote since before the Civil War, including the Congressional Union for Woman Suffrage and the National American Woman Suffrage Association. During the nineteenth and early twentieth centuries, Susan B. Anthony and Anna Howard Shaw were at the forefront of this movement. Their basic argument was that women's suffrage was necessary for a truly democratic society. Shaw wrote in 1914,

Our demand is suffrage for women on the same terms as for men. . . . The men of this country have established and maintained what they call a democracy. The basic idea of a democracy is, to say, that it shall be a government of the people, by the people, for the people. . . . But "people" has been translated to mean male citizens only. We ask, therefore, not that the established government be changed but that it shall be held to apply to women citizens as well as to men citizens.[19]

By August 1920, the Nineteenth Amendment was approved by the states providing citizenship for women and establishing their ability to participate in national politics.

At the same time, the U.S. sought to resolve issues of economic and political rights it began assuming a new international role. New philosophies suggested that the U.S was destined to assume a global leadership role. Alfred Mahan in *The Influence of Sea Power on History, 1660–1789,* wrote that great power status was achieved by the geographic location and national commitment of nations. A more common theme suggested that the

---

[17]Woodrow Wilson, "The Government and Business," *The Papers of Woodrow Wilson,* eds. Arthur Link, et al (Princeton, NJ: Princeton University Press, 1974), XVIII, 40.

[18]Anderson, *Jacobson's Development,* p. 483.

[19]Anna Howard Shaw, "Equal Suffrage—A Problem of Political Justice," *Annals of the American Academy of Political Science,* 56 (November 1914), 94. Reprinted by permission of Sage Publications, Inc.

U.S. was destined to control the world because of the political dominance of whites and the moral supremacy of Christianity. This view was evident in John Fiske's idea of the "manifest destiny" of Anglo-Saxons, John W. Burgess's Columbia University lectures on the superiority of "Anglo-Teutonic" people, and the Reverend Josiah Strong who argued Christianity and abstinence from liquor and tobacco would empower Anglo-Saxons to civilize the world.[20] These moral ideas can be seen to have laid the foundation for the American colonial empire. In 1899, the Spanish-American War ended with Spain's surrender of Guam, Puerto Rico, and the Philippines to the U.S., as well as Cuban independence. By 1903, the U.S. goal of building the Panama Canal was achieved through its support for Panama's succession from Columbia when the latter refused to endorse the project. These experiences supported the Roosevelt corollary to the Monroe Doctrine.

> Chronic wrongdoing, or an impotence which results in a general loosening of the ties of civilized society, may in America, as elsewhere, ultimately require intervention by some civilized nation, and in the Western Hemisphere the adherence of the United States to the Monroe Doctrine may force the United States, however reluctantly, in flagrant cases of such wrongdoing or impotence, to the exercise of an international police power.[21]

Traditional American diplomacy was further changed when President Wilson amended the Roosevelt corollary to include guarantees for constitutional democracy.[22]

America's international spirit was put to the test in World War I, for the U.S. had historically followed an isolationist policy. In 1917, the U.S. entered an alliance with foreign powers to fight a war. George Kirchwey argued this war was necessary in order for U.S. idealism to establish the American peace internationally.

> For the first time in human history a great nation has gone to war, has pledged all its power and resources, has staked its very existence for a purely ideal end. As the President has truly said, "We have no selfish ends to serve. We desire no conquest, no dominion. We seek no indemnities for ourselves, no material compensation for the sacrifices we shall freely make. We are but one of the champions of the rights of mankind. We shall be satisfied when those rights have been made as secure as the faith and the freedom of the nation can make them."[23]

---

[20]Caughey and May, *A History*, pp. 348–49.

[21]Ibid., pp. 389–90.

[22]Ibid., p. 436.

[23]George W. Kirchwey, "Pax Americana," *Annals of the American Academy of Political and Social Science* 72 (July 1917), 42. Reprinted by permission of Sage Publications, Inc.

Individuals like Kirchwey regarded World War I as the opportunity to reformulate international politics in terms of American ideas of democracy, freedom, and justice.

To others, World War I threatened the essence of American political culture, for the capital-intensive nature of modern warfare demanded that individual liberty and private property be subject to government needs. Two of the most powerful critics were William Jennings Bryan and Randolph Bourne. Secretary of State Bryan warned of the danger posed by loaning money to the Allies and letting Americans travel on Allied ships.[24] These actions had the potential for tying the U.S. to the Allied side by giving Americans a financial interest in who won the war and by forcing the U.S. government to protest any loss of American lives. Bourne, whom Beitzinger called "perhaps the most articulate dissenting voice in the war years," argued the war would destroy the American reform movement for it would force the regimentation of American life.[25] The premise of Bourne's philosophy was that human desire and energy were channeled by society and the state. In wartime, human creativity must be restricted so as to turn individuals into tools for the state's survival. According to Beitzinger, Bourne held that the state was "the organization of the herd to act offensively or defensively against another herd similarly organized."[26] Bourne's theory was vindicated when the U.S. entered World War I. Public dissension was regulated by Congress through the Espionage Act of 1917 and the Sedition Act of 1918. Leading opponents such as Eugene Debs were imprisoned. National boards were created to control food and industrial production in terms of the amount of goods produced, their cost, how much labor and management would be paid and which orders would be filled.[27] The American government assumed unprecedented authority.

In the following readings a broad range of subjects are presented which appeared in American politics during the period from 1880 to 1920. Works by Edward Bellamy, Lyman Trumball, William Jennings Bryan, Woodrow Wilson, Anna H. Shaw, George W. Kirchwey, and Randolph Bourne detail the major changes which occurred in American political theory, especially in regard to the relationship of individual rights, property, and governmental authority.

---

[24]From *The American Political Tradition* by Richard Hofstadter. Copyright 1948 by Alfred A. Knopf Inc. and renewed by Beatrice Hofstadter. Reprinted by permission of the publisher, pp. 260–61.

[25]Beitzinger, *A History*, p. 513.

[26]Ibid., p. 514.

[27]Jeanette P. Nichols and Roy F. Nichols, *The Growth of American Democracy* (New York: D. Appleton-Century Company, 1939), pp. 625–29.

Looking Backward: 2000–1887*

Edward Bellamy

"As I said," responded the doctor, "the subject is too large to discuss at length now, but if you are really interested to know the main criticisms which we moderns make on your industrial system as compared with our own, I can touch briefly on some of them.

"The wastes which resulted from leaving the conduct of industry to irresponsible individuals, wholly without mutual understanding or concert, were mainly four: first, the waste by mistaken undertakings; second, the waste from the competition and mutual hostility of those engaged in industry; third, the waste by periodical gluts and crises, with the consequent interruptions of industry; fourth, the waste from idle capital and labor, at all times. Any one of these four great leaks, were all the others stopped, would suffice to make the difference between wealth and poverty on the part of a nation.

"Take the waste by mistaken undertakings, to begin with. In your day the production of commodities being without concert or organization, there was no means of knowing just what demand there was for any class of products, or what was the rate of supply. Therefore, any enterprise by a private capitalist was always a doubtful experiment. The projector having no general view of the field of industry and consumption, such as our government has, could never be sure either what the people wanted, or what arrangements other capitalists were making to supply them. In view of this, we are not surprised to learn that the chances were considered several to one in favor of the failure of any given business enterprise, and that it was common for persons who at last succeeded in making a hit to have failed repeatedly. . . .

"The next of the great wastes was that from competition. The field of industry was a battlefield as wide as the world, in which the workers wasted, in assailing one another, energies which, if expended in concerted effort, as to-day, would have enriched all. As for mercy or quarter in this warfare, there was absolutely no suggestion of it. To deliberately enter a field of business and destroy the enterprises of those who had occupied it previously, in order to plant one's own enterprise on their ruins, was an achievement which never failed to command popular admiration. . . . Now nothing

---

*From Edward Bellamy, *Looking Backward: 2000-1887* in Thornton Anderson, *Jacobson's Development of American Political Thought*, (New York: Appleton-Century-Crofts, Inc., 1961), pp. 528–33.

about your age is, at first sight, more astounding to a man of modern times than the fact that men engaged in the same industry, instead of fraternizing as comrades and co-laborers to a common end, should have regarded each other as rivals and enemies to be throttled and overthrown. . . . The producers of the nineteenth century were not, like ours, working together for the maintenance of the community, but each solely for his own maintenance at the expense of the community. If, in working to this end, he at the same time increased the aggregate wealth, that was merely incidental. It was just as feasible and as common to increase one's private hoard by practices injurious to the general welfare. One's worst enemies were necessarily those of his own trade, for, under your plan of making private profit the motive of production, a scarcity of the article he produced was what each particular producer desired. It was for his interest that no more of it should be produced than he himself could produce. To secure this consummation as far as circumstances permitted, by killing off and discouraging those engaged in his line of industry, was his constant effort. When he had killed off all he could, his policy was to combine with those he could not kill, and convert their mutual warfare into a warfare upon the public at large by cornering the market, as I believe you used to call it, and putting up prices to the highest point people would stand before going without the goods. The day dream of the nineteenth century producer was to gain absolute control of the supply of some necessity of life, so that he might keep the public at the verge of starvation, and always command famine prices for what he supplied. . . . I assure you that the wonder with us is, not that the world did not get rich under such a system, but that it did not perish outright from want. This wonder increases as we go on to consider some of the other prodigious wastes that characterized it.

"Apart from the waste of labor and capital by misdirected industry, and that from the constant bloodletting of your industrial warfare, your system was liable to periodical convulsions, overwhelming alike the wise and unwise, the successful cut-throat as well as his victim. I refer to the business crises at intervals of five to ten years, which wrecked the industries of the nation, prostrating all weak enterprises and crippling the strongest, and were followed by long periods, often of many years, of so-called dull times, during which the capitalists slowly regathered their dissipated strength while the laboring classes starved and rioted. Then would ensue another brief season of prosperity, followed in turn by another crisis and the ensuing years of exhaustion. As commerce developed, making the nations mutually dependent, these crises became world-wide, while the obstinacy of the ensuing state of collapse increased with the area affected by the convulsions, and the consequent lack of rallying centres. In proportion as the industries of the world multiplied and became complex, and the volume of capital involved was increased, these business cataclysms became more frequent, till, in the latter part of the nineteenth century, there were two years of bad times to one of good, and the system of industry, never before so extended or so imposing, seemed in danger of collapsing by its own weight. . . .

"So far as considering the causes of the trouble inherent in their industrial system, your contemporaries were certainly correct. They were in its very basis, and must needs become more and more maleficent as the business fabric grew in size and complexity. One of these causes was the lack of any common control of the different industries, and the consequent impossibility of their orderly and coordinate development. It inevitably resulted from this lack that they were continually getting out of step with one another and out of relation with the demand. . . .

"A cause, also inherent in your system, which often produced and always terribly aggravated crises, was the machinery of money and credit. Money was essential when production was in many private hands, and buying and selling was necessary to secure what one wanted. It was, however, open to the obvious objection of substituting for food, clothing, and other things a merely conventional representative of them. The confusion of mind which this favored, between goods and their representative, led the way to the credit system and its prodigious illusions. Already accustomed to accept money for commodities, the people next accepted promises for money, and ceased to look at all behind the representative for the thing represented. Money was a sign of real commodities, but credit was but the sign of a sign. There was a natural limit to gold and silver, that is, money proper, but none to credit, and the result was that the volume of credit, that is, the promises of money, ceased to bear any ascertainable proportion to the money, still less to the commodities, actually in existence.... The great extension of the credit system was a characteristic of the latter part of the nineteenth century, and accounts largely for the almost incessant business crises which marked that period. Perilous as credit was, you could not dispense with its use, for, lacking any national or other public organization of the capital of the country, it was the only means you had for concentrating and directing it upon industrial enterprises. It was in this way a most potent means for exaggerating the chief peril of the private enterprise system of industry by enabling particular industries to absorb disproportionate amounts of the disposable capital of the country, and thus prepare disaster. Business enterprises were always vastly in debt for advances of credit, both to one another and to the banks and capitalists, and the prompt withdrawal of this credit at the first sign of a crisis was generally the precipitating cause of it.

"It was the misfortune of your contemporaries that they had to cement their business fabric with a material which an accident might at any moment turn into an explosive. They were in the plight of a man building a house with dynamite for mortar, for credit can be compared with nothing else. . . .

"Your business crises, Mr. West," continued the doctor, "like either of the great wastes I mentioned before, were enough, alone, to have kept your noses to the grindstone forever; but I have still to speak of one other great cause of your poverty, and that was the idleness of a great part of your capital and labor. With us it is the business of the administration to keep in constant employment every ounce of available capital and labor in the country. In your day there was no general control of either capital or labor, and a large part of both failed to find employment. `Capital,' you used to say, `is naturally timid,' and it would certainly have been reckless if it had not been timid in an epoch when there was a large preponderance of probability that any particular business venture would end in failure. . . . But for the same reason that the amount of capital employed at times of special insecurity was far less than at times of somewhat greater security, a very large proportion was never employed at all, because the hazard of business was always very great in the best of times.

"It should be also noted that the great amount of capital always seeking employment where tolerable safety could be insured terribly embittered the competition between capitalists when a promising opening presented itself. The idleness of capital, the result of its timidity, of course meant the idleness of labor in corresponding degree. Moreover, every change in the adjustments of business, every slightest alteration in the condition of commerce or manufactures, not to speak of the innumerable business failures that took place yearly, even in the best of times, were constantly throwing a multitude of men out of employment for periods of weeks or months, or even years. . . . Could there conceivably be a more conclusive demonstration of the imbecility of the system of private enterprise as a method for enriching a nation than the fact that, in an age of such general poverty and want of everything, capitalists had to throttle one another to find a safe chance to invest their capital and workmen rioted and burned because they could find no work to do?

"Now, Mr. West," continued Dr. Leete, "I want you to bear in mind that these points of which I have been speaking indicate only negatively the advantages of the national organization of industry by showing certain fatal defects and prodigious imbecilities of the systems of private enterprise which are not found in it. These alone, you must admit, would pretty well explain why the nation is so much richer than in your day. . . .

Speech at a Populist Meeting*

Lyman Trumbull

For ages the money power has controlled legislation the world over, and, I am sorry to say, has exercised a controlling influence in our land for many years. Laws which open the door to large fortunes by devise, by inheritance, or by speculation, have no tendency to promote the happiness of the people at large, and often not even the happiness of those for whose benefit they are made. If the accumulation of vast fortunes goes on for another generation with the same accelerated rapidity as during the present, the wealth of this country will soon be consolidated in the hands of a few corporations and individuals to as great an extent as the landed interests of Great Britain now are. Neither strikes of the laboring classes, which array against them the money power and the governmental power which controls, nor the governmental control of the great railroad and other corporations will remove the existing conflict between labor and capital, which has its foundation in unjust laws, enabling the few to accumulate vast estates and live in luxurious ease, while the great masses are doomed to incessant toil, penury and want. What is needed is the removal of the cause which permits the accumulation of the wealth of the country in few hands, and this can only be peaceably brought about by a change of the laws of property.

Of late years United States judges have assumed jurisdiction they would not have dared to exercise in the earlier days of the Republic. They now claim the right to determine the extent of their jurisdiction and enforce such orders as they think proper to make. These Federal judges, like sappers and miners, have for years silently and steadily enlarged their jurisdiction, and unless checked by legislation they will soon undermine the very pillars of the Constitution and bury the liberties of the people beneath their ruin. To vest any man or set of men with authority to determine the extent of their powers and to enforce their decrees is of the very essence of despotism. Federal judges now claim the right to take possession of and run the railroads of the country, to issue injunctions without notice, and to punish for contempt by fine and imprisonment any one who disputes their authority. It is to be hoped that Congress, when it meets, will put some check upon Federal judges in assuming control of railroads and issuing blanket injunctions and punishing people for contempt of their assumed authority. If this Congress does not do it I trust the people will see to it that Representatives are chosen hereafter who will.

*From Lyman Trumbull, "Speech at a Populist Meeting," *Public Opinion*, XVII, no. 29 (October 18, 1894), 687–88.

Speech Concluding Debate on the Chicago Platform*

William Jennings Bryan

Mr. Chairman and Gentlemen of the Convention: I would be presumptuous, indeed, to present myself against the distinguished gentlemen to whom you have listened if this were a mere measuring of abilities; but this is not a contest between persons. The humblest citizen in all the land, when clad in the armor of a righteous cause, is stronger than all the hosts of error. I come to speak to you in defense of a cause as holy as the cause of liberty— the cause of humanity.

Never before in the history of this country has there been witnessed such a contest as that through which we have just passed. Never before in the history of American politics has a great issue been fought out as this issue has been, by the voters of a great party. On the fourth of March, 1895, a few Democrats, most of them members of Congress, issued an address to the Democrats of the nation, asserting that the money question was the paramount issue of the hour; declaring that a majority of the Democratic party had the right to control the action of the party on this paramount issue; and concluding with the request that the believers in the free coinage of silver in the Democratic party should organize, take charge of, and control the policy of the Democratic party. . . .

When you (turning to the gold delegates) come before us and tell us that we are about to disturb your business interests, we reply that you have disturbed our business interests by your course.

We say to you that you have made the definition of a business man too limited in its application. The man who is employed for wages is as much a business man as his employer; the attorney in a country town is as much a business man as the corporation counsel in a great metropolis; the merchant at the cross-roads store is as much a business man as the merchant of New York; the farmer who goes forth in the morning and toils all day—who begins in the spring and toils all summer—and who by the application of brain and muscle to the natural resources of the country creates wealth, is as much a business man as the man who goes upon the board of trade and bets upon the price of grain; the miners who go down a thousand feet into the earth or climb two thousand feet upon the cliffs, and bring forth from their hiding places the precious metals to be poured into the channels of trade are as much business men as the few financial mag-

---

*From William Jennings Bryan, "Speech Concluding Debate on the Chicago Platform," *The First Battle* (Chicago: W.B. Conkey Company, 1896), pp. 199–209.

nates who, in a back room, corner the money of the world. We come to speak for this broader class of business men.

Ah, my friends, we say not one word against those who live upon the Atlantic coast, but the hardy pioneers who have braved all the dangers of the wilderness, who have made the desert to blossom as the rose—the pioneers away out there (pointing to the West), who rear their children near to Nature's heart, where they can mingle their voices with the voices of the birds—out there where they have erected schoolhouses for the education of their young, churches where they praise their Creator, and cemeteries where rest the ashes of their dead—these people, we say, are as deserving of the consideration of our party as any people in this country. It is for these that we speak. We do not come as aggressors. Our war is not a war of conquest; we are fighting in the defense of our homes, our families, and posterity. We have petitioned, and our petitions have been scorned; we have entreated, and our entreaties have been disregarded; we have begged, and they have mocked when our calamity came. We beg no longer; we entreat no more; we petition no more. We defy them. . . .

They tell us that this platform was made to catch votes. We reply to them that changing conditions make new issues; that the principles upon which Democracy rests are as everlasting as the hills, but that they must be applied to new conditions as they arise. Conditions have arisen, and we are here to meet those conditions. They tell us that the income tax ought not to be brought in here; that it is a new idea. They criticise us for our criticism of the Supreme Court of the United States. My friends, we have not criticised; we have simply called attention to what you already know. If you want criticisms, read the dissenting opinions of the court. There you will find criticisms. They say that we passed an unconstitutional law; we deny it. The income tax law was not unconstitutional when it was passed; it was not unconstitutional when it went before the Supreme Court for the first time; it did not become unconstitutional until one of the judges changed his mind, and we cannot be expected to know when a judge will change his mind. The income tax is just. It simply intends to put the burdens of government justly upon the backs of the people. I am in favor of an income tax. When I find a man who is not willing to bear his share of the burdens of the government which protects him, I find a man who is unworthy to enjoy the blessings of a government like ours. . . .

And now, my friends, let me come to the paramount issue. If they ask us why it is that we say more on the money question than we say upon the tariff question, I reply that, if protection has slain its thousands, the gold standard has slain its tens of thousands. If they ask us why we do not embody in our platform all the things that we believe in, we reply that when we have restored the money of the Constitution all other necessary reforms will be possible; but that until this is done there is no other reform that can be accomplished. . . .

We go forth confident that we shall win. Why? Because upon the paramount issue of this campaign there is not a spot of ground upon which the enemy will dare to challenge battle. If they tell us that the gold standard is a good thing, we shall point to their platform and tell them that their platform pledges the party to get rid of the gold standard and substitute bimetallism. If the gold standard is a good thing, why try to get rid of it? I call your attention to the fact that some of the very people who are in this convention today and who tell us that we ought to declare in favor of international bimetallism—thereby declaring that the gold standard is wrong and that the principle of bimetallism is better—these very people four months ago were open and avowed advocates of the gold standard, and were then telling us that we could not legislate two metals together, even with the aid of all the world. If the gold standard is a good thing, we ought to declare in favor of its retention and not in favor of abandoning it; and if the gold standard is a bad thing why should we wait until other nations are willing to help us to let go? Here is the line of battle, and we care not upon which issue they force the fight; we are prepared to meet them on either issue or on both. If they tell us that the gold standard is the standard of civilization, we reply to them that this, the most enlightened of all the nations of the earth, has never declared for a gold standard and that both the great parties this year are declaring against it. If the gold standard is the standard of civilization, why, my friends, should we not have it? If they come to meet us on that issue we can present the history of our nation. More than that; we can tell them that they will search the pages of history in vain to find a single instance where the common people of any land have ever declared themselves in favor of the gold standard. They can find where the holders of fixed investments have declared for a gold standard, but not where the masses have.

Mr. Carlisle said in 1878 that this was a struggle between "the idle holders of idle capital" and "the struggling masses, who produce the wealth and pay the taxes of the country;" and, my friends, the question we are to decide is: Upon which side will the Democratic party fight; upon the side of "the idle holders of idle capital" or upon the side of "the struggling masses?" That is the question which the party must answer first, and then it must be answered by each individual hereafter. The sympathies of the Democratic party, as shown by the platform, are on the side of the struggling masses who have ever been the foundation of the Democratic party. There are two ideas of government. There are those who believe that, if you will only legislate to make the well-to-do prosperous their prosperity will leak through on those below. The Democratic idea, however, has been that if you legislate to make the masses prosperous, their prosperity will find its way up through every class which rests upon them.

You come to us and tell us that the great cities are in favor of the gold standard; we reply that the great cities rest upon our broad and fertile prairies. Burn down your cities and leave our farms, and your cities will spring up again as if by magic; but destroy our farms and the grass will grow in the streets of every city in the country.

My friends, we declare that this nation is able to legislate for its own people on every question, without waiting for the aid or consent of any other nation on earth; and upon that issue we expect to carry every State in the Union. I shall not slander the inhabitants of the fair State of Massachusetts nor the inhabitants of the State of New York by saying that, when they are confronted with the proposition, they will declare that this nation is not able to attend to its own business. It is the issue of 1776 over again. Our ancestors, when but three millions in number, had the courage to declare their political independence of every other nation; shall we, their descendants, when we have grown to seventy millions, declare that we are less independent than our forefathers? No, my friends, that will never be the verdict of our people. Therefore, we care not upon what lines the battle is fought. If they say bimetallism is good, but that we cannot have it until other nations help us, we reply that, instead of having a gold standard because England has, we will restore bimetallism, and then let England have bimetallism because the United States has it. If they dare to come out in the open field and defend the gold standard as a good thing, we will fight them to the uttermost. Having behind us the producing masses of this nation and the world, supported by the commercial interests, the laboring interests, and the toilers everywhere, we will answer their demand for a gold standard by saying to them: You shall not press down upon the brow of labor this crown of thorns, you shall not crucify mankind upon a cross of gold. . . .

The Government and Business*

Woodrow Wilson

. . . We are being governed by many impulses, but we are not being governed by well thought out conclusions. It is certainly a time of excitement, of excited action which is being made more excited by excited speech; and in such a time there is special need that we should take counsel with one another as to what it is wise to do . . .

A perfect mania for regulation has taken hold of us. We have got in a fever of activity with regard to legislation; and I suspect that after having

*From Woodrow Wilson, "The Government and Business," The Papers of Woodrow Wilson, eds. Arthur Link, et al (Princeton, NJ: Princeton University Press, 1974), XVIII, 35–51.

acted we shall think; after having attempted a dozen remedies we shall then carefully set our selves down and ascertain whether any of the remedies remedy. It is not the wiser part to ask what it is that we want to remedy and what will be likely to remedy it?

Of course it is no longer debatable that there are a great many things to remedy. It is no longer debatable that a great many practices have sprung up under the modern conditions of business which are very undesirable practices indeed, very demoralizing to the public welfare, and very demoralizing to the men who engage in them—things not founded in righteousness, not founded in fair dealing, not founded in the right interpretation of law. And these things have been done under the cover of corporate organization. They do not seem to have been done so much by individuals as by combinations of individuals, which, in the old phrase, have no bodies to be kicked or souls to de damned—intangible, invisible, multiple persons, given their existence only by the theory of law, and not susceptible to ordinary moral standards.

In fact, we feel that we have lost the wrongdoers in the complex organization of modern business, and, instead of undertaking to find them again, we are undertaking to handle the organizations and not the persons, and so are changing the whole theory and practice of our legal system. For in respect of all things hitherto punishable it has been regarded as the sound theory of the law that the persons responsible should be punished, and not the business of the country. We have been trying to regulate the business when we should have been trying to regulate transactions. We have been trying to regulate the affirmative constructive administrative conduct of business when we should have been discriminating between those transactions which are detrimental to the public welfare and those which are not, seeking to check the one and to let the other go free of restraint. . . .

There is no doubt such a thing as predatory wealth but if wealth were all of it predatory—if every man were preying on every other man, a condition of things would arise which would be a condition of warfare and not of peace, a condition not of organization but of confusion and disorganization. Such a condition has not arisen, but these [there] are undoubtedly bad practices and it is none the less necessary, if we would moralize our business, that we return to a possible basis of morality.

Now morality is never corporate. Morality is never aggregate. The only way you get honest business is from honest men. I know that there are methods by which men cover the uncomfortable emotions of their consciences. I know that men accept in business which is corporate certain compromises which they conceive to have been forced upon them by the action of those with whom they must act in corporate transactions. I know that men salve their consciences by saying it was necessary to do this, that, or the other thing because they had to do it by way of compromise and in combination with others. But in the long run a man's conscience never lies easy under that kind of salve. It [is] necessary for every one of us, sooner or later, to go to bed. It is necessary for every one of us, sooner or later, to put out the light and lie down with our consciences. It is necessary, if men would retain the momentum of their best energy, that they should retain their respect for themselves when they are alone and closeted with their own consciences; and society itself cannot exist upon any other basis. Men know they are not going to be saved from responsibility by those who judge of the essence of the matter by any combination with others. They know they must be judged separately and individually, and there is no valid system of law which can be based upon any other feeling than that.

What I want particularly to point out this evening is this: We are making in our generation a radical choice by choosing between various sorts of practices. We are choosing between opposite sorts of principles. The principle upon which we shall choose our course of action, we of this generation, is a principle which will either retain or alter the character of our government. That is the serious aspect of the whole matter.

I have heard it said that certain kinds of governmental regulations must be adopted in order to stop the drift towards socialism in this country, and yet the very kinds of governmental regulation which are contemplated in such arguments are regulations which are themselves essentially socialistic in principle. After you start a little way on that road it is merely a question of time and choice as to how far you will go upon it. You can not, after you have got on the road, arbitrarily call a halt at any one point upon it. Let me proceed at once and tell you what I mean.

The regulation of the transactions is not socialistic in principle, no matter how far you carry it. If you say that the law shall prohibit such and such transactions, transactions of such and such kinds and classes, that is not socialistic; that has been time out of mind the process of law and is quite possible to be handled by the judicial machinery of the country. But if you propose that the government shall keep its hand on business by way of direct administrative regulation, through the instrumentality of commissions which will have it in their discretion to guide business in this direction or guide it in that, to determine which is best method and practice here, which the best there, you have adopted *in principle* the same thing as government ownership itself. You have not adopted government ownership with candid bravery; but you are on the way towards it. You are saying: Let the private individual have the burden and risk of the active administration, but let the government say what the character of the administration shall be. Let the individual take all the risks, let the individual spend all the money, but let the government say how the business should be conducted.

Now in principle there is no difference whatever between that and government ownership, no difference whatever between the direct regulation of business and the ownership of business enterprises. For the only safe way by which the government can pick its steps is by picking them upon the basis of experience, and the only thing that experience can yield is the revelation, item by item, of the things, the particular transactions, which society wishes to control.

What is it that is wrong with the business of this country? In the first place, certain monopolies, or virtual monopolies, have been established in ways which have been unrighteous and have been maintained in ways that were unrighteous; and have been used and intended for monopolistic purposes. In the second place, the business of the country has come near to being regulated, at one crisis and another, by what is no business at all, but the mere manipulation of those securities which represent business. The chief things that have gone wrong with the business of the country have not been based upon monopolistic undertakings at all, but have been based upon such things as over-capitalization and the foisting upon the public, that does not know the process by which this thing has been done, of securities that were not worth the purchase price that was paid for them. At the same time that purchase price, a perfectly artificial thing in itself, brought millions of dollars into the pockets of men who had managed the unrighteous transaction. Now the men who did these things are not always the men who administer the actual business of the country. In most instances they are not. . . .

What we need just now is a very peculiar thing, which I am afraid we are not very likely to get. We need the advice of very experienced corporation lawyers. What I mean to say is that the men who have stood inside the corporations as counsel and who have been trying to defend those corporations from the action of the law, are, as I know, some of them the chief critics of what our legislation has been. We ought not to heed their criticisms in the least unless they will come forward and say what the legislatures ought to do. They know what has gone wrong if anything has, and they know how to get at it if anybody does.

Now the situation is simply this. If these gentlemen will come forward and disclose the exact nature of such transactions and show the way in which they be limited or prohibited, if they will assist us to distinguish between the transactions which are legitimate and the transactions which are not legitimate, and show us how to make that discrimination in the prohibitions of the law, they will save their corporations from the mob, and will have saved this country from what may be a fatal period of experimentation. Are they going to do it?

I can speak very glibly about the theory of this thing and what ought to be done. But these gentlemen know in detail what is practicable to do and what ought to be done. If I were called upon at this moment to draw up any measure whatever, by way of suggestion, the first thing I would have to do would be to call them in to tell me what the measure ought to be. They know how to discriminate between one kind of transaction and another because they have been trying to steer their corporations on the leeward side of the law, and they know which is the leeward side and which is the windward side. Now I am a lawyer myself, and I haven't very much hope that they will do it. (Laughter). Almost all lawyers are on the defensive. Almost all lawyers think that the thing to do is to "stand pat" and defy the law, and see whether the legislator can do what he wants to do or not; and the reckoning justified by many past experiences is that he won't find a way to do it after all. But, gentlemen, there is blood in the eye of the American people now and they are not going to be stopped from wrecking something if you do not guide them into remedying something. You have the choice between wreckage and remedy.

Now I have a few ideas which are not vague on this subject. I believe that with regard to the administration of corporations it is possible to pick out the individual who is responsible. I do not know of any corporation which cannot itself pick out the person connected with its administration who is responsible when anything goes wrong. And if the corporation itself can pick out the responsible person I am sure the corporation can be induced to disclose the responsible person to the officers of the law. I am sure that if every corporation has in its own mind, in the mind of its own managers and owners, that which will enable it to put its hand on the man responsible for each transaction it can be made to disclose for the benefit of the public the requisite information, so that the officers of the law can find that man; and then you have found your man before the offense—for there is a certain play of hide and seek after the offense. After you have got your information and your fingers pointing to the man, and the transaction prohibited is engaged in, it is easy enough to get your man. . . .

If you undertake the old-fashioned program of finding and punishing the individual, what have you got to do? In the first place, you have got to have public officials who won't be respectors of persons. You must have public officials who will promptly, zealously, and fearlessly execute the law against anybody, no matter what the consequence is—men who will not exempt those whom they may consider serviceable to the community, but will proceed against anybody, in any circumstances, who breaks the law. I am afraid that is not the present situation. We hear of a great many discriminations as between individual and individual. There are many men in this country—I won't say many, but there are several—who are known to be responsible for certain outrageous transactions, against whom no attempt to put the law into operation has been made.

No government can regulate anything, gentlemen, unless that government is of the right sort and is thoroughly trustworthy. I remember talking with a member of a reform club not long ago, a reform club in the city of New York. He said that for twenty years he had been going to Albany to get reform measures passed and that little had been accomplished although many promising measures had been passed; and that he had the humiliating confession to make that, after all those twenty years of effort to get a good government by good legislation, he had found that the only way to get good government was to elect good men to conduct it; that the best laws did not operate successfully unless the best men were put behind them to execute them. . . .

I have been very much interested in the theory of government adduced by certain prominent persons. There is one very prominent person in the United States, for example, who won't trust corporations, but will, to any extent, trust the government of the United States. Now the government of the United States is made up of individuals just as a corporation is, and I have observed that there have been periods when corporations were made up of just as trustworthy persons as the government of the United States. Moreover the corporations have the advantage of understanding their own business. They must understand their own business or go into bankruptcy and the government of the United States has not yet produced a body of geniuses who can understand other people's businesses. . . . Until the government of the United States or the government of a state can understand a complex body, not of one business, but of a number of businesses, conducted by other persons for their profit, better than the persons whose fortunes are embarked in it understand it, they cannot by any discretionary measure justly regulate that business. . . .

Now history is inexorable. History does not indulge populistic parties. History has no atom of encouragement for socialistic processes. History says power, if you accumulate it in governors, will certainly sooner or later become oppressive and impossible to be borne. The only reign under which any self-respecting men can live is the reign, not of authority, but of law— the exact definition alike of his rights and of his obligations; definitions enforced by men whose object and interest are not political but judicial, who determine without administrative bias what is the true and ancient and lasting intent of the law of the land. The twenty-ninth clause of Magna Carta is just as permanent as any law of human nature, because it is founded in human nature.

There is no liberty unless a man's privileges be determined by the judgment of his peers and the law of the land. So soon as I have to go to Washington to ask how I may conduct my business I have ceased to live under an American polity. There is the no longer any difference between the polity which we established this government to escape and the polity which we ourselves, childishly, have returned to.

Government regulation? Yes, but through the ancient, the stable, the incorruptible instrumentality of law, not through the choice of executive officials. A country not to be upset by the scolding of magistrates but only to be upset by the corruption of its citizens—a country that knows its own mind, knows its own law, upholds its own magistrates is sure of the future because it is sure of its own principles.

Gentlemen, we shall not escape the necessity of making a fundamental choice. Wrong practices must be stopped, but they must be stopped in such a way that we shall not substitute the wrong of tyranny for the wrong of private oppression. I can resist my neighbor but I can not resist the government; and when the government is made strong against me and interferes in everything that I attempt to do, then my life is the life of a man enslaved and not of a man standing upon the ancient privileges of a free race. Have we not the self-possession to diagnose the case? Have we not the self-possession to determine exactly what it is that is the matter with us and that we want to correct? Have we not the intelligence and capacity to define the remedy in law? Have we not had courts which could be depended upon to enforce the law? I would despair of the intelligence of this people if I thought that there was more than one answer to that question.

The answer may not come soon. I admit to you in this presence that I am not hopeful of the immediate future; but I would be deeply hopeless of any future, immediate or remote, if we did not begin now to think straight about these things. We are going, apparently, to act first and think afterward; and God help us in the process of saving the fragments. But the sooner we begin to think the less the fragments will be scattered and the less impossible it will be to put them together again. The sooner we make up our minds that we are going to act upon tested principles and not upon doubtful experiments, the sooner we strip ourselves of individual interests and prejudices in the matter, the better. . . .

The real thing which a gathering of gentlemen like this should realize is that they must, for the salvation of their country, adjourn their own individual and particular interests for a very serious effort of public counsel; for we are on the eve of a political choice in this country which may be a permanent choice. We are upon the eve of a critical choice which may turn us in this direction or in that; and God help us if we do not know which direction we have chosen. We stand in the presence of the necessity of choosing a direction. We must recover by one process or another the ancient principles of morality, the ancient principles of public spirit, the ancient principles of common purpose, and then there will be no difficulty in putting a stop to the things which are against the public welfare. . . .

Equal Suffrage—A Problem of Political Justice*

Anna Howard Shaw

The franchise has been granted to women on equal terms with men in nine states of the United States and one territory, namely, Wyoming, Colorado, Utah, Idaho, Washington, California, Kansas, Arizona, Oregon, and Alaska. Everyone of the equal suffrage states is adjacent to one or more of the other suffrage states. Moreover, five of the states where equal suffrage amendments will be submitted to the voters in November border on one or more equal suffrage states. Surely no state would enfranchise its women, or would even seriously consider it, if equal suffrage had proved a failure just across the boundary line. Therefore, this geographical argument, as we suffragists call it, seems to us the very best one which can be urged as to the practical success of votes for women, proving, as it does, that the anti-suffrage bogies which make some impression in the East are merely ridiculous in the West where evil prophecies have given way before experience, and opinions are based on evidence, not on idle prejudice.

A similar practical demonstration of the results of equal suffrage has been made in Europe. For instance, in Norway tax-paying women were granted the municipal franchise in 1901, and the full franchise in 1907. In 1910 the municipal franchise was granted to all women, the full parliamentary franchise being extended to all women in 1913. If the Norwegian women had made a failure of their municipal suffrage, it is obvious that the parliamentary suffrage would not have been given them. If the tax-paying women had failed to demonstrate their patriotism and common sense, the non-tax-paying women would have failed to secure the franchise. The experience of Finland, whose women have had full suffrage since 1906, has been similar to that of Norway. . . .

These facts, demonstrating satisfaction with equal suffrage wherever it has been tried, together with the mass of favorable evidence which has been presented to the public through the impartial columns of our newspapers and magazines, would seem to make it unnecessary to discuss votes for women from the standpoint of expediency, even if one believed that a fundamental principle should be affected by questions of expediency.

I personally am convinced that the enfranchisement of women should be considered from the standpoint of justice and logic alone.

Our demand is suffrage for women on the same terms as for men. Let

*From Anna Howard Shaw, "Equal Suffrage-A Problem of Political Justice," *Annals of the American Academy of Political Science*, 56, November 1914, 93–98. Reprinted by permission of Sage Publications, Inc.

us see just what this means. The men of this country have established and maintained what they call a democracy. The basic idea of a democracy is, they say, that it shall be a government of the people, by the people, for the people. So far, so good. But "people" has been translated to mean male citizens only. We ask, therefore, not that the established principle of government be changed but that it shall be held to apply to women citizens as well as to men citizens.

In general, every male citizen of the United States, native born or naturalized, is entitled to vote, if he is 21 years of age and has been for a certain length of time a resident of the state and county where he desires to cast his ballot. Idiots and criminals are generally disfranchised. In some states there is a slight educational qualification—the ability to read and understand the constitution—and in a very few states a small property qualification. On the other hand, there are some states where an alien is entitled to vote as soon as he announces his intention to become citizen. But, with the exception of the provisions as to idiots, none of the causes for disfranchisement is such that a man can not overcome it or prevent it. He is not arbitrarily and irrevocably disfranchised, as women are simply because of their sex.

Occasionally, one hears a man say that the "ignorant men," or "the foreign-born men," or "the men of the lower classes" should not be allowed to vote, but no one makes any serious suggestion or prophecy of changing the form of government. Those who are dissatisfied with the present system apparently realize the futility of trying to take the franchise away from any class which has it, for, although the men of the present day do not stop to consider why they themselves vote, and seldom recall, except to quote at political meetings, the sentiments which stirred our forefathers—yet every man knows at heart that he could not be self-respecting if he were deprived of the ballot. He knows that whether the franchise is a right or a privilege, every citizen must have it in order to be free, since economic independence, intellectual independence, even spiritual independence can not exist without political freedom as a foundation.

Therefore, the question is not whether men should have a democratic form of government. They have already proved that it is the kind of government they want and the kind they intend to have, even though they make grievous mistakes in trying to live up to their ideals as to what a democracy should be. Nor is it pertinent to discuss whether the voter should meet certain educational, moral or property tests, because our only demand is that those tests be the same for men as for women. The question is, why should women, as women, be disfranchised? Or, in other words, why should women not have the ballot on the same terms as men, no matter what these terms are now or what they may be in the future?

There is no reason why they should not have it. If there were a reason, our opponents would have discovered it long ago. The fact that there is no reason explains why there is so much discussion of woman suffrage—discussion which plays all around the subject, but seldom hits it squarely. . . .

It seems to me very unfortunate that we suffragists should ever permit ourselves thus to over-qualify for the vote, which is exactly what we do when we prove or attempt to prove our fitness for the ballot, and our need of it, on any other ground than that of mere citizenship. We should say: The reason men are enfranchised is that, as citizens, they have a stake in the government. The reason women should be enfranchised is because, as citizens, they have a stake in the government. That is all there is to this question of woman suffrage.

But I admit that the temptation to over-qualify is very great because we know so much of the hardships and the ignominy which women have always suffered, and are still suffering, by reason of their political subjection; because we know of so many evils which we want to remedy—evils which affect all of society, as well as women alone; because we know so many fine women who are greatly handicapped in their work by their lack of power; because we are convinced that the world would be a much better and happier place if men and women could work on equal terms; because we know of the splendid results which can already be traced to the enfranchisement of women.

Yet such knowledge constitutes after all merely an added incentive for unlimited determination and ceaseless work. It is the inspiration which makes us force the reason for our enfranchisement to public attention; but it is not in itself the reason. . . .

There seems to be no difficulty in proving the justice and logic of equal suffrage to anyone willing and able to think clearly about it. The chief trouble lies in persuading people really to think about it at all. Many women, it must be admitted, do not appreciate the value of a vote. But men do not have the same excuse. They understand perfectly the power which the franchise gives, though they themselves do not make the most of it, and they believe in the principles of democracy. The difficulty lies in making them apply these principles to women.

It is indeed fearful and humiliating to belong to a class of people men can forget when speaking of fundamental privileges, but it is even more unfortunate to belong to a class of people men can forget without knowing they are forgetting anything. That is the position of women today. That is the only explanation of the attitude of the President of the United States, whose writings on democracy contain, perhaps, the best arguments ever made in favor of equal suffrage. The only trouble is that the President was not thinking of women when he made these arguments and, therefore, did not apply his conclusions to women as well as to men. There are many men who, like the President, think of us women merely as the wives, sisters and daughters of men, and in their thought of legislation they do not separate us from themselves and their interests. So they say of us in governmental affairs just as they say of us in the family life: "We take care of you; we look after your interests; your interests are safe in our hands." And, consequently, instead of opposing women suffrage because of sex antagonism, as is sometimes claimed, they really oppose woman suffrage on the ground of sex guardianship.

And that is where we women have lost all along, not by the antagonism of men, but by the guardianship of men. The idea that we are under tutelage, that we are taken care of, that a woman who works 16 hours a day is supported, is responsible for the conviction that women contribute nothing toward the upbuilding of the nation, and are, therefore, not entitled to an opinion on the nation's problems.

If men would divest themselves for one moment of the thought that women are related to them and other men, if they would think of women as they think of each other, as distinct human beings, with all the rights and privileges and desires and hopes and aspirations of human beings, then I doubt very much whether any man fundamentally sound and logical in his attitude toward great moral and political questions could ever again utter a democratic principle without recognizing its application to the womanhood of the nation.

Pax Americana*

George W. Kirchwey

The League to Enforce Peace has sprung full-armed from the brain of Woodrow Wilson. While the immediate occasion of our entry into the world war is "the reckless and lawless submarine warfare" which the German government has been waging against American commerce and the lives of our citizens, its purpose is declared by the President to be

> to vindicate the principles of peace and justice in the life of the world as against selfish and autocratic power and to set up amongst the really free and self-governed peoples of the world such a concert of purpose and of action as will henceforth insure the observance of those principles.

And again, in the same noble utterance from which this declaration is taken, he says:

> We shall fight for the things which we have always carried nearest our hearts—for democracy, for the right of those who submit to authority to have

*From George W. Kirchwey, "Pax Americana," *Annals of the American Academy of Political and Social Science*, Vol. 72 (July 1917), 40–48. Reprinted by permission of Sage Publications, Inc.

a voice in their own government, for the rights and liberties of small nations, for a universal dominion of right by such a concert of free peoples as shall bring peace and safety to all nations and make the world itself at last free. . . .

To what extent this growing purpose of the President has been shared by the American people, it would be vain to inquire. It had long been held by a small but influential section of the community, the majority of the "intellectuals," the professional classes and the leading newspapers. The great mass of the population, indifferent or reluctant from the beginning, has probably remained unconvinced to the end. But the end has come and it is safe to assume that the President's purpose is today the nation's purpose and that we are in the war not merely to protect our commerce and the lives of our citizens, but also to end the war which the German government is waging on mankind and, by cooperation with the governments now at war with Germany, to bring that government to terms.

In saying this I am not unmindful of the fact that the Congress, clearly representing the weight of public opinion of the country at large, has accepted, not willed, the war, and that only a small minority of either House put the seal of its approval on the wider purpose declared by the President. . . . Whether, as a people, we willed it or not, we are in the war and we are in it to the end. The only peace that we can now consider is a general peace that will make the world safe for democracy. For better or for worse, Woodrow Wilson has given the United States a new world policy.

If I am correct in this interpretation of the situation, two facts of momentous significance in their bearing on our national life and well-being as well as upon the future course of world-history come into view. The first is this: that for the first time in human history a great nation has gone to war, has pledged all its power and resources, has staked its very existence for a purely ideal end. As the President has truly said, "We have no selfish ends to serve. We desire no conquest, no dominion. We seek no indemnities for ourselves, no material compensation for the sacrifices we shall freely make. We are but one of the champions of the rights of mankind. We shall be satisfied when those rights have been made as secure as the faith and the freedom of the nation can make them." . . .

In the second place, our entry into the war "for such a cause" marks the abandonment, of our traditional and cherished policy of isolation and independence of world politics. Not at the close of the Civil War, not as the result of the Spanish War, but today has the United States become a part of the international system. No American will undervalue the advantages which that policy of proud isolation has conferred on humanity, or will see it pass wholly without regret. It has given security from foreign aggression to half a world. It has quarantined us against the fatal disease of militarism. It has made possible the growth to plenitude of power and prosperity of the greatest and most pacific democracy that the world has ever seen and has thus fitted it for the greater role which it has now assumed. But it has been a selfish policy, not less selfish—if less mischievous and hateful-than the predatory policy of the powers from whom it has kept us aloof. It has given us peace, but it has been the peace of Cain—"Am I my brother's keeper?" We have kept out of war ourselves, but we have done nothing to keep other nations out of war. . . .

At this point grave questions, sharp as the spear of Ithuriel, thrust themselves upon us. Is the issue between autocracy and democracy, between civilization and barbarism so clear in the present struggle that we could not refuse to take up the gage of battle? . . . Is war the only way, is it the best way, for our great, pacific democracy to champion the imperilled rights of mankind and strive for a better world order? On these questions, on which the sentiment of our people is so passionately divided, I express no opinion. . . .

Limiting our view, then, to the present war and its issues, what is the service that the high and disinterested purpose which we have avowed demands of us?

It requires, in the first place, that we shall wage the war nobly, generously and without bitterness. . . .

In the second place, as we fight only for the security of the nations against lawless aggression, our fight will be over as soon as that security has been attained, whether by crushing victory or by the voluntary submission of the enemy. . . .

In the third place, our government should not only withdraw from the war but should use all its influence to bring the war to a conclusion as soon as, in its opinion, a just and durable peace can be secured. We are fighting for a world-peace, not for a world-truce, and we cannot lend ourselves to terms of settlement which, because of their harsh or oppressive character, will have in them the seeds of future wars. . . .

In the fourth place, we should insist now, as the price of our active participation in the general war, that the Allies shall bind themselves to join with us in the creation of a true society of nations, from which no power, small or great, whether now friendly or hostile, shall be excluded. . . .

And, lastly, we must wage the war for democracy and the security of peace and justice at home as well as abroad. For the enemy, the selfish spirit of autocracy that lives by force and aggression is here in our midst as well as in Berlin, Vienna and Constantinople. . . .

And here we reach the height of the great argument. I have spoken of the high spirit of disinterestedness that has carried us into the war. But that should not surprise us nor anyone, friend or enemy, that knows us. As a recent writer has said:

> The truth is that the United States is the only high-minded Power left in the world. It is the only strong nation that has not entered on a career of imperial conquest, and does not want to enter on it. If the nations of Europe had entertained purposes as disinterested as those of the United States they would not

now be engaged in this butchery. There is in America little of that spirit of selfish aggression which lies at the heart of militarism. Here alone exists a broad basis for "a new passionate sense of brotherhood, and a new scale of human values." We have a deep abhorrence of war for war's sake; we are not enamored of glamour or glory. We have a strong faith in the principle of self-government. We do not care to dominate alien peoples, white or colored; we do not aspire to be the Romans of tomorrow or the "masters of the world." The idealism of Americans centers in the future of America, wherein we hope to work out those principles of liberty and democracy to which we are committed. . . . This political idealism, this strain of pacifism, this abstinence from aggression and desire to be left alone to work out our own destiny, has been manifest from the birth of the republic. We have not always followed our light, but we have never been utterly faithless to it.[1]

When such a people goes to war the act presents itself either as a great betrayal or as a sublime fulfilment, and the nations today and history tomorrow—not by our words but by our deeds—will judge us. What will be required of us is not victory—though for victory we must mightily strive—but fidelity to the principles that have made us a name among peoples. Victory achieved through the defeat of those principles will itself be defeat, however great the material triumph.

Shall we be able to keep our ideals unimpaired in this new old-world—this world of storm and stress, of militant wrong and triumphant power—in which we have now elected to play our part? To make war only when we must and then not for selfish ends but only for the common weal? To keep and strengthen justice and democracy at home even while we strive for democracy and justice abroad? To dream no dream of empire, to see no alluring vision of power but the vision of a world made safe for democracy and secured against outrage by the united will of enfranchised peoples? I do not know. But this I know, that the days of our cloistered virtue are well lost and that we cannot refuse the great adventure even though we gain the whole world and lose our own soul. And this, too, I know, that the greatest disaster that could befall mankind is not the sum of human misery which such a war as this brings in its train, nor yet the shameful legacy of hate and fear and mistrust that it leaves behind it, but the loss to humanity of those ideals of democracy, justice and peace which our Republic has represented in an evil world. And this, too, I know, that it rests wholly with us to keep our democracy true to the line marked out for it in Washington's farewell address:

> Observe good faith and justice toward all nations; cultivate peace and harmony with all. . . . It will be worthy of a free, enlightened and, at no distant period, a great nation, to give to mankind the magnanimous and too novel example of a people always guided by an exalted justice and benevolence.

[1]Roland Hugins, *The Possible Peace*, New York, 1916.

Conscience and Intelligence in War*

Randolph Bourne

The merely "conscientious objector" has absorbed too much attention from those who are concerned about understanding the non-popularity of our participation in the war. Not all the pacifist feeling has had an evangelical color. There is an element of anti-war sentiment which has tried to be realistic, and does not hope to defeat war merely by not doing something. Though events have been manipulated against it, this element neither welcomes martyrdom nor hopes to be saved for its amiable sentiments. And it is just this attitude, far more significantly "American" than "conscientious objection," that John Dewey has ignored in his recent article on "Conscience and Compulsion." The result has been to apply his pragmatic philosophy in its least convincing form.

His criticism is of the merely good and merely conscientious souls whose moral training has emphasized sentiments rather than specific purposes, and who are always found helpless before the coercion of events. His argument follows the well-known lines of his instrumental use of the intelligence for the realization of conscious social purpose. The conscience, he implies, is balked by an unpleasant situation, is futile unless it attaches itself to forces moving in another, and more desirable, direction. Dissatisfied with the given means or end, one chooses another alternative, either a new end to which the means may be shaped, or a new means to effect the desired end. But in applying this theory to the war situation, does not the philosopher ignore the fact that it is exactly in war that alternatives are rigorously limited? Is not war perhaps the one social absolute, the one situation where the choice of ends ceases to function? Obviously in a world of choice one may hope intelligently to select and manipulate some social mechanism by which a desired social arrangement may be brought about. But war always comes to seem just that urgent, inevitable crisis of the nation's life where everything must be yielded to one purpose. For a few months, the public may retain the illusion of freedom, of mastery over social forces. But as war continues, there comes the deep popular recognition that there is now but one end—victory; and but one means—the organization of all the resources of the nation into a conventional war technique. "Peace without victory" becomes a logical and biological contradiction. Belligerent peoples will have long ago realized that war is its own end, and that to paraphrase a popular ditty, they fight because they fight because

---

*From Randolph Bourne, "Conscience and Intelligence in War," *The Dial*, 63, no. 749 (September 13, 1917), 193–95.

they fight. This was the real basis of the opposition to the President's gesture for peace—the realization that though America might still be living in a pragmatic world, war had made Europe a realm of the absolute. And in our own country, war had not been with us for ten weeks before "peace without victory" changed officially into "conquer or submit!"

In wartime, there is literally no other end but war, and the objector, therefore, lives no longer with a choice of alternatives. The pacifist conscience attaches itself to no end because no end exists which connects with its desires. Plans and programmes may exist which have not to do with war, but they exist only in the realm of fantasy, not in the realm of practical politics. Peace comes through victory or exhaustion, and not through creative intelligence. The appeal to force removes everything automatically to a non-intelligent sphere of thinking and acting. Mr. Dewey is depressed at the number of conscientious young men who exchanged their "Thou shalt not kill" into an "Obey the law," though they saw the situation exactly as before. But his depression is due only to that inexorability which every pragmatist must resent. . . .

No social machinery exists to make dissent effective. Alternative ends are illusory. You can only accept, or rebel, or remain apathetic. This is not true of other social situations. It is true of war. If you are skeptical of the technique of war, or of the professed aims, a negative attitude is the only possible one. It may not be noble to concentrate on your own integrity, but it is perhaps better than to be a hypocrite or a martyr. And if pragmatists like Mr. Dewey are going to accept "inevitables," you at least have an equal right to choose what shall seem inevitable to you.

To many pragmatists the impotence of the pacifists in the period preceding the war has been a sore point. They are scolded for their lack of organization and their mere obstructiveness. Actually, they were fertile in constructive suggestions. But no social machinery existed for harnessing their conscience to action. The referendum would have been a slight democratic clutch. It was hooted out of court. Armed neutrality was foozled. The forces that were irresistibly for war had control of the war-making machinery. The pacifists sounded ridiculous and unreasonable, because the drive was the other way. The war suction had begun. Choices were already abolished, and the most realistic and constructive pacifism in the world would have been helpless.

In all this chain of events, those minds were able to retain a feeling of alternative forces and of free choice which were in sympathy with the announced purpose of the war and not temporarily hostile to its technique. The philosophy of creative intelligence still seemed to be working because there was no need to test its applicability. The dissenter, however, felt cruelly the coercive forces. Suppose I really believe that world peace will more likely come exactly "by not doing something," by a collusive neglect of imperialistic policy on the new Russian model. Suppose I believe that a federalism of sovereign nations will only mean more competitive wars. What forces are there then to which I can assimilate this war of ours, and so make my intelligence and conscience count for what little they may? Is not Mr. Dewey's case against the merely passive built on an assumption that if one chose freely one would choose the present inevitable forces? But the mind that is skeptical of these present forces,—is it not thrown back to a choice of resistance or apathy? Can one do more than wait and hope for wisdom when the world becomes pragmatic and flexible again?

DISCUSSION QUESTIONS

1. How did fundamentalists and revisionists disagree on the source of economic wealth and the role of government?
2. How did the Populist Party and Progressive movement differ in terms of constituencies and political agendas?
3. Why was the right to vote for women a major achievement in reforming the American political system?
4. How was World War I a major turning point in U.S. politics according to Kirchwey and Bourne?
5. Does the U.S. have a mission to bring democracy to the world?

Chapter 9

DEMOCRATIC AND ECONOMIC CRISIS

After World War I, production controls were eliminated and Americans enjoyed a higher standard of living than ever before. America returned to a period of normalcy. However, in 1929, the stock market crashed and the ensuing Great Depression set off a disruption in American society that brought into question the very nature of the relationship of individual liberty, government authority, and private property. As seen in Table 9–1, the percent of Americans unemployed nearly tripled between 1929 and 1930, and remained in double digits from 1931 through 1940. In comparison, unemployment reached double digit proportions for one year in the period from 1900 to 1929.[1]

Americans had believed in the importance of individualism in society, politics and economics since the Jeffersonian and Jacksonian presidencies. But during the 1930s, Americans looked to government as a means of coping with the severe economic collapse. However, the Hoover administration remained committed to the idea of individualism in a period when unemployment went from 3.2 percent to 23.6 percent. As Hofstadter, as well as Mason and Leach noted, the centerpiece of Hoover's philosophy was:

> That while we build our society upon the attainment of the individual, we shall safe-guard to every individual an equality of opportunity to take that position in the community to which his intelligence, character, ability, and

[1]*Historical Statistics of the United States, Colonial Times to 1957* (Washington, DC: U.S. Department of Commerce, 1975), p. 73.

TABLE 9-1   *Unemployment Rates, 1929–1942*

Year	Unemployed	Percent of Civilian Labor Force	Year	Unemployed	Percent of Civilian Labor Force
1929	1,550,000	3.2	1936	9,030,000	16.9
1930	4,340,000	8.7	1937	7,700,000	14.3
1931	8,020,000	15.9	1938	10,390,000	19.0
1932	12,060,000	23.6	1939	9,480,000	17.2
1933	12,830,000	24.9	1940	8,120,000	14.6
1934	11,340,000	21.7	1941	5,560,000	9.9
1935	10,610,000	20.1	1942	2,660,000	4.7

Historical Statistics of the United States, Colonial Times to 1957 (Washington, DC: U.S. Department of Commerce, 1975), p. 73.

ambition entitle him; that we keep the social solution free from frozen strata of classes; that we shall stimulate effort of each individual to achievement, that through an enlarging sense of responsibility and understanding we shall assist him in this attainment; while he in turn must stand up to the emery wheel of competition.[2]

The purpose of government was to ensure the ability of the individual to achieve by providing equality of opportunity. It was not the responsibility of government to promote economic well-being through increased regulation of industry or by expanding the level of federal expenditures during a depression. Indeed, the classic view was that government expenditures should be reduced during a depression to enable the reduction of taxes and thereby put additional funds into the hands of the public. In this regard, President Hoover concluded, expanded governmental spending would extend the Depression, for the resulting waste would suppress human creativity.

While I am a strong advocate of expansion of useful public works in hard times . . . there are limitations upon the application of this principle. Not only must we refrain from robbing industry and commerce of its capital, and thereby increasing unemployment, but such works require long engineering and legal interludes before they produce actual employment. Above all, schemes of public works which have no reproductive value would result in sheer waste.[3]

President Hoover displayed in the above passage a classic belief that the private sector could do more to ensure economic well-being than would

[2]From *The American Political Tradition*, by Richard Hofstadter. Copyright 1948 by Alfred A. Knopf, Inc. and renewed 1976 by Beatrice Hofstadter. Reprinted by permission of the publisher. P. 386. Alpheus Thomas Mason and Richard H. Leach, *In Quest of Freedom*, 2nd ed. (Englewood Cliffs, NJ: Prentice-Hall, Inc., 1973), p. 332.

[3]Herbert Hoover, "The Remedy for Economic Depression Is Not Waste, but the Creation and Distribution of Wealth," *The State Papers and Other Public Writings of Herbert Hoover*, ed., William Starr Myers (New York: Kraus Reprint Co., 1970), I, 578–79.

government policies. Rugged individualists tended to regard government intervention in the economy as leading to socialism, a charge which would haunt New Dealers in the 1950s. But in the 1932 election, President Hoover's campaign came under attack from all quarters because the administration's efforts failed to produce relief. As Caughey and May concluded the crisis grew worse until

> By 1932, nearly one man in four was out of work. A special federal census estimated that 15,000,000 were unemployed and looking for jobs. Whatever savings these men possessed had long ago disappeared. They could not meet mortgage payments or pay rent. Many moved in with relatives. Sometimes whole families had to live in garages or sheds or shacks built out of boards and sheets of rusty tin salvaged from a city dump.[4]

Hoover's philosophy was roundly criticized in the 1932 election. To Democrats, Hoover's administration had failed to adapt government to the crisis. To rugged individualists, government had expanded its role in the economy, under the guise of moderating the crisis, but had in fact increased its severity. The rugged individualism which had characterized American political thought for the previous hundred years ceased with Hoover's defeat.

Franklin Roosevelt was elected president to meet the economic crisis with his New Deal goal of reformulating the relationship between individual liberty, government authority, and private property. As Anderson noted, "the New Deal accepted capitalism but it also accepted the responsibility of the government for the health of the national economy, and in so doing it rejected laissez-faire."[5] Philosophically, the New Deal rejected the ideas of an expanding American economy with equality of opportunity in favor of government support for equality of outcome. President Roosevelt justified this change in his 1938 Commonwealth Club speech.

> A glance at the situation today only too clearly indicates that equality of opportunity as we have known it no longer exists. Our industrial plant is built; the problem just now is whether under existing conditions it is not over-built. Our last frontier has long since been reached, and there is practically no more free land.[6]

The individual no longer possessed the opportunities to achieve and therefore government intervention was paramount for continued economic

---

[4]John W. Caughey and Ernest R. May, *A History of the United States* (Chicago: Rand McNally, 1964), pp. 524–25.

[5]Thornton Anderson, ed., *Jacobson's Development of American Political Thought,* 2nd ed. (New York: Appleton-Century-Crofts, Inc., 1961), p.562.

[6]Franklin D. Roosevelt, "New Conditions Impose New Requirements upon Government and Those Who Conduct Government." *The Public Papers and Addresses of Franklin D. Roosevelt* (New York: Random House, 1938), I, 750.

expansion. Keynesian economics was adopted by the Roosevelt administration with its emphasis on government responsibility for full employment. In this regard, one finds an escalation of the number of people employed by the federal government in the 1930s from 605,496 in 1932, to 780,582 in 1935, finally to 953,891 in 1939.[7] President Roosevelt justified these changes and increased government involvement by concluding in 1938,

> The day of the great promoter or the financial Titan, to whom we granted anything if only he would build, or develop, is over. Our task now is not discovery or exploitation of natural resources, or necessarily producing more goods. It is soberer, less dramatic business of administering resources and plants already in hand, of seeking to reestablish foreign markets for our surplus production, of meeting the problem of underconsumption, of adjusting production to consumption, of distributing wealth and products more equitably, of adapting existing economic organizations to the service of the people.[8]

Whether Roosevelt's New Deal policies ended the Great Depression is highly questionable given the continued high unemployment levels as seen in Table 9–1. Yet at the same time, the fact Franklin Roosevelt was elected president four times suggested broad popular support for the New Deal policies. The effect on political theory was immense according to Mason and Leach.

> After 1932 the orientation of American political thought became basically collectivist. Thereafter, government enacted programs designed to promote the general welfare directly. It was recognized that no individual, no group, could profit or suffer without affecting the interests of all. Economic rights must be added to the roster of our freedoms, and government, rather than industrial ownership or management, be made the dominant power.[9]

Roosevelt's idea of greater government involvement in promoting the economic well-being of the American nation marked a major change in American politics. No longer was emphasis to be placed on the individual in effecting economic change or securing liberty in America.

Roosevelt's New Deal program was initially supported by pragmatists such as John Dewey. They saw in the New Deal a reformulation of the role of government in an industrial society which was designed to promote greater individual freedom. However, after 1935 the Roosevelt administration came under increasing criticism for expanding government authority without empowering American citizens. The centerpiece of Dewey's philosophy was the belief that human thinking capacity gives individuals the ability to change the physical and social environments in order to produce

[7]*Historical Statistics of the United States,* p. 710.

[8]Roosevelt, *The Public Papers,* pp. 751-52.

[9]Mason and Leach, *In Quest,* p. 362.

desired outcomes. The state functions to provide human beings with the ability to interact with each other and change the environment around them. Democracy maximizes this ability to interact and to achieve in relationship to the physical and social environment. Therefore government had a role in ensuring the quality of life, but not to the degree that it threatened to regiment people's lives and dictate what they could achieve. Despite the criticisms offered by pragmatists, Roosevelt's programs continued to accept and promote a belief in the democratic process as the basis of American politics.

Other Americans continued to accept a belief in the democratic process, to varying degrees, while rejecting both rugged individualism and New Deal programs. These individuals, of whom the most prominent were Father Charles E. Coughlin, Dr. Francis E. Townsend, and Senator Huey P. Long, proposed solutions which would have expanded government's role in redistrubuting wealth to promote prosperity beyond what was envisioned by the New Dealers. Father Charles E. Coughlin, a Roman Catholic priest, was especially critical of capitalism and the fact that banks were not nationalized, since they were the ultimate source of domination by the wealthy.[10] Dr. Francis E. Townsend called for adequate relief for the elderly by proposing a $200.00 a month pension.[11] Senator Huey P. Long proposed the "Share-the-Wealth" program which called for each family of modest means to be given $5000.00, paid for by a wealth tax "of the more prosperous citizens."[12] These proposals were adopted in diluted forms such as higher taxes on the wealthy and enactment of social security programs.

Among the most extreme solutions offered were the restructuring of the U.S. along the lines of fascist and communist societies. During the 1930s, when most countries were suffering a depression, the economies of fascist Germany and Italy, as well as that of the communist Soviet Union, expanded and their citizens living standards improved. Their success lead some Americans to conclude that fascism and communism were superior political and economic ideas. Individual freedom and democracy were seen in some quarters as having failed the test of the Great Depression. In this regard individualism was replaced by collectivism, private property by state planning or ownership, and democracy by totalitarianism.

One proposed philosophy was fascism, which had its origins in Italy during the 1920s. Hoover, in examining the philosophy of the fascism cited then Premier Mussolini's definition from the *Enciclopedia Italiana.*

> . . . Fascism combats the whole complex of democratic ideology and repudiates it. . . . Fascism denies that the majority by the simple fact that it is the

[10]Ibid., p. 360.
[11]Ibid.
[12]Ibid.

majority can direct human society, it denies that numbers alone can govern by means of periodic consultation. . . . Fascism denies in democracy the absurd conventional untruth of political equality . . . and the myth of "happiness" and indefinite progress. . . . Fascism has taken up an attitude of complete opposition to the doctrines of Liberalism born in the political field and the field of economics. . . . Let it be pointed out that all political hopes of the present day are anti-Liberal. . . .[13]

In the U.S., fascism was enunciated by Lawrence Dennis who argued that a national elite would dominate the American system through the raw power of the state rather than reasoning and convincing the people of a problem or solution. The individual, like property, would be at the service of the state. Dennis wrote,

The day has come when property must no longer assert any immunity from government taking and government commanding which a poor man cannot assert for his life or labor in war time when drafted from national defense. Fascism insists that property or capital and private economic enterprise must be called . . . as conscripts in time of war. And fascism insists that the term of service for both capital and labor is not for an emergency but a new and permanent scheme of social organization and operation.[14]

Fascism would ensure economic growth through government direction of the economy. Yet fascism did not require the elimination of private property. Instead, private property would be directed by the government.

An alternative strategy was proposed by Earl Browder in the form of communism and the establishment of the Soviet government of America. Browder, who ran for president in 1936 and 1940, argued

The primary concern of the Soviet Government will be production; this will be highly centralized, to realize the benefits of the highest technical achievements. All means of production will be socialized, taken out of private control. . . . Socialism is not only a revolution in economic life. It makes an entirely new human race. It takes this man who has been brutalized and degraded through the ages by the violence and oppression of class societies, frees him from his woeful heritage, carries over from the past only the achievements of the human mind and not its crimes and stupidities, and remakes man, molding him in the heat of socialist labor into a new social being.[15]

Property in a communist United States would be owned by the state, and individuals would be dependent on it for everything received. In the

---

[13]"Fascism," *Enciclopedia Italiana* in Herbert Hoover, *The Challenge to Liberty* (New York: De Capo Press, 1973), p. 66.

[14]Selected excerpt from page 137 from *The Coming of American Fascism* by Lawrence Dennis. Copyright 1936 by Harper & Brothers. Copyright renewed 1963 by Lawrence Dennis. Reprinted by permission of HarperCollins Publishers, Inc.

[15]Earl Browder, "A Glimpse of Soviet America," *What Is Communism?* (New York: The Vanguard Press, 1936), p. 231.

process, the worst attributes of capitalism would be removed from the American people. Whittaker Chambers described why people searched for something different in the 1920s.

> I had joined the Communist Party in 1924. No one recruited me. I had become convinced that the society in which we live, Western civilization, had reached a crisis, of which the First World War was the military expression, and that it was doomed to collapse or revert to barbarism. I did not understand the causes of the crisis, or know what to do about it.... In the writings of Karl Marx I thought that I had found the explanation of the historical and economic causes. In the writings of Lenin I thought I had found the answer to the question: What to do?[16]

The 1930s were one of the most pronounced periods of debate over the relationship of individual liberty, government authority, and private property. Government for the first time took on greater responsibility for the economy and promoting the well-being of the community. In the following writings by John Dewey, Franklin D. Roosevelt, and Lawrence Dennis, a series of divergent themes emerge representing the competing views presented during the Great Depression.

Renascent Liberalism*

John Dewey

Nothing is blinder than the supposition that we live in a society and world so static that either nothing new will happen or else it will happen because of the use of violence. Social change is here as a fact, a fact having multifarious forms and marked in intensity. Changes that are revolutionary in effect are in process in every phase of life. Transformations in the family, the church, the school, in science and art, in economic and political relations, are occurring so swiftly that imagination is baffled in attempt to lay hold of them. Flux does not have to be created. But it does have to be directed. It has to be so controlled that it will move to some end in accordance with the principles of life, since life itself is development. Liberalism is committed to an end that is at once enduring and flexible: the liberation of individuals so that realization of their capacities may be the law of their life. It is committed to the use of freed intelligence as the method of directing change. In any

---

[16]Whittaker Chambers, *Odyssey of a Friend, Whittaker Chambers to William F. Buckley, Jr.* ed. William F. Buckley, Jr. (New York: G.P. Putnam's Sons, 1969), p. 15.

*Reprinted by permission of The Putnam Publishing Group from *Liberalism and Social Action* by John Dewey. Copyright © 1935 by John Dewey. Renewed © 1962 by Roberta L. Dewey, pp. 56–93.

case, civilization is faced with the problem of uniting the changes that are going on into a coherent pattern of social organization. The liberal spirit is marked by its own picture of the pattern that is required: a social organization that will make possible effective liberty and opportunity for personal growth in mind and spirit in all individuals. Its present need is recognition that established material security is a prerequisite of the ends which it cherishes, so that, the basis of life being secure, individuals may actively share in the wealth of cultural resources that now exist and may contribute, each in his own way, to their further enrichment.

The fact of change has been so continual and so intense that it overwhelms our minds. We are bewildered by the spectacle of its rapidity, scope and intensity. It is not surprising that men have protected themselves from the impact of such vast change by resorting to what psycho-analysis has taught us to call rationalizations, in other words, protective fantasies. . . . But men have met the impact of change in the realm of actuality, mostly by drift and by temporary, usually incoherent, improvisations. Liberalism, like every other theory of life, has suffered from the state of confused uncertainty that is the lot of a world suffering from rapid and varied change for which there is no intellectual and moral preparation.

Because of this lack of mental and moral preparation the impact of swiftly moving changes produced, as I have just said, confusion, uncertainty and drift. Change in patterns of belief, desire and purpose has lagged behind the modification of the external conditions under which men associate. Industrial habits have changed most rapidly; there has followed at considerable distance, change in political relations; alterations in legal relations and methods have lagged even more, while changes in the institutions that deal most directly with patterns of thought and belief have taken place to the least extent. This fact defines the primary, though not by any means the ultimate, responsibility of a liberalism that intends to be a vital force. Its work is first of all education, in the broadest sense of that term. Schooling is a part of the work of education, but education in its full meaning includes all the influences that go to form the attitudes and dispositions (of desire as well as of belief), which constitute dominant habits of mind and character.

For, in the second place, insecurity is the natural child and the foster child, too, of scarcity. Early liberalism emphasized the importance of insecurity as a fundamentally necessary economic motive, holding that without this goad men would not work, abstain or accumulate. Formulation of this conception was new. But the fact that was formulated was nothing new. It was deeply rooted in the habits that were formed in the long struggle against material scarcity. The system that goes by the name of capitalism is a systematic manifestation of desires and purposes built up in an age of ever threatening want and now carried over into a time of ever increasing potential plenty. The conditions that generate insecurity for the many no longer spring from nature. They are found in institutions and arrangements that are within deliberate human control. Surely this change marks one of the greatest revolutions that has taken place in all human history. Because of it, insecurity is not now the motive to work and sacrifice but to despair. It is not an instigation to put forth energy but to an impotency that can be converted from death into endurance only by charity. But the habits of mind and action that modify insitutions to make potential abundance an actuality are still so inchoate that most of us discuss labels like individualism, socialism, and communism instead of even perceiving the possibility, much less the necessity for realizing what can and should be.

In the third place, the patterns of belief and purpose that still dominate economic institutions were formed when individuals produced with their hands, alone or in small groups. The notion that society in general is served by the unplanned coincidence of the consequences of a vast multitude of efforts put forth by isolated individuals without reference to any social end, was also something new as a formulation. But it also formulated the working principle of an epoch which the advent of new forces of production was to bring to an end. It demands no great power of intelligence to see that under present conditions the isolated individual is well-nigh helpless. Concentration and corporate organization are the rule. But the concentration and corporate organization are still controlled in their operation by ideas that were institutionalized in eons of separate individual effort. The attempts at cooperation for mutual benefit that are put forth are precious as experimental moves. But that society itself should see to it that a cooperative industrial order be instituted, one that is consonant with the realities of production enforced by an era of machinery and power, is so novel an idea to the general mind that its mere suggestion is hailed with abusive epithets—sometimes with imprisonment.

When, then, I say that the first object of a renascent liberalism is education, I mean that its task is to aid in producing the habits of mind and character, the intellectual and moral patterns, that are somewhere near even with the actual movements of events. It is, I repeat, the split between the latter as they have externally occurred and the ways of desiring, thinking, and of putting emotion and purpose into execution that is the basic cause of present confusion in mind and paralysis in action. The educational task cannot be accomplished merely by working upon men's minds, without action that effects actual change in institutions. The idea that dispositions and attitudes can be altered by merely "moral" means conceived of as something that goes on wholly inside of persons is itself one of the old patterns that has to be changed. Thought, desire and purpose exist in a constant give and take of interaction with environing conditions. But resolute thought is the first step in that change of action that will itself carry further the needed change in patterns of mind and character.

In short, liberalism must now become radical, meaning by "radical" perception of the necessity of thoroughgoing changes in the set-up of institutions and corresponding activity to bring the changes to pass. For the gulf between what the actual situation makes possible and the actual state itself is so great that it cannot be bridged by piecemeal policies undertaken *ad hoc*. The process of producing the changes will be, in any case, a gradual one. But "reforms" that deal now with this abuse and now with that without having a social goal based upon an inclusive plan, differ entirely from effort at re-forming, in its literal sense, the institutional scheme of things. The liberals of more than a century ago were denounced in their time as subversive radicals, and only when the new economic order was established did they become apologists for the *status quo* or else content with social patchwork. If radicalism be defined as perception of need for radical change, then today any liberalism which is not also radicalism is irrelevant and doomed. . . .

Liberalism has to assume the responsibility for making it clear that intelligence is a social asset and is clothed with a function as public as is its origin, in the concrete, in social cooperation. It was Comte who, in reaction against the purely individualistic ideas that seemed to him to underlie the French Revolution, said that in mathematics, physics and astronomy there is no right of private conscience. If we remove the statement from the context of actual scientific procedure, it is dangerous because it is false. The individual inquirer has not only the right but the duty to criticize the ideas, theories and "laws" that are current in science. But if we take the statement in the context of scientific method, it indicates that he carries on this criticism in virtue of a socially generated body of knowledge and by means of methods that are not of private origin and possession. He uses a method that retains public validity even when innovations are introduced in its use and application. . . .

The ultimate place of economic organization in human life is to assure the secure basis for an ordered expression of individual capacity and for the satisfaction of the needs of man in non-economic directions. The effort of mankind in connection with material production belongs, as I said earlier, among interests and activities that are, relatively speaking, routine in character, "routine" being defined as that which, without absorbing attention and energy, provides a constant basis for liberation of the values of intellectual, esthetic and companionship life. Every significant religious and moral teacher and prophet has asserted that the material is instrumental to the good life. Nominally at least, this idea is accepted by every civilized community. The transfer of the burden of material production from human muscles and brain to steam, electricity and chemical processes now makes possible the effective actualization of this ideal. Needs, wants and desires are always the moving force in generating creative action. When these wants are compelled by force of conditions to be directed for the most part, among the mass of mankind, into obtaining the means of subsistence, what should be a means becomes perforce an end in itself. Up to the present the new mechanical forces of production, which are the means of emancipation from this state of affairs, have been employed to intensify and exaggerate the reversal of the true relation between means and ends. Humanly speaking, I do not see how it would have been possible to avoid an epoch having this character. But its perpetuation is the cause of the continually growing social chaos and strife. . . . It can be brought about by organized social reconstruction that puts the results of the mechanism of abundance at the free disposal of individuals. The actual corrosive "materialism" of our times does not proceed from science. It springs from the notion, sedulously cultivated by the class in power, that the creative capacities of individuals can be evoked and developed only in a struggle for material possessions and material gain. We either should surrender our professed belief in the supremacy of ideal and spiritual values and accommodate our beliefs to the predominant material orientation, or we should through organized endeavor institute the socialized economy of material security and plenty that will release human energy for pursuit of higher values.

Since liberation of the capacities of individuals for free, self-initiated expression is an essential part of the creed of liberalism, liberalism that is sincere must will the means that condition the achieving of its ends. Regimentation of material and mechanical forces is the only way by which the mass of individuals can be released from regimentation and consequent suppression of their cultural possibilities. The eclipse of liberalism is due to the fact that it has not faced the alternatives and adopted the means upon which realization of its professed aims depends. Liberalism can be true to its ideals only as it takes the course that leads to their attainment. The notion that organized social control of economic forces lies outside the historic path of liberalism shows that liberalism is still impeded by remnants of its earlier *laissez faire* phase, with its opposition of society and the individual. The thing which now dampens liberal ardor and paralyzes its efforts is the conception that liberty and development of individuality as ends exclude the use of organized social effort as means. Earlier liberalism regarded the separate and competing economic action of individuals as the means to social well-being as the end. We must reverse the perspective and see that socialized economy is the means of free individual development as the end. . . .

It would be fantastic folly to ignore or to belittle the obstacles that stand in the way. But what has taken place, also against great odds, in the scientific and industrial revolutions, is an accomplished fact; the way is marked out. It may be that the way will remain untrodden. If so, the future holds the menace of confusion moving into chaos, a chaos that will be externally masked for a time by an organization of force, coercive and violent, in which the liberties of men will all but disappear. Even so, the cause of the liberty of the human spirit, the cause of opportunity of human beings for full development of their powers, the cause for which liberalism enduringly stands, is too precious and too ingrained in the human constitution to be forever obscured. Intelligence after millions of years of errancy has found itself as a method, and it will not be lost forever in the blackness of night. The business of liberalism is to bend every energy and exhibit every courage so that these precious goods may not even be temporarily lost but be intensified and expanded here and now.

New Conditions Impose New Requirements upon Government and Those Who Conduct Government*

Franklin D. Roosevelt

My friends:
    . . . I want to speak not of politics but of Government. I want to speak not of parties, but of universal principles. They are not political, except in that larger sense in which a great American once expressed a definition of politics, that nothing in all of human life is foreign to the science of politics. . . .

The issue of Government has always been whether individual men and women will have to serve some system of Government or economics, or whether a system of Government and economics exists to serve individual men and women. This question has persistently dominated the discussion of Government for many generations. On questions relating to these things men have differed, and for time immemorial it is probable that honest men will continue to differ.

The final word belongs to no man; yet we can still believe in change and in progress. Democracy, as a dear old friend of mine in Indiana, Meredith Nicholson, has called it, is a quest, a never-ending seeking for better things, and in the seeking for these things and the striving for them, there are many roads to follow. But, if we map the course of these roads, we find that there are only two general directions. . . .

So manifest were the advantages of the machine age, however, that the United States fearlessly, cheerfully, and, I think, rightly, accepted the bitter with the sweet. It was thought that no price was too high to pay for the advantages which we could draw from a finished industrial system. The history of the last half century is accordingly in large measure a history of a group of financial Titans, whose methods were not scrutinized with too much care, and who were honored in proportion as they produced the results, irrespective of the means they used. The financiers who pushed the railroads to the Pacific were always ruthless, often wasteful, and frequently corrupt; but they did build railroads, and we have them today. It has been

*From Franklin D. Roosevelt, "New Conditions Impose New Requirements upon Government and Those Who Conduct Government," *The Public Papers and Addresses of Franklin D. Roosevelt* (New York: Random House, 1938), I, 742–56.

estimated that the American investor paid for the American railway system more than three times over in the process; but despite this fact the net advantage was to the United States. As long as we had free land; as long as population was growing by leaps and bounds; as long as our industrial plants were insufficient to supply our own needs, society chose to give the ambitious man free play and unlimited reward provided only that he produced the economic plant so much desired.

During this period of expansion, there was equal opportunity for all and the business of Government was not to interfere but to assist in the development of industry. This was done at the request of business men themselves. . . . With this I agree; but I wonder whether they realize the implications of the past. For while it has been American doctrine that the Government must not go into business in competition with private enterprises, still it has been traditional, particularly in Republican administrations, for business urgently to ask the Government to put at private disposal all kinds of Government assistance. The same man who tells you that he does not want to see the Government interfere in business—and he means it, and has plenty of good reasons for saying so—is the first to go to Washington and ask the Government for a prohibitory tariff on his product. When things get just bad enough, as they did two years ago, he will go with equal speed to the United States Government and ask for a loan; and the Reconstruction Finance Corporation is the outcome of it. Each group has sought protection from the Government for its own special interests, without realizing that the function of Government must be to favor no small group at the expense of its duty to protect the rights of personal freedom and of private property of all its citizens. . . .

A glance at the situation today only too clearly indicates that equality of opportunity as we have known it no longer exists. Our industrial plant is built; the problem just now is whether under existing conditions it is not overbuilt. Our last frontier has long since been reached, and there is practically no more free land. More than half of our people do not live on the farms or on lands and cannot derive a living by cultivating their own property. There is no safety valve in the form of a Western prairie to which those thrown out of work by the Eastern economic machines can go for a new start. We are not able to invite the immigration from Europe to share our endless plenty. We are now providing a drab living for own people. . . .

Clearly, all this calls for a re-appraisal of values. A mere builder of more industrial plants, a creator of more railroad systems, an organizer of more corporations, is as likely to be a danger as a help. The day of the great promoter or the financial Titan, to whom we granted anything if only he would build, or develop, is over. Our task now is not discovery or exploitation of natural resources, or necessarily producing more goods. It is the soberer, less dramatic business of administering resources and plants already in hand, of seeking to reestablish foreign markets for our surplus production, of meeting the problem of underconsumption, of adjusting production to consumption, of distributing wealth and products more equitably, of adapting existing economic organizations to the service of the people. The day of enlightened administration has come. . . .

As I see it, the task of Government in its relation to business is to assist the development of an economic declaration of rights, an economic constitutional order. This is the common task of statesman and business man. It is the minimum requirement of a more permanently safe order of things.

Happily, the times indicate that to create such an order not only is the proper policy of Government, but it is the only line of safety for our economic structures as well. We know, now, that these economic units cannot exist unless prosperity is uniform, that is, unless purchasing power is well distributed throughout every group in the Nation. That is why even the most selfish of corporations for its own interest would be glad to see wages restored and unemployment ended and to bring the Western farmer back to his accustomed level of prosperity and to assure a permanent safety to both groups. That is why some enlightened industries themselves endeavor to limit the freedom of action of each man and business group within the industry in the common interest of all; why business men everywhere are asking a form of organization which will bring the scheme of things into balance, even though it may in some measure qualify the freedom of action of individual units within the business. . . .

I feel that we are coming to a view through the drift of our legislation and our public thinking in the past quarter century that private economic power is, to enlarge an old phrase, a public trust as well. I hold that continued enjoyment of that power by any individual or group must depend upon the fulfillment of that trust. The men who have reached the summit of American business life know this best; happily, many of these urge the binding quality of this greater social contract.

The terms of that contract are as old as the Republic, and as new as the new economic order.

Every man has a right to life; and this means that he has also a right to make a comfortable living. He may by sloth or crime decline to exercise that right; but it may not be denied him. We have no actual famine or dearth; our industrial and agricultural mechanism can produce enough and to spare. Our Government formal and informal, political and economic, owes to everyone an avenue to possess himself of a portion of that plenty sufficient for his needs, through his own work.

Every man has a right to his own property; which means a right to be assured, to the fullest extent attainable, in the safety of his savings. By no other means can men carry the burdens of those parts of life which, in the nature of things, afford no chance of labor; childhood, sickness, old age. In all thought of property, this right is paramount; all other property rights must yield to it. If, in accord with this principle, we must restrict the operations of the speculator, the manipulator, even the financier, I believe we must accept the restriction as needful, not to hamper individualism but to protect it.

These two requirements must be statisfied, in the main, by the individuals who claim and hold control of the great industrial and financial combinations which dominate so large a part of our industrial life. They have undertaken to be, not business men, but princes of property. I am not prepared to say that the system which produces them is wrong. I am very clear that they must fearlessly and competently assume the responsibility which goes with the power. So many enlightened business men know this that the statement would be little more than a platitude, were it not for an added implication. . . .

The Government should assume the function of economic regulation only as a last resort, to be tried only when private initiative, inspired by high responsibility, with such assistance and balance as Government can give, has finally failed. As yet there has been no final failure, because there has been no attempt; and I decline to assume that this Nation is unable to meet the situation.

The final term of the high contract was for liberty and the pursuit of happiness. . . . We know that liberty to do anything which deprives others of those elemental rights is outside the protection of any compact; and that Government in this regard is the maintenance of a balance, within which every individual may have a place if he will take it; in which every individual may find safety if he wishes it; in which every individual may attain such power as his ability permits, consistent with his assuming the accompanying responsibility. . . .

Faith in America, faith in our tradition of personal responsibility, faith in our institutions, faith in ourselves demand that we recognize the new terms of the old social contract. We shall fulfill them, as we fulfilled the obligation of the apparent Utopia which Jefferson imagined for us in 1776, and which Jefferson, Roosevelt and Wilson sought to bring to realization. We must do so, lest a rising tide of misery, engendered by our common failure, engulf us all. But failure is not an American habit; and in the strength of great hope we must all shoulder our common load.

State Absolutism*

Lawrence Dennis

THE State, through the instrumentalities of government, has to express and enforce the social plan which, for one country, has to be unique. We have already seen why the social plan for any one country has to be unique. This plan the State has to express and enforce through the instrumentalities of government. The methods by which the State does this may follow the liberal formula of the policeman State or the fascist formula of the executive State. In any event, the political power of the State has to be exercised in many matters without limitation if any type of social order is to be maintained. The point is that the power exercised by the totalitarian State in economic and social planning is no greater than the power of the State exercised in other ways under any other political system, or more simply still, that the social plan always requires exercises of the absolute power of the State.

The popular type of denunciation of fascism on the ground that it stands for State absolutism, or a State of unlimited powers, as contrasted with the liberal State of limited powers, is based on misrepresentation of the true nature of the liberal State. The issue between liberalism and fascism is not one of an absolute State versus a State of limited powers. The fact is that the powers of every State are in pure theory unlimited, except by physical impossibilities and by engagements the State chooses to respect in deference to the demands of certain class interests. The powers of the fascist State are unlimited as to doing certain things, while the powers of the liberal State are equally unlimited as to doing certain other things. The important differences between fascism and liberalism in this respect lie between those certain things which each State, respectively, does without limitation, or those fields of State action in which the State is inhibited by no limiting constitutional or legal engagement not to do certain things. . . .

The power of the liberal State to cause its citizens to be killed either in official or unofficial warfare abroad, through exercises of the discretionary power of the President over our armed forces, is absolutely unlimited by law or the courts. But it is a bulwark of liberal liberty that the President's power to regulate commerce, or to do any one of a thousand executive acts in the public interest, must be inhibited by the Constitution or subject to judicial review for its reasonableness. The President has virtually no limitations on his power to get us into war, through the conduct of foreign relations or the command of the armed forces, except such checks as legislative action might impose through impeachment or a failure to vote necessary funds.

The features of the liberal system we are now discussing are fundamental. It is constantly forgotten that the quintessence of liberalism and liberal liberties under a constitution is the maintenance of a regime of special or exceptionally favorable considerations for private property. Briefly, private property cannot be taken for public purposes, not even in war time, without an obligation to pay just compensation, while human life may be so taken without an obligation to pay any compensation. . . . This doctrine, of course, goes under a different name from that of special privilege for property. Its most popular identifying formula is "No taxation without representation." Of course, few people ever pause to inquire "Representation of whom and of what?"

The right of private property to be treated by the State with greater consideration than human life in the matter of conscription for public purposes is the essence of liberalism. This right, once established, becomes not only incompatible with the demands of humanity but also with the requisites of strong nationalism. An interesting sidelight, showing the power of this doctrine as a political principle, is the fact that good liberals before 1914 constantly speculated about the possibility of financing the next big war. But no liberal ever imagined that a war would be impossible because the State would be unable to mobilize the necessary man-power. A human life has no right to deny itself to its country, or to bargain with the State for a fair price, or have appeal to a neutral judiciary to fix for it a fair bargain with the State, according to the same theories of equity which are so extremely partial to property. . . .

The immunity of property from taking without just compensation is, of course, enjoyed in a legal sense quite as much by the man who has no money the State could take as by the man who has a million the State could take. Obviously, the protection of this immunity avails only to those who have enough money to be taken by the State, and whose money, as a practical matter, is taken, but in exchange for government bonds instead of the sort of compensation a conscript receives. Stripped of liberal verbiage of the law, and stated in terms of larger social results, the immunity liberalism gives to property but not to human life from taking by the State without just compensation, means that long wars result in a greater concentration of ownership of wealth, as a result of war financing by borrowing from the rich, whereas long wars would result in a drastic equalization of wealth if the funds needed were taken by levy from the only sources from which they can be taken.

It is one of the great propaganda and indoctrination achievements of the London shopkeepers and the Manchester mill owners, as well as of their American cousins, that it has been possible over a couple centuries of Anglo-Saxon liberal democracy to generalize the belief that the liberties of the people depend on the maintenance of liberal principles which operate to exempt wealth from sharing with personal service the burdens of the liberal state. It is amusing to see how poor devils who will never own anything that the State would find it worth while commandeering except their ability to serve as cannon-fodder will support a Constitution which protects capital from mobilization and social direction by the State except under conditions of profiteering by the capitalists. These poor devils do not realize that there is no clause in the Constitution which they, in their troubles, can ever invoke to check government impingement on their lives or to obtain government relief. When they turn to the Government, it is for a charity hand-out for which they can invoke no right granted them by the Constitution. Under the Constitution and under liberalism, there is a right not to have one's property taken without just compensation—i.e., compensation the courts approve of—but there is no such right for one's life, nor is there a right not to starve for want of work and lack of the instruments or facilities of production.

Indeed, what the Constitution protects is not the right of the hungry to eat but the right of the rich to keep what they have and to eat while the poor starve. Nothing augurs so impressively the end of liberalism today as the changing temper of those on relief who are coming more and more to feel and assert a vested right to be cared for by the State. To the extent the State is being forced by the demands of public order to grant relief—still on the theory of an emergency—it is creating a vested interest or a de facto right which the Constitution does not recognize and a right which a new social order must recognize. . . .

Ours is supposedly a government of delegated powers. The Federal Constitution nowhere delegates to the Federal Government the power to take property through condemnation proceedings in exercise of the right of eminent domain. But, in the opinion of the court—i.e., the Constitution of the United States—the Federal Government, by virtue of the fact that it is a national government, must have such power. The Federal Government may exercise this power inherent in government only in accordance with the social theory of the Court—i.e., the Constitution. In the social theory of the Court, government can properly take property through condemnation proceedings for an arsenal—but not for slum clearance or low cost housing. In the theory of the Court—i.e., the Constitution—the one is a public purpose and the other is not. . . .

The time has come when the limitations imposed by liberal theory on the sovereignty of the national State in respect of property rights, wealth, and economic activities generally, are no longer to be considered by a hard-thinking man of property as calculated to protect his interests in the long run. The day has come when property must no longer assert any immunity from government taking and government commanding which a poor man cannot assert for his life or labor in war time when drafted for national defense. Fascism insists that property or capital and private economic enterprise must be called to the colors as well as conscripts in time of war. And fascism insists that the term of service for both capital and labor is not for an emergency but a new and permanent scheme of social organization and operation. Fascism insists that the new social adventure cannot be conducted on the good liberal principle of having the State always buy the cooperation of the owners and managers of property, as well as of the workers, by paying the price which any economic factor is able to hold out for, in a bargain in which there is great inequality of bargaining power as between different individuals and groups.

The argument of this chapter has been that what is commonly thought of as more power over private property for the State does not mean any greater State absolutism than we have already, or, indeed, any new power over private property. It means new techniques, theories and methods in the application of State power and, also, the application of State power for the service of different interests and for the pursuit of different social objectives. In pure theory, or in concrete fact, fascism or any other political system, cannot be said to create new powers for the State or to give it powers it did not already possess. Fascism merely means that the State announces and adheres to the purpose of using the powers inherent in national sovereignty, or in the monopoly of force held by all government, to meet new needs and desires in new ways.

DISCUSSION QUESTIONS

1. Was the Great Depression the result of virtually unrestrained economic activity?
2. Why did individuals such as Herbert Hoover seek to limit the role of government in the economy?
3. How did Roosevelt's New Deal represent a continuation as well as a shift in federal policy?
4. Why were fascism and communism attractive philosophies in reviving the U.S.?
5. Does government regulation of property increase or decrease personal freedom?

Chapter 10

AMERICAN INTERNATIONALISM AND THE DOMESTIC THREAT

Bourne's forebodings about the impact of war on Americans were realized after the Second World War when the U.S. embarked on a crusade against Soviet communism. This anticommunist crusade saw restrictions placed on individual liberties, and to a lessor degree personal property rights, in order to strengthen the American government in its dealings with the Soviet Union.

The U.S. emerged from World War II as the only true superpower. Rather than retreating into isolation as in 1920, U.S. leaders perceived a Soviet threat to the nearly collapsed democracies of Western Europe and sought to educate the American public of it in order to prevent a return to isolationism. What emerged was an internationalistic outlook, but one which was anticommunist instead of anti-Soviet. According to Yergin,

> For Truman and many of his advisers, anticommunism meant primarily anti-Sovietism. That was not true, however, for a major part of the public, for which anticommunism was more broadly defined to include subversives "enemies within"—most imaginary—and even New Dealers and supporters of what would soon be called the Fair Deal.[1]

Judged in light of the need to prepare the U.S. for battle with the Soviet Union, individuals came under closer scrutiny. Individuals who had joined the American Communist Party were immediately suspected of being

---

[1]From *The Shattered Peace* by Daniel H. Yergin. Copyright © 1977, 1990 by Daniel H. Yergin. Used by permission of Viking Penguin, a division of Penguin Books USA Inc., p. 285.

agents of the Soviet Union. But so were the authors of New Deal policies, given their introduction of government involvement in the economy in an attempt to halt the Great Depression. Still others had their credibility questioned because they regretted the development of nuclear weapons. All these things occurred inside the U.S. at the same time the American Government was increasingly engaged in a war of wills with the Soviet Union for political supremacy.

The fear that there was a communist conspiracy to subvert the U.S. was evident to some by the failures of American foreign policy. Caughey and May noted in this regard,

> A series of events in 1948–1950 enhanced this impression (of the Communist menace) and led large numbers of people to accept the views that extremists put forward. One such event was the Communist coup in Czechoslovakia, for it appeared to demonstrate how powerful could be a relatively small number of dedicated party members. Another was the fall of China. The public had long conceived of the Chinese as peculiarly friendly to America, and wartime propaganda had pictured the Chinese as devoted to their hero, Chiang Kai-shek. It was incomprehensible that his regime should have fallen so swiftly; many could attribute it only to a failure of the United States to give Chiang adequate support; some were willing to believe the Communists in the American Government had engineered his collapse.[2]

This attitude was confirmed by the Rosenberg trial in which Julius and Ethel Rosenberg were convicted of providing nuclear secrets to the Soviet Union. The conclusion was obvious. Moscow was engaged in a world-wide subversive campaign which included directing American citizens to betray their country.

Quick to capitalize on this climate of fear and distrust was Senator Joseph R. McCarthy of Wisconsin, who in 1948 contended that high government officials had acquiesced to the presence of communists. Caughey and May quoted Senator McCarthy as stating,

> While I cannot take the time to name all of the men in the State Department who have been named as members of the Communist Party and members of a spy ring, I have here in my hand a list of two-hundred and five that were known to the Secretary of State as being members of the Communist Party and who nevertheless are still working and shaping the policy of the State Department.[3]

In an effort to weed the communists out of government both houses of Congress established special committees to investigate communist infiltration, the most notorious chaired by Senator McCarthy.

Distinctions between government and nation blurred with respect to

[2]John W. Caughey and Ernest R. May, *A History of the United States* (Chicago: Rand McNally, 1964), p. 676.

[3]Ibid., p. 678.

the perceived internal communist threat. Whereas historically one could be a loyal American and criticize the government, during the 1950s to ciritcize the government or a traditional feature of the American system suggested one possessed communist sympathies. One of the most prominent cases in this regard was that of Alger Hiss. In 1948, Hiss, a former member of the State Department and current president of the Carnegie Endowment for International Peace, was accused of being a communist agent by Whittaker Chambers, a former member of the American Communist Party. Hiss had been a member of Roosevelt's New Deal policy team, which had espoused government intervention in the economy, and as president of the Carnegie Endowment, sought peace in international affairs. Hiss's credibility was questioned by some who regarded his activities as subversive. In the late 1940s there also arose Whittaker Chambers's charge that Hiss had spied for the Communist Party. As Hiss noted in *The Court of Public Opinion*, individuals were accused in private meetings of a committee, information was not provided to the accused, and the charges appeared to be promoted by Republican tactics to discredit Democratic administrations.[4] However, to individuals like Whittaker Chambers there was no difference between socialists and communists in terms of their goals.

> It is a Western body of belief that now threatens the West from Russia. As a body of Western beliefs, secular and rationalistic, the intelligentsia of the West share it, and are therefore always committed to a secret emotional complicity with Communism of which they dislike, not the Communism, but only what, by the chances of history, Russia has added to it—slave labor camps, purges, MVD et al. . . . If they could have Communism without the brutalities of ruling that the Russian experience bred, they have only marginal objections. Why should they object? What else is socialism but Communism with the claws retracted?[5]

Who does one believe? Both Hiss and Chambers appeared sincere and committed to the ideas of American democracy. Yet both sought different solutions to the problems posed in the new age of American internationalism. The ensuing debate, which occurred in a period of nuclear tension, produced suspicions as to the loyalty of American citizens. In this context a very important question was raised in terms of, "How much security could an open, democratic nation have?"

The national security state came into being as a means of securing the U.S. Government against communist infiltration. But who was a communist? As shown, a communist was a person who supported the American

---

[4]Alger Hiss, "First Appearance Before the Committee, August 5, 1948," *In the Court of Public Opinion* (New York: Alfred A. Knopf, 1957), pp. 4–6.

[5]Whittaker Chambers, "Letter of August 5, 1954," in *Odyssey of a Friend, Whittaker Chambers' Letters to William F. Buckley, Jr.*, ed. William F. Buckley, Jr. (New York: G.P. Putnam's Sons, 1969), p. 68.

Communist Party, who believed in state control of the economy or who was seen as contradicting generally accepted American traditions. The broadness of this definition resulted in many Americans being labeled as subversives. Labor leaders who sought better pay for workers, civil rights activists who argued that liberties were denied to people because of their skin color and those who attended Communist-sponsored meetings during the Great Depression were classified as communists. Anything one did during the 1940s and early 1950s which was critical of the U.S. government or the American way of life opened one up to charges of being a subversive.

Some writers recognized that a restricted definition was necessary. Writing during this period, Arthur Schlesinger offered a different view as to what a communist was. "The only criterion for disloyalty is superior loyalty to another country, and that reservations about the capitalist system or skepticism concerning the wisdom of the business community are by themselves no evidence at all of external loyalties."[6] Individuals who have favored government regulation under the banner of the New Deal were not disloyal Americans according to Schlesinger.

What started out as an attempt to secure the world for democracy quickly developed as a pogrom of independent thought in the U.S. government, particularly state governments, attempted to weed out subversives by demanding that intellectuals, teachers, labor leaders, publishers, and members of the entertainment industry take loyalty oaths. Individuals who failed to do so or who had attended meetings of communist or left-leaning groups were labeled as untrustworthy. In this regard, Mason and Leach quoted former U.S. Attorney General Francis J. Biddle in describing how the loyalty program worked.

> Under the order [establishing the program] and regulations, charges were only as specific "as security considerations" would permit; the employee could only introduce such evidence as the [Loyalty Review] Board deemed proper; could cross-examine witnesses—but not informants; had no right to subpoena witnesses; and appeared before a board in his own department which in fact was also acting as a prosecutor. . . . [Cases were decided] on the "unsworn" reports in . . . secret files . . . purporting to connect [employees] . . . with Communism; not to knowledge, but on belief.[7]

Individuals who were regarded as subversive were fired and oftened blacklisted so as to prevent their employment by other businesses.

As seen, the political atmosphere of the 1940s and 1950s was charged by the perceived threat of communism to the point that individual liberty was substantially proscribed. Constitutional rights of freedom of speech

[6]Arthur M. Schlesinger, Jr., "What Is Loyalty? A Difficult Question," *The New York Times Magazine*, November 2, 1947, p. 51.

[7]Alpheus Thomas Mason and Richard H. Leach, *In Quest of Freedom*, 2nd ed. (Englewood Cliffs, NJ: Prentice-Hall, Inc., 1973), p. 374.

and press were visibly limited. Support for American values of freedom and individuality were readily available in motion pictures. Movies like *California Conquest* (1952) demonstrated the willingness of Americans to oppose foreign invasion by the Russians. Still other movies like *The Day the Earth Stood Still* (1951) suggested the existence of a psychosis within American society which led to distrust of anyone or anything which deviated from accepted American traditions.

Motion pictures were also a popular outlet for questioning government control of society. At a time when writers were blacklisted for deviant ideas, science fiction films were often the means of directing criticism of government policy. Particularly noteworthy was that scientific prowess did not justify policies which governments followed as seen in *Forbidden Planet* (1956). Human beings continued to be flawed and to make decisions that were not in the best interests of their security. Still other movies like *It Came From Beneath the Sea* (1955) and *The Incredible Shrinking Man* (1957) were notable for their latent criticisms of the politics and science which created nuclear weapons, but failed to foresee the effects of it on civilization. The criticism that science threatened to undermine American values was a theme of science fiction movies during the 1950s, but one which appeared as science fact during the 1980s and 1990s.

Largely hidden until the 1980s and 1990s was the fact that the American government approved of experiments on its citizenry under the guise of preparing to wage war with the U.S.S.R. Perhaps the most extreme example was Operation Sunshine which was designed to determine the long-term effects of human exposure to radiation. These tests ranged from exposure of stillborn babies to strontium 90, to the injection of radioactive materials into human beings. At other times, the government conducted above-ground nuclear tests without apparently warning the nearby communities, thus subjecting them to the effects of nuclear explosions. Moreover, the fact that nuclear production was more important than safeguarding the lives and property of those people who lived near these facilities has been clearly established during the last part of the twentieth century.

The apparent life and death struggle between American democracy and Soviet communism led to the acceptance of limitations on the rights of individuals and indirectly on property. Government assumed previously unheard-of powers in dealing with the perceived communist threat. The following readings by Alger Hiss, Whittaker Chambers, Arthur M. Schlesinger, Jr., and Howard M. Jones present some views of the period.

First Appearance Before the Committee, August 5, 1948*

Alger Hiss

IN AUGUST 1948 I was living in New York City. For the preceding year and a half I had been president of the Carnegie Endowment for International Peace. To accept that position I had resigned from the State Department, where I was director of the office responsible for proposing and carrying out our policies in the United Nations.

My new work was closely related to what I had been doing in Washington, for the Endowment had decided to concentrate its activities on support of the United Nations as the appropriate means of furthering Andrew Carnegie's aim, stated in 1910, "to hasten the abolition of international war, the foulest blot upon our civilization." The Endowment was conducting research and publishing analyses of the proceedings of the United Nations. In addition we were preparing a series of technical studies to assist the newly created United Nations with its own organizational problems and with the questions coming before it and its affiliated agencies.

On Monday, August 2, 1948, I returned to work at the Endowment's office in New York after a month's vacation with my family in a small Vermont village where we had spent our summers for many years. I had come down on the train alone, as my wife and son were staying in Vermont for a few more weeks. That evening a reporter reached me by telephone at my apartment. He told me that, according to information coming from the Committee on Un-American Activities of the House of Representatives, a man named Chambers was going to appear before the Committee the next morning and would call me a Communist. The reporter asked whether I had any comment.

I did not. The untruthful charge of Communism had been the lot of many who had been New Deal officials in the Washington of the 1930's and the early 1940's. I had not taken such charges seriously when made against others and I saw no reason why I or anyone else should pay much attention to a similar fanciful charge that might now be made against me.

The next morning, Tuesday, August 3, 1948, a witness named Whittaker Chambers appeared before the Committee and said that he was a senior editor of *Time* magazine but that years before he had been "attached" to "an underground organization of the United States Communist Party" in

---

*From Alger Hiss, "First Appearance Before the Committee, August 5, 1948," *In the Court of Public Opinion* (New York: Alfred A. Knopf, 1957), pp. 3–14.

Washington. He said that I had been a member of that group. I received this information about Chambers's testimony, while I was at work in my office, from numerous telephone calls from reporters for the press services and for individual papers. The volume of inquiry by the press was a surprise to me, but I was still inclined to treat the charges as more of a nuisance than anything else.

As I knew no one named Whittaker Chambers (I had heard the man's full name only once before, about a year earlier) and as I had belonged to no organization of the Communist Party, I told the newspapermen that what he said about my association with him was completely untrue, and that so far as I knew I had never even seen him.

At lunch I was advised by friends to ignore the Committee as a body whose activities were discounted by all sensible people. Nevertheless, I chose to make my denials not only to the newspapers but in the same setting where the charges had been made. Therefore, I sent a telegram to the Committee that same afternoon saying that I wanted to appear to deny Chambers's charges under oath. As I expected to be in Washington on Endowment business two days later, I suggested that I appear on that day, Thursday. . . .

Chambers's testimony was given just three months before the 1948 Presidential and Congressional elections. A few days prior to Chambers's public debut Miss Elizabeth Bentley had told the Committee her tale of Communist conspirators in government. For some months before the taking of any testimony, the more sensational newspapers had carried reports of promised disclosures by the Committee. In March the Committee had received from Congress (the first Republican Congress since 1932) the largest appropriation ($200,000) it had ever received in its ten years of existence. The election year 1948 had been chosen as a period of increased activity for the Committee; and the selected theme of that activity was Communist espionage. The Chairman of the Committee, Mr. J. Parnell Thomas, Republican, of New Jersey, said later that the Republican National Committee Chairman "was urging me in the Dewey campaign [Governor Dewey's 1948 presidential effort] to set up the spy hearings. At that time he was urging me to stay in Washington in order to put the heat on Harry Truman."[1]

In addition to the Chairman, the Committee had four other Republican members: Karl E. Mundt of South Dakota, John McDowell of Pennsylvania, Richard M. Nixon of California, and Richard B. Vail of Illinois. The Democrats were John S. Wood of Georgia, John E. Rankin of Mississippi, H. Hardin Peterson of Florida, and F. Edward Hebert of Louisiana. William S. White of *The New York Times* commented on August 15, 1948: "Likely as not, troubles for the Truman Administration will begin simultaneously with any hearing. The President has no really strong political supporter or

[1] *The New York Times*, February 8, 1954.

close friend on the committee's Democratic panel of four, and in that same panel he has certainly one of his most violent detractors, Representative John E. Rankin of Mississippi." . . .

The Committee accepted the day I had suggested, Thursday, and I went on to Washington the evening before. On arriving I obtained a transcript of Chambers's testimony. This gave me no more information as to what he was talking about than had the press accounts. He said nothing of the actual circumstances under which I had in fact met and known him by a different name, so that I still had no key to his identity, despite a slight sense of familiarity about some of his press photographs. An unknown man, with unknown motives, had chosen to call me a Communist. More specifically, he had asserted that I had been a Communist in the mid1930's.

Although I found no clues to Chambers's identity or to his motivation in his testimony, I found in reading the transcript indications of the Committee's attitude. Mundt, presiding in Thomas's absence, had, I noticed, asked Stripling whether he knew "the reason why" I was "removed from the State Department." Though Stripling had made the correction that he had no record that I had been removed, Mundt later in the hearing had volunteered, without correction, another prejudicial statement about me:

> There is reason to believe that he organized within that Department one of the Communist cells which endeavored to influence our Chinese policy and bring about the condemnation of Chiang Kai-shek, which put Marzani in an important position there. . . .

I had never known any Marzani. Not only had I never organized "cells" within the State Department, I had no connection with our China policy after 1944, a time when Chiang's pre-eminence was undisputed. My only functions before that time relating to China had been assisting in removing discriminatory aspects of our immigration policy, in negotiating a treaty of friendship with China, and in expediting lend-lease aid to China.

Upon bringing out my position with the Carnegie Endowment, Mundt had in addition contributed for the record the statement:

> . . . Certainly there is no hope for world peace under the leadership of men like Alger Hiss. . . .

It seemed to me plain enough that some members of the Committee were launched on a hunt for political sensations and that their attitude toward anyone charged with Communism would not be objective. I was annoyed at their biased comments about me, but I felt convinced that in spite of their attitude I would be able to show them promptly that they had been misled into hasty and unfair remarks. I had nothing to hide and, I thought, nothing to fear. A simple statement of facts would surely clear up the whole business. . . .

At the beginning of my testimony, I said that I had never been a member of the Communist Party or of any of its front organizations nor had I followed its line. I said also that, so far as I knew, none of my friends was a Communist and went on to add:

> To the best of my knowledge, I never heard of Whittaker Chambers until in 1947, when two representatives of the Federal Bureau of Investigation asked me if I knew him and various other people, some of whom I knew and some of whom I did not know. I said I did not know Chambers. So far as I know, I have never laid eyes on him, and I should like to have the opportunity to do so.

I had seen in the accounts of Chambers's testimony of August 3 several press photographs of him. There seemed to be a degree of familiarity about some of these. Perhaps I had met him at some large gathering and failed to catch, or now failed to recall, his name. Or perhaps he resembled someone I actually did know. At the time I had no further clues and I was curious to have a good look at him. I assumed that the Committee, having had for two days my request to testify, would have made arrangements for him to be present. My telegram had expressly stated: "I do not know Mr. Chambers. . . ." Had the procedure of confrontation been followed promptly to clear up the question of identity, I would in any colloquy that morning with Chambers unquestionably have been able, as I was two weeks later when I did see him, to recognize him as the free-lance writer George Crosley whom I had met fourteen years before, in the early days of the New Deal. . . .

In fact, however, the obvious practical step of letting me see Chambers was not taken for some time. Instead the Committee proceeded two days later to interrogate Chambers in secret about his claims of familiarity with my personal habits and then, again in secret, to go over the same topics with me on August 16. This procedure obscured what had actually happened, that I had indeed met Chambers fourteen years before but under a different name and in entirely different circumstances from those he asserted. Worse, the Committee's course built up over a two-week period the false impression that I had denied ever knowing Chambers under any name and in any circumstances. Though they did not then make it public, the Committee knew two days after my testimony that I had never known Chambers by his own name. He admitted this at a secret session held on August 7, but I did not learn of this until nine days later. The entire procedure followed by the Committee was ill-suited to an objective inquiry into the basic and preliminary question of whether I had ever known the man at all. . . .

But on August 5, as Crosley had not yet been recalled to my mind, these speculations had not yet occurred to me. I knew merely that a stranger had unaccountably said that I had been a member with him of a secret Communist group, that he had eventually come to my house to ask me to break with the Communist Party, that I had cried at separating from him that he was very fond of me. The situation seemed to me to be in the realm of fantasy and for that very reason, I could not but feel, would be dispelled by a simple assertion of reality. . . .

It seems clear that some members of the Committee, however, had a political stake in seeing to it that this fantasy should not be dispelled. No meeting with Chambers was arranged. Their attitude was revealed in a series of articles by Stripling that appeared in the Hearst press some months later (January 30 through February 26, 1949) and in the fall of 1949 in book form as *The Red Plot Against America*, edited by Bob Considine of International News Service (Hearst). Stripling reports that in an executive session (Congressional terminology for a closed meeting of the Committee) that followed my testimony, "the members looked at one another for a time, and you could have cut the gloom with a knife. `We're ruined!' one declared. . . . our espionage[2] inquiry plainly was tottering. President Truman took the occasion to call the hearing a 'red herring.' . . ."

Chambers, though not officially connected with the Committee, is also able to record this incident, adding the comment: "It was an election year, and the seat of every member of the Committee was at stake." Chambers further records that Nixon was "the man of decision who . . . made the Hiss Case possible" by insisting on additional hearings. Without apparent ironical intent, Chambers observes that the Committee "never faltered again."[3]

Letter of April 6, 1954*

Whittaker Chambers

Dear Buckley,

There are two Apparats, as you know—the Communist and the socialist. I believe that it is prevailingly the displeasure of the second Apparat that you are now suffering. It can be stated, simply as an objective fact, that Senator McCarthy is a Communist target, set up on a worldwide scale. Their aim in recognizing the possibilities of this target is, as so often with

---

[2]Though Chambers had expressly stated in his August 3 testimony that those he named "were specifically not wanted to act as sources of information," Stripling here reveals that the Committee had predetermined that its inquiry was to be a hunt for spies. Thomas, too, spoke of setting up "the spy hearings."

[3]Both Stripling and Chambers have, however, disclosed an additional occasion on which the Committee "faltered," and which revealed again the heavy investment the Committee had made in presenting a prejudged case as opposed to following an objective quest for facts.

*From Whittaker Chambers, "Letter of April 6, 1954," in *Odyssey of a Friend, Whittaker Chambers' Letters to William F. Buckley, Jr.*, ed. William F. Buckley, Jr. (New York: G.P. Putnam's Sons, 1969), pp. 56–63.

Communists, not merely negative (the destruction of an enemy), but positive (an issue and activity around which to recruit mass support). Incidentally a similar appraisal helps to determine my "neutralism" in the matter. Precisely because the Communists do not have the American masses with them on this issue, they must, to be effective, work up the "classes" to a pitch. Fortunately for the CP, the first Apparat, that is easy.to do. The second Apparat (socialism) is self-starting to a high degree, and the law of inertia can be counted on to do the rest with only a nudge now and then from the multitongued Agitprop. The socialist Apparat will eagerly do the rest. And almost everywhere and always, it is these people, rather than the masses, who have been the effective agents of Communist advance. Even when they are not the "classes" by origin, the socialists adapt themselves to the classes, and share their tone, habitats and superior venom. They are cobras, not pit vipers, like the Communists. They strike with some precision and grace; and their bite produces paralysis, rather than the agonized swelling and mortification of the rattlers. (There may always be a point, of course, at which the masses become decisive for the CP, but that is another story, though it would be a mistake not to bear it in mind.)

Now, the Communists recognized at once (or, more probably, after they had stirred things up a bit) that Senator McCarthy is a political godsend. The socialists like to note this disingenuously for their own political purposes, but the fact remains a fact. The reason is obvious. Not only does Senator McCarthy unite through fear the socialist Apparat and its far-flung freemasonry of fellow travelers (anybody who believes as an article of faith that a low voice is a sweet and modest thing in woman, and even in man; and that one does not bang one's spoon against one's cup whilst stirring one's tea). Equally important, Senator McCarthy *divides* the ranks of the Right. Historically, this is inevitable. There have been a series of these divisive leaders, varying in this or that set of details—Chiang Kai-shek, Syngman Rhee, General de Gaulle, etc. The Right, so long as it has vitality enough to fight back at all, must throw them up: they embody, inter alia, a way of fighting. Value judgments are not in point. The point is that their leadership never fails to divide the Right and unite the Left almost to the limits of its spectrum.

Senator McCarthy was almost made to order. He is a man, fighting almost wholly by instinct and intuition, against forces for the most part coldly conscious of their ways, means, and ends. In other words, he scarcely knows what he is doing. He simply knows that somebody threw a tomato and the general direction from which it came. His general tactic might be epitomized in Samson's bright thought of setting fire to the foxes' tails and sending them helter-skelter against the enemy.[1] A tactic not altogether

[1]Book of Judges 15:4.

ruled out in a minor skirmish in a guerrilla war—but it is not a strategy; and repetition dooms it, not only to defeat, but to boredom.

Yet the Senator represents the one force that all shades of the Left really fear. This does not contradict what I have written above about his tactical inadequacy. It results from the fact that, in the U.S., the Left must take power by deception. This is peculiarly true of the socialist Apparat. Deception and secrecy, for the Communist Apparat, are only certain methods, among others, of working. But for the socialist Apparat, deception and secrecy are prerequisites for the actual taking of power in the State, which they have held before (New and Fair Deals), and which they feel within an eyelash of taking, and permanently consolidating, soon again. That is, they stand within an inch of closing the capitalist phase of history in the U.S. (hence in the world), and of rooting their power in its vast, fertilizing dinosauric corpse. But there is one prime condition: they may not do it as socialists. They may do it only as something else, due to the ingrained American aversion to the word, socialism. By repeatedly lighting his foxes' tails and loosing them indiscriminately toward the Left, the Senator repeatedly calls the attention of the antisocialist masses to the fact that the socialist Apparat exists; and worse, that the socialist and Communist Apparats co-exist, blend at certain points of tactic and purpose; have been, and are, auxiliaries, although, no doubt, it is the socialist intention, as Franklin Roosevelt once noted for passing political effect, to lie in wait for the Communists on the day of reckoning. That day is the *Machtergreifung,* the seizure of power; and it is that seizure of power that the Senator constantly imperils. He alone on the Right, at this moment, *visibly* imperils it. So both Apparats, the cobras and the pit vipers, converge on him. . . .

But, as you know, I do not believe that the Senator has what it takes to win the fight for the Right. I believe that Richard Nixon may have some of what it takes. I believe it the more readily because the Left also believes it. Therefore, it sought to eliminate him at the start (of course, only as one detail of a wider strategy). Never suppose that the Left has finished with Nixon. But the Senator has proved a more available target; while Nixon has proved a more elusive strategist, and his methods and success are the more baffling (at least, momentarily) because they did not think he had it in him; and perhaps because they feel that they can eliminate him in the general wreck of the administration. For the present, that is sound tactics. But, once Senator McCarthy is pruned back, they will get on with the Vice President. As they will get on with me. One of the incidental values of Senator McCarthy as a target has been that he distracts attention from the Hiss Case, which remains the prime danger to the Left in that field. And this, both for what is past and because, if even one of the inner Hiss circle, say, Lee Pressman, should tell the truth, the political effect would be to blow the Left down for a season. . . .

Of course, in the larger sense, I believe that the bigger battle is lost in advance. This is nothing new with me. At heart, I have scarcely ever, if at all, believed anything else. My remark about "the losing side" aroused more concern among good folk than almost anything else in *Witness*. Moreover, I held this so strongly that in a passage, which so far as I know nobody has noticed, I said flatly that I felt that the cause I fought for was so powerless to help itself that even God had given up. This is the passage about my thoughts in the Wall Street district after the expert had mistakenly postdated the manufacture of the microfilm. I never really hoped to do more in the Hiss Case than give the children of men a slightly better, only slightly better, chance to fight a battle already largely foredoomed. I rejoice that I could make the effort, and I should rather never have lived than not have made it. But I had, and have, no illusion, or few. This is at the root of my endemic hopelessness, made deceptive to most people by my temperamental buoyancy. It is part of the climate that has taken vengeance on my heart—overweight and work are only incidental factors though of the kind that the secular world puts its faith in. This, too, was at the root of much of my vacillation in the past. . . .

These thoughts have been much re-enforced by the explosions in the Pacific,[2] which, like you, I cannot get out of my mind. I have long been convinced of that, too. Our faint hearts are all atremble with dread at the thought that what they are going to is a war. What they are really going to is the end of a civilization and an age. Now we see how. The solution lies with the Bombs, not with the arguments. But if it should not, if we should be so far gone in historical corruption as to outlaw the Bombs, gas, bacteria et al., the Communists will merely win over the slower haul. They will let us hang ourselves on our own base fears and parish-house morality. As Willi [Schlamm] says bitterly: "Malenkov will save civilization." . . .

Meanwhile, may things look up for you currently. I offer you a quotation with which to bait and lure your opponents in controversy. Offer it in exhibit and ask them if they too believe this: "It goes without saying that only a planned economy can make intelligent use of *all* a people's strength." If they agree, the author is Adolf Hitler (*Hitler's Secret Conversations*, Farrar, Straus, & Young, page 15). . . .

---

[2]The hydrogen bomb tests at Eniwetok.

Letter of August 5, 1954*

Whittaker Chambers

Dear Bill,

Thank you for the books, and, particularly, for your kindness in sending them. Camus is stunting in an intellectual glider, riding the currents of
the tricky, upper air. I admire his skill in the qualified way with which we
admire a skill we shall never be capable of, which seems to have little relevance to us, and which (perhaps because of our limitations) seems to have
little to do with reality. But Butterfield has both feet firmly on the ground. I
am reading him with interest. His grasp of what Marx means seems singular, coming from such a quarter; and my friend, John Chamberlain, should
be made to read that chapter every morning before breakfast.

Of course, I wrote you a long letter as soon as Camus came, and
added a few paragraphs with each Butterfield book. Yesterday, I did you
the kindness to burn it. From it I shall pick up only one point, touched on
by you in one of your letters. No, I no longer believe that political solutions
are possible for us. I am baffled by the way people still speak of the West as
if it were at least a cultural unity against Communism though it is divided
not only by a political, but by an invisible cleavage. On one side are the
voiceless masses with their own subdivisions and fractures. On the other
side is the enlightened, articulate elite which, to one degree or other, has
rejected the religious roots of the civilization—the roots without which it is
no longer Western civilization, but a new order of beliefs, attitudes and
mandates. In short, this is the order of which Communism is one logical
expression, originating not in Russia, but in the culture capitals of the West,
reaching Russia by clandestine delivery via the old underground centers in
Cracow, Vienna, Berne, Zurich and Geneva. It is a Western body of belief
that now threatens the West from Russia. As a body of Western beliefs, secular and rationalistic, the intelligentsia of the West share it, and are therefore always committed to a secret emotional complicity with Communism
of which they dislike, not the Communism, but only what, by the chances
of history, Russia has specifically added to it—slave labor camps, purges,
MVD et al. And that, not because the Western intellectuals find them unjus-
tifiable, but because they are afraid of being caught in them. If they could
have Communism without the brutalities of ruling that the Russian experi-

*From Whittaker Chambers, "Letter of August 5, 1954," in *Odyssey of a Friend, Whittaker Cham-
bers' Letters to William F. Buckley, Jr.*, ed. William F. Buckley, Jr. (New York: G.P. Putnam's Sons,
1969), pp. 67–68.

ence bred, they have only marginal objections. Why should they object? What else is socialism but Communism with the claws retracted? And there is positivism. What is more, every garage mechanic in the West, insofar as be believes in nuts and bolts but asks: "The Holy Ghost, what's that?" shares the substance of those same beliefs. Of course, the mechanic does not know, when he asks: "The Holy Ghost, what's that?" that he is simply echoing Stalin at Teheran: "The Pope—how many divisions has the Pope?" That is the real confrontation of forces. The enemy—he is ourselves. That is why it is idle to talk about preventing the wreck of Western civilization. It is already a wreck from within. That is why we can hope to do little more now than snatch a fingernail of a saint from the rack or a handful of ashes from the faggots, and bury them secretly in a flowerpot against the day, ages hence, when a few men begin again to dare to believe that there was once something else, that something else is thinkable, and need some evidence of what it was, and the fortifying knowledge that there were those who, at the great nightfall, took loving thought to preserve the tokens of hope and truth. . . .

What Is Loyalty? A Difficult Question*

Arthur M. Schlesinger, Jr.

We have heard a good deal in recent months about loyalty and Americanism. Spokesmen on one side proclaim that the American way of life is in imminent danger from any one who questions the eternal rightness of the capitalist system. Spokesmen on the other side proclaim that a sinister witch-hunt is already transforming the United States into a totalitarian police state.

The situation cries out for a little less hysteria and a little more calm sense. A calm survey surely reveals two propositions on which we can all agree: (1) that Americanism is not a totalitarian faith, which can impose a single economic or political dogma or require a uniformity in observance from all its devotees; but (2) that a serious problem for national security has been created by that fanatical group which rejects all American interests in favor of those of the Soviet Union.

In other words, the disciples of the Un-American Activities Committee and the leadership of the American Legion must be reminded that Americanism means something far richer and deeper than submission to their own collection of petty prejudices; and civil libertarians who honestly

*From Arthur M. Schlesinger, Jr., "What Is Loyalty? A Difficult Question," *The New York Times Magazine*, November 2, 1947, pp. 7, 48–51.

fear a witch-hunt must be reminded that in an imperfect world of spies and traitors a Government must be conceded the right of self-protection. We see here an inescapable conflict between civil liberty and national security, and we must face up to the problem of resolving the conflict.

What is Americanism? To get quickly to what its loudest exponents seem to regard as its basic point—private enterprise—there is nothing un-American about criticizing the capitalist system. Let us reveal the hideous secret: capitalism was not handed down with the Ten Commandments at Sinai. The Constitution of the United States does not ordain the economic status quo. It can well be argued that there is nothing in our fundamental law to prevent Congress from socializing all basic industry tomorrow; there is certainly nothing in our state laws to prevent public ownership.

Are we to assume that revelations concerning the sacrosanctity of private capitalism have been vouchsafed to the NAM and to the Republican party which were denied to the Founding Fathers? More than this, the basic tradition in American democracy—the tradition associated with such names as Jefferson, Jackson, Wilson, and the two Roosevelts—has been a fight on behalf of the broad masses against the economic excesses of capitalism and against the political aspirations of the business community. . . .

This insistence on the infallibility of capitalism and on the heresy of change finds no sanction in the usages of the American democratic tradition. It reaches its pinnacle of imbecility in such episodes as the attack on the film "The Best Years of Our Lives" as Communist-minded because it makes fun of the American business man, or in the standards employed by the Un-American Committee in their current Hollywood investigation. What havoc the rigid identification of Americanism with business worship would wreak upon the history and traditions of our country! Yet this very identification pervades altogether too much of the popular campaign against communism. Many conservatives are happily pouncing upon the Communist scare as an excuse for silencing all critics of business supremacy. . . .

Experience by now must have exposed the illusion that it is possible to work with Communists or fellow-travelers—with persons whose loyalties are signed, sealed and delivered elsewhere. . . . Again the record is clear. Herbert Morrison, hardly a reactionary, has borne testimony, for example, to the cases of Communist espionage which came to him as British Home Secretary at a time when Britain and Russia were fighting allies.

"It may be said that all countries spy, and it may be that they do," Morrison observed. "But there is a grave difference between the ordinary spying of the professional spy . . . and espionage through a political organization." The documents of the Canadian spy case report the techniques of Communist political corruption in fascinating and indisputable detail—in particular, the use of the "study group" as a way of feeling out the degrees of political fanaticism. . . .

It would be rash to assume that Moscow has its intelligence networks operating in every country except the one it has repeatedly named as its chief enemy—the United States. Certainly the American Communist party has made no secret of its belief that the United States should always follow the Soviet lead. As recently as September 1947, Political Affairs, the American Communist theological organ, made its usual references to the "fact" that "the policies of the Soviet Union before, during and since the anti-Axis war, have corresponded to the best interests of the American people."

In view of such repeated declarations, it becomes increasingly difficult to see how even Henry Wallace can continue saying, "The very few Communists I have met have been very good Americans." The presumption becomes overwhelming that the U.S.S.R. through the NKVD, its underground Communist cells and its front organizations, is commissioning agents to penetrate the "sensitive" branches of the Government, particularly the State Department, the Department of National Defense and the Atomic Energy Commission.

Let us then admit that a real danger exists. But the solution is surely not, on the one hand, to fire every one suspected of liberal leanings, nor, on the other hand, to fire only avowed and open Communists. The solution is rather to construct some means of ridding the security agencies of questionable characters, while at the same time retaining enough safeguards to insure against indiscriminate purges.

Discharge in advance of an overt act may seem a rough policy. Yet the failure to discharge suspicious persons may well imperil national security; it certainly would lead to the use of precautionary measures, such as wiretapping and constant shadowing which would bring the police state much nearer. Let us recall for a moment the situation in 1938. Obviously Nazis, their conscious fellow-travelers and soft-headed Americans who conceived Germany to be a much misunderstood nation had no business in the State Department; and liberals were correct in demanding their dismissal in advance of overt acts. I cannot see why this same principle does not apply today to the fellow-travelers of a rival totalitarianism.

Have we, in fact, a witch-hunt today? We must first discriminate between the wishes of some members of Congress and the intentions of the Executive. The most shocking actions of the Administration—notably the President's executive order, the State Department's loyalty code and some of the recent firings—have doubtless been motivated in great part by a desire to head off more extreme action from Congress. Yet this very process of appeasing the worst element in Congress has led to the compromise of principles which cannot be properly compromised in a democracy. Appeasement has produced throughout the Executive Branch an atmosphere of apprehension and anxiety that is fatal to boldness in government. . . .

Yet the executive order and the the State Department code are inexcusably defective. In particular, the recent action of the State Department in denying most of those discharged both the right to a hearing and the right to resignation without prejudice betrays a state of mind going beyond the requirements of security and entering the realm of persecution. The department must be able to terminate employment on suspicion; this can be done in a number of ways; but the department cannot be allowed to stigmatize individuals and wreck lives on suspicion.

. . . The final result can only be to enthrone the narrow, bureaucratic conformist at the expense of the courageous and independent public servant—and at the ultimate expense of the belief in human dignity which purports to be the main objective of our foreign policy.

Still, honest civil libertarians might better devote themselves, not to blanket abuse of any attempts to meet the problem but to the construction of alternatives which would better secure individual rights while still permitting the Government to deal effectively with the grim dangers of foreign espionage. . . .

The first constructive step, perhaps, would be to make a clear distinction between the rights of an American citizen and the rights of a government employee in a security agency. The private political views of a Hollywood writer, for example, hardly seem to be the proper consideration of the United States Government or a committee of Congress. An American citizen clearly must be protected in his right to think and speak freely—as a Communist, a Fascist or whatever he wants; but no rule of the Constitution or of common sense requires the State Department to employ him. . . .

The second step would be to hedge round the process of dismissal from security agencies with much firmer procedural safeguards. At some point in the process full power to summon witnesses and to weigh evidence must be concentrated. That point plainly must be, not the investigative agency, but a government review board to which all persons dismissed on security grounds can appeal. That board must acquaint the accused with the charges and permit him the protection of counsel. It must be able to obtain from the FBI full data concerning the reliability of the evidence; the situation is intolerable where the administrator must act on the basis of statements from informants identified only by letters, numbers or FBI code-names.

The board must have the further power to interrogate these informants. The problem of permitting the accused to confront the informants, however, is not so simple as it sounds. Espionage breeds counter-espionage; and government counter-espionage agencies simply cannot unveil their agents at every demand of a defense attorney. Where the evidence by itself is substantial, the review board cannot be expected to require confrontation. But, where the evidence is tenuous, the board must have the power of confronting the accused with the accuser. If the FBI does not think the case important enough to risk blowing a counter-espionage chain, it must choose between the chain and the conviction. . . .

The situation imposes a special responsibility, too, I think, upon the American left. Liberals who complain when Parnell Thomas fails to distinguish between liberals and Communists should remember that too often they have failed to make that distinction themselves. History by now has surely documented that distinction to the point of surfeit; the attack on the free Socialist parties in the recent Belgrade manifesto is only the most recent example of the deadly Soviet hostility to the non-Communist left.

The liberal movement in this country must reject the Communists as forthrightly as the British Labor party has rejected them; it must not squander its energy and influence in covering up for them. This is the dictate of strategy as well as principle. Whatever conservatism may say about Wilson Wyatt or Leon Henderson and Americans for Democratic Action, or about such labor leaders as Walter Reuther and David Dubinsky, it cannot combat them by smearing them as fellow-travelers.

But the situation imposes just as grave a responsibility upon American conservatives. They must remember that the only criterion for disloyalty is superior loyalty to another country, and that reservations about the capitalist system or skepticism concerning the wisdom of the business community are by themselves no evidence at all of external loyalties. The essential fight in Europe today, for example, is between socialism and communism; and socialism has many supporters and sympathizers in this country who are resolutely anti-totalitarian. If the leadership of this country were to be confined to men endorsed by the business community, then the United States would be doomed once more to that morass of confusion and failure into which business rule has invariably plunged us throughout our history.

There is no easy answer to this conflict of principles between civil liberty and national security. The practical results thus must depend too much for comfort upon the restraint and wisdom of individuals. This responsibility becomes only one aspect of the great moral challenge which confronts us. If we cannot handle this conflict of principle soberly and responsibly, if we cannot rise to the world crisis, then we lack the qualities of greatness as a nation, and we can expect to pay the price of hysteria or of paralysis.

Do You Know the Nature of an Oath?*

Howard Mumford Jones

Last October I received a telegram from the chairman of the English department of the southern branch of the University of California, commonly known as U.C.L.A., and attractively situated in Westwood in Los Angeles, not very far from the great Huntington Library in San Marino. This

*From Howard Mumford Jones, "Do You Know the Nature of an Oath?" Reprinted from *The American Scholar* Volume 20, Number 4, Autumn 1951. Copyright © 1951 by Phi Beta Kappa Society, pp. 457–67.

telegram asked whether I would be interested in accepting appointment to their summer faculty in 1951.

Since 1949 the University of California has been struggling in the coils of a situation which took initial shape when the Board of Regents decided to impose upon the faculty a so-called loyalty oath. Members of the faculty had already sworn to uphold the Constitution of the United States and the Constitution of California. The latter constitution prescribes an oath of the type usual for state officials—that is, they solemnly promise to support the Constitution and faithfully discharge their duties; and it then adds: "And no other oath, declaration, or test, shall be required as a qualification for any office or public trust." This language seems plain and clear; but the Regents, who had usually been of the opinion that a university professorship is neither a public office nor a public trust, decided that an additional oath was to be required of members of the University faculty and that they had the power to require it. They therefore instituted what is known as a loyalty oath, of their own devising.

This oath required the subscriber to swear that he does not believe in, and is not a member of, any party or organization that believes in, advocates, or teaches the overthrow of the United States government by force or violence. Such, at any rate, was the original form of this purgative declaration, which has been modified in the course of two unhappy years. As no member of the faculty was a member of any such party or organization, many professors refused to sign a statement so unnecessary and humiliating. The dispute began. . . .

When I received my telegram in October, I at once consulted two or three members of the California faculty who happened to be in Cambridge at the time. In the light of their advice and in the hope of enforcing the truth that contracts made in good faith cannot be arbitrarily terminated, I declined appointment at U.C.L.A. . . .

It is now canonical for me to state that I am not a member of the Communist party, that I have never been a member of the Communist party, that I have no intention of becoming a member of the Communist party, and that, to the best of my knowledge and belief, I am not now, I have not been, nor do I intend to become, a stooge for the Communist party. I have belonged at one time or another to random organizations which have since been called subversive, though I think I belong to no such organizations now, but in this connection it is important to observe that if you are of the liberal persuasion, if you want to accomplish some particular reform, and if you create an organization looking toward this purpose, you are commonly helpless as an individual to prevent anybody else from joining the organization; you are helpless to prevent somebody or other, in office or out, from calling such an organization subversive; and by and by you discover that sooner or later somebody finds this slur a convenient device for killing the liberal movement. I am also compelled to point out that as a matter of law the Communist party is a legal organization, that as a matter of principle the American Association of University Professors refuses to accept the theory that membership in any lawful political organization is *ipso facto* sufficient reason for discharging a professor, and that, in view of the express denial by officials of the American Communist party that they advocate the overthrow of the government by either force or violence, the courts have as yet reached no clear decision as to whether the overthrow of the government by force or violence is *ex hypothesi* an essential purpose of the American Communists. . . .

However, I am straying from the point. The increasing belief that loyalty oaths either produce or prove loyalty is one of the most remarkable phenomena of the last twenty-five years. The position of those who demand that loyalty oaths be imposed—usually upon other people—is simple, and emotionally understandable. They argue that not only public officials but any other important class of persons supposed to be influential—air-raid wardens, doctors, lawyers, librarians, teachers and the like—should take such an oath or leave their posts or their business. The theory is simple. The Constitution, state or federal, requires public officials to take an oath of office, doesn't it? Even Mr. Truman has to swear or affirm that he will faithfully execute his office and to the best of his ability preserve, protect and defend the Constitution. Do you think you're better than the president? If you're not a Red, why do you object to taking an oath? Aren't you a patriotic American? Why are you ashamed to prove you're loyal? Do you think we're going to entrust education (or the courts, or wounded boys in hospitals, or radio programs, or television, or public libraries) to disloyal Commies? People who might use the opportunity to overthrow the government by force or violence, or corrupt our youth, or mislead the voters, or distribute seditious literature, or promulgate atheism? . . .

The nation wants security. A psychology of fear is abroad. People are uneasy, and it seems to quiet their uneasiness if they can force other persons to take oaths. What is disturbing in this situation is that this apprehensiveness, this feeling that the Communist party or some other organization is somehow threatening our security, springs from a profound, widespread and popular distrust of democracy. It assumes that very few persons are to be trusted, that average human nature is corrupt, that men are more likely to be treasonable than loyal, corrupt than honest, conspiratorial than open, evil than good. The fact that the whole history of the United States up to now demonstrates the opposite conception—the conception, namely, that the relations between man and man are in the main honorable—somehow fails to persuade. Distrust remains. Distrust assumes that even if you allow Richard Roe and John Doe to do pretty much what they like as private persons (of course, within the laws and customs of the land), the moment you elevate Richard Roe and John Doe to posts of eminence or power or authority or responsibility, an irresistible impulse toward evil overcomes them, and to hamper this impulse, you must guard yourself against Richard Roe and John Doe as officials or teachers or lawyers or air-raid wardens or public librarians. . . .

I think the proponents of loyalty oaths are like this owl, hooting at the glorious sun and crying out, "Where is it?" Loyalty oaths neither create, nor prove, nor protect loyalty to the American tradition. They do not in the least help us to detect the traitorous or the criminal. Every lawyer I have talked to assures me that existing laws are ample to punish those who would betray their country or perjure themselves for treasonable purposes or otherwise be untrue to their American heritage. There are solemn occasions, indeed, when an oath is a proper and impressive ceremony, but the oftener oaths are required, the hastier the ceremony, the less impressive the oath, and the greater the temptation to regard the oath as a minor and meaningless legal convention. Loyalty oaths today are hampering government, weakening education, and restricting both the research work and the distribution of the fruits of research among the peoples of the earth. They will eventually induce among our people the same cynicism they induced in England in the seventh century and again in the eighteenth century, the same cynicism that was induced in this country by the Alien and Sedition laws.

If this nation is so feeble that its intellectual classes have to be plastered together by loyalty oaths, it will not survive by reason of these oaths. If there are those who think that only by loyalty oaths the democratic state can survive, I can but reply that these very persons, who demand this outward and formal proof of an inward and spiritual faith, are themselves false to the democratic spirit because they profoundly disbelieve the honesty of the average man; they are profoundly false to the axiom that every man is innocent until he is proven guilty; and they profoundly distrust the possibility of democracy itself. There have been, and there probably still are, traitors, perjurers and spies in the country, but they are a fraction of 1 per cent of the total population of decent, intelligent, God-fearing Americans. No conceivable loyalty oath is going to prevent the traitor, the perjurer or the spy from being what he is, just as no loyalty oath is going to help the police to expose him. As I am by faith a Jeffersonian democrat, defiant and unashamed, I cannot better conclude these remarks than by quoting a passage from the famous First Inaugural Address:

> If there be any among us who would wish to dissolve this Union or to change its republican form, let them stand undisturbed as monuments of the safety with which error of opinion may be tolerated where reason is left free to combat it. I know, indeed, that some honest men fear that a republican government cannot be strong; that this government is not strong enough . . . I believe this, on the contrary, the strongest government on earth. I believe it is the only one where every man at the call of the law, would fly to the standard of the law, and would meet invasion of the public order as his own personal concern. Sometimes it is said that man cannot be trusted with the government of himself. Can he, then, be trusted with the government of others? Or have we

Chapter 11

INDIVIDUAL RIGHTS AND LIBERTIES REDEFINED

The general trend towards greater government regulation of individual activities in the fight against communism was countered during the 1950s and 1960s by new movements which demanded equal rights for blacks and women. At times, these movements were regarded as communist front organizations because of their demand for a change from the traditional emphasis on equality of opportunity to equality of outcome. As authors of one American government textbook stated, "The history of civil rights in the United States is primarily the story of the search for social and economic equality."[1]

But how was this goal to be accomplished? Central in this regard was that the basic liberties and participatory rights of a minority must be protected the same as those of the majority. In addition, economic rights cannot be denied to someone because of skin color or gender. However, at the same time there were prominent individuals who argued that when a historic pattern of discrimination had existed it was impossible for there to be equality of opportunity. President Johnson made that forceful argument in stating:

> You do not take a person who for years has been hobbled by chains, liberate him, bring him up to the starting line of a race, and then say, "You are free to compete with all others," and still justly believe that you have been complete-

[1]Kenneth Janda, Jeffrey M. Berry, and Jerry Goldman, *The Challenge of Democracy*, 3rd ed. Copyright © 1992 by Houghton Mifflin Company, p. 576.

ly fair. Thus, it is not enough just to open the gates of opportunity; all our citizens must have the ability to walk through those gates.[2]

The movement to ensure civil liberties for blacks emerged most forcefully in the post–World War II period. Although slavery had ended with the Civil War, black Americans continued to lack economic and political rights. Economically, blacks continued to be among the poorest members of society for in the post–Civil War period they only received freedom and were not compensated for their bondage. Summing up the new form of slavery in the late nineteenth century, but in words applicable in the twentieth, Frederick Douglass was quoted by Cashman as writing that the black:

> Was free from the individual master but a slave of society. He had neither money, property, nor friends. He was free from the old plantation, but he had nothing but the dusty road under his feet. He was free from the old quarter that once gave him shelter, but a slave to the rains of summer and the frosts of winter. He was turned loose, naked, hungry, and destitute to the open sky.[3]

Politically blacks were often denied basic rights in the following century despite the provisions of the Thirteenth, Fourteenth, and Fifteenth Amendments to the Constitution.

After the return of the state governments to power in the 1870s, they institutionalized discriminatory practices. Poll taxes and literacy tests were implemented to prevent blacks from voting, and thereby eliminated the responsiveness of the political system to their needs. (These devices continued to be practiced into the 1960s when they were voided by the federal government and suffrage was expanded as seen in Table 11–1.) In addition, state governments produced Jim Crow laws that created "separate but equal" accommodations and facilities. Woodward discribed Jim Crow laws as

> The most elaborate and formal expression of sovereign white opinion upon the subject. . . . The code lent sanction of law to a racial ostracism that extended to churches and schools, to housing and jobs, to eating and drinking. Whether by law or by custom, that ostracism extended to virtually all forms of public transportation, to sports and recreations, to hospitals, orphanages, prisons, and asylums, and ultimately to funeral homes, morgues, and cemeteries..[4]

Blacks were legally separated from whites and placed in separate facilities, which were underfunded when compared to their white counterparts.

---

[2]Ibid., p. 603.

[3]Sean Dennis Cashman, *America in the Gilded Age*, 2nd ed. (New York: New York University Press, 1988), p. 153.

[4]C. Vann Woodward, *The Strange Career of Jim Crow*, 3rd ed. (New York: Oxford University Press, 1974), p. 7.

TABLE 11-1   *Voter Registration 1960–1975*

Year	Total for Eleven Southern States*	Alabama	Arkansas	Mississippi
1960				
White	12,276,000	860,000	518,000	478,000
Black	1,463,000	66,000	73,000	22,000
1964				
White	14,264,000	946,000	621,000	525,000
Black	2,164,000	111,000	95,000	29,000
1968				
White	15,702,000	1,117,000	640,000	691,000
Black	3,112,000	273,000	130,000	251,000
1971				
White	17,378,000	1,370,000	674,000	671,000
Black	3,449,000	290,000	165,000	268,000
1975				
White	19,429,000	1,486,000	797,000	866,000
Black	3,835,000	307,000	200,000	286,000

U.S. Bureau of the Census *Statistical Abstract of the United States: 1976* (97th edition) Washington, DC, 1976, p. 466.

*The eleven states were: Alabama, Arkansas, Florida, Georgia, Louisiana, Mississippi, North Carolina, South Carolina, Tennessee, Texas, and Virginia.

Political discrimination reinforced economic discrimination and together they prevented people from achieving because of skin color.

Efforts were made by the beginning of the twentieth century to repeal the discriminatory policies of racism and firmly establish the liberties guaranteed under the Thirteenth, Fourteenth and Fifteenth Amendments to the Constitution. Probably the most important was the 1954 Supreme Court ruling in *"Brown v. Board of Education"* that separate facilities were inherently unequal. The *Brown* ruling served to ignite the civil rights movement in that it demonstrated local and state policies of segregation were racist and unconstitutional.

The fact that segregation limited the liberties blacks could enjoy and their ability to prosper was taken up by several groups with different approaches toward achieving racial equality. Most prominent were the Southern Christian Leadership Conference (SCLC) and the Student Nonviolent Coordinating Committee (SNCC). Groups such as these worked to create the boycotts of the Montgomery bus lines, rallies to protest segregation, as well as student sit-ins of white-only lunch counters in Greensboro, North Carolina and throughout the South. Through the use of their buying power, blacks were able to attack the power structure which relegated them to the status of second class citizens.

Possibly the more dominant force during the 1950s and 1960s was the SCLC led by Martin Luther King, Jr., a Baptist minister and president of that organization. King sought to combat the discrimination practiced against blacks largely through acts of civil disobedience. Using the fact that the federal law was finally in agreement with the natural rights invested by God in all people, King argued that individuals had a right to refuse to obey discriminatory acts. King wrote,

> One day the South will know that when these disinherited children of God sat down at lunch counters, they were in reality standing up for what is best in the American dream and for the most sacred values in our Judaeo-Christian heritage, thereby bringing our nation back to those great wells of democracy which were dug deep by the founding fathers in their formulation of the Constitution and the Declaration of Independence.[5]

Nonviolence, or civil disobedience, was the key tactic, since it forced a community to reappraise its values when civil rights activists were attacked with water hoses and guard dogs as well as jailed. Thus white moderates were forced to reappraise their support for order over justice.[6]

Blacks were supported by some whites in ending segregationist policies. During the 1960s, a new orientation emerged in some black civil rights movements which Woodward identified as "black separatism."[7] Black separatism called for establishment of two societies, one black and one white. As Woodward noted, black separatists expressed differences over the "kind of separateness they wanted," but generally one finds a rejection of "integration, reconciliation, and assimilation as desirable aims of the race."[8] Over time, whites were alienated by black separatist tendencies.[9] During the mid-1960s, the idea of black separatism became prominent in the Congress of Racial Equality (CORE) and in SNCC, the latter under the leadership of Stokely Carmichael from 1966 to 1967.

While agreeing with King that blacks were discriminated against, and initially accepting nonviolent strategies, both SNCC and Carmichael increasingly favored "black power" during the 1960s. Black power held that black Americans had to liberate themselves as a group from white oppression, and thus preserve their identity. Carmichael wrote, "our concern for black power addresses itself directly to this problem, the necessity to reclaim our history and our identity from the cultural terrorism and depredation of self-justifying white guilt."[10] To achieve black power, Carmichael

---

[5]From Martin Luther King, Jr., "Letter from Birmingham Jail," *Why We Can't Wait* (New York: Harper & Row, Publishers, 1964), p. 99. Reprinted by arrangement with The Heirs to the Estate of Martin Luther King, Jr., c/o Joan Daves Agency as agent for the proprietor. Copyright 1963, 1964 by Martin Luther King, Jr., copyright renewed 1991, 1992 by Coretta Scott King.

[6]Ibid., pp. 129–30.

[7]Woodward, *The Strange*, p. 195.

[8]Ibid.

[9]Ibid.

[10]From Stokely Carmichael, "Toward Black Liberation," *The Massachusetts Review*, 7, no. 4 (Autumn 1966), 639.

held that blacks had to recognize being black made them different, and accept the need to organize for power as a community. Integration and ideas of equality of opportunity were regarded as attempts to buy blacks off from making further demands.[11] Over time, Carmichael's views on black power would dominate the activities of SNCC as well as the CORE.

The black civil rights movement during the 1950s and 1960s achieved several victories. Federal legislation in the form of the 1964 Civil Rights Act and the 1965 Voting Rights Act sought to end discrimination in terms of voting, public facilities, and employment. As seen in Table 11–1, the civil rights movement served to expand the number of blacks who voted in the south. Yet, even in the 1990s economic success has not been achieved by all blacks.

In the same period when an effort was being made to gain civil rights for blacks, another major struggle was taking place in the form of the women's movement. Women continued to be largely confined to the house in jobs as mother, wife, and housekeeper, or to low-paying jobs in business after achieving political equality through the Nineteenth Amendment. A philosophy of protectionism dominated American society in that there was "the idea that women must be sheltered from life's cruelties."[12] One finds the essence of protectionism in the comments of U.S. Supreme Court Justice Bradley in *Bradwell v. Illinois* (1873).

> The civil law, as well as nature herself, has always recognized a wide difference in the respective shperes and destinies of man and woman. Man is, or should be, woman's protector and defender. The natural and proper timidity and delicacy which belongs to the female sex evidently unfits it for many of the occupations of civil life. The constitution of the family ordinance, as well as in the nature of things, indicates the domestic shpere as that which properly belongs to the domain and functions of womanhood.[13]

The policy of protectionism continued to be practiced despite approval of the Nineteenth Amendment. While political equality was established in the Constitution, social and economic equality were lacking as demonstrated by Table 11–2 regarding the percent of college degrees awarded to females. Women tended to be denied opportunities in higher education for they were often stereotyped as either inferior or enrolling in college in order to find a husband. As shown in Table 11–2 (p. 233), women were a small percentage of the college enrollment in 1950. But after the women's movement took off they formed nearly half of the college population by 1980.

The fact women were discriminated against was brought out in stud-

---

[11]Ibid., pp. 642–65.
[12]Janda, Berry, and Goldman, *The Challenge* p. 597.
[13]*Bradwell v. Illinois,* 83 U.S. 130 (1873), 141.

ies conducted by the Commission on the Status of Women, formed by President Kennedy in 1963. As Pole noted,

> These studies brought to light a mass of evidence about the disadvantages of being a woman in the United States. Despite progress made over more than a century of agitation, may state laws still discriminated against women, especially when married, in matters of control over conjugal property, contractual rights, and the jobs women were allowed to do, all affecting a woman's basic independence as an economic, social, and moral being. Women were worse educated and more poorly paid and their status and expectations were generally lower than those of men in comparable situations.[14]

The work of the Commission confirmed Friedan's ideas that women were being denied the opportunities available to men because of the difference in gender, not because of their abilities. As a result the federal government began to promote policies aimed at ending discrimination of women performing similar jobs and to ensure women would not be relegated to certain positions or denied jobs because of their gender.[15]

The work of Betty Friedan was key to the realization that women lacked something which would enable them to be total human beings. Friedan, who wrote the statement of purpose for the National Organization of Women in June 1966 and served as its first president until 1970, concluded that American women "want something more than my husband and my children and my home."[16] Women desired to be treated as equals with men and to have the same opportunities as their male counterparts.

The basic premise of Friedan's criticism, that women wanted and desired equality with men, was shared by bell hooks. However, hooks took the feminist movement to task for what was viewed as feminist reactionism. Hooks argued that "Militant white women were particularly eager to make feminist movement privilege over men," not to achieve equality with men.[17] As hooks wrote,

> Sexist oppression is of primary importance . . . because it is the practice of domination most people experience, whether their role be that of discriminator or discriminated against, exploiter or exploited. It is the practice of domination most people are socialized to accept before they even know that other forms of group oppression exist. . . . Challenging sexist oppression is a crucial step in the struggle to eliminate all forms of oppression.[18]

---

[14]J.R. Pole, *The Pursuit of Equality in American History* (Berkeley: University of California Press, 1978), p. 315.

[15]Ibid., pp. 316–17.

[16]Reprinted from *The Feminine Mystique* by Betty Friedan, with the permission of W.W. Norton & Company, Inc. Copyright © 1974, 1973, 1963 by Betty Friedan, p. 27.

[17]From bell hooks, "The Significance of Feminist Movement," *Feminist Theory From Margin to Center* (Boston, MA: South End Press, 1984), p. 33.

[18]Ibid., pp. 35–36.

TABLE 11-2   *Education by Gender*

	1950	1960	1965	1970	1975	1980
Degrees Awarded*	497,000	477,000	664,000	1,271,000	1,666,000	1,731,000
To Males	75.7%	65.8%	61.6%	59.2%	56.1%	51.1%
To Females	24.3%	34.2%	38.9%	40.8%	43.9%	48.9%

U.S. Bureau of the Census, *Statistical Abstract of the United States: 1993* (113th edition) Washington, DC, 1993, p. 183.

*Degrees awarded are for Associate's, Bachelor's, Master's, Professional, and Doctor's degrees awarded by American colleges and universities.

Gender discrimination, according to hooks, was at the root of all forms of discrimination. Not only did hooks reject the way the feminist movement evolved, but implicitely criticized the ideas of Carmichael that first black people must recognize they are different. To hooks, the feminist movement must be inclusive by providing a new social order in which men and women were equals. This would mean that the elimination of "sexist oppression" was required to establish mutual understanding between men and women. Once established, these bonds would enable American society to be structured in order to end racism or poverty. Thus the elimination of gender discrimination would result in a fundamental reordering of American society and politics.

The women's movement would succeed in bringing greater attention to the traditional role of women and opening the way for them to move into male-dominated areas as shown in Table 11–2 regarding higher education. During the 1970s, the women's movement would reach a milestone with Congress's approval of the Equal Rights Amendment (ERA).[19] However, it also produced the backlash that hooks implicitly feared would come of a strategy perceived to be dedicated to women. When submitted to the state legislatures the ERA failed by three states to achieve ratification.

The civil rights movements not only produced attempts at remedying historic patterns of discrimination, but resulted in increases in federal authority. It should be remembered that discriminatory practices had been largely authorized by state and local governments. Federal intervention was generally the only means to ensure the safety of protestors and that reforms were made. By asserting federal supremacy, the U.S. government became responsible for social regulation. Graham noted in this regard, "In an unconscious yet seemingly symbiotic relationship, the civil rights movement, first led by blacks and then joined by women, formed the expanding edge of the new American administrative state."[20] The central government

---

[19]Despite congressional approval, the Equal Rights Amendment failed to be ratified by three-fourths of the state legislatures and effectively died in the 1980s.

[20]Hugh Davis Graham, *The Civil Rights Era* (New York: Oxford University Press, 1990), p. 7.

thus replaced the states as agents for achieving equality and federal administrative agencies assumed responsibility for operationalizing these goals.

As Janda, Berry, and Goldman noted, the movement towards government ensuring equality of outcome can be traced to the Office of Federal Contract Compliance which was created in 1965 to ensure employers doing business with the federal government did not discriminate. As such, the change in regulations during 1971, which called for the hiring of women and minorities, was based on the "government's notions of those groups' availability."[21] The civil rights movements for blacks and women during the 1950s and 1960s served to highlight the fact that various segments of the population were denied basic freedoms because of their minority status. Increasingly, the desire to ensure equality of outcome has led to greater government involvement. The legacy of these early movements, and government involvement, can also be seen in the realization that the civil rights of people who were members of labor organizations, physically impaired, elderly, or of different sexual orientations deserved protection. In this regard, the writings of Martin Luther King, Jr., Stokely Carmichael, Betty Friedan, and bell hooks, which are presented in the following pages, stand as prominent examples of the intellectual basis laid for the guarantee of individual liberties through expanded governmental involvement.

Letter from Birmingham Jail*

Dr. Martin Luther King, Jr.

MY DEAR FELLOW CLERGYMEN: April 16, 1963

While confined here in the Birmingham city jail, I came across your recent statement calling my present activities "unwise and untimely." Seldom do I pause to answer criticism of my work and ideas. If I sought to answer all the criticisms that cross my desk, my secretaries would have little time for anything other than such correspondence in the course of the day, and I would have no time for constructive work. But since I feel that you are men of genuine good will and that your criticisms are sincerely set forth, I want to try to answer your statement in what I hope will be patient and reasonable terms.

---

[21]Janda, Berry, and Goldman, The Challenge, p. 604.

*From Martin Luther King, Jr., "Letter from Birmingham Jail," Why We Can't Wait (New York: Harper & Row, Publishers, 1964), pp. 77–100. Reprinted by arrangement with The Heirs to the Estate of Martin Luther King, Jr., c/o Joan Daves Agency as agent for the proprietor. Copyright 1963, 1964 by Martin Luther King, Jr., copyright renewed 1991, 1992 by Coretta Scott King.

I think I should indicate why I am here in Birmingham, since you have been influenced by the view which argues against "outsiders coming in." I have the honor of serving as president of the Southern Christian Leadership Conference, an organization operating in every southern state, with headquarters in Atlanta, Georgia. . . . Several months ago the affiliate here in Birmingham asked us to be on call to engage in a nonviolent direct-action program if such were deemed necessary. We readily consented, and when the hour came we lived up to our promise. So I, along with several members of my staff, am here because I was invited here. I am here because I have organizational ties here.

But more basically, I am in Birmingham because injustice is here. Just as the prophets of the eighth century B.C. left their villages and carried their "thus saith the Lord" far beyond the boundaries of their home towns, and just as the Apostle Paul left his village of Tarsus and carried the gospel of Jesus Christ to the far corners of the Greco-Roman world, so am I compelled to carry the gospel of freedom beyond my own home town. Like Paul, I must constantly respond to the Macedonian call for aid. . . .

You deplore the demonstrations taking place in Birmingham. But your statement, I am sorry to say, fails to express a similar concern for the conditions that brought about the demonstrations. I am sure that none of you would want to rest content with the superficial kind of social analysis that deals merely with effects and does not grapple with underlying causes. It is unfortunate that demonstrations are taking place in Birmingham, but it is even more unfortunate that the city's white power structure left the Negro community with no alternative.

In any nonviolent campaign there are four basic steps: collection of the facts to determine whether injustices exist; negotiation; self-purification; and direct action. We have gone through all these steps in Birmingham. There can be no gainsaying the fact that racial injustice engulfs this community. Birmingham is probably the most thoroughly segregated city in the United States. Its ugly record of brutality is widely known. Negroes have experienced grossly unjust treatment in the courts. There have been more unsolved bombings of Negro homes and churches in Birmingham than in any other city in the nation. These are the hard, brutal facts of the case. On the basis of these conditions, Negro leaders sought to negotiate with the city fathers. But the latter consistently refused to engage in good-faith negotiation.

Then, last September, came the opportunity to talk with leaders of Birmingham's economic community. In the course of the negotiations, certain promises were made by the merchants—for example, to remove the stores' humiliating racial signs. On the basis of these promises, the Reverend Fred Shuttlesworth and the leaders of the Alabama Christian Movement for Human Rights agreed to a moratorium on all demonstrations. As the weeks and months went by, we realized that we were the victims of a broken promise. A few signs, briefly removed, returned; the others remained.

As in so many past experiences, our hopes had been blasted, and the shadow of deep disappointment settled upon us. We had no alternative except to prepare for direct action, whereby we would present our very bodies as means of laying our case before the conscience of the local and the national community. Mindful of the difficulties involved, we decided to undertake a process of self-purification. We began a series of workshops on nonviolence, and we repeatedly asked ourselves: "Are you able to accept blows without retaliating?" "Are you able to endure the ordeal of jail?" We decided to schedule our direct-action program for the Easter season, realizing that except for Christmas, this is the main shopping period of the year. Knowing that a strong economic-withdrawal program would be the by-product of direct action, we felt that this would be the best time to bring pressure to bear on the merchants for the needed change.

Then it occurred to us that Birmingham's mayoral election was coming up in March, and we speedily decided to postpone action until after election day. . . .

You may well ask: "Why direct action? Why sit-ins, marches and so forth? Isn't negotiation a better path?" You are quite right in calling for negotiation. Indeed, this is the very purpose of direct action. Nonviolent direct action seeks to create such a crisis and foster such a tension that a community which has constantly refused to negotiate is forced to confront the issue. It seeks so to dramatize the issue that it can no longer be ignored. My citing the creation of tension as part of the work of the nonviolent-resister may sound rather shocking. But I must confess that I am not afraid of the word "tension." I have earnestly opposed violent tension, but there is a type of constructive, nonviolent tension which is necessary for growth. Just as Socrates felt that it was necessary to create a tension in the mind so that individuals could rise from the bondage of myths and half-truths to the unfettered realm of creative analysis and objective appraisal, so must we see the need for nonviolent gadflies to create the kind of tension in society that will help men rise from the dark depths of prejudice and racism to the majestic heights of understanding and brotherhood.

The purpose of our direct-action program is to create a situation so crisis-packed that it will inevitably open the door to negotiation. I therefore concur with you in your call for negotiation. Too long has our beloved Southland been bogged down in a tragic effort to live in monologue rather than dialogue.

One of the basic points in your statement is that the action that I and my associates have taken in Birmingham is untimely. . . . My friends, I must say to you that we have not made a single gain in civil rights without determined legal and nonviolent pressure. Lamentably, it is an historical fact that privileged groups seldom give up their privileges voluntarily. Individuals may see the moral light and voluntarily give up their unjust posture; but, as Reinhold Niebuhr has reminded us, groups tend to be more immoral than individuals.

We know through painful experience that freedom is never voluntarily given by the oppressor; it must be demanded by the oppressed. Frankly, I have yet to engage in a direct-action campaign that was "well timed" in the view of those who have not suffered unduly from the disease of segregation. For years now I have heard the word "Wait!" It rings in the ear of every Negro with piercing familiarity. This "Wait" has almost always meant "Never." We must come to see, with one of our distinguished jurists, that "justice too long delayed is justice denied." . . .

We have waited for more than 340 years for our constitutional and God-given rights. The nations of Asia and Africa are moving with jetlike speed toward gaining political independence, but we still creep at horse-and-buggy pace toward gaining a cup of coffee at a lunch counter. Perhaps it is easy for those who have never felt the stinging darts of segregation to say, "Wait." But when you have seen vicious mobs lynch your mothers and fathers at will and drown your sisters and brothers at whim; when you have seen hate-filled policemen curse, kick and even kill your black brothers and sisters; when you see the vast majority of your twenty million Negro brothers smothering in an airtight cage of poverty in the midst of an affluent society; when you suddenly find your tongue twisted and your speech stammering as you seek to explain to your six-year-old daughter why she can't go to the public amusement park that has just been advertised on television, and see tears welling up in her eyes when she is told that Funtown is closed to colored children, and see ominous clouds of inferiority beginning to form in her little mental sky, and see her beginning to distort her personality by developing an unconscious bitterness toward white people; when you have to concoct an answer for a five-year-old son who is asking: "Daddy, why do white people treat colored people so mean?"; when you take a cross-country drive and find it necessary to sleep night after night in the uncomfortable corners of your automobile because no motel will accept you; when you are humiliated day in and day out by nagging signs reading "white" and "colored"; when your first name becomes "nigger," your middle name becomes "boy" (however old you are) and your last name becomes "John," and your wife and mother are never given the respected title "Mrs."; when you are harried by day and haunted by night by the fact that you are a Negro, living constantly at tip-toe stance, never quite knowing what to expect next, and are plagued with inner fears and outer resentments; when you are forever fighting a degenerating sense of "nobodiness"—then you will understand why we find it difficult to wait. There comes a time when the cup of endurance runs over, and men are no longer willing to be plunged into the abyss of despair. I hope, sirs, you can understand our legitimate and unavoidable impatience.

You express a great deal of anxiety over our willingness to break laws. This is certainly a legitimate concern. Since we so diligently urge people to obey the Supreme Court's decision of 1954 outlawing segregation in the public schools, at first glance it may seem rather paradoxical for us consciously to break laws. One may well ask: "How can you advocate breaking some laws and obeying others?" The answer lies in the fact that there are two types of laws: just and unjust. I would be the first to advocate obeying just laws. One has not only a legal but a moral responsibility to obey just laws. Conversely, one has a moral responsibility to disobey unjust laws. I would agree with St. Augustine that "an unjust law is no law at all."

Now, what is the difference between the two? How does one determine whether a law is just or unjust? A just law is a man-made code that squares with the moral law or the law of God. An unjust law is a code that is out of harmony with the moral law. To put it in the terms of St. Thomas Aquinas: An unjust law is a human law that is not rooted in eternal law and natural law. Any law that uplifts human personality is just. Any law that degrades human personality is unjust. All segregation statutes are unjust because segregation distorts the soul and damages the personality. It gives the segregator a false sense of superiority and the segregated a false sense of inferiority. Segregation, to use the terminology of the Jewish philosopher Martin Buber, substitutes an "I-it" relationship for an "I-thou" relationship and ends up relegating persons to the status of things. Hence segregation is not only politically, economically and sociologically unsound, it is morally wrong and sinful. Paul Tillich has said that sin is separation. Is not segregation an existential expression of man's tragic separation, his awful estrangement, his terrible sinfulness? Thus it is that I can urge men to obey the 1954 decision of the Supreme Court, for it is morally right; and I can urge them to disobey segregation ordinances, for they are morally wrong. . . .

Human progress never rolls in on wheels of inevitability; it comes through the tireless efforts of men willing to be co-workers with God, and without this hard work, time itself becomes an ally of the forces of social stagnation. We must use time creatively, in the knowledge that the time is always ripe to do right. Now is the time to make real the promise of democracy and transform our pending national elegy into a creative psalm of brotherhood. Now is the time to lift our national policy from the quicksand of racial injustice to the solid rock of human dignity. . . .

I wish you had commended the Negro sit-inners and demonstrators of Birmingham for their sublime courage, their willingness to suffer and their amazing discipline in the midst of great provocation. One day the South will recognize its real heroes. They will be the James Merediths, with the noble sense of purpose that enables them to face jeering and hostile mobs, and with the agonizing loneliness that characterizes the life of the pioneer. They will be old, oppressed, battered Negro women, symbolized in a seventy-two-year-old woman in Montgomery, Alabama, who rose up with a sense of dignity and with her people decided not to ride segregated buses, and who responded with ungrammatical profundity to one who inquired about her weariness: "My feets is tired, but my soul is at rest." They will be the young high school and college students, the young ministers of the gospel and a host of their elders, courageously and nonviolently sitting in at lunch counters and willingly going to jail for conscience' sake. One day the South will know that when these disinherited children of God sat down at lunch counters, they were in reality standing up for what is best in the American dream and for the most sacred values in our Judaeo-Christian heritage, thereby bringing our nation back to those great wells of democracy which were dug deep by the founding fathers in their formulation of the Constitution and the Declaration of Independence. . . .

I hope this letter finds you strong in the faith. I also hope that circumstances will soon make it possible for me to meet each of you, not as an integrationist or a civil-rights leader but as a fellow clergyman and a Christian brother. Let us all hope that the dark clouds of racial prejudice will soon pass away and the deep fog of misunderstanding will be lifted from our fear-drenched communities, and in some not too distant tomorrow the radiant stars of love and brotherhood will shine over our great nation with all their scintillating beauty. . . .

Toward Black Liberation*

Stokely Carmichael

One of the most pointed illustrations of the need for Black Power, as a positive and redemptive force in a society degenerating into a form of totalitarianism, is to be made by examining the history of distortion that the concept has received in national media of publicity. In this "debate," as in everything else that affects our lives, Negroes are dependent on, and at the discretion of, forces and institutions within the white society which have little interest in representing us honestly. . . .

Our concern for black power addresses itself directly to this problem, the necessity to reclaim our history and our identity from the cultural terrorism and depredation of self-justifying white guilt.

To do this we shall have to struggle for the right to create our own terms through which to define ourselves and our relationship to the society, and to have these terms recognized. This is the first necessity of a free people, and the first right that any oppressor must suspend. The white fathers

*From Stokely Carmichael, "Toward Black Liberation," *The Massachusetts Review*, 7, no. 4 (Autumn 1966), 639–51.

of American racism knew this—instinctively it seems—is indicated by the continuous record of the distortion and omission in their dealings with the red and black men. In the same way that southern apologists for the "Jim Crow" society have so obscured, muddied and misrepresented the record of the reconstruction period, until it is almost impossible to tell what really happened, their contemporary counterparts are busy doing the same thing with the recent history of the civil rights movement . . .

Traditionally, for each new ethnic group, the route to social and political integration into America's pluralistic society, has been through the organization of their own institutions with which to represent their communal needs within the larger society. This is simply stating what the advocates of black power are saying. The strident outcry, *particularly* from the liberal community, that has been evoked by this proposal can only be understood by examining the historic relationship between the Negro and White power in this country.

Negroes are defined by two forces, their blackness and their powerlessness. There have been traditionally two communities in America. The White community, which controlled and defined the forms that all institutions within the society would take, and the Negro community which has been excluded from participation in the power decisions that shaped the society, and has traditionally been dependent upon, and subservient to the White community.

This has not been accidental. The history of every institution of this society indicates that a major concern in the ordering and structuring of the society has been the maintaining of the Negro community in its condition of dependence and oppression. This has not been on the level of individual acts of discrimination between individual whites against individual Negroes, but as total acts by the White community against the Negro community. This fact cannot be too strongly emphasized—that racist assumptions of white superiority have been so deeply ingrained in the structure of the society that it infuses its entire functioning, and is so much a part of the national subconscious that it is taken for granted and is frequently not even recognized. . . .

It is more than a figure of speech to say that the Negro community in America is the victim of white imperialism and colonial exploitation. This is in practical economic and political terms true. There are over 20 million black people comprising ten percent of this nation They for the most part live in well-defined areas of the country—in the shanty-towns and rural black belt areas of the South, and increasingly in the slums of northern and western industrial cities. If one goes into any Negro community, whether it be in Jackson, Miss., Cambridge, Md. or Harlem, N.Y., one will find that the same combination of political, economic and social forces are at work. The people in the Negro community do not control the resources of that community, its political divisions, its law enforcement, its housing standards;

and even the physical ownership of the land, houses, and stores *lie outside that community.*

It is white power that makes the laws, and it is violent white power in the form of armed white cops that enforces those laws with guns and night-sticks. The vast majority of Negroes in this country live in these captive communities and must endure these conditions of oppression because, and only because, *they are black and powerless.* . . .

In recent years the answer to these questions which has been given by most articulate groups of Negroes and their white allies, the "liberals" of all stripes, had been in terms of something called "integration." According to the advocates of integration, social justice will be accomplished by "integrating the Negro into the mainstream of institutions of the society from which he has been traditionally excluded." It is very significant that each time I have heard this formulation it has been in terms of "the Negro," the individual Negro, rather than in terms of the community.

This concept of integration had to be based on the assumption that there was nothing of value in the Negro community and that little of value could be created among Negroes, so the thing to do was to siphon off the "acceptable" Negroes into the surrounding middle-class white community. Thus the goal of the movement for integration was simply to loosen up the restrictions barring the entry of Negroes into the white community. Goals around which the struggle took place, such as public accommodation, open housing, job opportunity on the executive level (which is easier to deal with than the problem of semi-skilled and blue collar jobs which involve more far-reaching economic adjustments), are quite simply middle-class goals, articulated by a tiny group of Negroes who had middle-class aspirations. It is true that the student demonstrations in the South during the early sixties out of which SNCC came, had a similar orientation. But while it is hardly a concern of a black sharecropper, dishwasher, or welfare recipient whether a certain fifteen-dollar-a-day motel offers accommodations to Negroes, the overt symbols of white superiority and the imposed limitations on the Negro community had to be destroyed. Now, black people must look beyond these goals, to the issue of collective power.

Such a limited class orientation was reflected not only in the program and goals of the civil rights movement, but in its tactics and organization. It is very significant that the two oldest and most "respectable" civil rights organizations have constitutions which *specifically* prohibit partisan political activity. CORE once did, but changed that clause when it changed its orientation toward black power. But this is perfectly understandable in terms of the strategy and goals of the older organizations. The civil rights movement saw its role as a kind of liaison between the powerful white community and the dependent Negro one. The dependent status of the black community apparently was unimportant since—if the movement were successful—it was going to blend into the white community anyway. We made no pretense of organizing and developing institutions of community power in the Negro community, but appealed to the conscience of white institutions of power. The posture of the civil rights movement was that of the dependent, the suppliant. The theory was that without attempting to create any organized base of political strength itself, the civil rights movement could, by forming coalitions with various "liberal" pressure organizations in the white community—liberal reform clubs, labor unions, church groups, progressive civic groups—and at times one or other of the major political parties—influence national legislation and national social patterns. . . .

The major limitation of this approach was that it tended to maintain the traditional dependence of Negroes, and of the movement. We depended upon the good-will and support of various groups within the white community whose interests were not always compatible with ours. To the extent that we depended on the financial support of other groups, we were vulnerable to their influence and domination.

Also the program that evolved out of this coalition was really limited and inadequate in the long term and one which affected only a small select group of Negroes. Its goal was to make the white community accessible to "qualified" Negroes and presumably each year a few more Negroes armed with their passport—a couple of university degrees—would escape into middle-class America and adopt the attitudes and life styles of that group; and one day the Harlems and the Watts would stand empty, a tribute to the success of integration. This is simply neither realistic nor particularly desirable. You can integrate communities, but you assimilate individuals. Even if such a program were possible its result would be, not to develop the black community as a functional and honorable segment of the total society, with its own cultural identity, life patterns, and institutions, but to abolish it—the final solution to the Negro problem. Marx said that the working class is the first class in history that ever wanted to abolish itself. If one listens to some of our "moderate" Negro leaders it appears that the American Negro is the first race that ever wished to abolish itself. The fact is that what must be abolished is not the black community, but the dependent colonial status that has been inflicted upon it. The racial and cultural personality of the black community must be preserved and the community must win its freedom while preserving its cultural integrity. This is the essential difference between integration as it is currently practiced and the concept of black power. . . .

SNCC proposes that it is now time for the black freedom movement to stop pandering to the fears and anxieties of the white middle class in the attempt to earn its "good-will," and to return to the ghetto to organize these communities to control themselves. This organization must be attempted in northern and southern urban areas as well as in the rural black belt counties of the South. The chief antagonist to this organization is, in the South, the overtly racist Democratic party, and in the North the equally corrupt big city machines. . . .

We must organize black community power to end these abuses, and to give the Negro community a chance to have its needs expressed. A leadership which is truly "responsible"—not to the white press and power structure, but to the community—must be developed. Such leadership will recognize that its power lies in the unified and collective strength of that community. This will make it difficult for the white leadership group to conduct its dialogue with individuals in terms of patronage and prestige, and will force them to talk to the community's representatives in terms of real power.

The single aspect of the black power program that has encountered most criticism is this concept of independent organization. This is presented as third-partyism which has never worked, or a withdrawal into black nationalism and isolationism. If such a program is developed it will not have the effect of isolating the Negro community but the reverse. When the Negro community is able to control local office, and negotiate with other groups from a position of organized strength, the possibility of meaningful political alliances on specific issues will be increased. That is a rule of politics and there is no reason why it should not operate here. The only difference is that we will have the power to define the terms of these alliances. . . .

The Problem That Has No Name*

Betty Friedan

THE PROBLEM LAY BURIED, UNSPOKEN, FOR MANY years in the minds of American women. It was a strange stirring, a sense of dissatisfaction, a yearning that women suffered in the middle of the twentieth century in the United States. Each suburban wife struggled with it alone. As she made the beds, shopped for groceries, matched slipcover material, ate peanut butter sandwiches with her children, chauffeured Cub Scouts and Brownies, lay beside her husband at night—she was afraid to ask even of herself the silent question—"Is this all?"

For over fifteen years there was no word of this yearning in the millions of words written about women, for women, in all the columns, books and articles by experts telling women their role was to seek fulfillment as wives and mothers. Over and over women heard in voices of tradition and

*Reprinted from *The Feminine Mystique* by Betty Friedan, with the permission of W.W. Norton & Company, Inc. Copyright © 1974, 1973, 1963 by Betty Friedan, pp. 11–27.

of Freudian sophistication that they could desire no greater destiny than to glory in their own femininity. Experts told them how to catch a man and keep him, how to breastfeed children and handle their toilet training, how to cope with sibling rivalry and adolescent rebellion; how to buy a dishwasher, bake bread, cook gourmet snails, and build a swimming pool with their own hands; how to dress, look, and act more feminine and make marriage more exciting; how to keep their husbands from dying young and their sons from growing into delinquents. They were taught to pity the neurotic, unfeminine, unhappy women who wanted to be poets or physicists or presidents. They learned that truly feminine women do not want careers, higher education, political rights—the independence and the opportunities that the old-fashioned feminists, fought for. Some women, in their forties and fifties, still remembered painfully giving up those dreams, but most of the younger women no longer even thought about them. A thousand expert voices applauded their femininity, their adjustment, their new maturity. All they had to do was devote their lives from earliest girlhood to finding a husband and bearing children. . . .

In the late fifties, a sociological phenomenon was suddenly remarked: a third of American women now worked, but most were no longer young and very few were pursuing careers. They were married women who held part-time jobs, selling or secretarial, to put their husbands through school, their sons through college, or to help pay the mortgage. Or they were widows supporting families. Fewer and fewer women were entering professional work. The shortages in the nursing, social work, and teaching professions caused crises in almost every American city. . . .

In the fifteen years after World War II, this mystique of feminine fulfillment became the cherished and self-perpetuating core of contemporary American culture. Millions of women lived their lives in the image of those pretty pictures of the American suburban housewife, kissing their husbands goodbye in front of the picture window, depositing their stationwagonsful of children at school, and smiling as they ran the new electric waxer over the spotless kitchen floor. They baked their own bread, sewed their own and their children's clothes, kept their new washing machines and dryers running all day. They changed the sheets on the beds twice a week instead of once, took the rug-hooking class in adult education, and pitied their poor frustrated mothers, who had dreamed of having a career. Their only dream was to be perfect wives and mothers; their highest ambition to have five children and a beautiful house, their only fight to get and keep their husbands. They had no thought for the unfeminine problems of the world outside the home; they wanted the men to make the major decisions. They gloried in their role as women, and wrote proudly on the census blank: "Occupation: housewife." . . .

If a woman had a problem in the 1950's and 1960's, she knew that something must be wrong with her marriage, or with herself. Other women were satisfied with their lives, she thought. What kind of a woman was she if she did not feel this mysterious fulfillment waxing the kitchen floor? She was so ashamed to admit her dissatisfaction that she never knew how many other women shared it. If she tried to tell her husband, he didn't understand what she was talking about. She did not really understand it herself. For over fifteen years women in America found it harder to talk about this problem than about sex. Even the psychoanalysts had no name for it. When a woman went to a psychiatrist for help, as many women did, she would say, "I'm so ashamed," or "I must be hopelessly neurotic." "I don't know what's wrong with women today," a suburban psychiatrist said uneasily. "I only know something is wrong because most of my patients happen to be women. And their problem isn't sexual." Most women with this problem did not go to see a psychoanalyst, however. "There's nothing wrong really," they kept telling themselves. "There isn't any problem. . . .

Gradually I came to realize that the problem that has no name was shared by countless women in America. As a magazine writer I often interviewed women about problems with their children, or their marriages, or their houses, or their communities. But after a while I began to recognize the telltale signs of this other problem. I saw the same signs in suburban ranch houses and split-levels on Long Island and in New Jersey and Westchester County; in colonial houses in a small Massachusetts town; on patios in Memphis; in suburban and city apartments; in living rooms in the Midwest. Sometimes I sensed the problem, not as a reporter, but as a suburban housewife, for during this time I was also bringing up my own three children in Rockland County, New York. I heard echoes of the problem in college dormitories and semi-private maternity wards, at PTA meetings and luncheons of the League of Women Voters, at suburban cocktail parties, in station wagons waiting for trains, and in snatches of conversation overheard at Schrafft's. The groping words I heard from other women, on quiet afternoons when children were at school or on quiet evenings when husbands worked late, I think I understood first as a woman long before I understood their larger social and psychological implications.

Just what was this problem that has no name? What were the words women used when they tried to express it? Sometimes a woman would say "I feel empty somehow . . . incomplete." Or she would say, "I feel as if I don't exist." Sometimes she blotted out the feeling with a tranquilizer. Sometimes she thought the problem was with her husband, or her children, or that what she really needed was to redecorate her house, or move to a better neighborhood, or have an affair, or another baby. Sometimes, she went to a doctor with symptoms she could hardly describe: "A tired feeling . . . I get so angry with the children it scares me . . . I feel like crying without any reason." (A Cleveland doctor called it "the housewife's syndrome.") A number of women told me about great bleeding blisters that break out on their hands and arms. "I call it the housewife's blight," said a family doctor in Pennsylvania. "I see it so often lately in these young women with four, five, and six children who bury themselves in their dishpans. But it isn't caused by detergent and it isn't cured by cortisone."

Sometimes a woman would tell me that the feeling gets so strong she runs out of the house and walks through the streets. Or she stays inside her house and cries. Or her children tell her a joke, and she doesn't laugh because she doesn't hear it. I talked to women who had spent years on the analyst's couch, working out their "adjustment to the feminine role," their blocks to "fulfillment as a wife and mother." But the desperate tone in these women's voices, and the look in their eyes, was the same as the tone and the look of other women, who were sure they had no problem, even though they did have a strange feeling of desperation. . . .

It is no longer possible to ignore that voice, to dismiss the desperation of so many American women. This is not what being a woman means, no matter what the experts say. For human suffering there is a reason; perhaps the reason has not been found because the right questions have not been asked, or pressed far enough. I do not accept the answer that there is no problem because American women have luxuries that women in other times and lands never dreamed of; part of the strange newness of the problem is that it cannot be understood in terms of the age-old material problems of man: poverty, sickness, hunger, cold. The women who suffer this problem have a hunger that food cannot fill. . . .

It is no longer possible today to blame the problem on loss of femininity: to say that education and independence and equality with men have made American women unfeminine. I have heard so many women try to deny this dissatisfied voice within themselves because it does not fit the pretty picture of femininity the experts have given them. I think, in fact, that this is the first clue to the mystery: the problem cannot be understood in the generally accepted terms by which scientists have studied women, doctors have treated them, counselors have advised them, and writers have written about them. Women who suffer this problem, in whom this voice is stirring, have lived their whole lives in the pursuit of feminine fulfillment. They are not career women (although career women may have other problems); they are women whose greatest ambition has been marriage and children. For the oldest of these women, these daughters of the American middle class, no other dream was possible. The ones in their forties and fifties who once had other dreams gave them up and threw themselves joyously into life as housewives. For the youngest, the new wives and mothers, this was the only dream. They are the ones who quit high school and college to marry, or marked time in some job in which they had no real interest until they married. These women are very "feminine" in the usual sense, and yet they still suffer the problem. . . .

How can any woman see the whole truth within the bounds of her own life? How can she believe that voice inside herself, when it denies the conventional, accepted truths by which she has been living? And yet the women I have talked to, who are finally listening to that inner voice, seem in some incredible way to be groping through to a truth that has defied the experts.

I think the experts in a great many fields have been holding pieces of that truth under their microscopes for a time without realizing it. I found pieces of it in certain new research and theoretical developments in psychological, social and biological science whose implications for women seem never to have been examined. I found many clues by talking to suburban doctors, gynecologists obstetricians, child-guidance clinicians, pediatricians, high-school guidance counselors, college professors, marriage counselors, psychiatrists and ministers—questioning them not on their theories, but on their actual experience in treating American women. I became aware of a growing body of evidence, much of which has not been reported publicly because it does not fit current modes of thought about women—evidence which throws into question the standards of feminine normality, feminine adjustment, feminine fulfillment, and feminine maturity by which most women are still trying to live.

I began to see in a strange new light the American return to early marriage and the large families that are causing the population explosion; the recent movement to natural childbirth and breastfeeding; suburban conformity, and the new neuroses, character pathologies and sexual problems being reported by the doctors. I began to see new dimensions to old problems that have long been taken for granted among women: menstrual difficulties, sexual frigidity, promiscuity, pregnancy fears, childbirth depression, the high incidence of emotional breakdown and suicide among women in their twenties and thirties, the menopause crises, the so-called passivity and immaturity of American men, the discrepancy between women's tested intellectual abilities in childhood and their adult achievement, the changing incidence of adult sexual orgasm in American women, and persistent problems in psychotherapy and in women's education.

If I am right, the problem that has no name stirring in the minds of so many American women today is not a matter of loss of femininity or too much education, or the demands of domesticity. It is far more important than anyone recognizes. It is the key to these other new and old problems which have been torturing women and their husbands and children, and puzzling their doctors and educators for years. It may well be the key to our future as a nation and a culture. We can no longer ignore that voice within women that says: "I want something more than my husband and my children and my home."

The Significance of Feminist Movement*

bell hooks

Contemporary feminist movement in the United States called attention to the exploitation and oppression of women globally. This was a major contribution to feminist struggle. In their eagerness to highlight sexist injustice, women focused almost exculsively on the ideology and practice of male domination. Unfortunately, this made it appear that feminism was more a declaration of war between the sexes than a political struggle to end sexist oppression, a struggle that would imply change on the part of women and men. Underlying much white women's liberationist rhetoric was the implication that men had nothing to gain by feminist movement, that its success would make them losers. Militant white women were particularly eager to make feminist movement privilege women over men. Their anger, hostility, and rage was so intense that they were unable to resist turning the movement into a public forum for their attacks. Although they sometimes considered themselves "radical feminists," their responses were reactionary. Fundamentally, they argued *that all men are the enemies of all women* and proposed as solutions to this problem a utopian woman nation, separatist communities, and even the subjugation or extermination of all men. Their anger may have been a catalyst for individual liberatory resistance and change. It may have encouraged bonding with other women to raise consciousness. It did not strengthen public understanding of the significance of authentic feminist movement.

Sexist discrimination, exploitation, and oppression have created the war between the sexes. Traditionally the battleground has been the home. In recent years, the battle ensues in any sphere, public or private, inhabited by women and men, girls and boys. The significance of feminist movement (when it is not co-opted by opportunistic, reactionary forces) is that it offers a new ideological meeting ground for the sexes, a space for criticism, struggle, and transformation. Feminist movement can end the war between the sexes. It can transform relationships so that the alienation, competition, and dehumanization that characterize human interaction can be replaced with feelings of intimacy, mutuality, and camaraderie.

Ironically, these positive implications of feminist movement were often ignored by liberal organizers and participants. Since vocal bourgeois white women were insisting that women repudiate the role of servant to others, they were not interested in convincing men or even other women

*From bell hooks, "The Significance of Feminist Movement," *Feminist Theory From Margin to Center* (Boston, MA: South End Press, 1984), pp. 33–41.

that feminist movement was important for everyone. Narcissistically, they focused solely on the primacy of feminism in their lives, universalizing their own experiences. Building a mass-based women's movement was never the central issue on their agenda. After many organizations were established, leaders expressed a desire for greater participant diversity; they wanted women to join who were not white, materially privileged, middle class, or college-educated. It was never deemed necessary for feminist activists to explain to masses of women the significance of feminist movement. Believing their emphasis on social equality was a universal concern, they assumed the idea would carry its own appeal. Strategically the failure to emphasize the necessity for mass-based movement, grassroots organizing, and sharing with everyone the positive significance of feminist movement helped marginalize feminism by making it appear relevant only to those women who joined organizations. . . .

Many contemporary feminist activists argue that eradicating sexist oppression is important because it is the primary contradiction, the basis of all other oppressions. Racism as well as class structure is perceived as stemming from sexism. Implicit in this line of analysis is the assumption that the eradication of sexism, "the oldest oppression," "the primary contradiction," is necessary before attention can be focused on racism or classism. Suggesting a hierarchy of oppression exists, with sexism in first place, evokes a sense of competing concerns that is unnecessary. While we know that sex role divisions existed in the earliest civilizations, not enough is known about these societies to conclusively document the assertion that women were exploited or oppressed. The earliest civilizations discovered so far have been in archaic black Africa where presumably there was no race problem and no class society as we know it today. The sexism, racism, and classism that exist in the West may resemble systems of domination globally but they are forms of oppression which have been primarily informed by Western philosophy. They can be best understood within a Western context, not via an evolutionary model of human development. Within our society, all forms of oppression are supported by traditional Western thinking. The primary contradiction in Western cultural thought is the belief that the superior should control the inferior. In *The Cultural Basis of Racism and Group Oppression,* the authors argue that Western religious and philosophical thought is the ideological basis of all forms of oppression in the United States.

Sexist oppression is of primary importance not because it is the basis of all other oppression, but because it is the practice of domination most people experience, whether their role be that of discriminator or discriminated against, exploiter or exploited. It is the practice of domination most people are socialized to accept before they even know that other forms of group oppression exist. This does not mean that eradicating sexist oppression would eliminate other forms of oppression. Since all forms of oppression are linked in our society because they are supported by similar institutional and social structures, one system cannot be eradicated while the others remain intact. Challenging sexist oppression is a crucial step in the struggle to eliminate all forms of oppression. . . .

Contemporary feminist analyses of family often implied that successful feminist movement would either begin with or lead to the abolition of family. This suggestion was terribly threatening to many women, especially non-white women. . . . While there are white women activists who may experience family primarily as an oppressive institution, (it may be the social structure wherein they have experienced grave abuse and exploitation) many black women find the family the least oppressive institution. Despite sexism in the context of family, we may experience dignity, self-worth, and a humanization that is not experienced in the outside world wherein we confront all forms of oppression. We know from our lived experiences that families are not just households composed of husband, wife, and children or even blood relations; we also know that destructive patterns generated by belief in sexism abound in varied family structures. We wish to affirm the primacy of family life because we know that family ties are the only sustained support system for exploited and oppressed peoples. We wish to rid family life of the abusive dimensions created by sexist oppression without devaluing it.

Devaluation of family life in feminist discussion often reflects the class nature of the movement. Individuals from privileged classes rely on a number of institutional and social structures to affirm and protect their interests. The bourgeois woman can repudiate family without believing that by so doing she relinquishes the possibility of relationship, care, protection. If all else fails, she can buy care. Since many bourgeois women active in feminist movement were raised in the modern nuclear household, they were particularly subjected to the perversion of family life created by sexist oppression; they may have had material privilege and no experience of abiding family love and care. Their devaluation of family life alienated many women from feminist movement. Ironically, feminism is the one radical political movement that focuses on transforming family relationships. Feminist movement to end sexist oppression affirms family life by its insistence that the purpose of family structure is not to reinforce patterns of domination in the interest of the state. By challenging Western philosophical beliefs that impress on our consciousness a concept of family life that is essentially destructive, feminism would liberate family so that it could be an affirming, positive kinship structure with no oppressive dimensions based on sex differentiation, sexual preference, etc. . . .

An important stage in the development of political consciousness is reached when individuals recognize the need to struggle against all forms of oppression. The fight against sexist oppression is of grave political significance—it is not for women only. Feminist movement is vital both in its power to liberate us from the terrible bonds of sexist oppression and in its potential to radicalize and renew other liberation struggles.

Feminist Revolution: Development through Struggle*

bell hooks

Today hardly anyone speaks of feminist revolution. Thinking that revolution would happen simply and quickly, militant feminist activists felt that the great surges of activity—protest, organizing, and consciousness-raising—which characterized the early contemporary feminist movement were all it would take to establish a new social order. Although feminist radicals have always recognized that society must be transformed if sexist oppression is to be eliminated, feminist successes have been mainly in the area of reforms (this is due primarily to the efforts and visions of radical groups like Bread and Roses and the Combahee River Collective, etc.). Such reforms have helped many women make significant strides towards social equality with men in a number of areas within the present white supremacist, patriarchal system but these reforms have not corresponded with decreased sexist exploitation and/or oppression. Prevailing sexist values and assumptions remain intact and it has been easy for politically conservative antifeminists to undermine feminist reforms. Many politically progressive critics of feminist movement see the impulse towards reforms as counter-productive. . . . Reforms can be a vital part of the movement towards revolution but what is important is the types of reforms that are initiated. Feminist focus on reforms to improve the social status of women within the existing social structure allowed women and men to lose sight of the need for total transformation of society. The ERA campaign, for example, diverted a great deal of money and human resources towards a reform effort that should have been a massive political campaign to build a feminist constituency. This constituency would have guaranteed the success of the ERA. Unfortunately, revolutionary reforms focused first and foremost on educating masses of women and men about feminist movement, showing them ways it would transform their lives for the better, were not initiated. Instead women involved with feminist reforms were inclined to think less about transforming society and more about fighting for equality and equal rights with men.

Many radical activists in the women's movement who were not interested in obtaining social equality with men in the existing social structure

*From bell hooks, "Feminist Revolution: Development through Struggle," *Feminist Theory from Margin to Center* (Boston, MA: South End Press, 1984), pp. 157–63.

chose to attack exploitative and oppressive sexist behavior. Identifying men as the villains, the "enemy," they concentrated their attention on exposing male "evil." One example of this has been the critique and attack on pornography. It is obvious that pornography promotes degradation of women, sexism, and sexualized violence. It is also obvious that endless denunciations of pornography are fruitless if there is not greater emphasis on transforming society and by implication sexuality. This more significant struggle has not been seriously attended to by feminist movement. The focus on "men" and "male behavior" has overshadowed emphasis on women developing themselves politically so that we can begin making the cultural transformations that would pave the way for the establishment of a new social order. Much feminist consciousness-raising has centered on helping women to understand the nature of sexism in personal life, especially as it relates to male dominance. While this is a necessary task, it is not the only task for consciousness-raising.

Feminist consciousness-raising has not significantly pushed women in the direction of revolutionary politics. For the most part, it has not helped women understand capitalism: how it works, as a system that exploits female labor and its inter-connections with sexist oppression. It has not urged women to learn about different political systems like socialism or encouraged women to invent and envision new political systems. It has not attacked materialism and our society's addiction to over-consumption. It has not shown women how we benefit from the exploitation and oppression of women and men globally or shown us ways to oppose imperialism. Most importantly, is has not continually confronted women with the understanding that feminist movement to end sexist oppression can be successful only if we are committed to revolution, to the establishment of a new social order. . . .

Although feminist rebellion has been a success it is not leading to further revolutionary development. Internally its progress is retarded by those feminist activists who do not feel that the movement exists for the advancement of all women and men, who seem to think it exists to advance individual participants, who are threatened by opinions and ideas that differ from the dominant feminist ideology, who seek to suppress and silence dissenting voices, who do not acknowledge the necessity for continued effort to create a liberatory ideology. These women resist efforts to critically examine prevailing feminist ideology and refuse to acknowledge its limitations. Externally the progress of feminist movement is retarded by organized anti-feminist activity and by the political indifference of masses of women and men who are not well enough acquainted with either side of the issue to take a stand.

To move beyond the stage of feminist rebellion, to move past the impasse that characterizes contemporary feminist movement, women must recognize the need for reorganization. Without dismissing the positive dimensions of feminist movement up to this point, we need to accept that there was never a strategy on the part of feminist organizers and participants to build mass awareness of the need for feminist movement through political education. Such a strategy is needed if feminism is to be a political movement impacting on society as a whole in a revolutionary and transformative way. We also need to face the fact that many of the dilemmas facing feminist movement today were created by bourgeois women who shaped the movement in ways that served their opportunistic class interests. We must now work to change its direction so that women of all classes can see that their interest in ending sexist oppression is served by feminist movement. Recognizing that bourgeois opportunists have exploited feminist movement should not be seen as an attack upon all bourgeois women. There are individual bourgeois women who are repudiating class privilege, who are politically progressive, who have given, are giving, or are willing to give of themselves in a revolutionary way to advance feminist movement. Reshaping the class politics of feminist movement is strategy that will lead women from all classes to join feminist struggle.

To build a mass-based feminist movement, we need to have a liberatory ideology that can be shared with everyone. That revolutionary ideology can be created only if the experiences of people on the margin who suffer sexist oppression and other forms of group oppression are understood, addressed, and incorporated. They must participate in feminist movement as makers of theory and as leaders of action. In past feminist practice, we have been satisfied with relying on self-appointed individuals, some of whom are more concerned about exercising authority and power than with communicating with people from various backgrounds and political perspectives. Such individuals do not choose to learn about collective female experience, but impose their own ideas and values. Leaders are needed, and should be individuals who acknowledge their relationship to the group and who are accountable to it. They should have the ability to show love and compassion, show this love through their actions, and be able to engage in successful dialogue. . . . Women must begin the work of feminist reorganization with the understanding that we have all (irrespective of our race, sex, or class) acted in complicity with the existing oppressive system. We all need to make a conscious break with the system. Some of us make this break sooner than others. The compassion we extend to ourselves, the recognition that our change in consciousness and action has been a process, must characterize our approach to those individuals who are politically unconscious. We cannot motivate them to join feminist struggle by asserting a political superiority that makes the movement just another oppressive hierarchy.

Before we can address the masses, we must recapture the attention, the support, the participation of the many women who were once active in feminist movement and who left disillusioned. Too many women have abandoned feminist movement because they cannot support the ideas of a small minority of women who have hegemonic control over feminist discourse—the development of the theory that informs practice. Too many women who have caring bonds with men have drifted away from feminist movement because they feel that identification of "man as enemy" is an unconstructive paradigm. Too many women have ceased to support feminist struggle because the ideology has been too dogmatic, too absolutist, too closed. Too many women have left feminist movement because they were identified as the "enemy." . . . To restore the revolutionary life force to feminist movement, women and men must begin to re-think and re-shape its direction. While we must recognize, acknowledge, and appreciate the significance of feminist rebellion and the women (and men) who made it happen, we must be willing to criticize, reexamine, and begin feminist work anew, a challenging task because we lack historical precedents. There are many ways to make revolution. Revolutions can be and usually are initiated by violent overthrow of an existing political structure. In the United States, women and men committed to feminist struggle know that we are far outpowered by our opponents, that they not only have access to every type of weaponry known to humankind, but they have both the learned consciousness to do and accept violence as well as the skill to perpetuate it. Therefore, this cannot be the basis for feminist revolution in this society. Our emphasis must be on cultural transformation: destroying dualism, eradicating systems of domination. Our struggle will be gradual and protracted. Any effort to make feminist revolution here can be aided by the example of liberation struggles led by oppressed peoples globally who resist formidable powers.

The formation of an oppositional world view is necessary for feminist struggle. This means that the world we have most intimately known, the world in which we feel "safe," (even if such feelings are based on illusions) must be radically changed. Perhaps it is the knowledge that everyone must change, not just those we label enemies or oppressors, that has so far served to check our revolutionary impulses. Those revolutionary impulses must freely inform our theory and practice if feminist movement to end existing oppression is to progress, if we are to transform our present reality.

DISCUSSION QUESTIONS

1. How were people discriminated against because of the color of their skin and/or their gender?
2. How did King and Carmichael agree on the problem and disagree on the solution?
3. How would Friedan and hooks agree on the origins of gender discrimination and disagree on the solution?

4. What role did economics play in racial and gender discrimination?
5. How can the idea of equality be established without penalizing people who have traditionally prospered at the expense of others?

Chapter 12

THE CONTINUING DEBATE

The dilemma of American political thought continues to exist in the late twentieth century as seen by the increasing contradictions between individual rights, government authority, and private property. American citizens possess an unparalleled freedom as seen by judicial, statutory, and constitutional guarantees. Yet economic achievement is lacked by many individuals, especially those who are members of historically discriminated groups. How can citizens be politically equal when liberty appears dependent on one's economic status? Conversely, how can one's economic status be controlled and yet allow the individual to be free? Government is often seen as the moderating agent in this struggle. But government is also part of the problem for its authority expands as a result of domestic and international crises, to a point where the federal government has eliminated all challengers for political dominance, particularly the states. Thus government is not the solution , for even a democraticly elected one can violate individual freedom. Ideally, in a free society the individual is respected by government, and private property is used to interest the members of society in promoting their well-bing as well as equality. In operationalizing justice, people have different opinions and ideal relationships often give way to reality. The dilemma remains to be resolved.

Individual liberty, while the key component of American political thought, cannot be the sole basis of a free society. When Locke formulated the idea of individual freedom the noblest qualities were believed to be possessed by human beings. In fact, human beings tend to abuse their compatriots when given the opportunity. Massive amounts of wealth served to empower a small minority in dominating the majority of Americans imme-diately after the Civil War. In a just system, people have to possess the free-dom to make their own choices. Those choices must not be allowed to con-trol or limit the freedom of others.

Government serves as the mediating body to ensure the freedom of one person does not become the tyranny of others. During the twentieth century the federal government has had successes in controlling the excess-es of wealth through the income tax and discrimination based on race or sex through statutory law. But the federal government is also a potential violator of liberties. One example is the confiscation of wealth from accused drug dealers. The degree of proof required to confiscate property appears much lower than for convicting individuals. Property must be proven inno-cent in order to free it from the government, as opposed to the individual who is innocent until proven guilty. Government limits the freedom of action for drug dealers by attacking their property. But the construct of pri-vate property is also attacked as a means for enhancing individual liberty vis-à-vis government.

Private property has generally been accepted as a given characteristic of the American political system in that it enhances individual liberty as well as motivates people to achieve both for themselves and society. The goal of property was key to the expansion of the American nation in the nineteenth century and the creation of intellectual property in the twentieth century. However, as previously stated, it also serves to empower some people over others. If this is indeed a problem of contemporary American society, then how much wealth should a person be allowed to possess? Or, who are the wealthy in our society?

Perhaps more questions are posed in the search for truth and justice than can be answered in terms of the American political system. After over three hundred years of searching for answers, the dilemma of American political thought remains: What is the proper mixture of individual free-dom, government authority, and private property to create a just political system? What is evident is that the dilemma continues to persist and in some cases has taken new forms.

The issue of individual freedom in the contemporary society can be seen in terms of diversity. American political theory has evolved from equality of opportunity under the Puritans, to the equality of political rights under the Lincoln and Wilson presidencies, to the equality of outcome at the present time. Perhaps no single issue better exemplifies this than the subject of cultural diversity. Generally speaking, cultural diversity has been based on the idea that American society is composed of people from diverse backgrounds and these differences incline them toward unique per-spectives. With the realization of political rights after the 1960s, these groups which were once discriminated against sought political and societal acceptance of their views.

The political relevance of cultural diversity has been of importance because of the origins of American political theory. According to Dorothy Ross, a Eurocentic-Americentric male elite has traditionally dominated the social sciences and inculcated in it their group's biases.[1] Established norms appear to be accepted as the rule, and since a Eurocentic-Americentric male elite created them, their biases are accepted as correct. Thus groups which did not share in the creation of canons are discriminated against. Ross wrote,

> To abolish canons in social sciences is to abolish any privileged form of the study of societies, whether embodied in textual canons or mainstream paradigms. What would be left is different kinds of studies of society, economy, polity, and history, studies that focus on particular kinds of issues, have different degrees of generality, practice different methods, and employ different personnel. Just as in various kinds of writing, these kinds of study carry with them appropriate standards of workmanship as well as pragmatic standards of truth.[2]

To abolish canons reopens the debate as to truth and empowers all participants in this search irrespective of gender or race. However, not all scholars agreed with Ross that the abolishment of contemporary standards was necessary. Thomas Sowell suggested that there exists a need to separate the issue of cultural diversity from ideological agendas. Specifically, "the entire history of the human race, the rise of man from the caves, has been marked by transfers of cultural advances from one group to another and from one civilization to another."[3] The historical result of cultural advances has been competition between different ideas with the fittest surviving.

The question of cultural diversity directly affects the norms of behavior and rights to be accorded to people in American society. Unlike 150 years ago, American society is no longer dominated by Christian males primarily of European extraction. Women, blacks, and Hispanics increasingly have assumed greater societal and political roles. Consequently, the norms of behavior which were once established no longer appear applicable to contemporary societal needs. Ultimately, the question becomes to what degree the federal government should force its concept of diversity on its citizens in order to ensure the well-being of all?

Changes in individual liberties have been paralleled by ones in the nature of property. Specifically, American society has changed from one primarily agrarian in which humans were considered property, to an industrial one in which labor was considered property. The industrial society of a

---

[1]Dorothy Ross, "Against Canons: Liberating the Social Sciences," *Society* 29, No. 1, 1991, 11–12. Reprinted with permission of Transaction Publishers.

[2]Ibid., p. 12.

[3]Thomas Sowell, "A World View of Cultural Diversity," *Society*, 29, No. 1 (November/December 1991), 37. Reprinted with permission of Transaction Publishers.

hundred years ago was denoted by a belief in laissez-faire economics, whereas in the contemporary period it has been state-sponsored capitalism. What should be the American government's role in providing access to society's wealth?

The American political system has since the founding of the U.S. been interconnected with questions of property and the economy. In the contemporary period, this association has provoked diverse conclusions as seen in the writings of Philip Green and Douglass C. North. Industrialization changed the way Americans think and work, especially in the last century with the employment of substantial portions of the population in industrial-urban settings. The very nature of industrialization has served to promote inequality between those who own the factories and those who work in them.

As Green noted, the crux of the problem has been that capitalism promised equality of opportunity, or inequality for the many, while democracy promised political equality for all.[4] The result was a continuous conflict in which the owners of the means of production used their wealth to achieve protection, whereas those with no wealth had only their vote. Accordingly, this was the source of political conflict.

> Since the most fundamental inequality in capitalist society is between the many who, owning no means of production, must work in order to live, and the few who own means of production and thus need not work in order to live, political conflict will focus on that inequality, unless it can be somehow deflected.[5]

Under such circumstances government must assume a basic role in redistributing wealth from the few to the many in order to secure a degree of individual equality.

However for North, contemporary problems of economic efficiency are not due to popular control over the national wealth, but the fact that government has increasingly sought to redistribute wealth through regulation. The result being according to North,

> More and more of the resources of the society are being tied up either in devoting time and effort to redistributing wealth and income in one's favor or in defensive measures by groups to prevent wealth and income from being redistributed away from them. As an ever-growing proportion of the resources of the society are devoted to these ends, they are withdrawn from productive effort.[6]

[4]"The Future of Equality," by Philip Green, from the April 25, 1981, issue of *The Nation*, pp. 490–91. Reprinted with permission from *The Nation* magazine. © The Nation Company, L.P.

[5]Ibid., p. 492.

[6]Douglass C. North, "Private Property and the American Way," *National Review*, 35, no. 13

With government assuming greater responsibility over property, the national economy has failed to grow dramatically. Increasingly, people have been unable to find goods at the desired prices resulting in greater demands on government for regulation and control. Thus while government seeks to promote individual equality through property regulation, its restrictions have produced scarcity.

The increasingly uncertain nature of individual liberties in the American system, coupled with that of private property, has seen an increase in the extent of governmental authority. Americans in the late twentieth century demand government solutions to societal problems and at the same time demand freedom from the regulation of their lives and property. The result is conflicting demands. Problems facing society such as drug use, rising crime, homelessness, and government overspending appear almost insurmountable. To James Q. Wilson, the problems of modern American society are due to prosperity, freedom, and democracy.[7] Prosperity has allowed Americans to exercise choice as to where they live or whether they engage in criminal activity.[8] Freedom has been expanded over the last thirty years to the degree that social institutions such as the police no longer impose the constraints they once did, while individuals, especially the young, have embraced "self-expression over self-control." Democracy has basically meant frustration, deriving not only from apparently conflicting popular demands, but from the division of governmental authority.[9] As Wilson wrote,

> Those expectations are that government should be nonintrusive and have a balanced budget; spend more money on education, health care, crime control and environmental protection; strike the right balance between liberty and order; and solve the problems of racism, drug abuse, school failures and senseless violence.[10]

American government appeared ill-prepared to meet these tough choices because of the competition between members of the legislative, executive, and judicial branches. Solving the social and political problems in the U.S. is therefore a difficult problem. Yet the federal government remains the only institution capable of tackling the existing problems.

The future of American political theory is uncertain. Will Americans be willing to surrender their liberties in exchange for greater government-supplied benefits? Will property once again be removed from government

---

[7]James Q. Wilson, "The Contradictions of an Advanced Capitalist State," *Forbes*, 150, no. 6 (September 14, 1992), 111. Reprinted by Permission of Forbes Magazine © Forbes Inc., 1992.

[8]Ibid., pp. 111–12.

[9]Ibid., p. 112.

[10]Ibid., p. 116.

regulation in an attempt to stimulate economic growth? Or will government itself collapse under its own weight and mismanagement? Such questions are best left to fortune tellers. What is certain is that questions of individual liberty, government authority, and private property will continue to dominate discussions of American politics into the next millennium. However, the following writings by Dorothy Ross, Thomas Sowell, Philip Green, Douglass C. North, and James Q. Wilson suggest what the future trends may be in resolving the dilemma of American political thought.

Against Canons: Liberating the Social Sciences*

Dorothy Ross

What bearing the canon debate has on the social sciences is not immediately obvious. The canon seems to be peculiarly the problem of humanistic disciplines that practice the hermeneutic method and define their field by a set of texts. The social sciences, at least in the United States, have located themselves between the humanities and the natural sciences, and mainstream social science since the 1920s has modeled itself self-consciously on natural science. As Thomas Kuhn pointed out some time ago, the natural sciences deliberately erase their historically paradigmatic texts. They teach rather out of textbooks that claim to embody in systematic form all the knowledge from prior texts that can be accepted as true.

With their divided allegiances, the social sciences exhibit both patterns. Mainstream social science has tried to substitute systematic textbooks for its historic body of texts, but the effort has not been altogether successful. The first self-consciously scientific textbook in American sociology, Park and Burgess's *Introduction to the Science of Sociology*, had to include large extracts from the seminal texts so that readers would know what the theory meant. Since then, these texts have usually survived in history-of-theory courses. A compilation of the classic texts that are taught in such courses would probably include at least the names of Adam Smith, Auguste Comte, Alexis de Tocqueville, John Stuart Mill, Herbert Spencer, Karl Marx, Max Weber, Franz Boas and John Maynard Keynes.

This list immediately reminds us that there is no single subject of "social science," only several social sciences, and national traditions within each. We are necessarily talking about multiple, overlapping, canons rather than a single construction. The different social sciences are also differently oriented toward a scientific mainstream and/or textual canon. While eco-

*From Dorothy Ross, "Against Canons: Liberating the Social Sciences," *Society*, 29, No. 1 (November/December 1991), 10–13. Reprinted with permission of Transaction Publishers.

nomics, with its mathematized neoclassical paradigm, seems now entirely given over to the scientific model, sociology, political science, and anthropology are sharply divided.

Still, there is one essential feature shared by both mainstream social sciences and their sometimes attendant textual canons that is relevant to the canon debate: each attempts to set up paradigms to govern work in their disciplines; each, therefore, privileges some kinds of work and excludes others. The critique of the literary canon is precisely an attack on its privileging of particular bodies and genres of work for legitimate study. The social sciences—both as mainstream orthodoxy and textual canon—can be defended and criticized on the same grounds. The scientific model of mainstream social science makes the classic texts themselves marginal, but where these texts exist as canonical works, they perpetuate many of the same exclusions as the mainstream.

Are there aspects of these social science canons that are worth defending and teaching? I think there are, but what I want to propose here is that they not be defended or taught as canonical. Let me begin then with the critique of the canon. On the face of it, the social sciences are, like many of the canonical literary texts, products of modern Western culture and likely to have absorbed the structural biases of that culture. . . .

The social sciences originated in the eighteenth and early nineteenth centuries as a kind of secular, elite learning that proposed to understand, manage, and reform the new modern society then coming into existence. As disciplines, they developed specialized discourses that claimed to be superior to the self-understandings of other elites, like the clergy, politicians, and businessmen, as well as the vast body of ordinary people. The subsequent history of the social sciences is in part a story of how they established legitimacy within the university curriculum and against competing voices in the public arena, and claimed the right to speak in the name of universal rationality. . . .

The social sciences have also been Eurocentric. Perhaps the deepest source of Eurocentric bias is the conception of history built into the framework of the social sciences at their inception. Modern society was understood to be an historically new phenomenon and a product distinctively of Western civilization. Adam Smith's *Wealth of Nations* refers constantly to the contrast between a modern Western society capable of progress, and primitive societies that have never developed that capacity, and stationary societies, like China, that seem to have lost it.

Western modernity, based in the progressive forces of capitalism, science, and democracy, was the model and the problem around which the social sciences formed, and Western modernity defined itself against the traditional societies in its own past and on its non-European periphery. This model held the possibility that the periphery, like the past, could be trans-

formed into modern societies of the Western type, a possibility that Western scholars were quick to exploit.

American social science has had its own exceptionalist version of this
narrative and was involved from the start in the national ideology that gave
America a unique place in history. After the 1890s, when social thinkers
attached American history to the progressive course of modern Western
society, America was placed at the forefront or quintessential center of
modern society and universal progress was cast in specifically American
shapes. . . .

The social science canons have also been in important ways masculine. In the nineteenth century, when European sociology wavered between
the realms of literature and science, sociological science was repeatedly cast
in masculine terms, literature in feminine. In gilded-age America, too, when
the social sciences established disciplinary foundations in the universities,
the gendered language of the culture identified hard facts and hard science
as masculine, sentiment, idealism, and imaginative insight as feminine.

Faced with new industrial conditions to which the inherited cultural
traditions no longer seemed to apply, American social scientists embarked
on a self-consciously realist, masculine course that would allow them to
engage the objective things in themselves. Professionalization and competition for status in the universities added other biases toward masculinity
and affected how fields were structured, what studies and what students
were encouraged. There was, for example, a remarkable group of young
women who took social science degrees at the University of Chicago and
Columbia University in New York at the turn of the century who managed
to question the biological bases of gender differences in behavior and plant
the seeds of modern feminism. The gender constraints of the culture, the
universities, and the social science professions, however, short-circuited
their careers. Those gender constraints have relaxed considerably since the
1960s, but they have hardly disappeared.

If the social science canons are biased in these (and other) ways, what
should be done? The easiest solution, in social science as in literature, is to
diversify the canons, allow in voices from the margins. Just as some individuals from society's out-groups obtained access to literary language and
produced works of literature, so too languages of social knowledge were
developed and social science languages were adapted by working class radicals, practical workers with the poor, university students from domestic
minorities and the imperial periphery, native informants turned anthropol-
ogist. These voices could easily be recovered and put in dialectical relationship with the classic texts and with mainstream paradigms. The problem
with this solution is that it is too easy. It is the time-honored liberal way of
letting new people in. In truth it is not easy in a practical sense, for there is
considerable backlash and inter-group tension in the universities, greatly

exacerbated by the political right and by subtle and not-so-subtle forms of racism and sexism in public discourse. The few racial extremists and intellectual provocateurs on the left have not helped matters either. As usual, the conservatives and a few radicals are making it hard for the liberals to save the canon.

Diversifying the canon is too easy a solution because it does not attack the existence of the canon per se. A good deal can be said for the radical critique. Dissolving the literary canon means dissolving the privileged category of literature and its ancient bifurcation of writing into high and low. What would emerge in its place would simply be different kinds of the social practice of writing. Such an outcome would by no means abolish standards. . . .

To abolish canons in social science is to abolish any privileged form of the study of societies, whether embodied in textual canons or mainstream paradigms. What would be left is different kinds of studies of society, economy, polity, and history, studies that focus on particular kinds of issues, have different degrees of generality, practice different methods, and employ different personnel. Just as in various kinds of writing, these kinds of study carry with them appropriate standards of workmanship as well as pragmatic standards of truth. In short, the radical critique of the canon leaves the social sciences in much the same position as Richard Rorty's critique of foundationalism leaves philosophy and as recent critiques of objectivity leave the discipline of history. (See AHR Forum in *American Historical Review*, June, 1991.)

Such an outcome would finally break open the lock that scientism has had on the social science mainstream. The kinds of work that now engage social scientists could go forward but with an awareness of their social and historical limitations and an appreciation of other kinds of work. Social scientists would be free to cross the disciplinary boundaries of the humanities as well as the sciences and join historians, philosophers, and students of writing and languages on related problems and using related methods. The classic texts would be more, rather than less, important in such a situation. Because the historicity, the social and conceptual boundedness of a variety of fields of study would be recognized, inquirers would have to study the original texts and contexts that shaped their questions and conceptual tools. Such study would disclose not only the limitations but in many cases, the continued relevance of these texts to the problems of modern society.

There is already a great deal of experimentation and cross-disciplinary reference going on in the social sciences, as there is in all the humanistic disciplines, where philosophers now analyze novels and poems, critics historicize the texts they study, social historians employ social science theories and methods, and scholars of gender employ post-structural theory. Natural scientists have for a long time been following their problems across disciplinary lines and have been setting up new fields with impunity. They, however, work with the assurance of a common scientific approach to problems. It may be that the humanistic disciplines are working toward a similar awareness of common grounding in hermeneutic and historicist approaches. The social sciences, standing athwart this divide, may well find their components moving in different directions. But they may also find new and renewed ways to make connections. The prospect is unsettling, but interesting.

A World View of Cultural Diversity*

Thomas Sowell

Diversity has become one of the most often used words of our time—and a word almost never defined. Diversity is invoked in discussions of everything from employment policy to curriculum reform and from entertainment to politics. Nor is the word merely a description of the long-known fact that the American population is made up of people from many countries, many races, and many cultural backgrounds. All this was well known long before the word "diversity" became an insistent part of our vocabulary, an invocation, an imperative, or a bludgeon in ideological conflicts.

The very motto of the country, *E Pluribus Unum*, recognizes the diversity of the American people. For generations, this diversity has been celebrated, whether in comedies like *Abie's Irish Rose* (the famous play featuring a Jewish boy and an Irish girl) or in patriotic speeches on the Fourth of July. Yet one senses something very different in today's crusades for "diversity," certainly not a patriotic celebration of America and often a sweeping criticism of the United States, or even a condemnation of Western civilization as a whole.

At the very least, we need to separate the issue of the general importance of cultural diversity—not only in the United States but in the world at large—from the more specific, more parochial, and more ideological agendas that have become associated with this word in recent years. I would like to talk about the worldwide importance of cultural diversity over centuries of human history before returning to the narrower issues of our time.

The entire history of the human race, the rise of man from the caves, has been marked by transfers of cultural advances from one group to another and from one civilization to another. Paper and printing, for example, are today vital parts of Western civilization, but they originated in China centuries before they made their way to Europe. So did the magnetic

*From Thomas Sowell, "A World View of Cultural Diversity," *Society*, 29, No. 1, 1991, 37–44. Reprinted with permission of Transaction Publishers.

compass, which made possible the great ages of exploration that put the Western hemisphere in touch with the rest of mankind. Mathematical concepts likewise migrated from one culture to another: trigonometry from ancient Egypt, and the whole numbering system now used throughout the world originated among the Hindus of India, though Europeans called this system Arabic numerals because it was the Arabs who were the intermediaries through which these numbers reached medieval Europe. Indeed, much of the philosophy of ancient Greece first reached Western Europe in Arabic translations, which were then retranslated into Latin or into the vernacular languages of the West Europeans.

Much that became part of the culture of Western civilization originated outside that civilization, often in the Middle East or Asia. The game of chess came from India, gunpowder from China, and various mathematical concepts from the Islamic world, for example. The conquest of Spain by Moslems in the eighth century A.D. made Spain a center for the diffusion into Western Europe of the more advanced knowledge of the Mediterranean world and of the Orient in astronomy, medicine, optics, and geometry.

The later rise of Western Europe to world preeminence in science and technology built upon these foundations, and then the science and technology of European civilization began to spread around the world, not only to European offshoot societies such as the United States or Australia, but also to non-European cultures, of which Japan is perhaps the most striking example.

The historic sharing of cultural advances, until they became the common inheritance of the human race, implied much more than cultural diversity. It implied that some cultural features were not only different from others but better than others. The very fact that people—all people, whether Europeans, Africans, Asians, or others—have repeatedly chosen to abandon some feature of their own culture in order to replace it with something from another culture implies that the replacement served their purposes more effectively. Arabic numerals are not simply different from Roman numerals, they are better than Roman numerals. This is shown by their replacing Roman numerals in many countries whose own cultures derived from Rome, as well as in other countries whose respective numbering systems were likewise superseded by so-called Arabic numerals. . . .

A given culture may not be superior for all things in all settings, much less remain superior over time, but particular cultural features may nevertheless be clearly better for some purposes—not just different.

Why is there any such argument in the first place? Perhaps it is because we are still living in the long, grim shadow of the Nazi Holocaust and are, therefore, understandably reluctant to label anything or anyone "superior" or "inferior." But we do not need to. We need only recognize that particular products, skills, technologies, agricultural crops, or intellectual concepts accomplish particular purposes better than their alternatives.

It is not necessary to rank one whole culture over another in all things, much less to claim that they remain in that same ranking throughout history. They do not.

Why do some groups, subgroups, nations, or whole civilizations excel in some particular fields rather than others? All too often, the answer to this question must be: Nobody really knows. It is an unanswered question largely because it is an unasked question. There is an uphill struggle merely to get acceptance of the fact that large differences exist among peoples, not just in specific skills in the narrow sense (computer science, basketball, or brewing beer) but more fundamentally in different interests, orientations, and values that determine which particular skills they seek to develop and with what degree of success. Merely to suggest that these internal cultural factors play a significant role in various economic, educational, or social outcomes is to invite charges of "blaming the victim." It is much more widely acceptable to blame surrounding social conditions or institutional policies.

But if we look at cultural diversity internationally and historically, there is a more basic question, whether blame is the real issue. Surely, no human being should be blamed for the way his culture evolved for centuries before he was born. Blame has nothing to do with it. . . .

What are the implications of a world view of cultural diversity on the narrower issues being debated under that label in the United States today? Although "diversity" is used in so many different ways in so many different contexts that it seems to mean all things to all people, there are a few themes that appear again and again. One of these broad themes is that diversity implies organized efforts at the preservation of cultural differences, perhaps governmental efforts, perhaps government subsidies to various programs run by the advocates of diversity.

This approach raises questions as to what the purpose of culture is. If what is important about cultures is that they are emotionally symbolic, and if differentness is cherished for the sake of differentness, then this particular version of cultural diversity might make some sense. But cultures exist even in isolated societies where there are no other cultures around—where there is no one else and nothing else from which to be different. Cultures exist to serve the vital, practical requirements of human life—to structure a society so as to perpetuate the species, to pass on the hard-earned knowledge and experience of generations past and centuries past to the young and inexperienced in order to spare the next generation the costly and dangerous process of learning everything all over again from scratch through trial and error—including fatal errors. Cultures exist so that people can know how to get food and put a roof over their head, how to cure the sick, how to cope with the death of loved ones, and how to get along with the living. Cultures are not bumper stickers. They are living, changing ways of doing all the things that have to be done in life.

Every culture discards over time the things that no longer do the job or which do not do the job as well as things borrowed from other cultures. Each individual does this, consciously or not, on a day-to-day basis. . . . Decisions about change, if any, seem to be regarded as collective decisions, political decisions. But this is not how cultures have arrived where they are. Individuals have decided for themselves how much of the old they wished to retain, how much of the new they found useful in their own lives.

In this way, cultures have enriched each other in all the great civilizations of the world. In this way, great port cities and other crossroads of cultures have become centers of progress all across the planet. No culture has grown great in isolation—but a number of cultures have made historic and even astonishing advances when their isolation was ended, usually by events beyond their control. . . .

We need also to recognize that many great thinkers of the past— whether in medicine or philosophy, science or economics—labored not simply to advance whatever particular group they happened to have come from but to advance the human race. Their legacies, whether cures for deadly diseases or dramatic increases in crop yields to fight the scourge of hunger, belong to all people—and all people need to claim that legacy, not seal themselves off in a dead-end of tribalism or in an emotional orgy of cultural vanity.

The Future of Equality*

Philip Green

The election of Ronald Reagan as President of the United States, following the installation of Margaret Thatcher as Prime Minister of Britain, confirmed that further advances in the direction of social and political equality are not on the immediate agenda in most advanced capitalist nations today. How can they be in the *sauve-qui-peut* atmosphere of inflation and the productivity crisis afflicting contemporary capitalism? In such a climate, and particularly in a nation with the individualist political traditions and fragmented political institutions of the United States, the idea of collective action for improvement and self-government languishes.

In times of crisis, too; the so-called inefficiency of public enterprise (as though any collective enterprise were ever un-wasteful) comes to the fore of public consciousness, for the simple reason that we are unable to vent our anger effectively on more fundamental sources of the crisis. The ineptitude

*"The Future of Equality," by Philip Green, from the April 25, 1981, issue of *The Nation*, 489–93. Reprinted with permission from *The Nation* magazine. © The Nation Company, L.P.

of conventional liberalism, real enough in recent years, becomes greatly inflated in the public eye (with a good bit of help from its opponents). Ironically, the tighter the stranglehold of "private" enterprise on our lives (and in few places is it tighter than in the United States), the more the public sector and public agencies must bear the burden of public unhappiness—not because they are less responsive than private enterprises but because they comprise the only social sector that is responsive to any extent at all. . . .

The ethos of capitalism is systematized inequality. From cradle to grave we subsist in a world of unequal incentives and rewards, of sharply stratified and omnipresent hierarchy. Very early we recognize that a satisfactory life will consist, for most of us, of fitting into some slot or other which is specifically defined as one rung on an ascending ladder of rewards and opportunities. Not to fit into that structure is to claim, literally, the status of misfit: a status likely to be unpleasant even for those whose only realistic alternative is the bottom rung of unskilled laborer.

Moreover, even those who suffer from it the most do not easily oppose or rebel against the system of inequality. As long as our social reward maintains us at a level at least of subsistence, that subsistence easily becomes an attractive bird in the hand compared with the hypothetical two in the bush promised by proponents of radical reform. At any given moment the alternative for most people is likely to seem either a continuation of a system in which they are surviving—even if (for many) uncomfortably—or a probable plunge into chaos if demands for a different system are taken too seriously. . . .

Unless the demand for equality is fueled by a natural tendency of the system toward growth (as in periods of general economic advance), or by real despair (as in periods of major depression), it remains off in the future, and no road seems to lead directly to it. Indeed, in the more usual periods of inflationary advance or of general but uneven economic development, segments of the working class are easily turned against each other in the name of protecting those marginal differences in position that differentiate them. In short, inequality as the predominant feature of capitalism comes to seem an inescapable necessity of life. . . .

Thus the system of material production (and relationships of material production) we call "capitalism" is also historically associated with a political and social system that we call "liberal democracy." Whereas the ethos of capitalism per se is inequality, the ethos of liberal democracy is equality. Despite vast economic divisions we learn that we are all citizens and in some sense equally citizens; that every citizen should count for one and none for more than one; that government is supposed to be of, by and for the people; and that the system promises worldly "success" to all of us who are not incorrigible idlers: every man (if not woman) can be a king. Authority is alleged to result only from merit, not from wealth, and wealth itself is justified as a reward for serving an important social function.

From the perspective of capitalist reality, liberal democratic "equality" must seem like a set of illusions, a pleasing facade hiding ugly but necessary truths. But from the perspective of liberal democracy, capitalist "reality" comes to seem a fraud, a betrayed promise, even if everyone knows that the promise was never intended seriously. "Equality of opportunity," though a truth for some, also remains clearly a myth for many; as such, it becomes a source of cynicism. Incredible disparities of income and power do not dwindle over time, or dwindle only slightly, no matter how hard those at the bottom of the ladder work to overcome them; wealth and power are flaunted in displays that have no conceivable relation to any vital social function. Born from that sense of betrayed promise, waves of egalitarianism, of demands for "more equality"—populism, socialism, or merely the inflationary demands of organized labor—periodically break upon the capitalist shore. In no capitalist nation can the public philosophy be described as simply either inegalitarian or egalitarian; the balance between the two moods always depends on which leaders or parties are prepared to press which demands at which historical junctures.

Since the legitimate capacity to make public policy stems, however tenuously, from the egalitarian institution of universal suffrage—majority rule—the actions of governing apparatuses partake of the same dualism found in the public philosophy. Since the introduction of universal manhood suffrage at least, in all capitalist societies those who control the state justify their actions sometimes in the name of more equality, sometimes in the name of equal growth in well-being for all—but hardly ever in the name of inequality. If a tax break is advocated for corporations, or the wealthy, that is done only in the name of increasing (allegedly) economic growth for the benefit of all. Special advantages for economic elites, as in the U.S. tax code, are introduced sub rosa, never proclaimed out loud. No one defends legislation by suggesting that the better class should be rewarded more and the inferior class less (except where the latter are alleged to be idle spongers); no legislator who hopes to advance in political life ever announces that his goal is to permanently maintain existing inequalities because some people naturally deserve more than others and it is morally right that they get it. Business elites in most capitalist societies spend a good deal of time and money vociferously denying that they exercise any independent power at all, political or economic; and even the most unregenerate opponents of social reform actually suggest that if only the right (i.e., laissez-faire) policies were followed, the gap between rich and poor would in the long run narrow rather than widen: this is the homage that vice self-consciously pays to virtue. . . .

Since the most fundamental inequality in capitalist society is between the many who, owning no means of production, must work in order to live, and the few who own means of production and thus need not work in order to live, political conflict will focus on that inequality, unless it can be somehow deflected. Those who think that the cause of equality will gain from the confrontation attempt to persuade the less-politicized majority that their real enemy is the economic elite: "big business," or "capitalists." Those who wish to deflect the conflict may attempt to persuade this same majority either that their real enemy is located abroad, in which case all classes would have a common interest in overriding their class differences; or that their real enemy is some other social group, a minority against whom they would do better to ally themselves with the business interest. Or both.

In effect, these are the two major, permanent alignments in any capitalist society, whatever names they go by at any moment and however well-organized and well-represented they actually are. Even when, as in the United States today, the egalitarian tendency is barely represented in one of the only two organized political parties, its lingering effects still offer about the only distinction between those parties. In this perennial conflict, members of the knowledge class—those who specialize in public writing and public talking—must necessarily play the major part on *both* sides: must present the arguments for and against more equality. Within that class the ideological contradictions of capitalist society are therefore played out.

The substance of these arguments, of course, varies with circumstances: fashions in debate vary as do fashions in everything else, and perhaps for similar reasons. Little more than a decade ago, most intellectuals, journalists and political activists assumed that the conditions inhibiting an approach to more equality were structural and thus in principle subject to attack. In a reformist tradition containing such diverse figures as Marx, Mill, Dewey, Tawney, Gunnar Myrdal and Franklin D. Roosevelt, the instrumentalities of government were seen by most people as the logical weapons for that attack. Opposition to egalitarianism centered on the alleged inefficiency or utopianism of nonmarket or cooperative economic practices, as well as on the notion that the autocratic Communist societies of Eastern Europe demonstrated both the unlikelihood of achieving real equality and the dangers apparently inherent in making the attempt. . . .

Thus during the 1970s the intellectual party of inequality gradually came to dominate the American dialogue, and this party opposes not only perfect equality but any further advances toward equality at all.

To a great extent, of course, that shift was a response to domestic and international developments adversely affecting the comparative wealth and power of many Americans as part of a national group and as individuals. But in some measure also that shift was heralded, inspired and continually promulgated by the academics and intellectuals who now command the front pages of the newspapers and prime time on public television.

The unchecked individualism which these new ideologues of inequality justify and express is false to the experience of most people, as the arguments that justify it are false to our knowledge of history and social relationships. But as an ideology which most people also accept from time to time it is still extremely potent; after all, billions of dollars are spent every year to propagate it. Therefore, inegalitarianism will continue to be the dominant intellectual tendency in the near future. To criticize the ideology of the new individualism will thus be to swim against the stream—but with the intention of recalling people, ultimately, to a different version of social reality which, when they stop to think about it, they will know to be true. The near future is not the only future. . . .

Private Property and the American Way*

Douglass C. North

CONSIDER SOME of the issues that faced the new American nation in the last decades of the eighteenth century. Decisions on these issues were not made in a vacuum; they were made in the context of material and intellectual developments in Britain in the previous centuries, as well as the immediate and urgent problems that faced a new nation. If the philosophical thought of Locke and Hobbes as embodied in the Declaration of Independence and the Constitution set the intellectual currents, the immediate issues of the 1780s specified many of the immediate problems and proposed solutions. The new nation emerged from the Revolutionary War deeply in debt, both to foreigners such as the French who helped with finances, munitions, and equipment, and to American citizens who had lent funds to the Continental Congress. These debts were of such magnitude that the question was raised—could they be paid? A second problem facing the economy was the promises given to soldiers of the Revolutionary War that they would receive substantial veterans benefits. Again, the ability to pay was in doubt. Should these contractual obligations simply be canceled? A third urgent demand for tax moneys after the war arose because pirates were preying on our shipping. The economic and political system that emerged from the Constitution and the subsequent interpretations of that document reflected the underlying currents. More than any other two men, John Marshall and James Madison expressed the issues that were to set the tone for nineteenth century America. John Marshall, as Chief Justice of the U.S. Supreme Court, was concerned with the problems that had threatened the rights of private property before the Constitution, when "a course of legislation had prevailed in many if not in all of the states which weakened the confidence of man in man and embarrassed all transactions between

*From Douglass C. North, "Private Property and the American Way," *National Review*, 35, no. 13 (July 8, 1983), 805–12.

individuals by dispensing with faithful performance of engagements." The strengthening of the institutions of private property consisted to a very important degree in legally limiting the power of government. The objective was to embody a set of comprehensive rules in an impersonal legal structure, rules that would not be subject to political whim and change by legislative bodies. Thus, the contract clause of the Constitution as interpreted by the Marshall Court was designed to rectify the insecurities of private property that had stemmed particularly from the behavior of the individual states that made up the confederacy.

If Marshall was primarily concerned with devising a formal structure of law that would make a market economy based on contract productive, Madison was concerned with devising a political structure that would prevent factions from dominating the system. . . . Madison wished to make it unprofitable for groups in society to devote their efforts toward redistributing wealth and income through the political process. In order to do this, a system of checks and balances was designed to make it extremely costly for any faction, whether a majority or a minority, to use the political system in this fashion. The tripartite system of government as well as the division between the two houses of legislature and that between the federal, state, and local governments all were designed to make the restructuring of property rights in order to redistribute wealth and income very difficult.

The result is what Willard Hurst in his *Law and the Conditions of Freedom in the Nineteenth Century* has characterized as "the release of energy." The structure of property rights in the context of the political organization encouraged individuals to undertake creative economic activity not only in technology but also in organizational forms that would enable society to realize the gains from growing markets and economies of scale, everywhere evident in the expanding American economy of the nineteenth century. . . .

Eventually, this nineteenth century world underwent a process of change; indeed, we are living in the midst of the transformation today. . . .

We have created an urban industrial society with a degree of interdependence—local, national, and international—of unprecedented scope. It has led to a tension with the structure of property rights, which was derived from a primarily agrarian decentralized world. We live in a world where externalities (an externality is a beneficial or harmful effect on a person not a party to a decision) are ubiquitous and where every person's actions are dependent on others. . . .

The Great Depression marked the end of one era. The basic assumptions underlying a market economy, that it operates to provide maximum welfare for its citizens and that no tinkering by government can improve upon it, were fundamentally shaken. The fumbling efforts of the Roosevelt Administration to devise programs that would produce recovery were complemented by a vast pattern of reforms in securities exchange and banking, labor relations, transportation, and public investment, which produced, what was called in the New Deal days, the alphabet soup of regulatory agencies. By the end of the 1930s the Federal Government's percentage of total gross national product was still small by modern comparisons, but its influence on the economy through the regulation of economic activity was far greater.

World War II not only irreversibly increased the relative size of the federal budget, but also changed the structure of power relationships among states, and led to the rise of the new superpowers. The federal budget rose most dramatically during and immediately after World War II, primarily as a consequence of military expenditures, but state and local governments have shown the sharpest rise in the last two decades. The composition changed too. Defense expenditures were no longer a rising proportion of total government spending. Rather, welfare costs and local services predominated.

This transformation was paralleled by a basic change in attitudes and beliefs. Skepticism about the effects of a market economy had been increasing long before the Great Depression of 1929. The muckrakers and the conservation movement both implied such doubts. And the groundswell of hostility to the market system that occurred with the Depression increased rather than diminished in the years after World War II. . . .

This capsule history cannot do justice as a description of the transformation that has occurred, but the results are more easily summarized. In very general terms, the benefits of using the political process to modify property rights have risen enormously as the government has come to occupy a key role in the whole economic process. Not only does government account for more than a quarter of gross national product, but government rules and regulations—federal, state, and local—are ubiquitous in modifying property rights. And as the benefits have risen, the costs of using the political system have declined. The regulatory commission and the government agency are key decision-makers now. It is no longer necessary to incur the prohibitive costs of influencing a majority of both legislative bodies as well as the executive in order to change property rights and redistribute wealth and income.

To be more specific, the benefits have risen because the income of individuals, the profits of firms, the wages and benefits of trade unions, the prices of agricultural goods, etc., are being decided daily within the governmental process. This is so because 1) government taxes take a major portion of society's income and wealth; 2) government is a major purchaser of goods and services; 3) transfer payments that shift income from one individual to another amounted, for example, to more than $86 billion in 1972–73; and 4) finally, changing taxes, rules, and regulations alter property rights that affect the income and wealth of every individual and group in the society. In this situation, access to governmental decision-making is essential.

The costs have fallen because the system of checks and balances has been replaced in many areas by government agencies and regulatory commissions. The cumbersome decision-making process envisioned by Madison has now been replaced by an individual or a commission.

Moreover, the rise in benefits and the fall in costs are not uniform throughout the system. The political structure favors large economic units (giant firms, trade unions, farm organizations) over small; dedicated single-purpose groups (passionate minorities) over more diffuse interests; and producers over consumers, to name but a few of the favored and disfavored groups.

Access to the governmental decision-making process is too large a subject to be treated in this brief essay. However, the consequences of this shifting emphasis of decision making from the market to government can be more briefly summarized. The most distinctive feature is the effort of all comers to attempt to get income and wealth at the expense of someone else. . . . Even a casual appraisal of the legislation passed at any level will reveal that the predominant trait of a good deal of it is redistribution of wealth and income. It may have other objectives as well, or the other objectives may simply be a disguise for efforts to get a slice of the pie at the expense of someone else. . . .

Does this mean that the consequences of the massive effort at redistribution have little or no effect on the economy? Not at all, just the reverse. The net effect may have been much smaller than one might first imagine, but the dead-weight effect on the economy is something else again. More and more of the resources of the society are being tied up either in devoting time and effort to redistributing wealth and income in one's favor or in defensive measures by groups to prevent wealth and income from being redistributed away from them. As an ever-growing proportion of the resources of the society are devoted to these ends, they are withdrawn from productive effort. That is the dead-weight loss. It should be noted in passing that this dead-weight loss does not show up in national income accounting. The manifestations of this phenomenon, however, are all around us in such developments as the enormous expansion of the legal profession and the conflicts among government bureaus with diverse and conflicting constituencies. . . .

What are the implications of the foregoing analysis for individual liberty? From my perspective, individual liberty is inextricably entwined with the options—the alternatives—available to individuals in a society. By this definition individual liberty has been seriously eroded. The choices of occupations, the decision to hire, fire, or promote employees, the exploitation of natural resources, the establishment of new enterprises, the determination of quality standards for products, the disposition of one's earnings all are increasingly more circumscribed than in the past. Yet clearly, this is an incomplete specification of the issue. What have we obtained in return—

greater economic security for individuals, a more desirable distribution of income, the reduction of environmental deterioration? Aside from the difficulty of agreeing about what is a desirable distribution of income, the assessment of these benefits (particularly as compared to hypothetical alternatives) would differ widely. I am somewhat skeptical about our successes in these directions. Yet obviously, we have experienced some degree of success. But the cost in terms of my definition of individual liberty has been substantial.

I would like to conclude on an even more sober note. Individual liberty is clearly a "good" in itself. But it is also an essential means to a desirable end. In a world of uncertainty, no one knows the correct path to follow, whether it is in the pursuit of economic well-being or other desirable objectives. But diversity—decentralized decision-making—assures the society that many alternative paths will be pursued and therefore raises the odds that success will be achieved. The varieties of creative talent and ideas that the individuals in a society possess must have ready and easy access to expression. Competition and decentralized decision-making contribute as much to that process as does equality of opportunity. Centralized decision-making, large-scale bureaucracy and monopolistic privilege operate in the reverse direction. The latter appears to me to be the path we are following. We are reducing our options with consequences that have foreboding implications for our long-run survival.

The Contradictions of an Advanced Capitalist State*

James Q. Wilson

Karl Marx thought that the contradictions of capitalism were the inevitability of declining profits and exhausted markets. He got it only slightly wrong: Those turned out to be the problems of *communist states*. The problems of advanced capitalist, democratic societies are not economic at all, they are political and cultural.

The U.S. has pursued happiness with greater determination and more abundant success than any other nation in history. For 45 years it waged, with steady resolve and remarkable forbearance, a Cold War that preserved the security of the Western world without sacrificing its liberty in the process. So remarkable has been our achievement that millions of people from every corner of the globe have come here to be part of America. And

*From James Q. Wilson, "The Contradictions of an Advanced Capitalist State," *Forbes*, 150, no. 6 (September 14, 1992), 110–18. Reprinted by Permission of *Forbes* Magazine © Forbes Inc., 1992.

what have they found? A nation of grumpy citizens, convinced that their country, or at least its government, has gone to hell in a hand basket. . . .

Before trying to explain why the public is so grumpy now, I think it worth asking why they were so euphoric before. Maybe low public confidence in government is the norm and the high confidence that existed in the 1950s was the abberation. It's not hard to imagine why we felt so good then. We had just waged, with great success, an immensely popular war for a manifestly good cause; at the end of the war we were indisputably Top Nation, with a currency that was the world's standard, a productive capacity that was unrivaled, export markets that took everything we produced and begged for more and a monopoly on the atom bomb.

My guess is that Americans have usually been suspicious of their politicians and that the Eisenhower-era euphoria was unusual, perhaps unprecedented. I'd like to believe that because I find it troubling that Americans might normally be so silly as to think they could always trust officials in Washington to do the right thing.

But even if we discount the slide on the grounds that we were overdue for a return to normalcy, there are features of the current anger that strike me as more troublesome than anything we can attribute to the post-Ike hangover.

One is the condition of our inner cities. It is not just that they are centers of unemployment, high crime rates, school dropouts and drug abuse; that has, alas, always been the case. Today, however, the problems seem more pervasive, more widespread and more threatening than in the past. Once there were bad neighborhoods to be avoided; elsewhere, life was, if not prosperous, at least orderly. Today the signs of decay seem omnipresent—panhandlers and graffiti are everywhere, senseless shootings can occur anywhere and drug use has penetrated even the best schools.

To cope with these problems in the past we have relied on the schools and the police. But today that reliance seems misplaced; the schools don't teach students, the police can't maintain order.

Indeed, the government as a whole seems to be out of control. It has a huge peacetime deficit at which politicians feebly gesture; the number of interest groups besieging Congress has risen tenfold since 1960; we are entertained by the prospect of legislators easily writing bad checks when many ordinary folk find it impossible to write good ones; everybody knows that the nation faces serious problems, but the only issue on which Congress has been able to break out of its policy gridlock has been doling out favors to the savings and loan industry; the presidential race confronts us with the wearying spectacle of candidates exchanging personal barbs and policy bromides.

While I think there is some exaggeration in most of these complaints, there is much truth in all of them. To this extent the public's grouchiness is well founded. Why do these problems exist?

There are three reasons: prosperity, freedom and democracy.

Prosperity. For a century or more, dangerous drugs have been consumed. Middle-class people used opium, jazz musicians used heroin, stockbrokers sniffed cocaine. But starting in the 1960s, these drugs moved out of the elite markets and entered the mass market. The reason was that the nation had become prosperous enough so that ordinary people could afford them. The discovery of crack cocaine in the early 1980s brought that drug within the reach of almost everyone. . . .

The inner city has always been a haven for criminals who could take advantage of its anonymity, disorder and low-cost housing. So long as they had to search out their victims on foot, the victims were neighbors. The availability of cheap automobiles put everyone within reach of burglars and robbers. As these offenders began to share in the general prosperity, they were able to replace fists with guns and cheap Saturday-night specials with modern semiautomatic weapons. . . .

What frustrates many Americans, I think, is that their hard-earned prosperity was supposed to produce widespread decency. They had been taught to believe that if you went to school, worked hard, saved your money, bought a home and raised a family, you would enjoy the good life. About this they were right. But they also thought that if most people acted this way their communities would improve. About this they were not right. What produced the good life for individuals did not produce it for cities.

The reason is that prosperity enabled people to move to the kinds of towns Americans have always wanted to live in—small, quiet and nice. As the middle class moved out to the suburbs they took with them the system of informal social controls that had once helped maintain order in the central cities. As employers noticed that their best workers were now living outside these cities, they began moving their offices, stores and factories to the periphery.

Prosperity not only enhanced the purchasing power of urban criminals, it deprived them of the legitimate jobs that had once existed as alternatives to crime and it emancipated them from the network of block clubs, PTAs and watchful neighbors that are the crucial partners of the police.

As we Americans got better off individually, our cities got worse off collectively. This was probably inevitable. But it left us feeling angry and cheated.

Freedom. Freedom in the last 30 years has undergone an extraordinary expansion in at least two ways. The powers exercised by the institutions of social control have been constrained and people, especially young people, have embraced an ethos that values self-expression over self-control. The constraints can be found in laws, court rulings and interest-group pressure; the ethos is expressed in the unprecedented grip that the youth culture has on popular music and entertainment.

One should not exaggerate these constraints. The police, for example, must now follow much more elaborate procedures in stopping, arresting and questioning suspects. This is burdensome, but it is not clear that it has materially reduced their ability to solve crimes or arrest criminals. Most homicides, robberies and burglaries are solved because there is eyewitness testimony or physical evidence; confessions are not typically the critical determinant of a successful prosecution. An important exception involves consensual crimes, such as drug dealing. Lacking a victim or a witness, many prosecutions depend on undercover drug purchases or overheard conversations, and what can be purchased or overheard is now far more tightly regulated....

Many of the same restraints have reduced the authority of the schools. Disorderly pupils can still be expelled, but now with much greater difficulty than once was the case. The pressure to pass students without demanding much of them has intensified. As the freedom of students has grown, that of teachers has shrunk. The immense bureaucratic burdens on classroom teachers have deprived them of both time and power, with the result that they have both less time in which to teach and less authority with which to make teaching possible.

The expansion in personal freedom has been accompanied by a deep distrust of custodial institutions. The mentally ill were deinstitutionalized in the belief that they would fare better in community mental health clinics than in remote asylums, but there weren't enough clinics to treat the patients, the patients were not compelled to enter the clinics and their families were unequipped to deal with them. The mentally ill and the drug dependent now constitute a majority, it is estimated, of homeless adults on the streets.

Democracy. Americans have two chief complaints about our government. One is that it seems unable or unwilling to cope adequately with the costs of prosperity and the darker side of freedom. The other is that it has not managed to extend that prosperity and freedom to everyone. These two views are not in principle incompatible, but many Americans suspect that in practice they are. That is one reason, I think, that race relations are, at least rhetorically, so bad. Whites think the government is too tolerant of crime, gangs, drug abuse and disorderly behavior; blacks think it is too preoccupied with law and order and not concerned enough with ending racism and widening opportunities. Public reaction to the Los Angeles riots expressed that tension.

But even if that tension did not exist, it is not clear that democracy, American style, could effectively meet popular expectations. Those expectations are that government should be nonintrusive and have a balanced budget; spend more money on education, health care, crime control and environmental protection; strike the right balance between liberty and order; and solve the problems of racism, drug abuse, school failures and senseless violence. . . .

If people are asked how the government can reconcile more spending, lower taxes and a balanced budget, the answer they give is clear: Eliminate waste, fraud and mismanagement. That no amount of waste reduction, fraud detection and bureaucratic reorganization can possibly achieve this reconciliation seems beside the point. . . .

In making policy in a highly participatory system, officials will have no incentive to say that the government shouldn't tackle a problem or doesn't know how to solve it and every incentive to claim that government must "do something" and that they know just what to do. As a result, we have crime bills that don't reduce crime, drug abuse bills that don't curb drug abuse, education bills that don't improve learning and disability insurance that can't define "disability." The more such things are done, the more interest groups will have an incentive to organize lobbying efforts and open offices in Washington. The more such offices are opened, the more pressure there will be for more bills and the smaller the chances that any given bill will make much sense.

What Americans don't see is a constitutional system at work in an era of big government and mass participation; what they do see are the things that they don't like about politics.

They see interminable, expensive, attack-based campaigns. They don't see the fact that campaigns would be very short (about two months), much less expensive and (perhaps) less attack-based if we didn't have primary elections or caucuses, if party managers picked candidates and if candidates had to run defending a party record.

They see special-interest groups proliferating. They don't see that these organizations are simply the most visible form of popular participation in government, participation that cannot be extended to individuals without also extending it to groups, and they don't see that having many interests is a *result*, not the cause, of big government.

They see American politicians accused of lying, corruption and self-dealing. They don't see the lying, corruption and self-dealing in parliamentary regimes, and they don't see it because there are not in those places the checks and balances and incessant rivalries of American-style democracy that provide politicians with an incentive to expose such misconduct.

They see a government that cannot solve the critical problems of our time. They don't see that no other free government has solved those critical problems, either. European democracies run big deficits (often they are, relative to GNP, bigger than ours), are equally baffled by youth disorders and drug abuse and have made even less progress in combatting racism.

What, a citizen may ask, do we get out of all of this confusion, pettiness, incompetence and gridlock?

Prosperity, freedom and democracy.

Cheer up, Americans. You are right to be grumpy, but there is no system for governing a large, free and complex society such as ours that is likely to do much better or make you less grumpy. If you don't believe it, travel.

On your travels you will meet countless people who want to know how to immigrate to the U.S. You will discover that our standard of living, in purchasing power equivalents, is the highest in the world. You will discover that among the larger democracies, our tax rates are the lowest in the world. You can talk to conservative leaders in England, Germany and Sweden who will speak enviously of a nation, America, that has managed to keep the economic burden of social welfare programs so small. (Relatively small, anyway.) American environmental regulations, though sometimes poorly designed and badly administered, set the standard for most of the world.

If you get arrested abroad, you will appreciate the constraints on the American police. The Swiss and the Swedes may strike you as civilized people, and they are, but I would not advise you to provoke the police in Geneva or Stockholm. If it irritates you that members of Congress pay themselves so much and have such large staffs, try getting your problems solved by a member of the British House of Commons or the French Chamber of Deputies. You will discover that those skilled debaters and bright intellects can't really do very much for you. As individuals, they don't have much power. And not having much power, it stands to reason that they won't be able to vote themselves big salaries or large staffs. If you don't want your legislators to have many perks, strip them of their power—which necessarily includes the power to help you.

And when you get home, look up the public opinion polls that compare how Americans feel about their country and its institutions with how many Europeans feel about theirs. By then you may not be surprised to learn that Americans have much more confidence in their institutions, public and private, than Germans, Frenchmen or Spaniards have in theirs. And you may not be surprised to learn that by majorities of roughly two-to-one Americans are more inclined than many Europeans to say that they are very proud to be citizens of their country and willing, if necessary, to fight for it.

DISCUSSION QUESTIONS

1. How can Americans best achieve equality?
2. In achieving equality, should property be regulated by government? How would Green and North see this issue?
3. What should government's powers be in creating equality?
4. What do you see as the solution to the dilemma of American political thought as phrased by Wilson, or as presented in this reader?

BIBLIOGRAPHY

ORIGINAL SOURCES OF READINGS

Adams, Abigail, "Abigail Adams's Letter to John Adams, March 31, 1776," in *The Book of Abigail and John*, pp. 120–21, edited by L.H. Butterfield, March Friedlaender, and Mary-Jo Kline. Cambridge, MA: Harvard University Press, 1975.

Bellamy, Edward, *Looking Backward: 2000–1887*, in *Jacobson's Development of American Political Theory*, pp. 528–33, edited by Thornton Anderson. New York: Appleton-Century-Crofts, Inc., 1961.

Bourne, Randolph, "Conscience and Intelligence in War," *The Dial*, 63, no. 749 (September 13 1917), 194–95.

Bryan, William Jennings, "Speech Concluding Debate on the Chicago Platform," *The First Battle*, pp. 199–209. Chicago: W.B. Conkey Company, 1896.

Calhoun, John C., "A Disquisition on Government," in *The Works of John C. Calhoun*, vol. 1, pp. 1–107, edited by Richard K. Cralle. New-York: D. Appleton & Company, 1854.

Carmichael, Stokely, "Toward Black Liberation," *The Massachusetts Review*, 7, no. 4 (Autumn 1966), 639–51.

Carnegie, Andrew, "Wealth," *The North American Review*, 148, no. 391 (June 1889), 653–64.

Chambers, Whittaker, "Letter of April 16, 1954," in *Odyssey of a Friend, Whittaker Chambers' Letters to William F. Buckley, Jr.*, pp. 56–63, edited by William F. Buckley, Jr. New York: G.P. Putnam's Sons, 1969.

———, "Letter of August 5, 1954," in *Odyssey of a Friend, Whittaker Chambers' Letters to William F. Buckley, Jr.*, pp. 67–68, edited by Wiliam F. Buckley, Jr. New York: G.P. Putnam's Sons, 1969.

Dennis, Lawrence, "State Absolutism," *The Coming American Fascism*, pp. 130–39. New York: Harper & Brothers Publishers, 1936.

de Tocqueville, Alexis, "The Sovereignty of the People in America," *Democracy in*

America, pp. 55–58, edited by Richard D. Heffner. New York: Mentor Books, 1956.

Dewey, John, "Renascent Liberalism," *Liberalism & Social Action*, pp. 56–93. New York: Capricorn Books, 1963.

Douglass, Frederick, "Lecture on Slavery, No. 1," in *The Life and Writings of Frederick Douglass*, vol. 2, pp. 132–39, edited by Philip S. Foner. New York: International Publishers, 1950.

———, "Lecture on Slavery, No. 2," in *The Life and Writings of Frederick Douglass*, vol. 2, pp. 139–49, edited by Philip S. Foner. New York: International Publishers, 1950.

Emerson, Ralph Waldo, "Politics," *Essays*, pp. 163–83. New York: United States Book Company, 1890.

Fitzhugh, George, "The Universal Trade," *Cannibals All! Or Slaves Without Masters*, pp. 15–20, edited by C. Vann Woodward. Cambridge, MA: The Belknap Press of Harvard University Press, 1960.

Friedan, Betty, "The Problem That Has No Name," *The Feminine Mystique*, pp. 11–27. New York: Dell Publishing Company, 1974.

Garrison, William Lloyd, "Prospectus of the Liberator, Volume VIII," pp. 140–44 in *Documents of Upheaval*, ed. Truman Nelson. New York: Hill and Wang, 1966.

Green, Philip, "The Future of Equality," *The Nation*, 232, no. 16 (April 25, 1981), 489–93.

Hamilton, Alexander, "The Federalist No. 21," in *The Federalist Papers*, (2nd ed.), pp. 45–49, edited by Roy P. Fairfield. Baltimore, MD: The Johns Hopkins University Press, 1981.

———, "The Federalist No. 84," in *The Federalist Papers*, (2nd ed.), pp. 259–69, edited by Roy P. Fairfield. Baltimore, MD: The Johns Hopkins University Press, 1981.

Hiss, Alger, "First Appearance Before the Committee, August 5, 1948," *In the Court of Public Opinion*, pp. 3–14. New York: Alfred A. Knopf, 1957.

hooks, bell, "The Significance of Feminist Movement," *Feminist Theory From Margin to Center*, pp. 33–41. Boston, MA: South End Press, 1984.

———, "Feminist Revolution: Development Through Struggle," *Feminist Theory From Margin to Center*, pp. 157–63. Boston, MA: South End Press, 1984.

Howard, Martin, Jr., "A Letter From a Gentleman at Halifax," in *Pamphlets of the American Revolution, 1750–1776*, vol. 1, pp. 532–44, edited by Bernard Bailyn. Cambridge, MA: The Belknap Press of Harvard University Press, 1965.

Hutchinson, Anne, "Statement of Mistress Anne Hutchinson," in *The Antinomian Controversy, 1636-1638*, (2nd ed.), pp. 271–73, edited by David D. Hall. Durham, NC: Duke University Press, 1990.

Jay, John, "The Federalist No. 2," in *The Federalist Papers*, (2nd ed.), pp. 5–9, edited by Roy P. Fairfield. Baltimore, MD: The Johns Hopkins University Press, 1981.

Jones, Howard Mumford, "Do You Know the Nature of an Oath?" *The American Scholar* 20, no. 4 (Autumn 1951), 457–67.

King, Martin Luther, Jr., "Letter from Birmingham Jail," *Why We Can't Wait*, pp. 77–100. New York: Harper & Row, Publishers, 1964.

Kirchwey, George W., "Pax Americana," *Annals of the American Academy of Political and Social Science*, 72, (July 1917), 40–48.

Lawrence, William, "The Relation of Wealth to Morals," *World's Work*, 1, (January 1901), 286–92.

Lincoln, Abraham, "Speech at Peoria, Illinois," in *The Collected Works of Abraham Lincoln*, vol. 2, pp. 247–83, edited by Roy P. Basler. New Brunswick, NJ: Rutgers University Press, 1953.

Madison, James, "The Federalist No. 10," in *The Federalist Papers*, (2nd ed.), pp.

16–23, edited by Roy P. Fairfield. Baltimore, MD: The Johns Hopkins University Press, 1981.

———, "The Federalist No. 51," in *The Federalist Papers*, (2nd ed.), pp. 158–63, edited by Roy P. Fairfield. Baltimore, MD: The Johns Hopkins University Press, 1981.

Mayhew, Jonathan, "Concerning Unlimited Submission and Nonresistance to the Higher Powers," in *Pamphlets of the American Revolution, 1750–1776*, vol. 1, pp. 215–47, edited by Bernard Bailyn. Cambridge, MA: The Belknap Press of Harvard University Press, 1965.

North, Douglass C., "Private Property and the American Way," *National Review*, 35, no. 13 (July 8, 1983), 805–12.

O'Sullivan, John L., "Introduction," *The United States Magazine and Democratic Review*, 1, no. 1 (1838), 1–15.

Otis, James, "The Rights of the British Colonies Asserted and Proved, of the Political and Civil Rights of the British Colonists," in *Pamphlets of the American Revolution, 1750–1776*, vol. 1, pp. 441–70, edited by Bernard Bailyn. Cambridge, MA: The Belknap Press of Harvard University Press, 1965.

Paine, Thomas, "Thoughts on the Present State of American Affairs," in *The Life and Works of Thomas Paine*, vol. 2, pp. 122–50, edited by William M. Van der Weyde. New Rochelle, NY: Thomas Paine National Historical Association, 1925.

Randolph, Edmund, "A Letter of His Excellency Edmund Randolph, Esquire, on the Federal Constitution," in *The Complete Anti-Federalist*, vol. 2, pp. 86–98, edited by Herbert J. Storing. Chicago, IL: University of Chicago Press, 1981.

Roosevelt, Franklin D., "New Conditions Impose New Requirements upon Government and Those Who Conduct Government," *The Public Papers and Addresses of Franklin D. Roosevelt*, vol. 1, pp. 742–56. New York: Random House, 1938.

Ross, Dorothy, "Against Canons: Liberating the Social Sciences," *Society*, 29, no. 1 (November/December 1991), 10–13.

Schlesinger, Arthur M., Jr., "What Is Loyalty? A Difficult Question," *The New York Times Magazine*, November 2, 1947, 7, 48–51.

Shaw, Anna Howard, "Equal Suffrage—A Problem of Political Justice," *Annals of the American Academy of Political Science*, 56, (November 1914): 93–98.

Sowell, Thomas, "A World View of Cultural Diversity," *Society*, 29, no. 1 (November/December 1991), 37–44.

Sumner, William G., "Consolidation of Wealth: Economic Aspects," *The Independent*, 54, no. 2787 (May 1, 1902), 1036–40.

Thoreau, Henry D., "Civil Disobedience," *The Works of Thoreau*, pp. 789–808, edited by Henry Seidel Canby. Boston, MA: Houghton Mifflin Company, 1937.

Trumbull, Lyman, "Speech at a Populist Meeting," *Public Opinion*, XVII, no. 29 (October 18, 1894), 687–88.

Williams, Roger, "The Bloody Tenent of Persecution," in *The Puritans*, pp. 216–17, edited by Perry Miller and Thomas H. Johnson. New York: American Book Company, 1938.

Wilson, James Q., "The Contradictions of an Advanced Capitalist State," *Forbes*, 150, no. 6 (September 14, 1992), 110–18.

Wilson, Woodrow, "The Government and Business," in *The Papers of Woodrow Wilson*, vol. 18, pp. 35–51, edited by Arthur Link, et al. Princeton, NJ: Princeton University Press, 1974.

Winthrop, John, "A Modell of Christian Charity," in *The Puritans*, pp. 195–99, edited by Perry Miller and Thomas H. Johnson. New York: American Book Company, 1938.

Yates, Robert, "Essays of Brutus, I," in *The Complete Anti-Federalist*, vol. 2, pp.

363–72, edited by Herbert J. Storing. Chicago, IL: University of Chicago Press, 1981.

———, "Essays of Brutus, II" in *The Complete Anti-Federalist*, vol. 2, pp. 372–76, edited by Herbert J. Storing. Chicago, IL: University of Chicago Press, 1981.

REFERENCE SOURCES

Adams, Abigail, "Abigail Adams's Letter to John Adams, May 7, 1776," in *The Book of Abigail and John*, pp. 126–27, edited by L.H. Butterfield, March Friedlaender, and Mary-Jo Kline. Cambridge, MA: Harvard University Press, 1975.

Adams, Charles Francis, Jr., "An Erie Raid," *The North American Review*, 112, no. 231 (April 1871), 241–91.

Anderson, Thornton, ed., *Jacobson's Development of American Political Thought*, (2nd ed.). New York: Appleton-Century-Crofts, Inc., 1961.

Aristotle, *Politics*, in *Great Political Thinkers: Plato to the Present*, pp. 92–126, edited by William Ebenstein and Alan O. Ebenstein. Orlando, FL: Holt, Rinehart and Winston, 1991.

Bailyn, Bernard, ed., *Pamphlets of the American Revolution, 1750–1776*, vol. 1. Cambridge, MA: The Belknap Press of Harvard University Press, 1965.

Beard, Charles, *An Economic Interpretation of the Constitution of the United States*. New York: The Macmillan Company, 1913.

Beitzinger, A.J., *A History of American Political Thought*. New York: Dodd, Mead & Company, 1972.

Bradwell v. State of Illinois, 83 U.S. 130 (1873), 130–42.

Browder, Earl, "A Glimpse of Soviet America," *What Is Communism?*, p. 226–35. New York: The Vanguard Press, 1936.

Calhoun, John C., *The Fort Hill Address of John C. Calhoun*, Richmond, VA: The Virginia Commission on Constitutional Government, 1960.

Cashman, Sean Dennis, *America in the Gilded Age* (2nd ed.). New York: New York University Press, 1988.

Caughey, John W., and Ernest R. May, *A History of the United States*. Chicago, IL: Rand NcNally, 1964.

Chambers, Whittaker, *Odyssey of a Friend, Whittaker Chambers' Letters to William F. Buckley, Jr.*, edited by William F. Buckley, Jr. New York: G.P. Putnam's Sons, 1969.

Debs, Eugene V., "The Issue," *Writings and Speeches of Eugene V. Debs*, pp. 293–310, edited by Joseph M. Bernstein. New York: Hermitage Press, Inc., 1948.

Dennis, Lawrence, *The Coming American Fascism*. New York: Harper & Brothers Publishers, 1936.

Dreier, Peter. *Today Journal*, February 14, 1986, p. 11, in Kenneth Janda, Jeffrey M. Berry, and Jerry Goldman, *Challenge of Democracy* (3rd ed.), p. 277. Boston, MA: Houghton Mifflin Company, 1993.

Dye, Thomas R., and L. Harmon Zeigler, *The Irony of Democracy* (4th ed.). North Scituate, MA: Duxbury Press, 1978.

Ebenstein, William, and Alan O. Ebenstein, *Great Political Thinkers: Plato to the Present* (5th ed.). Orlando, FL: Holt, Rinehart and Winston, 1991.

"Fascism," *Enciclopedia Italiana* in Herbert Hoover, *The Challenge to Liberty*. New York: Da Capo Press, 1973.

Fowler, Robert Booth, and Jeffrey R. Orenstein, *An Introduction to Political Theory*. New York: HarperCollins College Publishers, 1993.

Graham, Hugh Davis, *The Civil Rights Era*. New York: Oxford University Press, 1990.

Historical Statistics of the United States, Colonial Times to 1957. Washington, DC: Department of Commerce, 1975.

Hobbes, Thomas, *Leviathan*, in *Great Political Thinkers: Plato to the Present* (5th ed.), pp. 407–24, edited by William Ebenstein and Alan O. Ebenstein. Orlando, FL: Holt, Rinehart and Winston, 1991.

Hofstadter, Richard, *The American Political Tradition* (2nd ed.). New York: Vintage Books, 1989.

Hoover, Herbert, "The Remedy for Economic Depression Is Not Waste, but the Creation and Distribution of Wealth," pp. 572–83. *The State Papers and Other Public Writings of Herbert Hoover*, vol. 1, edited by William Starr Myers. New York: Kraus Reprint Co., 1970.

Ireton, General Henry, *Debates on the Putney Project*, pp. 8–22, in *Free Government in the Making* (3rd ed.), edited by Alpheus Thomas Mason. New York: Oxford University Press, 1965.

Jackson, Andrew, "Veto Message of the Renewal of the Bank of the United States' Charter," in Alpheus Thomas Mason, *Free Government in the Making* (3rd ed.), p. 443. New York: Oxford University Press, 1965.

Janda, Kenneth, Jeffrey M. Berry, and Jerry Goldman, *Challenge of Democracy* (3rd ed.). Boston, MA: Houghton Mifflin Company, 1993.

Locke, John, *Two Treatises of Government*, in *Great Political Thinkers: Plato to the Present* (5th ed.), pp. 435–54, edited by William Ebenstein and Alan O. Ebenstein. Orlando, FL: Holt, Rinehart and Winston, 1991.

Marx, Karl, and Friedrich Engels, *The Communist Manifesto*, in *Great Political Thinkers: Plato to the Present* (5th ed.), pp. 737–55, edited by William Ebenstein and Alan O. Ebenstein. Orlando, FL: Holt, Rinehart and Winston, 1991.

Mason, Alpheus Thomas, and Richard H. Leach, *In Quest of Freedom* (2nd ed.) Englewood Cliffs, NJ: Prentice-Hall, Inc., 1973.

Miller, Perry, and Thomas H. Johnson, eds., *The Puritans*. New York: American Book Company, 1938.

Nichols, Jeanette P., and Roy F. Nichols, *The Growth of American Democracy*. New York: D. Appleton-Century Company, 1939.

Otis, James, "The Rights of the British Colonies Asserted and Proved, of the Political and Civil Rights of the British Colonists," in *Pamphlets of the American Revolution, 1750–1776*, vol. 1, pp. 419–82, edited by Bernard Bailyn. Cambridge, MA: The Belknap Press of Harvard University Press, 1965.

Padover, Saul K., assembled and arranged, *The Complete Jefferson*. Freeport, NY: Books for Libraries Press, 1969.

Penn, William, "An Address to the Civil Magistrate for Redress," in *The Select Works of William Penn*, vol. 3, pp. 27–44. New York: Kraus Reprint Co., 1971.

Plato, *The Republic*, in *Great Political Thinkers: Plato to the Present* (5th ed.), pp. 30–80, edited by William Ebenstein and Alan O. Ebenstein. Orlando, FL: Holt, Rinehart and Winston, 1991.

Pole, J.R., *The Pursuit of Equality in American History*. Berkeley: University of California Press, 1978.

Rainboro, Colonel, *Debates on the Putney Project*, pp. 8–22, in *Free Government in the Making* (3rd ed.), edited by Alpheus Thomas Mason. New York: Oxford University Press, 1965.

Russell, Bertrand, *A History of Western Philosophy*. New York: Simon & Schuster, 1945.

Seligman, Edwin R.A., *The Economic Interpretation of History* in Charles Beard, *An Economic Interpretation of the Constitution of the United States*, p.15. New York: The Macmillian Company, 1913.

Statistical Abstract of the United States, 1976. Washington, DC: U.S. Bureau of Foreign and Domestic Commerce, 1976.
————, *1993*. Washington, DC: U.S. Bureau of Foreign and Domestic Commerce, 1993.
Storing, Herbert J., ed., *The Complete Anti-Federalist*. Chicago, IL: University of Chicago Press, 1981.
Tinder, Glenn, *Political Thinking* (5th ed.). New York: HarperCollins Publishers, 1991.
Whitman, Walt, "Introduction" to *Leaves of Grass* in A.J. Beitzinger, *A History of American Political Thought*, p. 333. New York: Dodd, Mead & Company, 1972.
Woodward, C. Vann, *The Strange Career of Jim Crow* (3rd ed.). New York: Oxford University Press, 1974.
Yergin, Daniel, *Shattered Peace*. New York: Penguin Group, 1990.